This is a new edition of Geoffrey Parker's much admired illustrated account of how the West, so small and so deficient in natural resources in 1500, had by 1800 come to control over one third of the world. This edition incorporates new material, including a substantial 'Afterword' which summarizes the debate which developed after the book's first publication.

From reviews of the first edition (1988):

'... a work of superb scholarship ... a brisk and engaging account that illuminates virtually every aspect of warfare in this watershed period'.
   Gordon A. Craig in *New York Review of Books*

'... a succinct but dense study with the rare distinction of being packed with information, rich in argument, and yet well organized and clear'.
   John Childs in *The Times Literary Supplement*

'... a major work of military historiography which will influence the outlook of Professor Parker's fellow practitioners for years to come'.
   John Keegan in *The Daily Telegraph*

From reviews of the second edition (1996):

'... a genuinely admirable book, and every student of military history, whatever his specialisation, ought to read it.'
   Thomas M. Barker in *The Journal of Military History*

'A second, updated edition of Geoffrey Parker's *The Military Revolution* deserves a warm and thoughtful welcome by all historians ... I strongly commend this book.'
   Weston F. Cook Jr in *The Journal of Military History*

The military revolution

The Lees Knowles Lectures 1984

Given at Trinity College, Cambridge

The military revolution

Military innovation and the rise of the West, 1500–1800

SECOND EDITION

GEOFFREY PARKER

The Ohio State University

CAMBRIDGE
UNIVERSITY PRESS

CAMBRIDGE UNIVERSITY PRESS
Cambridge, New York, Melbourne, Madrid, Cape Town, Singapore, São Paulo,
Delhi, Tokyo, Mexico City

Cambridge University Press
The Edinburgh Building, Cambridge CB2 8RU, UK

Published in the United States of America by Cambridge University Press, New York

www.cambridge.org
Information on this title: www.cambridge.org/9780521479585

First published 1988
Reprinted 1988 and 1989
Second edition 1996
15th printing 2011

Printed in the United Kingdom at the University Press, Cambridge

A catalogue record of this publication is available from the British Library

British Library Cataloguing in Publication data
Parker, Geoffrey, 1943–
The military revolution: military innovation
and the rise of the West, 1500–1800.
1. Militarism – History
I. Title

355′0213′09 U2.1.2.

Library of Congress Cataloguing in Publication data
Parker, Geoffrey, 1943–
The military revolution: military revolution: military innovation and the rise
of the west, 1500–1800 / Geoffrey Parker. – 2nd ed.
p.   cm.
"The Lees Knowles lectures, 1984, given at Trinity College,
Cambridge" – Half t.p.
ISBN 0 521 47426 4. – ISBN 0 521 47958 4 (pbk.)
1. Military art and science – Europe – History – 16th century.
2. Military art and science – Europe – History – 17th century.
3. Military art and science – Europe – History – 18th century.
1. Title.
U39.P37   1996
355′.0094′0903 dc20   95 24970 CIP

ISBN 978-0-521-47426-9 Hardback
ISBN 978-0-521-47958-5 Paperback

For Michael Roberts

Contents

Illustrations

Acknowledgements

Sir Lees Knowles, whose generous donation to his old Cambridge college helped to finance the lectures on which this book is based, was born in Lancashire in 1857. He went from Rugby School to be a Trinity pensioner in 1875 and read Law, being called to the Bar in 1882. But he was also a keen athlete, becoming a blue in three separate events and President of the Cambridge University Athletic Club; as late as 1901, he captained the Oxbridge Athletic team which toured North America. But by then, Lees Knowles was a Member of Parliament, having won Salford for the Conservatives in 1886 (by a mere 3,399 votes to 3,283 – a reminder of how small constituencies then were). He had also served for five years as Parliamentary Secretary to the Board of Trade in Lord Salisbury's third ministry, and was created a knight baronet in 1903. At the outbreak of World War I, although almost sixty years old, he at once joined the Lancashire Fusiliers and had risen to the rank of Lieutenant-Colonel by 1918. He died ten years later.

It might seem that there is little here to warm the heart of a man born in Nottingham, of Yorkshire parents, who cares little for politics, prefers the navy to the army, and has never been noted for his physical fitness. But Sir Lees Knowles was also a keen student of the Past, and he wrote a number of works on eighteenth- and nineteenth-century military history. They still merit attention because, although most of them concerned only those campaigns which involved his own regiment, they were very carefully researched. First, he travelled extensively to the places that he wrote about – visiting, for example, the area around Minden while he prepared a book on the battle there in 1759, and searching out historians of the German regiments which had fought alongside, or against, the Lancashire Fusiliers. He also mastered the languages of all the major participants in the various histories that he wrote, becoming fluent in Italian, French and German.

In preparing this book, I have done my best to follow the methods of Sir Lees Knowles. But two factors now complicate both foreign travel and linguistic achievement. First, living abroad has become so expensive that few scholars can finance prolonged research overseas from their own resources. I therefore thank the Travel and Research Fund of St Andrews University, the Japan Society for the Promotion of Science, the British Academy, and the Carnegie trust for the Universities of Scotland, all of which contributed most generously to the cost of my research in Asia, Africa, Europe and America. I am also most grateful to the Study Leave Committee of St Andrews University, which generously granted five weeks' leave of absence to permit me to complete my work on the lectures and to reside in Cambridge whilst I gave them; and to the Master and Fellows of Trinity College, Cambridge, who invited me to deliver the Lees Knowles lectures on military history for 1984, and provided me with splendid hospitality and strong support while I did so. The second obstacle to writing a general work which touches on the history of many countries is the diversity of languages. In the world today, it is said, there are no less than 2,796 different written languages (India alone has over fifty, written in fourteen different scripts). No historian can hope to master all of them; and yet to concentrate on only a few, especially if all are Western, is to risk introducing distortion and bias. There is no shortage of Eurocentric works; the world does not need another. So during my travels, I tried to meet as many local historians as possible in order to become acquainted, through them, with local perspectives and writings on the themes covered in this book. In Japan, I was very fortunate to meet Professor Hayami Akira of Keio University (Tokyo). On my first visit, in 1983, he showed me how profoundly the military revolution of early modern Europe had affected the countries of East Asia, and he introduced me to several colleagues who (like Professor Hayami) helped to correct my Eurocentric outlook: Professors Iwao Seiichi, Hamashita Takeshi, Hora Tomio, Ann B. Jannetta and Ronald P. Toby. Professor Hayami also secured for me, on my second visit to Japan, the services of an able research assistant, Hamano Kiyoshi, who read and translated into English for me the leading Japanese sources on early modern military matters. I thank them all.

Concerning the military balance in South Asia during this period, I was grateful to receive advice, and references to relevant literature, from Professors C. R. Boxer, Ashin das Gupta, Hsu Cho-yun, Peter Marshall, M. N. Pearson, Evelyn Rawski, Jonathan Spence and Niels Steensgaard. For Africa, I am likewise grateful for illumination from Dr John Lonsdale and Mr James de V. Allen. On European warfare at home, I owe special thanks to Dr. Simon Adams, who originally suggested to me the topic of these lectures, gave me much helpful advice whilst I was writing them, and provided invaluable comments on the typescript. I am also most grateful to Professor Sir John Hale, whose works on early modern warfare I have found a constant source of inspiration and information, and who read through the typescript for me and made many helpful comments; and to Professor John Kenyon, Professor Bruce Lenman, Professor John Lynn, Dr Colin Martin, Dr Jane Ohlmeyer, Dr Hamish Scott and Dr Sanjay Subrahman yam, all of whom also read through my typescript and helped me to correct many (though not, I fear, all) of my errors and misconceptions.

Innumerable drafts of this work have been expertly typed and retyped by Nancy Wood, without whose dedicated assistance and shrewd comments the text would have been much the poorer; Kim Everett prepared a final draft; Jane Ohlmeyer helped with the maps; and Bill Davies and Susie Wood-house of Cambridge University Press provided expert editorial support. I thank them all too. But my principal debt in preparing this book is to Michael Roberts, who provided encouragement and support for my work for almost thirty years, both by letter and in personal discussions. It is as a token of gratitude and esteem that I dedicate this volume to him.

Preface to the second edition

Many studies of the military revolution have appeared since the typescript of this book was finalized: several monographs and numerous articles – the best of the latter republished in Clifford J. Rogers, *The military revolution debate* (Boulder, 1995). In preparing a revised edition of this work, however, it did not seem appropriate to integrate the new findings into the original text and notes, since they reflect the state of my knowledge in 1987: had I known then what I know now, I would have written a somewhat different – no doubt better – book. I have therefore changed only errors of fact and updated only works which were then 'forthcoming' and have now appeared in print. Instead, I have tried to address subsequent scholarship in a new section, the 'Afterword' (pp. 155–75), and on p. 247 I have noted the most important new works to appear on the subject.

I would like to thank the following for suggestions and supplementary information: Leonard Blussé and Ben Cox from the Netherlands; Truls Holmsen from Norway; Sanjay Subrahmanyam from the Delhi School of Economics; Bernard S. Bachrach from the University of Minnesota; and David W. Baeckelandt, John F. Beeler, Teresa A. Hiener, John A. Lynn and Ronald P. Toby from the University of Illinois.

Preface to the 1999 reprint

I have taken advantage of this reprint of the revised edition of *The Military Revolution* to correct some misprints and to update a few references. I also cite new works on the subject in the 'Afterword' and in the 'Bibliographical note' on p. 247. I thank Russell Hart and Jeff Seiken of the Ohio State University and Gábor Agoston of Georgetown University for bringing several of them to my attention. How I wish I could present a copy of this edition to Michael Roberts, my friend and mentor for almost thirty years, but he died at the age of 88 on New Year's Eve 1996.

Principal areas affected by the Military Revolution

0   100   200   300 km
0   100   200 miles

Culloden × Auldearn
Alford ×   • Aberdeen
× Inverlochy
Killiecrankie ×
Tippermuir × Perth Dundee
Stirling • St Andrews
Kilsyth ×   • Dunbar
Glasgow   Eyemouth
Edinburgh• Berwick-
Prestonpans × upon-Tweed
Philiphaugh

Londonderry •

Charlemount •   • Hillsborough
Enniskillen • Benburb ×
Clontibret × × Yellow Ford

Boyne × • Drogheda
Trim •
Dublin •

Smerwick •   IRELAND

Kinsale •

Marston Moor ×
× Preston   Hull

Newark •
WALES   ENGLAND

Worcester ×   × Naseby
× Edgehill
• Oxford
London
Bristol •   Reading   The Downs
Portsmouth
Lostwithiel •   • Plymouth
× Beachy Head

La Hogue ×

Bygdeå
SWEDEN
Stockholm •
SCOTLAND   RUSSIA
Moscow •
IRELAND
Smolensk •   Tula •
ENGLAND   Danzig ×
× Kirchholm
× Klushino
THE   POLAND   Belgorod •
Poltava ×
Brest •   EMPIRE   Zamość •
FRANCE
× Coutras   HUNGARY
Turin   × Mohács
PORTUGAL   × Pavia   OTTOMAN
× Salces   Florence ×
Siena •   × Ravenna
SPAIN   Civitavecchia • Rome •   Constantinople
Granada •   Naples •   Cannae   EMPIRE
Cadiz •
Oran • Algiers •

Ivry
FRANCE
R. Loire
× Poitiers
• La Rochelle

1 *The military revolution in Europe* began in the lands ruled by the Habsburgs and their arch-enemy, the king of France. From there it spread: first westwards, in the sixteenth century, to England; and then eastwards, in the seventeenth, to the rest of the Holy Roman Empire,

DENMARK

SWEDEN

POLAND

Stralsund

HOLSTEIN

Terschelling ×
Kijkduin ×

× Wittstock

VERDEN/
• BREMEN

• Berlin

Amsterdam •

Schenckenschans

Breda • • 's Hertogenbosch

Breitenfeld ×

• Torgau

en-op-Zoom

Turnhout

Antwerp
Aalst •Dendermond Julich
udenaarde •Brussels

× Ramillies

× Malplaquet

Roeroi

Metz

Frankenthal •

Nancy

Héricourt ×

Grandson

× Morat

Lützen ×

• Siegen

Ehrenbreitstein

• Hanau

× Alte Veste/
Nuremberg

Mannheim
•Heidelberg

Nördlingen ×

Neuburg
• Ingolstadt

Blenheim × Rain

• Augsburg

• Munich

× Tuttlingen

Palmanova

THE

• Prague

R. Danube

Vienna

EMPIRE

Bicocca

Spanish Road

Milan ×

× Marignano

Venice •

Spanish Road

Rhine

to Poland, to Russia. But other areas – such as Ireland, Scotland and central France –
remained relatively untouched until after 1700.

Montréal

NEW ENGLAND

New Netherland

FLORIDA

AZTEC EMPIRE

Tenochtitlán

Havana

Atlantic

Barbados

MOROCCO

Tondibi
✗

SONGHAI
EMPIRE

GUINEA

Pacific

Cajamarca•

INCA EMPIRE

Ocean

Ocean

Ocean

CHILE

2 *The military revolution abroad* also occurred in phases. The new military methods of the Europeans were used successfully overseas against the native peoples of the Americas from the sixteenth century, against those of Siberia, Southeast Asia and Sub-Saharan Africa from

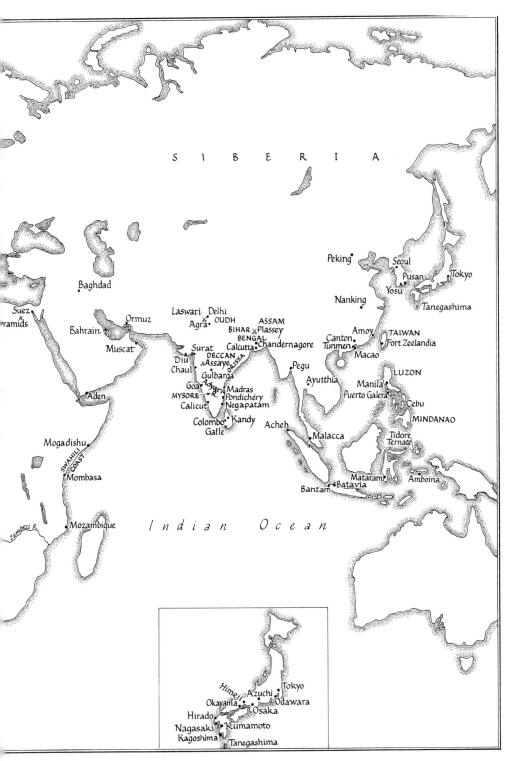

S I B E R I A

Peking
Seoul
Pusan Tokyo
Yosu
Nanking Tanegashima

Baghdad

Suez
ramids
Ormuz
Laswari Delhi
Bahrain
Agra× ×OUDH ASSAM
Muscat BIHAR ×Plassey Amoy TAIWAN
BENGAL Canton Fort Zeelandia
Diu Surat DECCAN Calcutta Chandernagore Tunmen
Chaul ×Assaye ORISSA Macao
Gulbarga Pegu LUZON
Goa Adyar Ayutthia Manila
Aden R. Madras Puerto Galera
MYSORE Pondichéry Cebu
Calicut Negapatam MINDANAO
Colombo Kandy Acheh Tidore
Galle Malacca Ternate

Mogadishu
SWAHILI Amboina
COAST Mataram
Mombasa Bantam Batavia

Zambezi R. Mozambique Indian Ocean

Himeji Azuchi Tokyo
Okayama Odawara
Hirado Osaka
Nagasaki Kumamoto
Kagoshima Tanegashima

the seventeenth, and against those of India from the eighteenth. But even the countries least
intimidated by the warriors of early modern Europe – China and Japan – to some extent
copied the military innovations of the Westerners.

xix

Introduction

'This,' wrote Fulvio Testi, an Italian poet, in 1641, 'is the century of the soldier'. But what century in European history was not? Hardly a decade can be found before 1815 in which at least one battle did not take place. Thus between 700 and 1000 AD, the surviving Western chronicles scarcely mention a year in which hostilities did not break out somewhere, and wartime outweighed peacetime by a factor of about five to one. In the eighteenth century, too, there were only sixteen years during which the continent was entirely at peace.[1] Yet amid this apparent consistency, the early modern period stands out as unusually belligerent. In the sixteenth century there were less than ten years of complete peace; in the seventeenth there were only four. The years between 1500 and 1700, according to a recent study of the incidence of war in Europe, were 'the most warlike in terms of the proportion of years of war under way (95 per cent), the frequency of war (nearly one every three years), and the average yearly duration, extent, and magnitude of war'. During the sixteenth century, Spain and France were scarcely at peace; while during the seventeenth, the Ottoman Empire, the Austrian Habsburgs and Sweden were at war for two years in every three, Spain for three years in every four, and Poland and Russia for four years in every five.[2]

Recent explanations of this unusual readiness to resort to armed conflict have almost always centred around the idea of a 'military revolution' in early modern Europe. The concept was first examined (and christened) in a dazzling inaugural lecture by Michael Roberts, entitled 'The military revolution 1560–1660' and delivered at the Queen's University of Belfast in January 1955. Four changes in the art of war during the period were singled out as critical. First came a 'revolution in tactics': the replacement of the lance and pike by the arrow and musket, as the feudal knights fell before the firepower of massed archers or gunners. Associated with this development were a marked growth in army size right across Europe (with the armed forces of several states increasing tenfold between 1500 and 1700), and the adoption of more ambitious and complex strategies designed to bring these larger armies into action. Fourth and finally, Roberts's military revolution dramatically accentuated the impact of war on society: the greater costs incurred, the greater damage inflicted, and the greater administrative challenges posed by the augmented armies made waging war far more of a burden and far more of a problem than ever previously, both for the civilian population and for their rulers.

There were, of course, many other novelties in early modern warfare – such as the creation of specialized military education and of military academies, the articulation of positive 'laws of war', and the emergence of an enormous literature on the art of war; but tactics, army size, strategy and impact were perceived by Roberts as the key developments. Like so many other inaugural lectures, this novel contribution would probably have been immediately forgotten had Sir George Clark, in his 1956 Wiles Lectures at Belfast (published two years later as *War and society in the seventeenth century*), not singled out the idea for special praise as the new orthodoxy.[3] For the next two decades, almost every work on early modern Europe that mentioned warfare included a paragraph or two which largely repeated Roberts's argument. But since 1976 there have been some criticisms. It has been suggested that Roberts paid insufficient attention to naval developments; that he grossly underestimated the importance of siege warfare throughout early modern times; that he exaggerated the impact of the reforms effected in the Swedish army under Gustavus Adolphus; that he overlooked the parallel but independent changes made in the French, Dutch and Habsburg armies.[4] These criticisms all concern the intrinsic reasons (as it were) for military change in early modern times; but there has also been some revision of Roberts's analysis of the wider implications of the military revolution. Some subsequent writers have claimed that the severe administrative and logistical problems posed by the need to build more fortresses and more warships, and to raise and equip more troops, in effect caused a revolution in government from which emerged, in the eighteenth century, the modern state.[5]

In view of all these objections, some may wonder whether it is justifiable to speak of a 'military revolution' at all. Perhaps too much coherence, too much importance, has been attached to a series of gradual and modest adjustments to the constantly changing demands of war? This issue, however, is easily resolved by comparing early modern Europe's experience with another, undoubted, 'military revolution' some two thousand years before.

The decline of the Chou dynasty in the eighth century BC gave rise to a large number of mutually antagonistic feudal states all over China. Between 770 and 221 BC there were only 127 years entirely free of hostilities: not for nothing is the period known to historians as the 'Warring States Era'. But the nature, duration and intensity of those wars changed radically over time. In the sixth and seventh centuries BC battles, normally fought by rival concentrations of chariots, rarely involved more than 10,000 men; by the third century, however, field armies had grown tenfold, and the total armed forces of the major states approached 1 million.[6] As in early modern Europe, this dramatic increase was associated with important tactical changes: aristocratic charioteers armed with bows gradually gave way to massed conscript infantry armed with spears and swords of iron (assisted by smaller numbers of horse archers). Naturally, military changes of this magnitude presented chronic problems of supply and command which forced the warring states to reshape their political structure; and so most governments changed from something resembling a large household, with most important offices in the hands of the ruler's relatives or leading noblemen, into an autocratic state run on behalf of a despotic prince by a salaried bureaucracy, carefully indoctrinated (from the fifth century BC onwards) with Confucian principles and recruited according to merit from all social classes.

With the aid of this new civil service, and thanks to the larger armies, wars now became longer, less numerous yet more decisive. Between 722 and 464 BC, there were only thirty-eight years of peace (1 year in 6) while between 463 and 221, there were eighty-nine (1 year in 2.5); but during the latter period the number of independent states steadily dwindled. Between 246 and 221 BC, the able Prince Cheng of Ch'in destroyed the other six remaining states and created a unified empire with perhaps 50 million inhabitants and a standing army of well over 1 million. A uniform penal code and administrative structure were applied to the whole empire; a system of roads and canals, a single coinage, and a standardized written language were created; and the first Great Wall, running for 3,000 kilometres along China's northern frontier, was begun. But perhaps the most revealing monument to the power of China's first emperor was his mausoleum, larger than the pyramids of Egypt, built near his capital. It was guarded by an army of 6,000 life-size terracotta figures. Their different faces reflected the diversity of ethnic types within the empire; but the standard uniforms (with colour-coded insignia denoting their unit) and the mass-produced weapons of the emperor's warriors attested to the formidable centralization and efficiency achieved. The 'military revolution' of the Ch'in established a system that endured, with remarkably little change, for two millennia.[7]

The resemblance between this sequence of events and the European military revolution is striking. Both involved a massive manpower growth, a profound change in tactics and strategy, and an intensified impact of war on society. Both, too, required equally profound changes in the structure and philosophy of government. If one be deemed to have constituted a revolution, then so must the other. Admittedly, the changes in early modern Europe did not usher in a military system that lasted, more or less intact, for centuries; but, on the other hand, they not only transformed the conduct of war at home but also decisively accelerated the progress of Europe's expansion overseas. The superior military organization of the Ch'in enabled them to conquer all of China; that of the West eventually allowed them to dominate the whole world. For in large measure 'the rise of the West' depended upon the exercise of force, upon the fact that the military balance between the Europeans and their adversaries overseas was steadily tilting in favour of the former; and it is the argument of this book that the key to the Westerners' success in creating the first truly global empires between 1500 and 1750 depended upon precisely those improvements in the ability to wage war which have been termed 'the military revolution'. That is my principal justification for subjecting the whole question to renewed scrutiny.

So this book is not, and is not intended to be, a general history of the art of war in early modern times. Those who seek a discussion here of the impact of war on society, of the 'costs' of war to the societies that fought them, of the literature on the limits to war, or of the reciprocal relations between a state and the military system it supported, will be disappointed. But all these matters have been admirably covered elsewhere.[8] Instead I have concentrated on those elements of Europe's military history that shed light on a different problem: just how did the West, initially so small and so deficient in most natural resources, become able to compensate for what it lacked through superior military and naval power?

My story begins with a survey of the various ways in which the Europeans fought their wars in the sixteenth and seventeenth centuries, as the rapid spread of firearms transformed the conduct of both offensive and defensive operations, with due regard for those areas that seemed largely unaffected by the military revolution as well as for those that lay at its heart (chapter 1). Chapter 2, by contrast, does focus on these more 'advanced' areas, most of them in the west of Europe, in order to examine the logistical problems which better fortifications and bigger armies created, and how they were overcome. However, the arms-race between the various Western powers took place by sea as well as by land; and the 'military revolution' here offered the European states an opportunity to extend their conflicts far beyond their own shores. At first this escalation remained confined to encounters at sea, with attacks by one European flotilla upon another in the North Atlantic, the Mediterranean, the Caribbean and, eventually, the Indian Ocean (chapter 3). But, before long, the Europeans abroad searched for native allies, and thereby spread their enmities to the other continents. With them they took their new military methods and, as these steadily improved, they gradually gained superiority over all their opponents: over the Americans in the sixteenth century, over most Indonesians in the seventeenth, over many Indians and Africans in the eighteenth. In the end, only Korea, China and Japan held out against the West until the Industrial Revolution in Europe and America forged some new tools of empire – such as the armoured steam-ship and the rapid-fire gun – to which even East Asia at first possessed no effective reply (chapter 4).

This volume concludes with a brief examination of the process by which the armies and navies of the early modern states metamorphosed into those of the industrial age, capable of imposing – and, for nearly a century, of maintaining – Western influence and Western ways on almost the entire world. That saga, of course, has been well told by others, most notably by Daniel R. Headrick in *The tools of empire: technology and European imperialism in the nineteenth century* (Oxford, 1981). Headrick explained how the Western states increased their global empires from about 35 per cent of the world's land surface in 1800 to 84 per cent in 1914. His story makes compelling reading; it does not need retelling. My objective, therefore, is rather different: I seek to illuminate the principal means by which the West acquired that first 35 per cent between 1500 and 1800.

1

The military revolution revisited

'We must confesse,' wrote Sir Roger Williams in his *Briefe discourse of Warre* in 1590, 'Alexander, Caesar, Scipio, and Haniball, to be the worthiest and famoust warriors that ever were; notwithstanding, assure your selfe, . . . they would neuer have . . . conquered Countries so easilie, had they been fortified as Germanie, France, and the Low Countries, with others, have been since their daies.' For Williams, a commander with long experience of war in the Spanish, Dutch and English armies, the proliferation of a defensive system which was more or less impervious to attack, constituted a crucial difference between the wars of his day and those of all preceding periods. In the view of Williams, and of many of his contemporaries, the introduction of geometric fortifications, and of the firearms that made them necessary, revolutionized warfare to such an extent that nothing valuable was to be learnt from past precept.[1]

Naturally, this extreme view was not universally accepted. For every military writer of the Renaissance who rejected the usefulness of ancient examples, there was another who extolled them. Classical treatises were frequently reprinted and translated – especially those composed in the periods when the Roman empire was under threat from external invasion – and their ideas were taken over and adapted to modern conditions by sympathetic military theorists such as Justus Lipsius.[2] But both 'ancients' and 'moderns' were unanimous in their contempt for the intervening millenium between the fall of Rome (476) and the fall of Constantinople (1453): the Middle Ages were considered to be totally devoid of interesting examples or parallels. According to Niccolo Machiavelli, a Florentine of the early sixteenth century with considerable experience of military organization, the wars of the immediately preceding generations had been 'commenced without fear, continued without danger, and concluded without loss'. And later writers have often been led by this and other such statements to dismiss medieval armies as 'mere crowds' which were 'totally, gloriously indisciplined', and have denied that "'generalship" and "planning" are concepts that can usefully be applied to medieval warfare'.[3]

But this is nonsense. The armies of the Middle Ages were subject to just that same tension between offensive and defensive techniques from which strategy, and military innovation, spring. Particularly after the proliferation of stone-built castles in western Europe, which began in the eleventh century, all the necessary ingredients for strategic thinking were present because, wherever the new fortresses were built, military leaders were compelled to increase the size of their armies, to improve the discipline and lengthen the service of their men, and to pursue a strategy of carefully calculated attrition (perhaps for several years on end).[4] According to the foremost authority on the matter, 'the true end of military activity became the capture and defence of fortified places'. By the twelfth century:

An invader could control an area while he occupied it with an army; but if he took no strong place then his control ended with the withdrawal of his forces. The primary objective of an invader who came to annex territory was to take its fortified points. It was not then, as now, to destroy or to paralyse the enemy forces in order that he might impose his will in all things on the ruler whose lands he was attacking.[5]

In the military balance between defence and offence, the former had clearly become predominant. There was therefore, for the time being, little need to change the design of fortifications: the vertical style of Château Gaillard, built in the twelfth century, clearly belongs to the same family as Coucy castle in the thirteenth, the Paris Bastille in the fourteenth, or Prior Hepburn's walls around St Andrews cathedral in the early sixteenth century (plate 1). And the operations required to capture these places, whether by blockade, battery or assault, also changed relatively little. War, in the zone of castles and fortified towns, long remained primarily an affair of manoeuvres, skirmishes and protracted sieges.[6]

I

This stalemate was temporarily terminated by the invention of powerful siege guns in the fifteenth century. At first, the appearance of only one might lead to the immediate surrender of a garrison: Berwick-upon-Tweed's Scottish soldiers surrendered in 1405 after the single English bombard had fired a single round. And, indeed, the sight of weapons like 'Mons Meg', cast for the duke of Burgundy in 1449 and now at Edinburgh Castle, must have been terrifying: it was over three metres long, weighed 8.5 tons, and hurled a stone shot 500 millimetres in diameter (plate 2).[7] But weapons like these had a limited future in the West. In the first place, they were so huge and unwieldy that they could only be transported by water: they could strike terror only into towns and forts accessible by sea or river. Second, there were some fortifications against which, either because of natural defences or skilful design, even the largest bombard was powerless.

1 *St Andrews in Fife* was the seat of the Primate of Scotland, whose ecclesiastical capital was heavily fortified in the 1530s. But the walls, although constructed some time after the first bastions had gone up in Italy, were built on the traditional 'vertical' defensive principle of the Middle Ages, designed to keep out human assault rather than artillery bombardment.

The castle of Coucy in northern France, for example, erected on a rock outcrop between 1225 and 1230 and arguably the largest fortress ever built in Europe, boasted walls up to 7.5 metres thick, which even in the mid-seventeenth century proved impervious to both mines and artillery bombardment. However, in the course of the fifteenth century, the French Crown achieved success against its enemies by concentrating several smaller guns, rather than a few large ones, against fortresses defended by conventional high walls and round towers. In the 1440s and 50s, the English-held towns in Normandy and Aquitaine were reduced by mobile artillery; then in 1487–8, the fortresses of Brittany – although partially adapted to accommodate artillery for defence – were battered into submission. Meanwhile, in Spain, thanks to their command of a siege-train of some 180 guns, the 'Catholic Kings' Ferdinand and Isabella were able to reduce within ten years (1482–92) the Moorish strongholds in the kingdom of Granada that had defied their forebears for centuries. It seemed as if the age of 'vertical defence' was now over.[8]

The Italian architect and humanist, Leon Battista Alberti, was the first to divine the correct response to the bombard. His treatise *De re aedificatoria*, composed in the 1440s, argued that defensive fortifications would be more effective if they were 'built in uneven lines, like the teeth of a saw', and

2 Mons Meg was a bombard cast in the Netherlands in the 1440s for the duke of Burgundy. Although it weighs more than eight tons, it was transported safely to Edinburgh; but deployment on campaign proved more difficult. In 1497, for example, 100 workmen and 5 wrights, as well as a special team of oxen, were assigned to 'Mons' during the Scottish campaign against Norham (on the Border). A pipe band played as the great gun moved majestically down the High Street of Edinburgh, but just outside the city walls she broke down and three days were required to repair the carriage. As a rule, bombards could only be brought into action when they could be transported to the target by water.

even speculated that a star-shaped configuration might be best. But few rulers paid heed; indeed Alberti's treatise remained unpublished until 1485. It was only in the last decades of the century that a number of Italian states began to build fortifications capable of withstanding artillery bombardment. A few (usually fairly small) included angled bastions – the Rocca near Ostia; Brolio and Poggio Imperiale in Tuscany; Castel San Angelo at Rome. But far more were constructed to the traditional design, albeit on such a massive scale that the largest of them (such as the Sforza citadel at Milan) remained defensible for two centuries and more.[9]

The catalyst of major change was the French invasion of the peninsula in 1494–5. Charles VIII brought to Italy an army of 18,000 men and a horse-drawn siege-train of at least forty guns. Even contemporaries realized that this marked a new departure in warfare: in 1498 the Venetian Senate

declared that 'the wars of the present time are influenced more by the force
of bombards and artillery than by men at arms' and frantically set about
acquiring firearms.[10] Other states soon followed suit and, within a few years,
the French invasion was seen as a watershed. According to the Florentine
diplomat and historian, Francesco Guicciardini, writing in the 1520s:

Before the year 1494, wars were protracted, battles bloodless, the methods followed
in besieging towns slow and uncertain; and although artillery was already in use,
it was managed with such lack of skill that it caused little hurt. Hence it came
about that the ruler of a state could hardly be dispossessed. But the French, in
their invasion of Italy, infused so much liveliness into our wars that, up to the
[present], . . . whenever the open country was lost, the state was lost with it.

In a later work, Guicciardini again attributed all the major changes in the
art of war in Italy to the French and their guns:

They were planted against the walls of a town with such speed, the space between
the shots was so little, and the balls flew so quick and were impelled with such
force, that as much execution was done in a few hours as formerly, in Italy, in
the like number of days.[11]

With their aid, cities once considered impregnable were captured with ease.
According to Niccolo Machiavelli, writing in 1519, from 1494 onwards 'No
wall exists, however thick, that artillery cannot destroy in a few days'.[12]

But Machiavelli and Guicciardini were wrong. Even as they wrote, military
architects were evolving a new system of defence against gunfire. The process,
whose culmination is shown in figure 1, was roughly as follows. First, the
walls were made both lower and thicker; but this meant that the defenders,
although better protected against bombardment, could no longer watch the
ground immediately below them and so became more vulnerable to a surprise
assault. Effective flanking fire was therefore needed, and it could only be
provided by constructing gun-towers which projected at an angle beyond
the walls and carried artillery which could not only cut down any assault
on the main defences, but also keep the enemy's siegeguns at bay and cover
the blind spots around the neighbouring bastions. Although many alternative
designs were tried, the construction of quadrilateral, angled bastions at regular intervals along all walls, first attempted around the Papal port of Civitavecchia in 1515, was found to offer the best system of mutually supporting
fields of fire.[13] As time passed, further refinements were added. Thus, it was
found that the addition of a wide and deep ditch both helped to keep the
enemy's artillery at a greater distance and made it more difficult to sink
a gunpowder mine under the walls. Naturally, all these advantages were
multiplied once further fortifications were constructed to defend the ditch.
So either pill-boxes (known as 'casemates') were added within, if the ditch
was dry, or detached triangular bastions (known as 'ravelins') were built
beyond, if it was wet. Finally, strategic areas immediately outside the walls

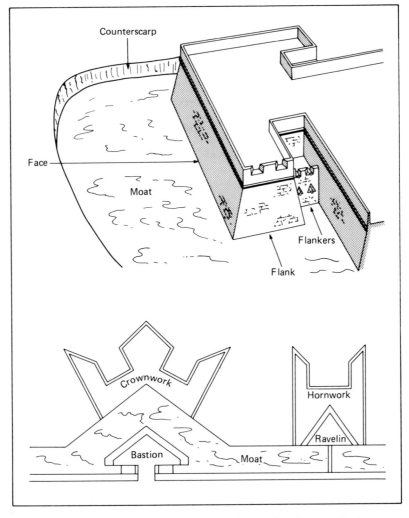

1 *The bastion* was the dominant feature of the new style of defensive fortifications that developed in early modern Europe. Built squat and solid, behind a wide moat, two of its sides pointed outwards and carried heavy artillery to keep besiegers at bay, while the other two stood at right angles to the main wall and bristled with lethal anti-personnel weapons As artillery ranges improved, further fortifications – ravelins, crownworks and hornworks – were added in order to improve defensive capacity.

might be linked with the main defensive system by enclosing them in special extensions ('crownworks' or 'hornworks'); while larger fortified centres could also maintain a series of outlying redoubts (of the same, star-shaped, design, but smaller) intended both to keep lesser enemies at bay and, at the same time, to dominate the villages on which the main garrison depended for supplies and recruits. In this way, major strongholds (such as Turin or Milan) could control up to eighty square kilometres of territory.

The cost, however, was stunning. The scheme to surround Rome with a belt of eighteen powerful bastions was abandoned in 1542 when the construction of one bastion alone was found to have cost 44,000 ducats (about £10,000). Palmanova, built on the Venetian frontier in Friuli in the 1590s, was originally intended to have twelve bastions; but this was soon reduced to nine on the grounds of cost. It was a wise decision: the Republic of Siena had lost its independence forty years earlier largely because its leaders embarked upon a programme of fortification that they could not afford. In 1553, faced with the threat of imminent attack by its enemies, it was decided that seventeen towns, including Siena, would be equipped with new bastions and ramparts. But labour, funds and building materials for such a major project were all so hard to come by that, when the invasion occurred in 1554, few of the projected defence works were complete; and yet the Republic had spent so much on fortification that it had no resources left either to raise a relief army or even to hire and man a fleet to succour its coastal fortresses. So in April 1555, after a gruelling ten-month siege, Siena surrendered unconditionally and was, after a short period of occupation, annexed by her neighbour, Florence. The military revolution had led directly to extinction.[14]

Cautionary tales such as this impeded the spread of the new defensive system (known as the *trace italienne*). Although bastions were built around many fortifications in Spanish Italy, the first to be constructed in Spain itself (at Sabiote) only dates from 1543. Instead, lower walls and scarped towers were sunk into a massive ditch in order to present the smallest possible target for artillery fire.[15] It was not until the 1530s that angled bastions spread across the Alps. By then, however, over 100 Italian engineers were working in France under the direction of Girolamo Marini, and later of Antonio Melloni, on improving the kingdom's northern defences. By 1544, fifteen strongholds along the border with the Netherlands had been provided with new-style fortifications, and were defended by 1,012 artillery pieces (the capital value of the latter alone amounting to about £50,000 sterling).[16] At the same time, other Italians were at work in the Habsburg Netherlands: at Breda for Count Henry of Nassau, at Antwerp for the city council, and along the southern frontier for the Emperor Charles V. Once again, the cost was appalling- for example, the seven-kilometre enceinte of Antwerp with nine bastions and five monumental gates, cost one million florins (about £100,000) – but considerations of national security, as usual, overrode taxpayers' protests.

Between 1529 and 1572, some 43 kilometres of modern defences had been built in the Netherlands: 4 citadels, 12 entirely new circuits of walls, and 18 substantially new circuits, at a total cost of about 10 million florins (£1 million). By 1648, when the Low Countries' Wars ended, only a handful of major settlements remained without bastions.[17] The same process took place slightly later overseas, but the Italian inspiration remained the same. From the 1580s onwards Giovanni Battista Antonelli designed and directed the construction of bastion fortifications at Havana, San Juan de Ulua and Fort Augustine in Florida for the Spaniards, while Giovanni Battista Cairati built forts at Mombasa, Bassein and Damao for the Portuguese.[18]

But how were strongholds such as these to be attacked? There are a few examples in early modern warfare of a well-fortified place being taken by surprise (as, in the Low Countries' Wars, the towns of Holland fell to the Sea Beggars in 1572), or by storm (as with the capture of Antwerp in the 'Spanish Fury' of 1576), or by treachery (as at Aalst, sold to Spain by its English garrison in 1582). But such strokes of good fortune for the besiegers were relatively rare. Normally the capture of a stronghold defended by the *trace italienne* required months, if not years, and a chain of siegeworks had to be built and manned until either the defenders were starved out, or trenches were advanced near enough to the walls to permit close-range bombardment and an assault, or else tunnels were excavated under a bastion where gun-powder mines could be planted (plate 3). Numerous examples of each technique fill the annals of early modern warfare; but the one thing they all had in common was longevity. Thus the Spanish siege of Breda in the Low Countries, which began in August 1624, involved surrounding the city with a double line of fortifications defended by 96 redoubts, 37 forts and 45 batteries. Not a shot seems to have been fired against the bastions and horn-works of Breda itself: the city surrendered nine months later, in May 1625, through simple starvation.[19] This was relatively short by the standards of the Low Countries' Wars! The port of Ostend, in Flanders, had been block-aded for more than three years – from July 1601 until September 1604 – and was eventually forced to surrender only when the Spanish besiegers edged close enough to capture some of the outworks and created a breach capable of being assaulted.[20] On the other hand, the Dutch siege of 's Herto-genbosch in 1629 began in late April, but it was not until mid-July that the outlying redoubts around the city were all taken. Only then could mining and bombardment commence against the city's own walls; and only on 11 September was a mine sprung, under one of the main bastions, which created a breach capable of being stormed. The 3,000-man garrison surrendered three days later.[21]

To secure up to 50,000 besiegers from disturbance as they tunnelled and mined normally required a double chain of fortifications around the block-aded centre – one ring to keep the defenders in, the other to keep any relief forces out (plate 4). Since these were normally constructed some way beyond the range of the artillery mounted on the walls of the beleaguered town – which might be 1,500 metres long – the siegeworks about a major town could be very extensive indeed. Those erected by the Dutch around 's Herto-genbosch in 1629, for example, stretched for forty kilometres.[22]

3 *Sapping and mining* were just as important in reducing places defended by bastions as artillery. But here, too, there were problems: moving a bombard the size of 'Mons Meg' may have been a Herculean labour, but so was the excavation of a tunnel large enough and long enough to enable a gunpowder mine to be planted under some part of the fortifications under siege. (From Leonhard Fronsperger, *Kriegsbuch,* III [Frankfurt, 1573], CLXVI v.)

Clearly to carry out an operation like this, and at the same time defend one's own fortresses from attack, called for unprecedented concentrations of both men and munitions. Thus although the siege of 's Hertogenbosch itself tied down only 25,000 men, the need to defend the numerous fortified centres of the Republic itself required an increase in Dutch army size from 71,443 in February 1629, to 77,193 in April, and to 128,877 in July.[23] And, even then, the town held out for three more months.

After the Renaissance, therefore, much of western Europe seemed locked into a military system in which offence and defence were almost exactly balanced. There were some further improvements to fortifications in the seventeenth century, but they did not render the earlier versions obsolete, as the bastion had almost instantly outmoded most medieval walls; indeed, several early modern fortresses continued to be seen as strategically important until the 1920s. Yet in the year 1722, J. D. Durange, a military engineer at Jülich, published a treatise which found fault with each of the 118 different methods of fortification previously put forward by some seventy individual

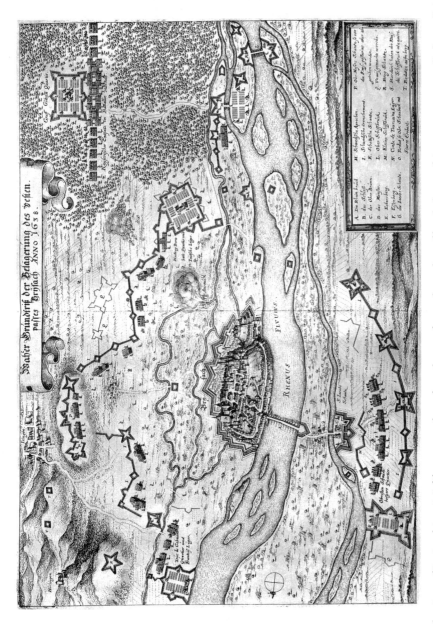

4 *The siege of Breisach* in 1638, like many others, lasted several months and so offered plenty of time to arrange a relief expedition. But this was easier said than done: a besieging army, given time, could build for itself a position almost as impregnable as the beleaguered town. Thus, although a powerful relief army approached the siegeworks and camped close by (*upper right*), it could not dislodge the besiegers and, eventually, Breisach was starved into surrender.

authors. Needless to say, he proceeded to offer a further (119th) method of his own.[24] And in this he was partly justified, for many bizarre designs were the work of armchair mathematicians and economists, or of civilian architects, rather than of military engineers. But that was not the whole story. The 'military revolution' had, in effect, created strategic problems to which there was no easy solution. A heavily defended fortress or town, sheltering perhaps 10,000 men and supported by lesser strongholds in the vicinity, was far too dangerous to be left in the wake of an advancing army: it had to be taken, whatever the cost. And yet there was no short-cut to capture, however powerful the besieging army might be. This simple paradox rendered battles more or less irrelevant in all areas where the new fortifications were built, except (as often occurred) when they were fought between a besieging army and a relief column, so that the result decided the outcome of the siege – as at St Quentin (1557), Nordlingen (1634), Rocroi (1643), Marston Moor (1644), the Dunes (1658), or Vienna (1683). And for every battle fought, there were numerous sieges. In the words of Roger Boyle, Lord Broghill and Orrery, writing in the 1670s:

Battells do not now decide national quarrels, and expose countries to the pillage of the conquerors, as formerly. For we make war more like foxes, than like lyons; and you will have twenty sieges for one battell.[25]

Even John Churchill, duke of Marlborough, who in his campaigns of the 1700s expressly sought opportunities to give battle, only fought four major actions during his ten campaigns; but he conducted thirty sieges.

However Marlborough's battles, with thin ranks of musketeers firing at each other in lines running for several kilometres, were totally different in nature from the predominantly cavalry encounters of (say) the Crusaders or the Capetians. For the revolution in siege warfare during the Renaissance was accompanied by a revolution in field warfare, as tactics which relied on the direct use of brute force (headlong charges, hand-to-hand combat) gave way to the use of firepower. The transition began, like the change in fortress design, in the fifteenth century; and it likewise began in Italy. The English had, since the wars of Edward I (1272–1307), used volleys of arrows in battle as well as cavalry charges and, when they attempted to conquer France under Edward III (1327–77), their archers secured a string of striking victories over the French mounted knights. Even in the early fifteenth century, the French resisted the logical implications of their ill-success: at Agincourt, in 1415, the vanquished Valois host still numbered two men-at-arms to every archer. But eventually they changed their minds. In the great military ordinance of 1445, the composition of the royal army was established at two archers for every man-at-arms.[26]

It was in this context of increased reliance on missiles that the attractions of the gun became obvious. Small-calibre firearms – both hand-held and on carriages – first appeared on the battlefields of Europe in the fourteenth century but, in terms of accuracy and range, they long remained inferior to the bow. Indeed, the English persisted until well into the sixteenth century in preferring the longbow to the gun; and although King James IV of Scotland in 1508 acquired a 'hand culverin' (for stalking deer at Falkland, shooting seabirds on the Isle of May, and target practice in the great hall of Holyrood House), he and his army brought scarcely any firearms to their catastrophic defeat at Flodden five years later.[27] Even Charles the Rash, duke of Burgundy, who maintained an army in which firepower predominated, still trusted to archers rather than to gunners: in 1471 his army numbered 1,250 men-at-arms, and 1,250 pikemen, as against 5,000 archers and 1,250 hand-gunners. The majority of these troops were salaried professionals (many came from abroad, above all from England and Italy), and they were defeated only because – at Hericourt, Morat, Grandson, and Nancy – they were taken at a disadvantage by a far larger enemy force of pikemen. In the final battle, for example, at which Charles lost his life in January 1477, the Burgundian army of at most 4,000 men faced an allied host of at least 20,000. Guns played a minor part in the outcome. But the new weapons were immediately welcomed in Italy. In the numerous battles between the Italian states in the fifteenth century, firearms became ever more prominent until, in 1490, the Venetian Republic decided to replace all its crossbows with guns and, in 1508, to equip its newly formed militia with gunpowder weapons. The armies of other states soon travelled the same road.[28]

The performance of these early firearms, however, still left much to be desired: a well-trained archer could discharge ten arrows a minute, with reasonable accuracy up to 200 metres, but the arquebus of the earlier sixteenth century took several minutes to reload and was accurate only up to 100 metres. And yet, for all that, the gun remained attractive because it required virtually no training for use. As J. F. Guilmartin put it: 'Where a few days and a good drill sergeant might suffice to train a reasonably good arquebusier, many years and a whole way of life were needed to produce a competent archer'.[29] Undoubtedly the introduction of the musket in the 1550s, beginning with the Spanish regiments in Italy, accelerated the process, since the new weapon could throw a 2-ounce lead shot with sufficient force to penetrate even plate armour 100 metres away.[30] Gradually, the musketeer became master of the battlefield and drove off most other military specialists. The first to go were the broadswordsmen, whose skill with their double-handed claymores had struck terror into most enemies: there are few references to them after 1515. The halberd vanished shortly afterwards and, for a time, even cavalry became relatively scarce. Machiavelli believed that the ideal army should have twenty foot soldiers for each horseman, and in the later sixteenth century some armies did indeed approach this ratio (see page 69 below). Crossbowmen had largely disappeared by the mid-century, and even

England finally dropped longbows in favour of handguns during the 1560s. Although a rearguard action was fought in favour of the longbow by some armchair strategists, their case was not generally heeded: in Robert Barret's *Theory and practice of modern wars*, a military treatise of 1598, 'a gentleman' reminded 'a captain' that Englishmen in the past had done well enough with the longbow; to which the captain witheringly replied, 'Sir, then was then, and now is now. The wars are much altered since the fiery weapons first came up.'[31]

But although archers gave way to musketeers, pikemen remained. In the course of the fourteenth and fifteenth centuries, the armed forces of the Swiss cantons had demonstrated that tightly formed squares of pikemen could defeat both cavalry charges and attacks by other infantry units. Indeed for a time, after the crushing defeat of the Burgundians in the 1470s, the Swiss pikemen were reckoned invincible and the troops of many German and Italian states were ordered to imitate them.[32] But firearms succeeded where the knights had failed: a pike square might be proof against cavalry, but it offered an easy target to field artillery and handguns. At Ravenna (1512), Marignano (1515), and Bicocca (1522) gunfire inflicted serious casualties on the massed pikemen.[33] Not surprisingly, within a few years, most nations had added files of 'firelocks' to defend their pike squares, although at first the ratio was only about one to three. But, as the century advanced, and the effectiveness and reliability of firearms improved, some armies added a few specialist companies of 'shot' (combined musket and arquebus) to existing regiments.[34] Eventually, by the 1650s, most units comprised shot and pike in a ratio of three or four to one.[35]

It was now the pikemen who protected the musketeers, thanks to the musket's lamentably slow rate of fire. By the beginning of the seventeenth century, it would seem, an experienced musketeer could get off one round every two minutes; but against a cavalry charge that meant, in effect, only one round between the enemy coming into effective range and the onset of hand-to-hand combat.[36] There were only two ways of changing this situation. One was to improve the musket's accuracy. Although some authorities have denied it, this was a genuine alternative, for rifled sporting guns existed which were capable of hitting game at a considerable distance. In war, these were often put in the hands of snipers. In 1633, for example, an English soldier at the siege of Rijnberg in the Netherlands was highly impressed by the accuracy of the enemy sharpshooters: 'Let but the topp of an old hatt appeare' above the parapet, he wrote, 'and you shall presently have three or four bulletts shott into it.'[37] Rifled guns, however, required an even longer reloading time, for the bullet and charge were far harder to ram down the barrel. But, in the 1590s, the commanders of the Dutch army, Counts Maurice and William Louis of Nassau, suddenly realized that there was another way of increasing the musketeers' rate of fire: if their men were

5 *The European countermarch* was first suggested by William Louis of Nassau in a letter to his cousin Maurice, written in Groningen on 8 December 1594 (see the last line of the document). The Count, who had just read Aelian's description of the drill practised by the Roman army, argued that six rotating ranks of musketeers could replicate the continuous hail of fire achieved by the javelin and sling-shot throwers of the Legions. In the event, ten ranks were needed at first to maintain constant fire, but musketry volleys soon became the standard battle tactic of European armies. (The Hague, Koninklijke Huisarchief, MS. A22-1XE-79.)

drawn up in a series of long lines, the first rank firing together and then retiring to reload while the following ranks came forward and did the same, a continuous hail of fire would be maintained to keep the enemy at bay. We can date the Dutch discovery of the 'volley' technique very precisely: it first appeared, in diagrammatic form, in a letter from William Louis to his cousin Maurice dated 8 December 1594 (plate 5), and the author asserted that he had derived the idea from an assiduous study of the military methods of the ancient Romans.[38]

The development of volley fire had a critical impact upon battle tactics. To begin with, it was now imperative for armies to spread out during battle, both to maximize the effect of outgoing fire and to minimize the target for incoming fire. The battlefields of medieval Europe had often measured only 1 kilometre across, with up to 10,000 men packed into very tight formations;

but under volley fire this would be suicidal, and so early modern battles gradually came to be fought by men drawn up in ranks that were as long and thin as possible. This, in turn, had important consequences. First, changing a pike square perhaps fifty deep into a musketry line only ten deep inevitably exposed far more men to the challenge of face-to-face combat, calling for superior courage, proficiency and discipline in each individual soldier. Second, it placed great emphasis on the ability of entire tactical units to perform the motions necessary for volley-firing both swiftly and in unison.[39]

The answer to both problems was, of course, practice. Troops had to be trained to fire, countermarch, load and manoeuvre all together. The counts of Nassau therefore divided their army into far smaller formations – companies of 250 with eleven officers were reduced to 120 men with twelve officers; regiments of 2,000 were replaced by battalions of 580 – and taught them to drill. The journal of a member of Maurice's general staff, Anthonis Duyck, reveals the Dutch troops on active service during the 1590s almost constantly at their 'exercises', forming and reforming ranks, drilling and parading in the manner advocated in Roman times by military writers like Vegetius and Aelian, and subsequently by the political philosopher Justus Lipsius in his *De militia romana*, published in 1595.[40]

In 1599, Maurice of Nassau secured funds from the States-General to equip the entire field army of the Republic with weapons of the same size and calibre and, at about the same time, his cousin John began work on a new method of advanced military training: the illustrated drill manual. Count John analysed each of the different movements required to manipulate the principal infantry weapons, gave each of them a number, and prepared a sketch of how each should be performed. There were fifteen drawings for the pike, twenty-five for the arquebus, and thirty-two for the musket (plate 6). In 1606–7, the whole scheme was recast – now there were thirty-two distinct positions for the pike, forty-two for the arquebus and forty-three for the musket – and a sequence of numbered pictures was engraved and published, under Count John's supervision, in Jacob de Gheyn's *Wapenhandlingen van roers, musquetten ende spiessen* [*Arms drill with arquebus, musket and pike*] (Amsterdam, 1607). The book rapidly went through numerous editions in Dutch, and was soon translated into Danish, German, French and English (plate 7).[41]

Even before de Gheyn, however, the fame of Maurice's drill had spread beyond the Dutch Republic. In 1603, Louis de Montgomery, lord of Courbouzon, devoted a chapter of his book on tactics to 'the evolutions and exercises that are used in the Dutch army'; and for many years after the appearance of the *Wapenhandlingen* few works on warfare failed to mention the new methods. Thus John Bingham's English edition of *The tactics of Aelian* (London, 1616) included an appendix entitled 'The exercises of the English in the service ... of the United Provinces of the Low Countries'.[42] And the

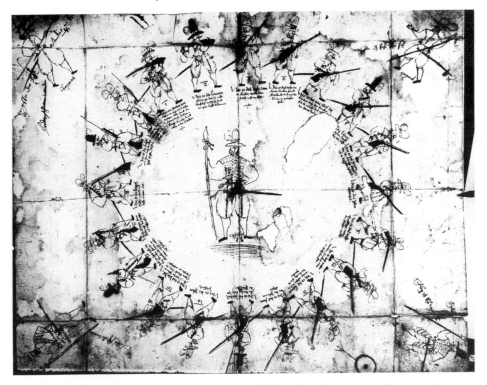

6 *The* Kriegsbuch *of John of Nassau* (a brother of William Louis) was an early recognition of the main difficulty caused by volley-fire: the need to train troops to reload more swiftly. In this early sketch, Count John envisaged twenty positions, here shown simultaneously; in later versions, however, this was expanded to 25 positions for the arquebus and 32 for the musket, each of them illustrated separately and in greater detail. In 1607 his sketches were revised by a professional engraver, Jacob de Gheyn, who published them under his own name. (Wiesbaden, Staatsarchiv, MS. K924 pp. 109f.)

presence of numerous foreign units – Scottish, German and French as well as English – and of innumerable individual foreign volunteers in the Dutch army, certainly aided the spread of Maurice's innovations to other lands. So did the supply of Dutch military instructors to friendly foreign states. Brandenburg requested, and received, two Dutch experts in 1610; others were later sent to the Palatinate, Baden, Württemberg, Hesse, Brunswick, Saxony and Holstein.[43]

Meanwhile in 1616 Count John of Nassau opened a military academy at his capital, Siegen, to educate young gentlemen in the art of war: training took six months, and arms, armour, maps and models for instruction were provided by the school. The first director of the *Schola militaris*, Johan Jakob von Wallhausen, published several manuals of warfare, all of them explicitly based on Dutch practice (the only system taught at Siegen).[44] Even the traditional-minded Swiss, who had retained a strong preference for pikes, were

7 *The exercise of arms*, first published in the Netherlands in 1607, was an immediate best-seller and did much to popularize the new military methods of the Dutch. The English edition, dedicated to Henry Prince of Wales, only required changes to the title page and introduction: the numbered sequence of engravings of course remained the same.

forced to take note: in 1628 the Berne militia was reorganized on unashamedly Dutch lines, with smaller companies and greater firepower.[45] As time passed, drill became more complex – a German military manual of 1726 illustrated seventy-six separate positions for loading and firing a musket where de Gheyn in 1607 had depicted only forty-two – but it was still recognizably the same as the method devised by John, Maurice and William Louis of Nassau more than a century before.[46]

To some extent, however, the full value of the Nassau tactical reforms remained unrealized in the Netherlands, since the Dutch army was seldom exposed to the supreme test of battle. Although the cousins diligently studied accounts of the battle of Cannae in 216 BC, where 40,000 Carthaginians had overwhelmed 70,000 Romans, the ambiguous outcome of their two pitched encounters – at Turnhout in 1597 and at Nieuwpoort in 1600 – suggests that they had not entirely mastered the formula for total victory. But a quarter of a century later, Gustavus Adolphus of Sweden demonstrated its full potential. In the first place, thanks to constant drill and practice in the course of the 1620s reloading speeds in the Swedish army were improved to the point where only six ranks of musketeers could maintain a continuous barrage. Second, firepower was greatly increased by the addition of a copious field artillery. Whereas the Dutch army at Turnhout in 1597 deployed a mere four field guns, and at Nieuwpoort three years later only eight, Gustavus Adolphus took eighty with him to Germany in 1630.[47] These guns were standardized on three calibres (24-, 12.- and 3-pounders) and some were even supplied with cartridges already attached, for speedier loading. The 3-pounders, of which every regiment was issued with four, could fire up to twenty rounds an hour – not much slower than a musketeer.[48] Moreover, where the Dutch tended to use the countermarch defensively, against an advancing enemy, the Swedes used it to attack. According to the Scottish colonel, Robert Monro, who fought in the Swedish army for six years, Gustavus made his first rank advance ten paces before they fired. They then stopped to reload where they stood until the other 'rancks advance before them and give fire after the same manner, till the whole troop hath discharged and so to beginne againe as before ...; ever advancing to an enemie, never turning backe without death, or victorie'.[49] Finally, Gustavus also trained his cavalry to charge home with swords drawn, rather than to skirmish with pistols and carbines from a distance (as most German horsemen preferred to do).[50]

The superiority of the Swedish military system was fully demonstrated at the battle of Breitenfeld, just outside Leipzig, in September 1631. A veteran Imperialist army, numbering 10,000 horse and 21,400 foot and commanded by an experienced general (Count Tilly), was drawn up in squares thirty deep and fifty wide, supported by twenty-seven field guns. The Swedes and their German Protestant allies, however, had fifty-one heavy guns and every regiment was reinforced by its four light field pieces; their 28,000 foot were drawn up in six ranks, covered by 13,000 cavalry. In the event, the German troops fighting with Gustavus broke after the first hour, but the Swedish reserve marched across in perfect order and took their places. In the second hour's fighting, and in the rout that followed, two-thirds of the Imperial army and all its guns were lost, and 120 of their standards were captured and sent back to decorate the Riddarholm church in Stockholm.[51] Further major Swedish victories followed at Lützen (1632), Wittstock(1636), Breitenfeld II (1642) and Jankov (1645), accompanied by a host of lesser encounters from which the Swedes almost always emerged victorious. Not surprisingly, their methods were soon copied by other major armies in Europe (plate 8).

Already at Lutzen, in November 1632, the Imperialists (under Albrecht von Wallenstein) had thinned out their lines, perfected volley firing, and added field artillery. After this, most other states began to acquire large numbers of Swedish guns – up to 1,000 a year were being exported by the 1650s, mostly for sale in Amsterdam[52] – and the musket remained the 'queen of the battlefield' for over two centuries.

II

So the military revolution of early modern Europe possessed a number of separate facets. First, the improvements in artillery in the fifteenth century, both qualitative and quantitative, eventually transformed fortress design. Second, the increasing reliance on firepower in battle – whether with archers, field artillery or musketeers – led not only to the eclipse of cavalry by infantry in most armies, but to new tactical arrangements that maximized the opportunities of giving fire. Moreover these new ways in warfare were accompanied by a dramatic increase in army size. Ferdinand and Isabella of Spain conquered Granada in 1492 with a force exceeding 60,000 men, and their grandson Charles V commanded perhaps 100,000 against the Turks in Hungary in 1532, and almost 150,000 overall at the time of his unsuccessful siege of Metz in 1552. And where Spain led, her principal enemy was forced to follow: Charles VIII of France had invaded Italy in 1494 with 18,000 men, but Francis I attacked in 1525 with 32,000 and Henry II captured Metz in 1552 with 36,000. By the 1630s, the armed forces maintained by the leading European states totalled perhaps 150,000 each and, by the end of the century, there were almost 400,000 French soldiers (and almost as many again ranged against them). The ancillary services of armies also increased dramatically: for example, where the French royal artillery in the 1440s consumed only 20,000 pounds of powder annually and was supervised by 40 gunners, a century later it consumed 500,000 pounds and required the services of 275 gunners.[53] However, all the evidence for radical military change, whether in army size, fortifications, or firearms, comes from the lands of the Habsburgs or of their neighbours: from Spain, Italy, the Netherlands, and France. That was the heartland of the military revolution.[54] But what of the other regions of Europe: how did the character of warfare develop there in early modern times?

The key variable appears to have been the presence or absence of the *trace italienne* in a given area, for where no bastions existed, wars of manoeuvre with smaller armies were still feasible. And, for a long time, outside the 'heartland' there was a marked reluctance to introduce the new

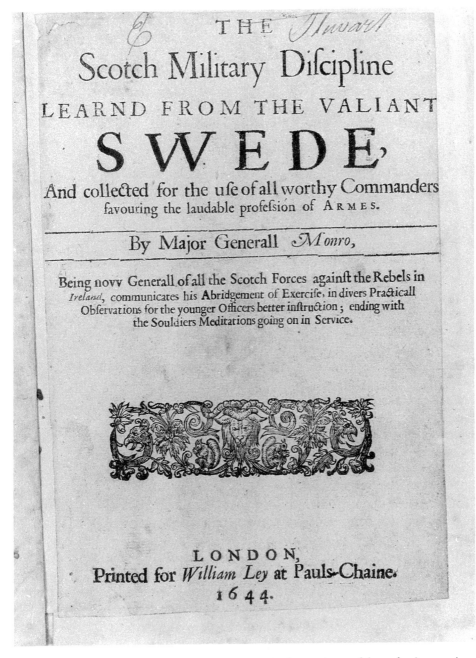

THE *Illustrat*
Scotch Military Difcipline
LEARND FROM THE VALIANT
SWEDE,
And collected for the ufe of all worthy Commanders favouring the laudable profeffion of ARMES.

By Major Generall *Monro,*

Being novv Generall of all the Scotch Forces againft the Rebels in *Ireland,* communicates his Abridgement of Exercife, in divers Practicall Obfervations for the younger Officers better inftruction; ending with the Souldiers Meditations going on in Service.

LONDON,
Printed for *William Ley* at Pauls-Chaine.
1644.

8 *The Scotch military discipline* (London, 1644) was in fact a reissue of the author's memoirs of 1637, entitled *Monro his expedition with the worthy Scots regiment call'd Mackays*. Most of the volume was still taken up with a chronicle of the regiment's service in Germany between 1626 and 1633, but it did contain Monro's thoughts on the art of war. Since the 1,500 copies printed in 1637 were not all sold, it was evidently hoped that a title more appropriate to wartime would shift the rest.

defensive systems. Thus in Germany, a few towns commissioned new walls during the confrontation between the emperor and his Protestant subjects in the 1540s and 50s; but after that there was a half century of peace, during which virtually no new military constructions were erected. Then after 1600 all this changed again, as religious tension within the Empire rose once more: first the Protestants began to build new citadels and fortresses (the Elector Palatine, for example, at Frankenthal, Heidelberg and Mannheim); then the Catholics, suitably alarmed, followed suit (the Elector of Trier at Ehrenbreitstein, the bishop of Speyer at Philippsburg, the duke of Bavaria at Munich and Ingolstadt). Elsewhere, large cities which had always been fortified updated their defences, while new centres of economic activity (mining towns, manufacturing locations) and new capital cities (Neuburg, Hanau, Julich) found it prudent to acquire up-to-date protective walls for the first time. But there were hundreds of other towns in Germany which perceived no strategic threat until the outbreak of the Thirty Years War in 1618. Even then, the war remained relatively localized for some time, and the ease with which many towns changed hands in the 1620s and 30s confirms the evidence of Matthaeus Merian's contemporaneous bird's-eye views: that there were still relatively few bastion defences in central Europe.[55] That is the main reason why there were so many battles in the Thirty Years War, and why so many campaigns covered thousands of miles and consisted mainly of complex manoeuvres designed to force one's enemy either to fight or to retreat into devastated areas where his troops might starve. The Swedish main army under Gustavus Adolphus covered almost 1,600 kilometres in the course of 1631 and 1632, and fought four major battles – Breitenfeld, Rain, Alte Veste and Lützen – while the successors of these men in the last three years of the war, from the battle of Jankov to the siege of Prague, covered even more ground.[56]

The *trace italienne* made slow progress, in Germany and elsewhere, not merely because of the cost (although for some states that was deterrent enough), but also through the difficulties of keeping up to date. Thus Henry VIII of England, fearing a general invasion from the Continent, drew up a detailed 'Device' in February 1539 for improving the defences of eastern and southern England and of the English outposts in France. An impressive series of twenty-eight new forts were built and many older ones were refurbished all around the coasts. But the work was entrusted by the king to his native master-craftsmen, rather than to professional architects from abroad, and the results were outdated even before they were completed. With their concentric hollow keep and bastions, liberally endowed with gunports (Sandgate Castle boasted over sixty artillery and sixty-five handgun embrasures), these edifices certainly maximized the potential for offensive firepower; but they possessed poor defensive capacity (plate 9). Hollow walls could not withstand heavy bombardment and round bastions proved an easy

9 *Henry VIII's south coast defences*, c. 1539. The king's decision to break with Rome in the 1530s certainly provided the state with vast new resources, in the shape of confiscated church lands; but it also created new expenditures to match, since Protestant England was plunged into a 'cold war' with both France and the Habsburg empire. A chain of new fortresses was designed and built to defend the south-east from invasion but, unfortunately, all of them (like this design for the 'castle for the Downes' near Dover) were made of hollow concentric rings rather than solid angular bastions. (BL, Cotton MS. Augustus, I.i.20.)

prey to mine and sap. Yet Henry remained convinced that he knew best. When a Portuguese engineer in 1541 criticized the reconstructed defences of Guines as unsound, the king crisply dismissed him as 'an ass who did not understand his business'. But four years later, shaken by the massive (albeit unsuccessful) French invasion of the Solent, Henry at last accepted that a new generation of fortifications, with angled bastions, ravelins and the rest, would be required. Eyemouth, Portsmouth and other places of strategic importance were hastily (though expensively) fortified. However, when the next invasion scare came – in 1588 – these defences, too, were deemed outdated and another round of spending was required to renovate, augment and extend them (though even this would almost certainly not have been enough to protect Elizabethan England, if the Spanish Armada had landed). As one of the queen's advisors remarked, it was too little and too late: Elizabeth seemed to share 'the opinion of the Lacedemonians, that fortifying of towns doth more hurt than good'.[57]

Certainly a 'Lacedemonian' policy saved money and, with few exceptions, rulers tended to sanction the building of new fortifications only in times of crisis. Indeed, the decision to build bastions was usually a clear sign of imminent war. Thus in England, only a few places possessed modern fortifications in 1642, on the eve of the Civil Wars – Berwick, Hull, Portsmouth and Plymouth – and all of these were on the coast, whereas most of the fighting took place inland. So after the war began, several key towns (such as the rival capitals, Oxford and London) and some strategically located country houses were provided with a full enceinte; while other less important centres were simply surrounded with a chain of redoubts (sometimes linked by a rampart, as at Newark, Bristol and Reading, but usually not).[58] When such strong points came under attack, a major siege on continental lines was required: the royalist garrison of Newark, for example, supported by outlying redoubts at Shelford, Belvoir Castle, Thurgaton, Wiverton Hall and Norwell, easily withstood the siege maintained by some 7,000 Scottish and 9,000 Parliamentarian troops in 1645–6.[59] But most places of strategic significance during the English Civil War were enclosed (rather than defended) by outdated medieval walls wholly susceptible to artillery bombardment. It is therefore strange to find that relatively few places were in fact reduced by gunfire until 1645. The explanation, however, is simple. Given the highly unsettled state of most of the kingdom during the early war-years, with powerful detachments from both sides roaming the roads, it was extremely hazardous to convey a siege-train across the country. One risked losing it (as Parliament did at Lostwithiel in 1644, forfeiting forty heavy guns to the king). Most towns, therefore, were taken by storm – just as in the Middle Ages – with no preliminary battery; while the few remaining strongholds were bombarded by only a handful of big guns at any one time. Thus against Lathom House in Lancashire, Parliament could bring, in 1644, only one

80-pound mortar, one 27-pounder and one 15-pounder siege gun; against Pontefract, in 1645, there were only three heavy guns (they fired 1,400 rounds but failed to make a breach); and against Scarborough, in the same year, a single 64-pounder 'cannon royal' made no impression at all.[60] Only after the victory at Naseby (June 1645) was the Parliamentary army able to move its siege train around at will.[61] The wars in Scotland were little different: Aberdeen (1645) and Dundee (1651) were taken by storm, while Glasgow, Perth and Stirling capitulated before a shot was fired. None had replaced their medieval walls.[62]

The position in Ireland during the 1640s illustrates the contrast between the old and new ways in warfare even more starkly. Until the twelfth century, there were no stone castles in the island at all, but they soon proliferated – especially after 1430 when the government offered a subsidy to anyone who would build a tower eleven or more metres high within five years. By 1500 there were reputedly 400 in County Limerick alone, and Ireland simply bristled with castles. Although some were merely towerhouses, others were very large indeed, such as the castle of Trim, built between 1210 and 1250 with walls 3 metres thick and 12 metres high, or the walls and castle of Drogheda, also built in the thirteenth century, which were roughly the same. But these high, thin defences were of little use against artillery. Drogheda withstood a three-month siege in 1641–2 by an Irish army; but Oliver Cromwell took it by storm seven years later, even though it was defended by 3,000 veteran troops, because he was able to concentrate the fire of eleven siege and twelve field guns against its ancient walls.[63] However Cromwell's army was less successful in Ulster, where immigrants from Scotland and England had settled in strength since 1603, protecting their settlements with fortifications that were far more modern. Under Elizabeth, the local lords had built 'tower-houses' like those of Scotland (indeed, many, such as Enniskillen Castle [plate 10] were built by masons hired from Scotland); but under James VI and I, defences with bastions, moats and artillery platforms were begun. The Enniskillen tower-house (or what remained of it) was surrounded with ramparts; so was the new settlement at Londonderry (with a circuit of walls more than a kilometre in circumference, defended by a moat and forty heavy guns); and star-shaped sconces were constructed to protect the new 'plantations' at Charlemount, Hillsborough and elsewhere. But the settlers were short of firearms to defend their modern walls: a survey of the weapons owned by the English and Scots in Antrim and Down in 1630 showed that only 99 of the 4,255 adult males recorded there possessed guns, while only 2,416 owned swords or pikes, and 1,839 were unarmed.[64] So in the course of the Ulster rebellion of 1641, most of the modern forts fell for lack of defenders, and only the larger settlements held out.

During the 1650s, many of the 'rebel fortresses' in Ireland were destroyed; but a considerable number of new ones were constructed in strategic places,

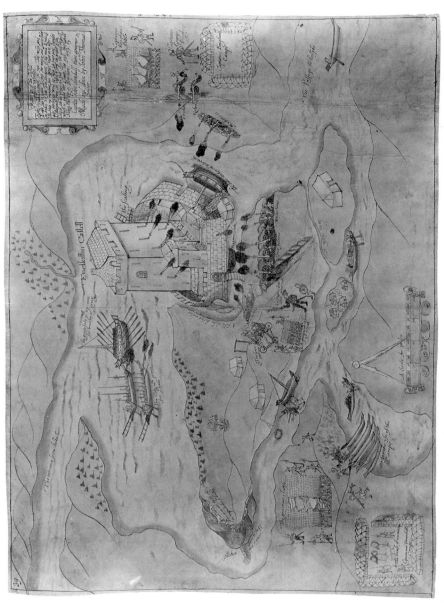

10 *The siege of Enniskillen* (Co Fermanagh) in 1594 showed that the military revolution was only partially understood in Tudor Ireland. The detailed drawing by an English participant, made to inform the London government, shows the use of heavy artillery (*right*), a siege engine (*lower left*) and armed galleys (*upper left*). But the English camp is still shown unfortified and, in the end, scaling ladders were evidently required to take the tower-house. The illustration helps to explain why the English took nine years to suppress Tyrone's rebellion. (BL, Cotton MS. Augustus, I.ii.39.)

11 *Charles Fort, Kinsale*, built in the 1670s to secure a harbour in the south-west of Ireland
that had twice been used as a base for hostile invasion, shows that the *trace italienne* was
becoming known in even relatively remote parts of Europe by that date. But although known,
it was still imperfectly understood, for a report from an engineer with continental experience
in 1686 considered that (although well-built) Charles Fort had been situated in an indefensible
spot, overlooked by higher ground, and would require a further £23,000 to complete.

according to continental principles (and, indeed, mostly to an identical quadrilateral design, with a bastion at each of the four angles).[65] Then in 1668
the government decided to fortify the harbour of Kinsale, which had already
been used as a bridgehead for invasion by Spanish troops in 1601–2. and
by Royalist forces in 1649: Charles Fort, Kinsale, completed in the 1670s,
contained six huge bastions and enough barrack accommodation for a large
garrison (plate 11). Nevertheless, in the 1680s, the government in London
became concerned that other parts of Ireland might also be easily captured
by invaders. So an experienced engineer, Thomas Phillips, was sent to inspect
all existing defences. His report, submitted in March 1686, made depressing
reading. There were, he said, far too many castles in Ireland, and yet none
of them – including Charles Fort – were strong enough to withstand a
siege. Moreover they were not situated in the right places because, Phillips
observed wryly, 'attempts and disturbances seldome are where places are

prepared'. Thus, even if every strategic centre were to be fortified in the latest fashion:

there are yett twice as many more unsecured, soe that it will be endlesse to think to fortifie all places that require it. For the more fortifications, the greater the army, and the greater the number of fortifications, the more the army is disperst [in garrisons] and of less use.

Phillips therefore proposed the construction of six fortresses only, each of massive proportions, capable of sheltering a powerful army and of withstanding a major siege.[66] But when the next rebellion came, in 1689–90, none of the new super-fortresses had becn built, and even Charles Fort fell with scarcely a blow. The full *trace italienne* only came to Ireland – and to Scotland – in the eighteenth century, with the construction of offensive bastion-defences large enough to shelter a force capable of mounting a counter-attack in case of rebellion or invasion.[67]

The British Isles, then, were a zone where the transformation in fortification and siegecraft was incomplete, gradual and relatively tardy. Naturally, this had a marked effect on the art of field warfare. Ireland, where bastion-defences were almost non-existent, was, of course, the most backward – as indeed it had been throughout the Middle Ages. In the fourteenth century Jean Froissart noted that 'It is hard to find a way of making war on the Irish effectively for, unless they choose, there is no one there to fight, and there are no towns to be [taken]'.[68] But once the Irish chiefs began to live in stone castles during the fifteenth century, there was more to attack (and to defend) and mercenary troops, above all from Scotland, were hired in large numbers both to assault neighbouring chiefs and to resist the periodic invasions of the English. Firearms, however, still remained a rarity. The first recorded use of either handguns or ordnance in Ireland dates from the 1480s; and, even then, the mountains, bogs and forests of the interior made it almost impossible to deploy siege pieces inland. Instead, both sides frequently adopted a policy of 'beastliness'. In the 1570s an English commander, Sir Humphrey Gilbert, openly engaged in counter-insurgency terrorism and (according to his personal chronicler):

tooke this order infringeable, that whensoever he made any ostyng, or inroad, into the enemies Countries, he killed manne, woman and child, and spoiled, wasted and burned, by the grounde, all that he might; leavyng nothing of the enemies in saffetie, which he could possibllie waste or consume . . .

The same savage treatment was extended to any invaders allied to the Irish: thus the 400 Italian and Spanish auxiliaries who surrendered to an English force at Smerwick in 1580 were almost all massacred in cold blood, as were the 3,000 Spaniards from the Armada who, eight years later, were forced ashore by storms.[69]

It was partly the effectiveness of English brutality, made possible by an overwhelming superiority in firepower, that eventually convinced the Irish leaders of the need to embrace the gunpowder revolution. Although he never acquired siege guns, Hugh O'Neill, earl of Tyrone, hired English and Spanish captains in the 1580s specifically to train his 10,000 or so native troops in the use of the musket, and he purchased firearms and ammunition on a large scale in England and Scotland, as well as from fugitive soldiers and corrupt offficials in Ireland. Thanks to these measures, soon after he rebelled against Queen Elizabeth, Tyrone's men inflicted a heavy defeat on the English at Clontibret in 1595. They did so again at the Yellow Ford in 1598 and, towards the end of that year, were able to launch raids on the suburbs of Dublin. But then a new commander, Charles Blount, Lord Mountjoy, began to use against Tyrone the painstaking strategy of attrition that he had witnessed in the Low Countries' Wars. He avoided battles, fearing that his troops might be defeated. Instead a chain of autonomous, well-stocked fortresses was placed around mid-Ulster, from each of which powerful garrisons carried out raids systematically to destroy the crops and stores on which Tyrone's war-effort depended. Even the arrival of a Spanish expeditionary force of 3,500 men at Kinsale in 1601, which forced Mountjoy to march south, did not reduce England's stranglehold on Ulster. Early in 1602 the Spaniards surrendered and Tyrone, his field army destroyed in battle as it tried to reach Kinsale, followed suit the next year. It was a great victory, for it established English rule over the whole of Ireland for more than three hundred years.[70]

However, even though the English eventually managed to apply the military revolution in Ireland, they still lagged far behind continental practice at home. Above all there was, until relatively late, very little use of field artillery. In some battles of the English Civil War, such as Naseby (1645) or Preston (1649), neither side deployed field guns at all; while at other times they only seemed effective when defending an entrenched position against frontal attack.[71] There was nothing to match Gustavus Adolphus's concentration of 90 artillery pieces at the crossing of the Lech in 1632 or Torstensson's brilliant re-alignment of his field batteries to win the battle of Wittstock in 1636.

But this failure was not entirely for want of trying. There were, for example, numerous British attempts to imitate the light and mobile 3-pounders popularly known as 'leather guns'. The technique of casting a thin metal barrel, bound with rope and encased in a tough leather sheath, was first perfected in Zurich in 1622. By 1627 leather guns were being made in Sweden, and before long they were to be found, often mounted in twos and threes, in general use in the Swedish army. From there they spread to other forces, and examples are still to be found in the museums of Paris, Berlin and elsewhere. But the largest single collection of leather guns – nineteen in number,

12 *Leather guns* were an unsuccessful attempt to create a mobile field artillery. This battery of four, cast in Scotland in the 1630s, still shows the way in which leather and rope were 'sweated' on to a metal barrel, much as steel guns were to be made in the nineteenth century. But, unlike steel guns, the casing of leather guns proved a poor conductor and they soon overheated. The fact that they were nevertheless used repeatedly in action (at least until 1689) reflects the military backwardness of Scotland at this time.

with forty-two barrels – lies today in Scotland's National Museum of Antiquities (plate 12). They were not preserved, however, because of their success in battle; on the contrary, they survived because they proved useless in action on behalf of the Covenanting armies at Dunbar (1650) and Worcester (1651), and so were captured. It was a measure of the government's unpreparedness after the 'Glorious Revolution' of 1688 that, the following year, they were nevertheless taken out to be used at Killiecrankie against the Jacobite rebels led by John Graham of Claverhouse, Viscount Dundee. Many exploded at the third round, and the rest were insufficient to stop the dramatic charge of the Jacobite Highlanders.[72]

The truth is that leather guns did not work. Their rope and leather bindings were poor conductors, and caused the barrels, however well made, to over-heat. But it is doubtful whether *any* conventional weapons of the day could have stopped 'Bonnie Dundee' and the Highland Charge. For, after delivering a single musket volley, as much to create a smoke screen as to kill adversaries, the clansmen threw down their firearms and regrouped in wedges before racing forward with only a targe (to thrust aside English bayonets) and a sword (to cut English throats). As the defeated general at Killiecrankie, Hugh Mackay, later observed:

The Highlanders are of such a quick motion, that if a battalion keep up his fire till they be near to make sure of them, they are upon it before our men can come to their second defence, which is the bayonet.

On the other hand, as another unsuccessful commander – General Hawley – observed shortly before his defeat at the battle of Falkirk in 1746, firing at the Highland Charge too soon was also fatal.

If the fire is given at a distance you probably will be broke, for you never get time to load a second cartridge; and if you give way, you may give your foot [up] for dead, for they [the Highlanders], being without a firelock or any load, no man with his arms, accoutrements, etc., can escape them, and they give no Quarter ...[73]

So throughout the seventeenth and early eighteenth centuries, numerous encounters occurred in which troops equipped with all the tools of the military revolution were put to flight by the headlong charge of a horde of clansmen armed only with traditional weapons – under the marquis of Montrose and Alastair MacColla from Tippermuir to Kilsyth in 1644–5; under Claverhouse at Killiecrankie in 1689; under 'Bonnie Prince Charlie' at Prestonpans and Falkirk in 1745–6. And the Highland Charge was only stopped at Culloden, later in 1746, because the Hanoverian army possessed, on that occasion, considerable field artillery, overwhelming numerical super-iority, and (above all) improved fire-control. This time the rear rank of muske-teers fired first, when the clansmen were about twelve metres away, and the other two ranks only fired after that, when the enemy was at point-blank range (plate 13).[74] Although the Highlanders were to charge successfully once more – at the battle on the Heights of Abraham, in 1759, which wrested Canada from French control – elsewhere the infantry regiments of the line with their salvoes reigned supreme on the battlefields of Europe.[75]

The military revolution was also slow to affect warfare in other areas on the periphery of Europe. When Charles X of Sweden found himself at war with Russia in 1656 his army in Finland – numbering some 10,000 infantry – was obliged to learn to operate on skis in order to protect the frontier in winter. They can have had little time for drill or volley fire.[76] Beyond and between the fortresses along the Ottoman–Habsburg border in

13 *The Highland Charge* was used successfully by Scottish clan warriors for over a century before the decisive defeat at Culloden in 1746. The Jacobite soldiers again managed to come close to the Hanoverian musketeers on that occasion, but volley-fire at close range destroyed them. It is interesting to note that the artist, who used some of the clansmen captured at Culloden as his models, showed them dressed in plaids of many different types and hues: the idea of individual 'clan tartans' was invented after the '45. (From David Morier, 'An incident in the rebellion of 1745: Culloden'.)

Hungary, a peculiar system of frontier warfare grew up in the century after 1560 in which the main military preoccupations became cattle and prisoners – preoccupations that are accurately reflected in surviving local documents, which record the number and value of livestock captured or lost in meticulous detail but reserve the greatest detail for the prisoners. Military rank, distinguishing marks, names and aliases (such as 'Ali the Beast' or 'Crazy Yusuf') were all carefully noted, for this was the real objective of the war. Prisoners' ransoms were big business on the Hungarian frontier: they often produced profits far in excess of the costs of a campaign.[77]

The wars fought on the eastern half of the Great European Plain likewise remained deeply resistant to military innovation. In the early seventeenth century, for example, there were still ten horsemen for every foot soldier in the Polish army, and this was perfectly reasonable, given the nature of Poland's enemies: after the secularization of the Teutonic Order in 1525, German expansion along the Baltic coast largely ceased whilst almost simultaneously, after the defeat of Hungary at Mohács in 1526, the threat from the Tatars and the Turks increased. Against the horsemen of the south, it made sense for Poland to strengthen her cavalry, rather than her infantry and artillery, and to concentrate on armies that could win battles rather than conduct sieges. Even in the 1600s, the Polish cavalry proved able to destroy the Swedes when they invaded (at Kirchholm in 1605 and at Klushino in 1610). But these successes induced a false sense of security. In 1621, on the eve of a new Swedish invasion, the *trace italienne* was to be found in Poland only around some Baltic ports (as at Danzig) or on the estates of a few great magnates (as at the new town of Zamość, where the Italian Bernardo Morando built new walls with seven bastions between 1587 and 1602). That is why the Swedish onslaught in the 1620s initially made such good progress. Several outraged books and pamphlets were promptly written by Polish propagandists, excoriating the invaders for their 'unchivalrous deceit' in raising ramparts around their camps 'as though they needed a grave-digger's courage to conceal themselves', and deploring their painstaking siege techniques as 'Kreta robota [mole's work]'.[78] But, mole's work or not, Crown Prince Wladislaw was immediately dispatched to the Netherlands to learn about these deceitful tactics at first hand. He was followed by Polish engineers, such as Adam Freitag who, in 1631, published at Leiden an international classic on developments in military fortification – *Architectura militaris nova et aucta* – before returning home to put his ideas into practice.[79] By then, in the wake of Sweden's successes in Livonia and the Empire, the Polish army had also been reorganized on Western lines. The infantry was reinforced with special musketeer units (who, even though most of their soldiers were native Poles, were known as 'foreign troops'). At the same time, a number of gunnery manuals based on Western experience were published in Polish, and the various types of artillery pieces were standardized, including field guns modelled on Swedish equivalents. Then, a full programme of gun casting was initiated: in 1637 there were 222 artillery pieces in the royal arsenals, but two years later there were 320.[80] In addition, a series of special military maps of all frontier areas was drawn up by the royal cartographer, Fryderyk Getkant, showing the theatre of operations for possible future wars, together with the points of potential strength and weakness. Nevertheless, the work was slow: the nobles who dominated the Polish state resisted any measure that might enhance the power of the monarchy – whether it was hiring foreign mercenaries, arming serfs, or fortifying royal cities. In 1655, therefore, the royal army was so unprepared and the fortifications of Warsaw so primitive that the Swedes captured the city in a cavalry raid![81]

The progress of the military revolution was no faster in Russia. Although artillery was used from the late fourteenth century onwards, both guns and infantry remained relatively unimportant in the army of the Tsars until the seventeenth century: even in 1600, according to a recent authority, 'Russia's basic orientation was still toward steppe warfare, with horsemen and bows and arrows ... Muscovy had not yet made a full commitment to the gunpowder revolution'.[82] The change began, as in the West, with the construction of new fortifications which could only be reduced through lengthy sieges. Smolensk, for example – built between 1595 and 1602 with the aid of 150 million bricks, 620,000 facing stones, and 1 million loads of sand – was defended by walls that were 5 metres thick, up to 19 metres high, and 6.5 kilometres long. Already, in 1550, the Moscow government had seen the need for a permanent infantry corps, and founded the *streltsy*, who used handguns. At first, there were only 3,000, drawn from the gentry class, but by 1600 there were 20,000 of them and by 1632 there were almost 34,000. But not all the *streltsy* served in the army (many carried out police and local defence duties instead); and during the War of Smolensk (1632–4), fully one-half of the Russian field army was composed of 'new formation regiments' – mercenaries recruited abroad and fighting with linear tactics, as in the West. Between 1630 and 1634, the government raised ten of these regiments of foreigners – some 17,400 men in all, equipped with muskets and supported by field artillery. Although the 'new formation' units were disbanded after the war ended, in the 1650s they were revived. There were 60,000 foreign troops in Russian service by 1663 and 80,000 by 1681, supported by the weapons turned out by a Dutch-run arms factory at Tula and the arsenal of flintlocks and field guns amassed in the Moscow Kremlin and elsewhere. These troops operated according to the *Military Instructions* issued in 1649 by Tsar Alexei Romanov, which were based on those of Maurice of Nassau. Meanwhile, French Huguenot and Dutch military engineers directed the massive work of restoring and extending the defensive curtain known as the Belgorod line, along the southern frontier of Muscovy.

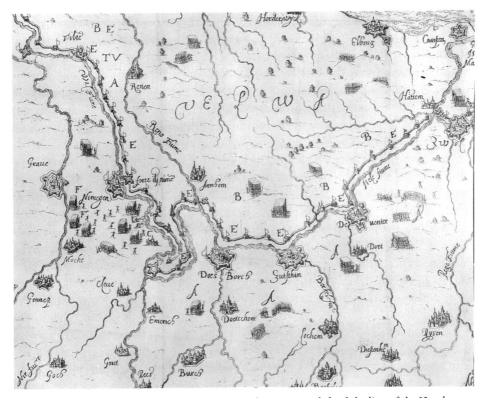

14 *The Great Wall of the Dutch Republic* was built in 1605 to defend the line of the IJssel
and Waal rivers against invasion by the Army of Flanders, commanded by Ambrosio Spinola.
It consisted of wooden redoubts linked by an earthen rampart, and was clearly shown in
the map drawn by one of Spinola's Italian subordinates. In the event, in 1606 the Spanish
army almost broke through the wall and invaded the Veluwe, and thus prompted the Dutch
Republic to agree to a cease-fire the following year. (From P. Giustiniano, *Delle guerre di
Fiandra, libri VI* [Antwerp, 1609], fig. 75.)

By 1653 its ravelins and bastions stretched 800 kilometres across the
boundary of forest and steppe where, in a new sense, Europe met Asia.[83]

III

The decision to invest in this latter-day Hadrian's Wall, paralleled in the
West by the line of connected wooden redoubts built along the IJssel in
1605–6 by the Dutch Republic (plate 14), serves as a reminder that the
greater part of military expenditure and military resources in every early
modern state went not on offence but on defence.[84] However large a nation's
field army might be, the forces deployed elsewhere in fortresses, subordinate
theatres, and around the capital were normally greater; and however much
it might cost to launch the front-line troops on a campaign, the expense of
constructing and defending up-to-date fortifications was usually greater.[85]

It is very easy to underestimate the number of soldiers tied down in garrisons and 'sideshows', as a consideration of the military events in Germany during the year 1632 demonstrates. All the history books dwell upon the three great confrontations that took place between the main field armies – at Rain, at the Alte Veste and at Lützen – yet none of these were truly decisive, for the war dragged on for a further sixteen years. Moreover, far more troops were always in service outside the main armies than ever marched with them. Thus in November 1632, the month of Lützen, Gustavus Adolphus directed the operations of 183,000 soldiers in Europe: but 62,000 were scattered all over northern Germany in ninety-eight permanent garrisons; 34,000 were left in Sweden, Finland and the Baltic provinces; and 66,000 operated as independent, regional forces in the Empire. The king therefore fought and died in battle at the head of a mere 20,000 men. The Imperialists' dispositions were similar: 18,000 men at Lützen itself, a further 40,000 operating elsewhere, and no less than 43,000 more in garrisons. Even at the war's end, in 1648, the majority of Sweden's army was tied down in 127 garrisons all over Germany, with a further 95 towns and fortresses defended by the troops of her allies.[86]

Likewise, in the Spanish Army of Flanders, up to half the troops deployed to defend the South Netherlands were regularly kept in garrisons. In the year 1639, for example, the army maintained 208 separate garrisons, from the 1,000 men stationed in Dunkirk down to the ten men who guarded the lonely fort on a dike near Ghent called 'La Grande Misere'. In all, defence accounted for 33,399 men, at a time when the total strength of the army, even on paper, was only 77,000.[87] It was the same with the Dutch: the greater part of the Republic's army was tied down in garrisons that were sometimes considerably larger than the civilian populations they defended.[88] The constant hostilities between the neighbouring garrisons of each side represented the commonest form of military action during the Low Countries' Wars, as a glance at the memoirs of Roger Williams, Francis Vere, or James duke of York (to name but three English participants) swiftly proves.[89] Indeed, when the struggle was at its height, between 1589 and 1598, some local commanders seemed to be fighting their own war. Martin Schenck van Nijdeggen, for example, by 1589 was reported to be using his fortified base at Schenckenschans on the Lower Rhine to undertake 'various exploits, more to raise some money or to take a good prisoner than for any other reason'. Meanwhile, in the north-east, Colonel Francisco Verdugo had reconquered much of Friesland and Groningen for Spain with the aid of an impoverished skeleton army which was forced to live largely off the country. Sometimes his companies were reduced to a strength of ten (although, according to Verdugo's memoirs, they were nevertheless deployed in traditional order: two musketeers as an advance guard, three pikemen and the captain in the centre, and three women and a secretary in the rear).[90]

In France, at the same time, the military commander and theorist Blaise de Monluc described war in his day as nothing more than a series of 'fights, encounters, skirmishes, ambushes, an occasional battle, minor sieges, assaults, escalades, captures and surprises of towns'.[91] This was perhaps a slight exaggeration – there were both numerous battles and major sieges during the French Religious Wars – but once regular troops were withdrawn from the provinces to join a field army, the initiative in each locality devolved upon the garrisons and the irregular forces that were left.[92] Half a century later, the military character of the English Civil War was remarkably similar. Despite the attention that has been devoted to the numerous pitched battles, especially where Oliver Cromwell was involved, local operations by regional forces were both more numerous and more important than has usually been recognized. From 1642 until 1646 a bitter, dirty war went on in most of the shires of England and Wales between the various opposing garrisons, with each local commander striving to destroy his enemy's resources while preserving his own. During the early years, even quite small strongholds in the less accessible parts of the kingdom (such as the Welsh border counties) could maintain a respectable sphere of influence. Most were garrisoned, it has been observed, 'for reasons of local security rather than as part of any major tactical or strategic thinking', and many seemed to exist simply to extract money from a locality. And yet their cumulative impact was considerable. Edgehill in 1642 was lost by the Parliamentary army largely because of the need to send out troops to garrison Hereford, Northampton and Coventry; while Naseby in 1645 was lost by the king largely because he left 1,500 men to defend Leicester, captured two weeks before, and refused to call in reinforcements from surrounding fortresses (such as Newark, defended by 4,000 men).[93] By the middle of 1645 there were eighty Royalist garrisons in England and Wales, and perhaps as many Parliamentary ones – eighteen in Shropshire, eighteen in Oxfordshire and so on. Taken together, they must have tied down over half the total forces involved in the Civil War.[94]

Der kleine Krieg was thus as much the staple of early modern warfare in many parts of Europe as pitched battles and protracted sieges. By the side of the spectacular confrontations and campaigns, any complete military history of the age must consider the countless 'small wars' in which numerous concentrations of troops, although often only a few hundred strong, aimed to 'damage the enemy without trying to force a decision by battle'.[95]

This complex pattern of warfare, in which *guerilla* was as important as guerra, only came to an end with the demolition of the network of strongholds which sustained it. France, significantly, led the way. Henry IV destroyed a number of castles and forts after 1593, as outlying provinces were pacified at the end of the Religious Wars; likewise, during the 1630s, Richelieu razed over a hundred fortresses in the south, after the suppression of a wave of

Huguenot and aristocratic rebellions.[96] The advantages of this policy were evident to all, and it was widely followed. During the English Civil War, both sides ruthlessly destroyed strongholds in areas where military activity had ceased, even before the war was over, in order to free men for the field army. Thus the eighteen Shropshire garrisons of May 1645 (fourteen Royalist and four Parliamentary), had shrunk to eleven by October (three Royalist and eight Parliamentary), and to only two by 1647. The rest were evacuated, and their defences destroyed. After the end of the war, fortifications in central England were demolished in large numbers. It is true that the surviving garrisons (mostly along the coasts) tended to be substantial; but the overall total of men involved was far smaller.[97]

The dangers of leaving too many forts in being were dramatically demonstrated during the 1670s by events in the Baltic region. The lands in Germany acquired by Sweden during and after the Thirty Years War lacked any natural frontier – indeed, Swedish territory was often so indistinguishable from its neighbours that boundary posts had to be erected. And, within these somewhat arbitrary borders, only long chains of fortresses at first seemed to offer a path to security. However the cost of maintaining the numerous garrisons was crippling and, in the 1670s, the defence of the Swedish duchies of Verden and Bremen collapsed precisely because there were too many strongholds and not enough troops could be found to defend them. Most of the score or so forts held by the Swedes were isolated, besieged, and starved out – the smaller ones, which fell first, being used subsequently to threaten the larger ones. In the 1680s, therefore, many of these forts were either abandoned or destroyed.[98]

However, all this was as nothing compared with the systematic demilitarization of central France under Louis XIV. Following the Fronde (1648–53) and the War of Devolution (1667–8), the ministers of the Crown became concerned by the large number of fortresses that had to be manned. Some were in the interior, defending once-important centres now far from danger; others were on the frontiers, where the gains made at the Peace of the Pyrenees (1659) and of Aix-la-Chapelle (1668) had left France with a number of precarious enclaves deep in enemy territory. Early in 1673, with another war under way, Louis XIV's chief military engineer, Sebastien Le Prestre de Vauban, proposed a rationalization of French defences. 'This confusion of friendly and enemy fortresses mixed up pell-mell with one another does not please me at all,' he wrote. 'You are obliged to maintain three in place of one.'[99] Vauban christened his ideal the *pré carré* (the square field) and over the next thirty years he urged his master to acquire – whether by conquest, exchange or treaty – retain and fortify such places as provided France with (as far as possible) a frontier that ran in a straight line. French engineers built or rebuilt 133 strongholds which either closed to the enemy various points of entry to the kingdom, or else facilitated entry by French forces into neighbouring territory. Hence the massive scale of Vauban's fortifications: they were designed to be big enough to shelter sufficient supplies and troops for offensive as well as defensive operations. It is not always realized, however, that the corollary of the *pré carré* was the creation of a virtually demilitarized zone in the inland provinces, through the destruction or studied neglect of 600 or so other walled cities and fortresses in the interior of the kingdom – including Paris, whose fortifications the government ordered to be demolished in 1670.[100] As Vauban later put it, ten fewer fortresses meant 30,000 more men for the king's field army; and the increase in the size of Louis XIV's armed forces was thus due as much to the strategic vision of Vauban, who freed more men for the campaign, as to the ingenuity and zeal of Louvois, who secured more recruits.[101]

And so to conclude: warfare in early modern Europe was certainly transformed by three important, related developments – a new use of firepower, a new type of fortifications, and an increase in army size. But the timing of the transformation was far slower, and the impact less total, than was once thought. Most of the wars fought in Europe before the French Revolution were not brought to an end by a strategy of extermination, but (to use the language of Hans Delbruck) through a strategy of attrition, via the patient accumulation of minor victories and the slow erosion of the enemy's economic base. There were, to be sure, a few exceptions – the Schmalkaldic War of 1547–8, the war of Ostia in 1557, the war of Saluzzo in 1600; but such conflicts ended swiftly because the forces of a major state recently at war were pitted against those of a smaller one that had become isolated. The classic conflicts of the age of military revolution were all 'long wars' made up of numerous separate campaigns and 'actions': the Italian wars, which lasted for much of the period between 1494 and 1559; the French Religious Wars, which dragged on with but few intermissions from 1562 to 1598, and then broke out again in 1621–9; the 'Eighty Years War' in the Netherlands, which involved continuous hostilities between 1572 and 1607 and again between 1621 and 1647; the 'long war' in Hungary in 1593–1606. It is sometimes suggested that the conflicts of the seventeenth and early eighteenth centuries became shorter and more decisive – that generals now sought to achieve a rapid victory through decisive battles (as if somehow in earlier generations they had not).[102] But wars still eternalized themselves: the Thirty Years War lasted from 1618 to 1648 in spite of Breitenfeld, Lutzen and Nordlingen; the 'other thirty years war' between France and Spain dragged on between 1629 and 1659 in spite of Rocroi and Lens; the Great Northern War endured from 1700 to 1721 in spite of Poltava; the War of the Spanish Succession continued from 1701 to 1713 in spite of Blenheim, Ramillies, Oudenaarde and Malplaquet. The only real difference was that the later wars were fought with ever larger and more expensive armies than the earlier ones. And in these increases in size and cost lay the principal explanation of the longevity: strategic thinking had become crushed between the sustained growth in army size and the relative scarcity of money, equipment and food.[103] In the age of the military revolution, the skill of individual governments and generals in supplying war often became the pivot about which the outcome of armed conflict turned.

2

Supplying war

Tristram Shandy's Uncle Toby, as is well known, had a hobby-horse ('an hobby horse well worth giving a description of') one part of which was 'the Prodigious armies we had in Flanders' during the wars of William III in the 1690s. Laurence Sterne, his creator, hoped that Uncle Toby's obsessive military ideas, first brought to public attention in the 1760s, might 'swim down the gutter of Time' and achieve immortality; and, indeed, we find them again in the writings of an influential French military theorist of the Enlightenment, Count Guibert, whose hobby-horse, in the *Essai général de tactique* first published in 1772, was likewise the changes in the art of war caused by *'les armées . . . prodigieusement plus nombreuses'* which had arisen in Europe in the days of Louis XIV.[1]

Most later students of military history have been impressed in their turn by the growth of European armies during the later seventeenth century; and with good reason, for their size did indeed increase to unprecedented levels at precisely that time. But there was another period of rapid growth unmarked by both Sterne and Guibert, considerably earlier, during the reign of the Emperor Charles V (see page 24 above). In the year 1552, for example, the emperor's advisers calculated that they were supporting 22,200 cavalry and 87,000 infantry in Germany and the Low Countries; together with more than 24,000 soldiers in Lombardy, and at least a further 15,000 in Naples, Sicily, North Africa and Spain – a grand total of 148,000 men.[2] This total seems to have remained, for more than a century, a threshold beyond which no individual European state could pass. It is true that, in the year 1625, Philip IV of Spain claimed to be supporting, in his various dominions, armed forces that totalled 300,000 regular troops plus 500,000 militiamen; but no detailed breakdown of this figure was offered, and no subsequent computation of the king's soldiers seems able to raise the total above 150,000, spread over half of western Europe – which is almost exactly the same as the total controlled by his great-grandfather, Charles V, seventy years before.[3] 150,000 was also the size of the army of Philip IV's principal enemy, France, during the wars of the 1640s and 50s. Not until the 1670s did the French armed forces exceed 200,000. But that was the beginning of the major manpower revolution remarked on by Guibert (and Uncle Toby), for the size of Louis XIV's army rose to 273,000 in 1691 and to 395,000 in 1696 (at which point soldiers were even more numerous in France than clerics, and almost one adult Frenchman in four was in the ranks). Louis's enemies struggled to match this escalation until, by 1710, the total number of troops simultaneously on foot in Europe has been estimated at 1.3 million.[4]

Today, military concentrations such as these seem insignificant; but in early modern Europe they were unprecedented. They posed problems of recruitment, supply and deployment that no government in Christendom had previously had to face. And yet, eventually, all the obstacles were overcome. The early modern states may have lacked the resources to wage a war of extermination; but they could certainly keep on fighting, with ever-larger armies, often on more than one front and sometimes overseas, for years at a time. In the course of the seventeenth century, between 10 and 12 million Europeans became soldiers. But how, precisely, was this feat achieved: how were the large, semi-permanent armies raised; how were they financed; and how were they supplied?

I

The first problem was the easiest to solve. Few governments in early modern Europe seem to have experienced much difffculty in raising an army. Between 1701 and 1713, for example, about 650,000 Frenchmen entered the armies of Louis XIV. Some of them, as we shall see, were in effect conscripts, impressed into service against their will; but by far the majority, whether of French or foreign origin, were volunteers. Volunteers, however, were easier to find at some times than at others. The 'bounty' (or premium) paid to each man on enlistment varied over time in step with both the seasonal demand for agricultural labour and the annual variation in food prices, because both affected the availability of recruits. It was usually necessary to pay more during seed-time and harvest, when there was plenty of alternative work available, or when the price of bread was high. Thus in 1706, a year of relatively low prices, the 'winter premium' was around 50 *livres* per man; but in 1707 it dropped to 30 *livres* because food was more scarce – indeed the entire orchestra of the Marseilles opera joined up together in December, forming a sort of 'chums platoon', because, they confessed, they were all 'dying of hunger'. Then, in the winter of 1708–9, despite France's crushing defeat at Oudenaarde the previous year, recruits could be had for as little as 20 *livres* a head because of the high cost of living and, as the French commander, Marshal Villars, later observed:

It might well be said that 'it's an ill wind that blows nobody any good', for we could only find so many recruits because of the misery of the provinces ... One could well say that the misfortune of the masses was the salvation of the kingdom.

Finally, in 1710, after the worst winter in a hundred years, men enlisted without even asking for a premium: the price of bread rose so high that the army offered the starving poor one of their few chances of survival.[5]

Most of these recruits came, like the recruits before and after them, from three broad areas: the mountains, the towns, and the war-zone itself. Upland pastoral villages have traditionally been the nursery of armies, and this seems to have been especially true during the seventeenth century. The primacy of the other two locations – the towns and the war-zone – is more surprising, but it is fully demonstrated by a study of some 1,500 veterans recruited into the French army during the Thirty Years War: of those born in France, 52 per cent came from the towns (which contained less than 15 per cent of the French population), and the rest were peasants, mainly from villages in the north and north-east, near to the main theatres of operations and the main garrison centres.[6] This same pattern appears even more clearly in the eighteenth century, when the records of the French army become truly plentiful. On the one hand, recruits from the frontier provinces heavily outnumbered those of the interior – whereas 1,200 soldiers per 10,000 citizens were provided by Lorraine and Burgundy in the east, less than 150 per 10,000 came from Brittany in the west. On the other, between 35 and 40 per cent of the army came from the towns, with a growing preponderance of soldiers recruited in Paris.[7]

The wide range of motives which impelled men, in France and elsewhere, to join armies of their own free will was cogently expressed by the experienced Venetian general, Giulio Savorgnan, in 1572. Men enlisted, he asserted, 'To escape from being craftsmen [or] working in a shop; to avoid a criminal sentence; to see new things; to pursue honour (though these are very few) ... all in the hope of having enough to live on and a bit over for shoes, or some other trifle that will make life supportable'.[8] Perhaps this was an oversimplification because there were in fact other reasons for joining up; but certainly hardship and want were the most prominent.

Many men chose the army because it offered employment at a time when civilian life did not. Those who had already left their villages and tried, unsuccessfully, to make a living in the towns; those who could not, or would not, follow the trade or calling of their fathers; those thrown out of work by economic recession; those whose crops had been devastated by natural or human agency – for all of these, an enlistment bounty paid in cash and a new suit of clothes, plus the promise of pay and plunder to follow, might appear an attractive alternative to a civilian existence in which work and wages were often hard to come by, and the risk of being looted by passing soldiers, or bankrupted by heavy taxes, was high.

A second major group of volunteers comprised those who desired a 'change of scenery'. Some were impelled by a temporary crisis at home – such as debt (which the enlistment bounty could be used to liquidate), the threats of an irate father (or putative father-in-law), or the prospect of appearing before some ecclesiastical or secular court.[9] Others, however, simply desired to see the world, to fight for a cause, or to add some military experience to their general education. Thus Sir James Turner, who fought for both Denmark and Sweden during the 1630s, confessed that he went to the wars because 'a restles desire [had] enter'd my mind to be, if not an actor, at least a spectator of these warrs which at that time made so much noise over all the world'. On the other hand Robert Monro, author of the first regimental history in the English language, entitled *Monro his expedition with the worthy Scots regiment call'd Mackays*, claimed that although he and his men went to fight in the Thirty Years War partly through a desire for travel, adventure, and military experience under an illustrious leader, they marched above all to defend the Protestant faith, and to vindicate the claims and honour of Elizabeth Stuart, their king's sister and the wife of Frederick, the 'Winter King' of Bohemia.[10]

But Monro's men had another reason for going to the wars: they were commanded to do so by their clan chief, for they were almost all called Mackay. Likewise, many of the Scots troops brought into Swedish service in 1631 by James, marquis of Hamilton were called Hamilton; and several members of the Leslie family from Aberdeenshire fought together in Germany and Russia during the 1630s.[11] It was the same in France: even when the king's army rose to 400,000, recruiting by officers of their personal 'lieges' still played an important part in securing volunteers. Colonels (who often succeeded their relatives in command of a regiment) employed either kindred or neighbours as their captains and, at least until the 1740s, recruited their vassals as often as possible. Clearly, adding a 'feudal bond' to normal military obligations could only strengthen the cohesion of units.[12] And as this method of recruiting waned, another rose to take its place: an increasing number of men chose the army as their professional career. There was, of course, nothing new in this. Many medieval warriors – not merely the knights, but also a significant number of the mercenary bands – followed the calling of their fathers, uncles and brothers; but as the armed forces of more and more countries became permanent, so the proportion of military dynasties grew.[13]

Nevertheless, the supply of individual volunteers was never enough to maintain armies during a prolonged war, and governments therefore resorted to three additional techniques of raising men: recruiting entire units in other areas of Europe and making them fight far from their homes; enlisting the soldiers of a defeated enemy in their own army; and, when all else failed, conscripting local men against their will. The first was the most common. The Spanish Habsburgs, in particular, favoured a system of military expatriation, raising troops in one area specifically to fight in another. Units were regularly recruited in Spain to serve in the garrisons of Spanish Italy (Naples,

Sicily and Lombardy); then, after a period of basic training there, they might be sent on to serve in the Netherlands, in Germany, or on the Mediterranean galley fleet.[14] Perhaps 25 per cent of the troops in the Spanish Army of Flanders, throughout the later sixteenth and the seventeenth centuries, had previously served their apprenticeship elsewhere; and certainly more than 50 per cent had been recruited outside the country in which they fought. Conversely, troops raised in the Netherlands – and elsewhere in northern Europe – were sent to serve in Spain (especially during the 1630s and 40s). [15]

The French army, for its part, eagerly received entire regiments of foreign troops recruited by sympathetic or allied governments. In his *Political testament*, for example, Cardinal Richelieu commented that 'It is almost impossible to undertake major wars successfully with French troops alone', and he favoured an army which included 50 per cent foreign troops. In the event, perhaps 20 per cent of the armies of both Louis XIII and Louis XIV were recruited abroad: 25,000 Irish soldiers are believed to have fought for France between 1635 and 1664, alongside numerous German and Swiss regiments. The armies of Louis XV likewise normally included a foreign component of about one-fifth.[16] The Dutch Republic also relied upon foreign formations to strengthen its military effectiveness: there were French, English, German and Scottish brigades in the Dutch army throughout the seventeenth century (and beyond).[17] The same 'nations' also provided troops for the Swedish army.

There had been Scottish regiments in Scandinavia as early as the 1560s, and perhaps 25,000 Scotsmen crossed the sea to serve the 'Protestant cause' in central Europe between 1626 and 1632 in the armies of either Christian IV of Denmark or Gustavus Adolphus of Sweden (plate 15). They, and the smaller French and English contingents, were heavily outnumbered, however, by the troops raised by Denmark and Sweden in Germany.[18]

Some of these 'volunteers' nevertheless came under duress: they were criminals who (in effect) accepted military expatriation as an alternative to execution. In 1605, for example, the Scottish government, exasperated by the lawlessness of the Graham clan in the Borders, sentenced 150 men of that name to be sent to the wars in the Netherlands, in the hope that most of them would die there. [19] In 1627 the Lord of Spynie was empowered to impress into his regiment (raised under licence for Denmark) all 'strong, able, and counterfeit limmers called Egyptians [sc. gypsies]', as well as all 'strong and sturdy beggars and vagabonds, masterless men and idle loiterers, who want [sc. lack] trades and calling and competent means to live upon [sc. the unemployed]'. Any who showed reluctance were to be imprisoned until transport was ready. The previous year, the recruits for Mackay's regiment had been augmented by some prisoners from the Tolbooth of Edinburgh 'sometimes called Macgregor' (a name then synonymous with outlaw) who were taken to Leith docks under heavy guard and made to swear before embarkation

In folchem Habit Gehen die 800 In Stettin angekommen Irrländer oder Irren.

Es ift ein Starckes dauerhafftigs Volck behilfft fich mit geringer fpeiß hatt es nicht brodt fo Effen fie Würtzeln, Wans auch die Notturfft erfordert Können fie des Tages Uber die 20 Teütfcher meilweges lauffen, haben neben Mufqueden Jhre Bogen vnd Köcher vnd lange Meffer.

15 *A Scots clan regiment in Germany, 1631.* 'In such garments go the 800 Irish who arrived in Stettin' claims the print issued by George Köler of Nuremburg. It provides the first known illustration of Highland ('Irish') dress, and depicts Alexander Hamilton's regiment of Scots and Irish infantry, which landed near Stettin in August 1631 as part of the Marquis of Hamilton's expedition to assist Gustavus Adolphus's campaign in Germany. As in plate 13, nothing here suggests that clansmen then dressed in some sort of tartan uniform.

'that they shall never return again within this kingdom under pain of death'. In 1629, finally, Colonel Sir James Spens received 47 convicted felons (including one woman) from the prisons of London: in their case, enlistment brought a pardon for all crimes, but only on condition that those pardoned emigrated for ever.[20]

The volunteers most sought after by all governments, however, were neither the jail-birds nor the glory-seekers, but the veterans: those who had already mastered the trade of arms and become professional soldiers. Such men often passed, at high wages, from one army to another as opportunity or occasion called. Thus several Englishmen – including Sir Roger Williams, William Garrard and Humphrey Barwick: all subsequently authors of influential military treatises – served in both the Spanish and the Dutch armies in the Netherlands, as well as in England; while Philip II's redoubtable commander, Julian Romero, fought (along with about 1,000 other Spanish mercenaries) in Scotland as part of the English army of occupation in 1545–6 and 1547–51.[21] In the 1590s there was hot competition between the Army of Flanders, the army of the French Catholic League, and the Imperial forces in Hungary for suitable veterans, and high rewards were offered to those prepared to move from one service to another. It was much the same in the 1640s, with wars afoot in the greater part of Europe: English, Scottish and Irish troops on the continent, for example, were offered strong inducements to come home and fight in the Civil Wars.[22]

There were good reasons for this. The history of the small force victoriously commanded by James Graham, marquis of Montrose, fully demonstrates the impact that veteran forces could have on a war. In the twelve months following his arrival in Scotland in August 1644, Montrose and his army of Scottish and Irish volunteers travelled some 3,000 kilometres around the kingdom and, in a remarkable sequence of six battles (at Tippermuir, Aberdeen, Inverlochy, Auldearn, Alford and Kilsyth), destroyed much of the military strength of the Scots government. Historians have been puzzled by these victories, all of them won against forces that were far more numerous and better equipped; and much has been attributed to the charismatic leadership of Montrose and his principal Irish lieutenant, Alastair MacColla. The vanquished Scots were also perplexed: 'We are amazed [wrote one of them after Alford] that it should be the pleasure of God to make us fall this fifth time, before a company of the worst men in the earth'; 'We pray the Lord [wrote another] to discover the cause ... why our forces ... have received defeat upon defeat, even these five times, from a despicable and inconsiderable enemy'.[23] But the enemy was neither 'despicable' nor 'inconsiderable'. Although Montrose may have commanded only 3,000 men (or less) during most of his victorious campaign, perhaps two-thirds of them were veterans of the fighting in Ulster in 1641–2 and some had served in the Spanish Army of Flanders too: they had been specially recruited from among the Irish regiments in the Low Countries, with Spanish permission, and ferried over to Scotland in two frigates hired at Dunkirk. The unfortunate Scots were defeated by no ordinary troops.[24]

The advantage of hiring veterans was obvious, particularly in a country which, like Stuart Britain, had itself experienced a generation of peace. Indeed, such was the need for trained troops that it even became common for the defeated or captured soldiers of one side to be taken into service by their enemies. After the great Parliamentary victory of Naseby, for example, although many Royalist soldiers, captured either after the battle or at the subsequent surrender of garrisons, were recruited forthwith by agents acting for the French or Spanish crowns, many more joined the victorious New Model Army. Sir Thomas Fairfax, the Parliamentary commander, was quite unabashed: 'I found you had made them good soldiers,' he observed sanctimoniously to a surrendered Royalist officer, 'and I have made them good men'.[25] During the Thirty Years War in Germany, this was also standard practice: prisoners of war were encouraged to join the ranks of the victors en masse, in spite of religious and political differences, so that the percentage of veterans in each unit sometimes rose to astonishing proportions. Thus in one of the Bavarian regiments for which we have particularly good records, only 15 per cent of the troops were already veterans in 1624, but this had increased to 30 per cent in 1639, 50 per cent in 1643 and 66 per cent in 1647.[26] Nevertheless, there were obvious dangers in encouraging yesterday's enemies to become today's bodyguards. Sir James Turner expressed the misgivings of many governments and generals when he wrote in his *Memoirs* of those who had 'swallowed without chewing, in Germanie, a very dangerous maxime, which militarie men there too much follow; which was, that so we serve our master honestlie, it is no matter what master we serve'.[27]

It was to avoid the dangers inherent in such a philosophy that most early modern states tried to raise at least a few exclusively national formations by means of conscription. The commonest method, especially in the case of troops required for service overseas (like the Scottish soldiers noted above), was to draft either criminals or the unemployed. There is no doubt that a substantial number of the 40,000 English troops raised for service abroad between 1588 and 1595, and of the 50,000 drafted between 1624 and 1627 for the expeditions to the Netherlands, Spain and France, were 'undesirables' recruited against their will by magistrates who were compelled by government order to supply a fixed quota of men.[28] And in Scotland, two of the regiments raised by the Covenanters in 1640 for operations against England were composed exclusively of 'adulterers, furnicators, thieves, murderers, drunkards [and] sabbath breakers, who were given up by the minister of every parish' to the recruiting officers.[29] When these and other similar measures proved inadequate, governments might also call up members of the local militia (units raised exclusively for defensive duties at home). But this – whether ordered by Louis XIV of France, Philip IV of Spain, or Charles I of England – proved so unpopular that it was attempted only as a last resort, and even then only for a short period.

The sole permanent form of compulsory military service to be found in early modern Europe was the *indelningsverk* or allocation system, introduced into Finland and metropolitan Sweden during the reigns of Charles IX and Gustavus Adolphus. A first scheme of universal impressment was attempted in the 1600s, when registers listing all men over the age of 15 were compiled. Then, after 1620, a fixed ratio was established whereby one soldier had to be provided, equipped and fed by each parish for every ten eligible male parishioners. However, some social groups remained more likely than others to be drafted: those absent from the meetings held to select the soldiers were automatically conscripted, while those who were noblemen, clerics, miners, armaments workers or the only sons of widows were exempt. Inevitably, most Swedish soldiers were therefore peasants: in the voluminous (but as yet little analysed) records of the Swedish and Finnish forces who fought in the Thirty Years War, *bonde* (peasant farmer) is by far the commonest entry in the enrolment lists. Each year the government specified the overall number of recruits required, and allocated a quota to each province and parish. The totals may seem small – 13,500 in 1627; 11,000 in 1628; 8,000 in 1629; 9,000 in 1630 – but it must be recalled that Sweden was a small country, with a total population of perhaps only 1.5 million. The cumulative impact of compulsory recruiting on isolated communities could be disastrous. The parish of Bygdeå in northern Sweden, for example, provided 230 young men for service in Poland and Germany between 1621 and 1639, and saw 215 of them die there, while a further five returned home crippled. Although the remainder – a mere ten men – were still in service in 1639, it is unlikely that any of them survived to see the war's end, nine years later. Enlistment, in effect, had become a sentence of death: of the 27 Bygdeå conscripts of the year 1638, mustered on 6 July before being sent to Germany, all but one were dead within the year. Not surprisingly, this sustained one-way human traffic had highly deleterious consequences for Sweden's population. The number of adult males in Bygdeå, for example, decreased by 40 per cent, from 468 in 1621 to 288 in 1639; and the age of the conscripts gradually fell as more and more teenagers were drafted. Of the conscripts of the year 1639, half were only fifteen years old and all but two were under eighteen. By 1640, the number of households in Bygdeå headed by women had increased sevenfold, whilst every available adult male was either on the conscription lists, already in the ranks, or too crippled to serve (see figure 2).[30]

Was this high military wastage typical? Certainly, there is much indirect evidence to suggest that a high proportion of those sent to serve in armies abroad never returned. In 1601, for example, Lord Mountjoy (Queen Elizabeth's successful commander in the Irish wars) justified his decision to allow defeated Irish rebels to enlist in foreign armies because 'it hath ever been seen that more than three parts of the four of these countrymen do never return, being once engaged in any such voyage'. More recently, a leading demographer has offered some support for this high estimate: working from the hypothesis that the total military mortality rate must have been roughly ten times the total of deaths in battle, Jacques Dupâquier concluded that probably one out of every four or five soldiers who enlisted in early modern Europe died each year on active service.[31] However the surviving records of some armies suggest that this figure may be too high. On the one hand, the wastage rates recorded in figure 3 indicate a total loss from *all* sources, including desertion, of under 20 per cent annually; on the other, casualties from fighting could be extremely heavy.[32] Thus at the battle of Marston

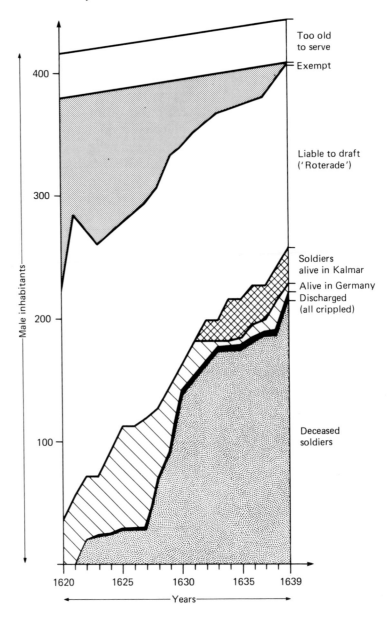

2 *Bygdeå recruiting costs* 1620–39. The demographic history of the parish of Bygdeå in northern Sweden reveals the terrible social costs of the expansionist policies pursued by Gustavus Adolphus and his daughter. In 1620 the parish provided 36 soldiers for the wars, and there were also 36 in 1639, but in between 230 men were conscripted, of whom all but 15 died in service (and 5 of these were discharged as too crippled to serve further). At the same time, the number of adult males available for service but not yet drafted fell until it was scarcely enough to keep the village's economy going.

Moor in 1644, perhaps 20 per cent of the Royalist army was killed on a single day, amounting to about 4,000 men (although the impact was heightened by the fact that, in the judgement of an eye-witness, 'there were two gentlemen to one ordinary soldier that was slain'). At the battle of Freiburg in southwest Germany, in the same year (according to the Bavarian commander, Johann Werth) 'In the twenty-two years I have been involved in the carnage of war, there has never been such a bloody encounter [as this]': the overall casualties were probably 5,000 on each side. But this was a low figure by the standards of Louis XIV's wars. At Malplaquet, in 1709, where the victorious allies again lost roughly 25 per cent of their strength, this amounted to 24,000 dead.[33] Sieges were equally destructive of men. Thus during the blockade of Stralsund in 1648, Mackay's Scots regiment was on duty under fire for six weeks continuously and, during this period, of 900 men in the regiment, 500 were killed and a further 300 (including their lieutenant-colonel and chronicler, Robert Monro) were injured. Losses among the besiegers could also be catastrophic. Gaspar de Coligny, an experienced French commander of the mid-sixteenth century, commented that 'large cities are the graveyard of armies', because so many troops died in the trenches surrounding them; and the commandant of Saint Jean d'Angely in 1569 boasted, when he surrendered after a long siege, that his prolonged defence had caused more than 10,000 enemy troops to die beneath its walls. Perhaps this was an exaggeration, but there are many other appalling (yet more reliable) figures to hand. Thus, according to the records of the paymaster of the army sent by Charles I of England to relieve La Rochelle in 1628, of the 7,833 soldiers who embarked at Portsmouth in June, 409 were lost almost at once in the landing on the Ile de Ré, 100 in the trenches, and 120 by dysentery; 3,895 more died either in an ill-fated assault on a French position or in the final retreat (during which 'Our men spoiled one another, and more were drowned than slain'); and, finally, a further 320 men went missing. Only 2,989 survived the campaign – 38 per cent of the initial force – to return home to Portsmouth in October.[34]

Perhaps the 320 were deserters. Although desertion from an expeditionary force overseas was not easy, after a few weeks in the trenches without pay or food, even veterans were ready to take almost any risk in order to escape. Thus, at the siege of Bergen-op-Zoom by the Army of Flanders in 1622 almost 40 per cent of 20,600 men encamped around the town were lost; but of these, at least one-third (2,500 men) adopted the desperate remedy of deserting to the town under siege. There they pleaded for 'a little bread and a little money' with, if possible, a passage home. One Italian deserter who staggered in towards the end of the siege was asked 'Where have you come from?'. 'D'infierno', he replied: 'From Hell'.[35]
Desertion indeed exercised the most volatile and unpredictable influence on an army's strength. Conditions of service could become so appalling that,

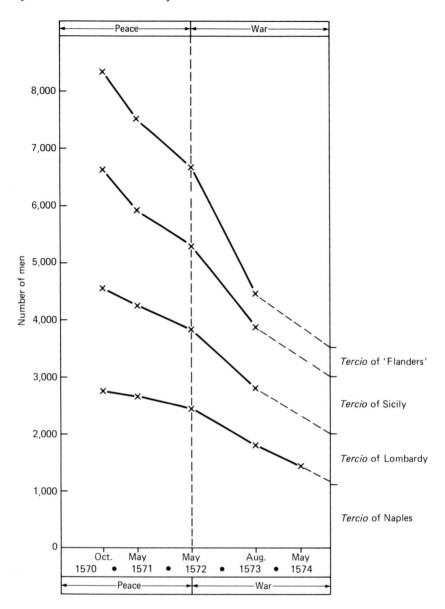

3 *Wastage rates among front-line troops* in the sixteenth and seventeenth centuries show remarkable consistency. Among the Spanish veterans garrisoned in the Netherlands during the 1570s (above), the outbreak of serious hostilities in April 1572 caused remarkably little increase in wastage rates (with the exception of the *tercio de Flandes*, the unit with the least number of veterans). In war, as in peace, desertion and disease rather than enemy action were responsible for most losses. The average attrition rate for elite trained troops, whether Spaniards in the Netherlands or the Scots and Austrians in Germany half a century later (right), was around 2 per cent per month, or roughly a quarter of total strength per year.

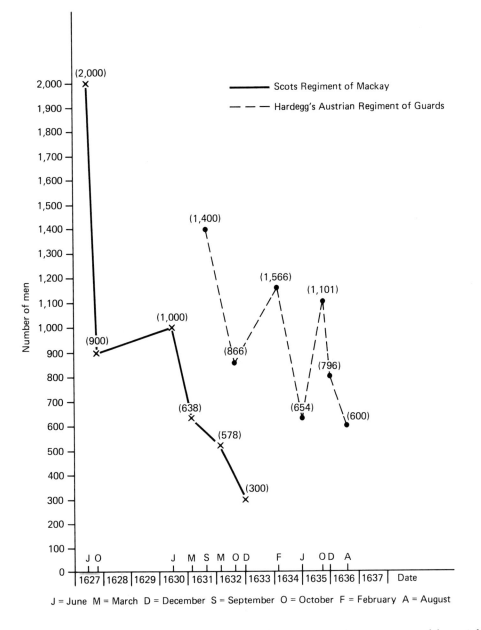

Number of men

(2,000) ×

━━━━━ Scots Regiment of Mackay

━ ━ ━ Hardegg's Austrian Regiment of Guards

(1,400)

(1,566)

(1,101)

(1,000) ×

(900) ×

(866)

(796)

(638) ×

(654)

(600)

(578) ×

(300) ×

J O   J M S M O D   F J OD A

1627 1628 1629 1630 1631 1632 1633 1634 1635 1636 1637   Date

J = June M = March D = December S = September O = October F = February A = August

in certain places and at certain times, almost an entire army would vanish into thin air. Thus between 1608 and 1619, no less than 4,211 Spanish soldiers from the garrison of Oran (in North Africa) chose to desert and surrender themselves into captivity with their Muslim adversaries, rather than continue to defend the city entrusted to them. At Algiers they were well fed and cared for, until a ransom was provided by one of the many Iberian charitable organizations dedicated to rescuing Christians from bondage among the infidel.[36] And the desertion rate in other Spanish armies was, on occasion, even higher. In the spring of 1576, the Spanish Army of Flanders shrank from perhaps 60,000 men in June to no more than 11,000 in November; and in the 1630s some units were losing up to 7 per cent of their manpower each month through desertion. Likewise in the Spanish Army of Extremadura, created to defend Castile from rebellious Portugal after 1640, wastage rates of 90 per cent were occasionally reported.[37] Matters were little better in the French army. Thus, in 1635, the French forces operating in the South Netherlands were found in October to number only 10,000 instead of their paper strength of 26,500; and in the following year the Army of Champagne, reportedly 14,200 strong, had actually fallen to 6,000 by June. The situation deteriorated still further as the war continued – the average effective strength of a French infantry company (theoretically 120 men) fell from fifty men in 1637–8 to twenty-one in 1642–7.[38]

Variations in troop strength of this magnitude made it almost impossible for generals and governments to be sure of the exact size of their armed forces at any given time. Recent studies of the French army under Louis XIII have clearly demonstrated that neither the king nor his ministers possessed any clear notion of how many troops they commanded. In the course of the year 1635, orders were apparently issued to raise 134,000 infantry and 21,000 cavalry, in order to produce an effective strength at the front of just 60,000 and 9,000 respectively; and it was taken for granted, throughout the war with Spain, that in order to bring 1,200 soldiers to the front, it was necessary to recruit 2,000, since initial wastage was expected to run at 40 per cent. But even this was no more than a working hypothesis: it was not based on any detailed study of musters and reviews.[39] Eventually, the problem was only brought under control by imposing draconian penalties on deserters, and on those who assisted them. Between 1684 and 1714 some 16,500 illegal fugitives from the army were brought in chains to Marseilles (making up in most years almost half the total of convicts serving on the King's galleys), and the desertion rate in Louis XIV's armies at last declined.[40]

Of course, another way to reduce desertion was to offer the troops a chance to enrich themselves; and, indeed, plunder and booty were regarded as one of the legitimate rewards that every soldier had a right to expect. They could be acquired in many different ways. The first, and certainly the easiest, was simply to extract payments from civilians under threat of death, torture or destruction. Villages along main roads were particularly vulnerable – some being looted several times in the course of a war – and even a small contingent of soldiers could extort considerable profit.[41] Travelling merchants also constituted a soft target. In January 1638, for example, a convoy of Augsburg and Nuremberg merchants with seven wagons, returning home from the Leipzig fair, was ambushed by about 200 cavalry troopers. The soldiers demanded £500 in cash; the convoy rashly offered less than £100, and the troops at once attacked and plundered the wagons. They killed several merchants, seized 80 horses which they loaded with booty, and destroyed everything else. It was the seventh wagontrain belonging to Nuremberg merchants to be lost in twelve months, and a further sixteen similar incidents were recorded before the end of the Thirty Years War in 1648.[42]

Acquiring plunder in such ways, at the expense of isolated and often unarmed civilians, offered soldiers enrichment at little personal risk; but the rewards (as well as the risks) were far increased by defeating enemy troops. A battle might produce thousands of prisoners, whose personal effects immediately became the property of the captor, and whose ransoms would be divided between him and his commanders in a fixed proportion.[43] Even greater opportunities for gain were provided by the capture of an enemy town. Although there were some dissenting voices, most military experts agreed that towns could be legitimately sacked if they refused to surrender before the besiegers brought up their artillery.[44] After that happened, if the town were captured, its inhabitants forfeited liberty, property and even life, thereby turning every soldier in the victorious army into a prince. Thus the Spanish troops who returned to Italy in May 1577, six months after the notorious sack of Antwerp, took with them 2,600 tons of booty (and also remitted home large sums of money, some of it derived from ransoms, by letters of exchange); while the plunder accumulated by Cromwell's Ironsides during their victorious Scottish campaign from the battle of Dunbar in September 1650 up to the sack of Dundee a year later was enough to fill 60 ships.[45]

But such events were relatively rare. More frequently, campaigns consisted of prolonged manoeuvring for several months, followed by a siege which lasted into the winter and resulted in a negotiated surrender producing little in the way of 'storm-money' for the exhausted and dispirited besiegers. As a cynical French commentator wrote in 1623, for every soldier who grows rich by war 'you will find fifty who gain nothing but injuries and incurable diseases'.[46] A long and unsuccessful campaign could easily result in the disintegration of an entire army, either through catastrophic desertion, or through mutiny.

Revolts against authority by all or part of an army on active service were relatively frequent in early modern times. The Spanish Army of Flanders was probably the most unruly, for it mutinied 45 times between 1572 and 1609 (often following the surrender of a town on terms that seemed to the troops over-generous, as at Haarlem in 1573 or Zierikzee in 1576). But there were also numerous outbreaks of unrest in other armies that were mobilized for long periods, especially when on active service (or scheduled for active service) abroad. The Swiss and German mercenaries who fought in the Italian wars (1494–1559), the Elizabethan forces in Ireland and the Netherlands in the later sixteenth century, the Swedish army in Germany during the 1630s and 40s, the New Model Army in 1647–9 when threatened with further duties in Ireland, and the troops of the Austrian Habsburgs detailed for service in Spain in the 1650s, were all afflicted by mutinies which temporarily crippled their fighting potential and often resulted in mass migration from the army once the grievances were settled. Even the mutineers who stayed on might insist, additionally, on changing their units in order to avoid the risk of victimization by their former officers.[47]

This combination of heterogeneous methods of recruiting, high wastage rates, and considerable mobility within the ranks soon destroyed any sense of corporate identity among the individual formations of every early modern army. As each unit wasted away, the survivors were incorporated into others, creating – in the phrase of Marin Sanuto, a Venetian diarist of the early sixteenth century – Noah's Ark armies: volunteers and felons, international brigades, local militiamen, vassals, lieges and conscripts from many lands were all jumbled up together.[48] Matters were little different in the seventeenth century. One Bavarian regiment in 1644, for example, included soldiers from sixteen different countries, including fourteen Turks.[49] But one can make too much of this fragmentation: even such a markedly cosmopolitan force would still possess a high degree of military experience and efficiency. The variety of backgrounds complicated the task of giving orders, but that was about all: those who came into contact with the veterans seldom doubted their effectiveness.

Far more debilitating than linguistic or national diversity was the desperate recruitment of troops who were physically unequal to the strain of war. Thus in March 1636 the commander of the Army of Flanders ordered that, in future, all new infantry companies raised in the Low Countries were to consist of one-quarter pikemen and three-quarters musketeers. The use of the smaller and lighter arquebus or caliver was to be discontinued. Yet in February 1643, just before the invasion of France that was crushed at Rocroi, the army's High Command noted that 'it is now necessary, on account of the shortage of recruits, to accept some young and weak men, who can be of some service [now] and could learn to use ... the musket later.' The arquebus was therefore re-introduced, and up to twenty-five of the feebler men in each company were permitted to use it.[50] For the French army, too, finding enough tall soldiers was a problem. In 1685, Louis XIV's minister of war, Louvois, was forced to abandon height requirements for recruits, except for Guards regiments: '*Sa Majeste' ne veut point que l'on mesure les soldats,*' he informed the army inspectors, because otherwise enough recruits would never be found (scarcely surprising, given the fact that the French population in the seventeenth century appears to have been, on average, some five centimetres shorter than today). Even in the eighteenth century, when attempts to recruit tall men were re-introduced, in a random sample of 3,508 French soldiers in the year 1716, only ten men attained the height of

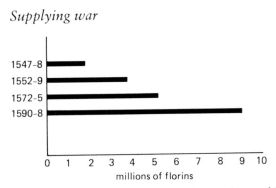

4 *The rising cost of waging war.* The average annual expenditure of Spain on fighting abroad rose inexorably over the course of the sixteenth century: the Schmalkaldic war of 1547–8 cost scarcely 2 million florins (£200,000) a year; but the war against France in the Netherlands in the 1550s was already double that; and the war during the 1590s against France, England and the Dutch Republic (in the Netherlands alone) consumed more than 9 million florins a year. Nor did the escalation in costs end there: by 1630, according to the military experts of most European states, it cost five times as much to put a soldier in the field as it had done a century before.

1.94 metres (6 'pieds') – measured in shoes – and of almost 8,000 in the year 1737, only fifty-nine. No one stood taller. In the army of the Austrian Netherlands, a little later (1786–7), out of 9,655 recruits, only 404 attained this height.[51]

II

But whatever their stature, and however they had enlisted, the soldiers of early modern Europe required to be paid, cared for, and equipped. This was, of course, a problem shared by armies in other ages; but certain factors conspired to make matters worse in the sixteenth and seventeenth centuries. To begin with, not only were there now more soldiers and more weapons in each army, but their unit cost had also increased (see figure 4). In the words of a Spanish minister in the Netherlands in 1596:

If comparison be made between the present cost to His Majesty [Philip II] of the troops who served in his armies and navies, and the cost of those of [his father] the Emperor Charles V, it will be found that, for an equal number of men, three times as much money is necessary today as used to be spent then.[52]

And, thanks to the 'strategy of attrition' favoured by most commanders of the day, the money was required for far longer. As the Italian political theorist, Giovanni Botero, wrote in 1605: '[Nowadays] war is dragged out for as long as possible, and the object is not to smash but to tire; not to defeat but to wear down the enemy. This form of warfare is entirely dependent on money.' 'The manner of making war at the present time,' echoed one of Spain's leading soldier-diplomats, the marquis of Aytona, in 1630, '... is reduced to a sort of traffic or commerce, in which he who has most money wins'. And a little earlier, another soldier-diplomat, Don Bernardino de Mendoza, had given as a general rule in his *Theory and practice of war*, that 'victory will go to whoever possesses the last *escudo*'.[53]

But the last escudo might be hard to find. Today, governments are criticized when defence spending reaches 17 per cent (France), 29 per cent (the United States) or 41 per cent (Israel) of total public expenditure. However military outlays were far higher in early modern times. In the 1700s, Louis XIV appears to have devoted 75 per cent of his revenues to war, while Peter the Great spent 85 per cent. Even more extreme was the situation of the English Republic during the 1650s, where no less than 90 per cent of public spending seems to have gone on the army and navy. And still this was not enough: the New Model Army's pay remained in arrears (£1.3 million in 1659); the Navy was owed almost as much (£1 million by 1660); the tax-payers complained; and the government never seemed to have enough cash – 'The great want is money, which puts us to the wall in all our business' complained Secretary of State Thurloe in 1658.[54] And of course, in addition, most of the major towns in all these countries were forced to devote similarly large proportions of their resources to the construction, maintenance and defence of new bastion-studded walls (see page 12 above).[55]

Louis XIV's France, Petrine Russia and Cromwellian Britain were all, how-ever, states of a particular type: on the one hand, they were unpopular and isolated abroad and found it difficult (if not impossible) to raise foreign loans to finance their wars; on the other, their power and resources at home were so great that they could support a sizeable standing army for several years on end. Governments with more modest domestic revenues at their disposal were forced to adopt other solutions. The government of Tudor England, for example, spent heavily on its wars with France and Scotland between 1538 and 1552: £3.5 million, according to the Privy Council itself, most of it expended in 1542–50, at the rate of almost £450,000 a year. Since the Crown's revenues at this time were only about £200,000 annually, a massive deficit was rapidly created. Part of the shortfall was bridged by the sale of the church lands confiscated after Henry VIII's breach with Rome (monastic lands worth £800,000 – perhaps two-thirds of the total secularized – had been sold by 1547); and part was provided by new taxes, forced loans and confiscations. But a large sum still had to be raised at interest on foreign money markets: by 1552 £500,000 was outstanding, and the capital was not entirely repaid until 1578.[56]

The Habsburgs, too, had to sell their assets in order to finance war; although the principal 'windfall' revenue at their disposal was not church lands, but American treasure. With the aid of regular shipments of bullion from Mexico and Peru, Charles V managed to raise loans of unprecedented size in the financial centres of western Europe. Between 1520 and 1532, he borrowed 5.4 million ducats (over £1 million sterling), an annual average of 414,000; but during his war against France and the Turks between 1552 and 1556 he borrowed 9.6 million (over £2 million sterling), an annual average of almost 2 million ducats. The cost of the loans rose, as well as their size: from an average of 18 per cent annual interest on loans taken in the 1520s to almost 49 per cent in the 1550s.[57] The charges all had to be met from future revenues and, at his accession in July 1556, Charles's son, Philip II, discovered that all his Spanish revenues had been pledged to repay loans, or pay interest, up to and including the year 1561. So in June 1557, Philip issued a 'decree of bankruptcy' which unilaterally converted all these short-term loans at high interest into long-term redeemable annuities (*juros al quitar*) at 5 per cent interest. Then in 1560, after borrowing heavily for three more years in order once more to defeat the French, the king repeated the manoeuvre; and in 1575, 1596, 1607, 1627, 1647 and 1653, he and his successors did so yet again. Naturally the bankers whose capital was thus confiscated bitterly resented the king's breach of faith, and for some time after each decree they refused to lend any further funds; but the Crown always won them over again by the simple expedient of refusing to pay any interest at all on existing loans or juros until new loans were advanced. This clumsy and brutal system enabled the Spanish government to increase its funded debt from 6 million ducats in 1556 to 180 million (approximately £36 million sterling) a century later.[58]

But it was a poor way to win a war. Time and again, the temporary bankruptcy of the Spanish Crown caused the failure of her military operations. The suspension of payments in 1575 deprived Philip II of the means to follow up the Army of Flanders's successful operations against the Dutch rebels, and within nine months produced a mutiny among his unpaid troops which destroyed all royal control in the Netherlands. The bankruptcy of 1627 likewise resulted in military paralysis in the Low Countries, allowing the Dutch to take 's Hertogenbosch, Wesel, and numerous towns in Westphalia occupied by Spanish forces. For the Dutch, by this time, were able to support a large and effective army for as long as necessary.[59] They had devised a novel form of fund-raising that was to prove their salvation.

During the first half of the sixteenth century, the provincial States of Holland began to accept collective responsibility for war-loans secured on the yield of future taxes: payment of interest and eventual redemption were offficially guaranteed. Since the interest rates offered were high, and the security good, there was a notable inflow of capital, both from domestic and outside investors.[60] In the seventeenth century, even though the interest rates fell (by stages) from 10 per cent in 1600 to 4 per cent in 1655, the Dutch Republic was still able to borrow on the open market as much money for war as it required. In the 1630s, for example, it was estimated that the tax revenues of Holland (by far the richest province) amounted to 11 million florins annually (over £1 million sterling), while expenditure on war was about 12 million and interest charges absorbed a further 7 million. There was thus an annual deficit of around 8 million florins, financed by loans which, by 1652, after the end of the long war with Spain, stood at 132 million florins (roughly £13 million sterling). Although much of this was quickly paid off, redemption was (according to the English ambassador Sir William Temple) not at all popular with investors who, far from rejoicing when the Republic resolved to 'pay off any part of the Principal ... receive it with tears, not knowing how to dispose of it to interest, with such safety and ease'. So successful was the Dutch 'financial revolution' that in the 1690s it was transplanted to England, where it enabled William III and his allies to withstand the superior resources of Louis XIV's France. Under William's successor, Queen Anne, the British government spent £93.6 million between 1702 and 1713 in the war against Louis XIV, of which no less than 31 per cent was raised by borrowing.[61]

III

But all this lay in the future. For most European governments of the sixteenth and seventeenth centuries, the problems caused by the increase in army size and by the price revolution proved too great for immediate solution. The traditional system of paying each soldier his due in person was gradually abandoned in favour of some form of administrative devolution, by which governments paid private contractors and entrepreneurs to supply the military services which they could no longer afford to organize for themselves.[62]

By the end of the sixteenth century, several states had begun to recruit and supply their armies – particularly units required to serve abroad – through private contractors; but during the Thirty Years War the system reached its apogee, with some 1,500 individuals raising troops all over Europe, under contract, for one or more warlords. Between 1630 and 1635, perhaps 400 military enterprisers were active, raising and maintaining fully equipped regiments, brigades and (in the case of Wallenstein and Bernard of Saxe-Weimar) even whole armies on behalf of governments which lacked either the financial or human resources to do the job themselves. The basic qualification of these military entrepreneurs was economic power. Military success was, somewhat surprisingly, not a prerequisite, for some leaders (such as Ernest Count of Mansfelt or Dodo von Knyphausen) seem to have led their armies from one defeat to another while nonetheless managing to hold their troops together through sheer organizational skill. But to achieve success, a military enterpriser also needed wealth. Wallenstein advanced over six million thalers (£1.25 million) to the emperor between 1621 and 1628; Bernard of Saxe-Weimar in 1637 estimated his personal fortune at 450,000 thalers; the Imperialist commander, Henrik Holck, once a poor man, returned to his native Denmark in 1627 rich enough to pay 50,000 thalers in cash for an estate on Funen; and the Swedish general Konigsmarck, who had formerly served as both a page and a common soldier, died in 1663 with assets worth almost 2 million thalers.[63] However the credit of even these individuals was not inexhaustible; they could not continue to pay their men indefinitely from their own resources. Indeed, they could not afford to pay their men very much at all: most of the soldiers who fought in the Thirty Years War agreed to serve for wages that were scarcely higher than those of farm hands. Instead, armies raised by contractors were supported by a complicated scheme of military finance, originally perfected by the Dutch and Spanish commanders fighting in the Netherlands. The first essential ingredient was a regular (even if inadequate) input of cash from the state treasury. In a famous letter of January 1626, written at the beginning of his first generalship, Wallenstein informed the Imperial Finance Minister that he would need 'a couple of million thalers every year to keep this war going'.[64] But this money was not paid directly to the troops: it was required solely to maintain Wallenstein's personal credit, and to repay the sums he had advanced to the men under his command.

The system of military devolution was bitterly satirized in a celebrated novel about the war: *The adventures of Simplicissimus the German*. The author, Hans Jakob Christoffel von Grimmelshausen, devoted to the subject an elaborate simile, which compared the army hierarchy on pay-days to a flock of birds in a tree.[65] Those on the topmost branches, he claimed:

> were at their best and happiest when a commissary-bird flew overhead and shook a whole panfull of gold over the tree ... for they caught as much of that as they could and let little or nothing at all fall to the lowest branches; so that, of those who sat there, more died of hunger than of the enemy's attacks.

In fact Grimmelshausen's vision was somewhat distorted, because the birds on the lowest branches – the army's rank and file – actually received considerable sustenance by other means. In the first place, armies on the move normally secured the food and other supplies they needed from the civilian population through whom they passed. Plunder alone was too wasteful: for an army to 'live off the country', the exploitation of local resources had to be controlled and systematized. In its simplest form, this procedure was known as *Brandschatzung* (or, in the Netherlands, *Brandschatting*): 'fire-money'. An army threatened to set fire to, or sack, a community unless it produced (in effect) a ransom either in cash or in commodities required by the troops (plate 16). In return for its contribution, the town or village might receive a letter of protection guaranteeing that it would not be subjected to further demands from any forces of the same side (in areas of frequent or constant hostilities, villages might have to make regular payments to the neighbouring garrisons of both sides as 'protection money').[66] And from there it was but a short step to the fully fledged 'contributions system': a

16 *The Brandmeister*. Securing money for armies from civilian populations under threat of arson was singularly effective when houses were built of wood and thatched with straw. It is true that, as in the Vietnam War, what was easily burnt could also be easily rebuilt; but the destruction of the food supplies and tools stored in the houses was far more serious. (From Fronsperger, *Kriegsbuch*, III, fo. LXVIII.)

permanent military tax levied by the army from all the communities within a certain radius of its presence. Under the direction of a skilled and ruthless commander, such as Parma or Wallenstein, 'contributions' could be made to supply the troops' every need – food, clothes, lodgings, munitions, transport – the exact mechanics and amounts of the goods and services supplied being worked out between the regimental and company clerks on the one hand, and the local magistrates on the other. In areas frequently visited by troops, such as the Low Countries or central Germany, an 'early warning system' developed among communities along an army's projected line of march, so that the necessary provisions could be prepared in advance. If, finally, prior liaison between military and civilian administrators seemed unlikely to produce sufficient victuals, merchants from areas unaffected by the war might be persuaded to step in. Thus some generals in the Dutch and German wars purchased cattle in bulk from Switzerland, or cloth from England; and Wallenstein organized the regular delivery of beer, bread, clothes and other necessaries to his army from his own extensive estates in Bohemia.[67] All these various expedients were essential for, as Michel le Tellier, French Secretary of State for War, observed: 'to secure the livelihood of the soldier is to secure victory for the king'. By the 1640s, most military administrators reckoned to supply two-thirds of their troops' wages in kind.[68]

This system at least kept the armies fed, equipped and clothed; but it was by no means perfect. In the first place, few contractors were able to provide sufficient artillery from their own resources. For reasons of both national security and exorbitant cost most states, however much they might rely on the services of contractors for their other military needs, deemed it essential to create a stock of field and siege guns that was entirely their own; and few contractors, for their part, could afford to add an artillery train that might inflate the total costs of a campaign by as much as 50 per cent.[69] A second limitation of the system of military devolution was that much of the equipment actually supplied by the contractors was far from satisfactory. Perhaps this was inevitable, since an army of 30,000 combatants, for example, would need at the outset 30,000 suits of clothes and 60,000 shoes, 30,000 swords and helmets, an appropriate number of pikes, armour, muskets (with all necessary accoutrements), and ammunition. As any soldier knows, even today no quartermaster can guarantee that each and every one of these items will be issued in full working order and perfect condition. Nevertheless, some items supplied to early modern armies were inexcusably defective. For example, the English forces in Ireland fighting against the troops of the earl of Tyrone between 1594 and 1603 were constantly threatened with disaster because of inadequacies in supply. In 1599, the earl of Essex urged that any new levies sent from England should bring their own arms 'for here in service the arms decay faster than the men; and the store that was [recently] brought over is already so much diminished that to any new levy it will afford but little help'. Admittedly, Essex was in a particularly difficult situation: he had arrived in Ireland in the wake of a major English defeat (the Yellow Ford, near Armagh, in August 1598) and had increased the total forces of Elizabeth in Ireland from perhaps 4,000 to over 18,000. Since Ireland was unable to supply munitions itself, all that Essex's men needed required to be shipped out from England; so between 1598 and 1601, fourteen major armament convoys (each of some thirty seven-ton carts) were sent from London, via Chester or Bristol, to Dublin.

Mountjoy's victories over Tyrone in Ulster and over his Spanish allies at Kinsale in 1601–2 (page 33 above) were as much the result of superior supply as of superior generalship.[70]

But military efficiency, to be effective, must be constantly maintained. Part of the problem in the 1590s was the unpreparedness of the government to face a new war in Ireland: after almost thirty years of peace, it took time to become fully mobilized. Nevertheless, after the victory in 1603 (and an agreement with Spain the following year) the military establishment built up with so much effort was soon allowed to decay so that, when war broke out again in the 1640s, there were once more insufficient munitions to go round, or else not enough of the right sort. Roger Boyle, lord Broghill, a commander in Ireland during the Civil War, complained that his musketeers almost lost one battle because the shot supplied was too large for the weapons available, so that some men 'were forced to gnaw off much of the lead [while], others to cut their bullets, in which much time was lost, the bullets flew a less way and more uncertainly; and, which was worse, so many pauses animated the enemy by making him think our courages cooled.'[71]

Part of Broghill's embarrassment stemmed from a lack of standardization due to the differing provenance of his small arms – some made locally, some captured from the enemy, some supplied from England (and those, too, by no means uniform). But the real problem lay in the general shortage of arms throughout Britain upon the outbreak of the Civil Wars, after so many years of peace. When Charles I led his army out of Shrewsbury in September 1642, a sympathetic eye-witness lamented that some of his infantry were armed with 'but pitchforks and such like tools, and many only with good cudgels', while in the whole army 'there was not one pikeman had a corslet, and very few musketeers who had swords.'[72] For some time after this, Royalist soldiers were equipped by the constables of loyal villages, who were required to send the parish store of powder, arms and armour – some of it, no doubt, half a century old – to the Ordnance Office in Oxford. Then, in the summer of 1643 when these reserves were consumed, recourse was made to continental contractors. It was not always a move for the better. The lugubrious description of a consignment of 1,000 muskets brought over from France to Weymouth in 1644 illuminates the problem:

They are of three or four score sundry bores – some pistol bores, some carbine bores, some little fowling pieces, and all the old trash that can be rapt together.

But, on the other hand, the weapons delivered direct from the continent under contract by reliable arms manufacturers were usually excellent in quality. There were few complaints, either, about local supplies obtained once the war was properly underway: the king esteemed highly the 200 muskets and 30 pairs of pistols produced each week by the gunsmiths of Bristol.[73] Even though the speed with which weapons wore out exasperated the generals

– 'It is inconceivable what these fellows were always doing with their arms', complained a petulant Ralph Hopton in September 1643: 'they appear to be expended as fast as their ammunition' – nevertheless the Royalist army, like its Parliamentary and Scottish enemies, always seems to have been able to secure enough munitions to keep on fighting. Once a steady and substantial demand developed, production and distribution of armaments improved until it was satisfied.[74]

The supply of war-horses for armies followed much the same course, although the story is complicated by the fact that cavalry was not of equal importance in European warfare at all times and in all places. The Muslim onslaught on Europe in the eighth century had led the Franks to adopt cavalry, rather than infantry, as their principal arm, and to introduce a new, larger, warhorse to carry their fully armed warriors into battle: the *destrier*. By the fourteenth century, thanks to careful selective breeding, these warhorses had become very large indeed – perhaps 17 hands high, like their lineal descendant the 'shire horse'. But, at precisely this moment, a movement away from cavalry-based armies began in England. Already, by the 1350s, relatively few destriers were being bred there and, instead, English armies trusted for victory to their archers.[75] The verdict of battle at Crecy (1346), Poitiers (1356), Agincourt (1415), and countless other lesser encounters confirmed that a charge by heavy cavalry could be stopped by archery volleys (see p. 16 above). But still the knights survived.[76] *The Bandes d'Ordonnance*, whose creation in 1445 has been hailed as the origin of the French standing army, were predominantly composed of heavy cavalry; and when King Charles VIII launched his rash invasion of Italy in 1494 (page 24 above), his 18,000 men included 12,000 cavalry. Even Francis I, at Pavia in 1525, commanded 6,000 cavalry in his army of 32,000.[77] But after this (and it should be recalled that Francis I and many of his knights were captured by their enemies at Pavia), the number of heavy cavalry in west European armies declined rapidly both relatively and absolutely until, by the last quarter of the century, they had almost totally disappeared. Of course all armies still needed horsemen, whether for scouting and skirmishing or for attack in battle; and sometimes, as under Henry IV of France at Coutras (1587) and Ivry (1590), a cavalry charge could still win battles. But for about a century after the battle of Pavia, few Western armies had more than 10 per cent of their men fighting on horseback. When France went to war against the Habsburgs in 1635, orders were issued to raise 132,000 infantry but only 12,400 cavalry, and each operational army was seen (ideally) as 10,500 foot and 2,500 horse. Even in the 1640s, an experienced officer like George Monck still believed that mounted troops should constitute only one-quarter or one-fifth of an army engaged principally in siege warfare.[78]

From the standpoint of supply, all this was just as well: the cost of a warhorse capable of carrying a knight in full armour represented between six and twenty-six months' wages for the owner; and each cavalryman might require up to three new mounts per year (for even in billets or in garrisons, contemporaries reckoned that 'One rainstorm, one cold night or one frost is enough to kill a horse not under cover'). Naturally, on active service, losses would be far higher: at the battle of Dendermonde in 1452, one commander had five horses killed from under him; almost two centuries later, at the battle of Lützen in 1632, the Imperialist general Ottavio Piccolomini lost seven of his horses in the course of the day, Captain Sydnam Poyntz lost three, and King Gustavus Adolphus's magnificent charger 'Streiff', which had cost 1,000 thalers (about £200), was mortally wounded.[79] So the maintenance of large cavalry units posed serious problems. In 1592, after the daring relief of Rouen by the Spanish Army of Flanders, almost two-thirds of the cavalry lacked mounts. During the English Civil War, quartermasters on both sides resorted to theft, confiscation and compulsory purchase in order to mount their troopers: even before Edgehill the king found it necessary to impose the death penalty on any former owner caught trying to retrieve his horse from the Royalist camp. And in Spain, even as the outbreak of war with France appeared inevitable, early in 1635, Philip IV instructed his ambassador in Paris to purchase as many French cavalry horses as he could whilst there was still time. A few years later they were being bought and shipped to Spain from as far afield as Denmark.[80] But (yet again) both England and Spain had experienced a long period of domestic peace, during which horse-breeding for war had been allowed to lapse. After a few years of continuing hostilities, these acute supply problems gradually eased. In the course of the Civil Wars, the Royalist main army was able to increase its cavalry component from 2,500 horse (or one-fifth of the total force) at Edgehill in October 1642, to 4,500 (or one-half of the total) at the second battle of Newbury two years later. Meanwhile the Parliamentary army in the West, under Sir William Waller, managed to mount all its infantry for the 1644 campaign, in the interests of mobility; and the northern campaign of 1645 was fought mainly by large bodies of cavalry moving rapidly from one threatened town to another.[81] In the 1650s, after the war, the continuing production of English horses was so high that export restrictions – rigorously enforced since Tudor times – were lifted and, from Sandwich alone, some 500 horses annually were exported to the Continent.[82] Some of these went to Spain, where the heavy losses incurred in the wars against France and Portugal ran to several thousand mounts a year; but, there too, a crash breeding programme produced an increasing number of locally raised steeds for the expanding cavalry component in Philip IV's armies. The army of Extremadura, throughout the 1650s, seems to have consisted of around 5,000 men, of whom 3,000 were mounted.[83] The presence of a steady and predictable demand thus once more solved the problem of supply: when Europe's armies needed large numbers of horses again on a regular basis, large numbers could in time be produced.

Precisely the same process can be detected in the supply of military clothing. During the English Civil War, for example, both sides were at first prepared to accept civilian contributions paid in kind. Food, lodging and clothes were therefore supplied direct to the army against receipts issued by the local commanders, and garments for the Royalists seem to have been sent to a special magazine, established in January 1643 in the Oxford Schools of Music and Astronomy, where a team of tailors and seamstresses turned them into military dress. But it seems unlikely that their efforts managed to clothe entire regiments – let alone entire armies – in raiment of a single colour There were several reasons for this. To begin with, the need for a uniform was still not universally recognized, for as long as a large part of the army wore armour, uniforms were redundant. And then, even after buffcoats replaced breastplates, it had to be recognized that no large group of men who began a campaign in clothes of the same colour and design would still be wearing them at the end. It did not take long to ruin coats and breeches when one had to live like Thomas Raymond, who fought with the Dutch army in 1633:[84]

One night I had nothing to keepe me from the cold wett ground but a little bundle of wett dryed flax, which by chance I litt on. And soe with my bootes full of water and wrapt upp in my wett cloake, I lay as rounde as a hedgehogg, and at peep of day looked llke a drowned ratt.

Worn-out or damaged clothes would be replaced by the troops from any source available – from fallen comrades, from civilians (whether by purchase or plunder), even from the enemy. In 1651, it was desired that Charles II's Scottish Lifeguards 'might all of them have cottes of one colour'; but when a supply-ship bearing replacement uniforms for their English adversaries was blown off course and captured, the Scots gladly made use of them![85] The continental armies of the day were no better. When, in 1647, the French secretary of state for war issued regulations for clothes to be made for Louis XIV's armies, he specified three fittings and the quantities for each (one-half 'normal'; one-quarter 'large'; one-quarter 'small'), but said nothing about colour.[86] The only way, therefore, that commanders could distinguish their troops from those of the enemy was by making all those on the same side wear a coloured marker – usually a sash, a ribbon, or a plume. The soldiers of the Habsburgs, whether Spanish or Austrian, always wore a red token; those of Sweden wore yellow; those of France wore blue; those of the Dutch (and, initially, of the English parliament in the 1640s) wore orange.[87] It is sometimes asserted that the English New Model Army was the first to dress entirely in uniform; a red top-coat, it is said, was worn by every man after 1645. But though this was certainly the intention, it proved impossible to achieve. As usual, once a campaign was under way, men replaced damaged items of clothing as best they could. At both Dunbar (1650) and Worcester (1651), it was still necessary for the New Model to have distinguishing marks (in both cases 'to have no white about us')[88]; and in 1655, after a solemn audience with Cromwell in Whitehall Palace, the Swedish ambassador reported that the Protector's Guards 'were drawn up outside in the square, and on both sides of the street: ... pretty handsome young men, but they were not in livery. Each was clad in his particular colour, mostly grey'.[89] So much for the redcoat army!

Nevertheless, the situation was changing. When, in 1645, the Imperial generalissimo Count Gallas placed an order with Austrian clothiers to supply 600 uniforms for his men, he attached a sample of the exact material and specified the colour (pale grey) to be copied. He also sent samples of powder-horns, and cartridge belts to be manufactured *en masse* by local suppliers. Once permanent regiments were created, as they were in Sweden and Austria in the 1620s, or in England and France in the 1660s, uniforms made better sense. Yet again, only the guarantee of constant, predictable demand produced a standard dependable supply.[90]

The creation of standing armies also gave rise to other innovations – led by the Spanish army of Flanders, the first large permanent force in Europe (it remained constantly mobilized from 1567 until 1706). To begin with, it supported the first permanent military hospital in modern Europe, at Mechelen (Malines) in Brabant. The duke of Alva set up a hospital for sick Spanish troops in the city immediately after his arrival in the Netherlands in 1567, but it was dismantled after about a year and, even following the outbreak of war in 1572, nothing took its place. One of the principal grievances of the Spanish mutineers in 1574, 1575 and 1576 was precisely that 'Many soldiers have suffered and died [in the war] because there was nowhere for them to be cured when they fell sick. Most of them would have recovered had there been medical assistance [and a hospital].'[91] But it was not until 1585 that a permanent hospital was reopened in Mechelen with (eventually) a staff of 49 and some 330 sickbeds (plate 17). There, soldiers were cured, with remarkable success, of everything from diseases like syphilis and malaria, through psychological disorders and battle trauma, to severe combat injuries (plate 18). The Spanish authorities, it must be admitted, acted only partially from charitable motives. There was also a compelling cost-benefit factor to consider – it was cheaper by far to cure a wounded veteran in the Netherlands than to train and transport a replacement from Spain (especially since the cost of the hospital was financed, in part, by the troops themselves: one *real* per month deducted from every soldier's monthly wage plus, from 1596 onwards, the yield of fines imposed on officers and men for blasphemy). The same combination of altruism and cost-efficiency was responsible for

17 *Inside the military hospital at Mechelen.* A manuscript account of the Netherlands war in the 1590s, compiled by an Austrian traveller Paulus Marsteller, included a special chapter on the large hospital for sick and wounded soldiers established at Mechelen in Brabant in 1585. At the time, it was the only permanent establishment of its kind in Europe and, for almost a century, it remained so. (Vienna, Osterreichische Nationalbibliothek, Cod. Vindob. 8905 fo. 51. The text reads 'Vertzaichnüs aller bevelchshaber so in dem Veltspital dienen mitsambt iren besoldüngen'.)

the Army of Flanders's excellent record on ransoming and exchanging its soldiers when captured by the enemy (from 1609, men were even paid full wages for the period of their captivity).[92] But it was charity alone which seems to have led the same army to establish a special home for its crippled veterans (the 'Garrison of Our Lady of Hal') which in 1640 numbered 346 men; to have established a sort of 'Public Trustee' (*Depositario General*) in 1596 to administer and execute the testaments of all soldiers who died

Serratura.

18 *The tools of a military surgeon* varied little between the sixteenth century and the nineteenth: saws, a brace-and-bit, a large number of instruments long, sharp and thin .... An incision with a knife and a few strokes of the saw were enough to amputate a leg – as Hans von Gersdorff's manual of military surgery (the first illustrated surgical treatise printed in Europe) graphically showed. One patient (standing, right) holds the stump of a successfully amputated hand, while another loses a leg. He appears to be unconscious (either from pain, or some drug contained in the cloth over his face) although anaesthetics, as such, were unknown to early modern surgeons and their patients. (H. von Gersdorff, *Feldbuch der Wundarznei* [Strasbourg, 1517], LXIX.)

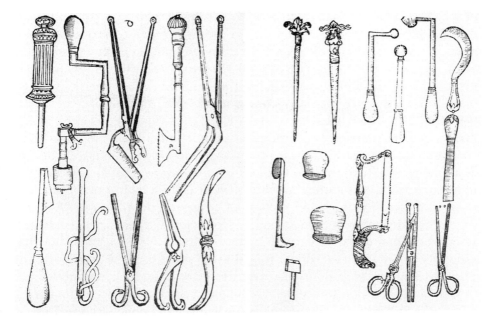

in service; to have maintained a full chaplaincy service; and to have paid the full arrears of pay, and sometimes also a pension, to the widows and orphans of those captured or killed in action.[93] Other states eventually followed suit – France with the Hotel des Invalides (for both injured and old soldiers) from 1670; Britain with the military hospitals at Kilmainham (Dublin) from 1681 and at Chelsea (London) from 1684. But Spain led the way.[94]

IV

At least the problems of providing an army with clothes, horses, weapons, and hospital care were transient, however: they caused a crisis once or twice a year, not every day. The tasks of feeding and lodging the troops were of a very different magnitude. To begin with, every soldier required bread, and in most armies the daily ration was reckoned at 1.5 pounds a day (or a 3-pound loaf every two days). In addition, about 1 pound of meat, cheese, or fish, and 6 pints of beer (or 3 pints of wine) were laid down as the standard daily ration in most armies. But to translate these norms into reality required great effort and skill, for a garrison of 3,000 might be larger than the town on which it was billeted, and a field army of 30,000 required more food than all but the largest cities of the day.[95] To produce the 45,000 pounds – twenty tons – of bread required every day to feed such an army, over 10,000 pounds of flour had to be baked daily. To provide 30,000 pounds of meat required the slaughter of some 1,500 sheep or 150 bullocks every day – a surprisingly high figure, due to the small size of livestock in early modern times.[96] Admittedly, when the army was not on campaign, it could be quartered on the population over a large area, so that the supply problem for any given community was kept within bounds.[97] And when the troops moved along a route that was known in advance, suitable victuals could be prepared beforehand. The 'Spanish Road', for example, used by troops marching from Lombardy to the Low Countries between 1567 and 1620, represented the acme of early modern troop movement: thousands of men at a time were able to travel the 700 or so miles between Milan and Brussels in five to seven weeks with remarkably few casualties, thanks to the arrangement of a fixed itinerary and a chain of magazines in advance.[98] At other times, provided there were roads suitable for wheeled transport, considerable reserves of food could be carried along with the army's baggage. But this, too, was easier said than done: for an army of 30,000, the transportation of a week's supply of flour, the ovens to bake it (each consisting of 500 bricks), and the wood to fire them, demanded some 250 carts and a corresponding number of draught animals.[99] It was seldom possible to find everything necessary in one place at the same time. When the Dutch army – one of the best organized of its day – marched through hostile territory in Brabant in 1633, its mobile ovens 'answered not expectation, they not being able with a whole week's cooking to furnish the army on[e] day's bread'.[100]

There were a number of alternatives to this dilemma. One was to campaign close to the sea, or to a navigable river, so that bulk supplies of food could be brought in by water transport: this was certainly the strategy adopted by Oliver Cromwell in his initial conquest of Ireland (1649) and of Scotland (1650). But there came a point after which an enemy had to be pursued into territories far from waterways. Cromwell, and his able successor in Scotland George Monck, solved this problem by making each soldier carry enough bread or biscuit in their knapsacks to keep them for a week, with a supply of cheese (plus a reserve of biscuit) carried on a train of packhorses (there being no roads in the Highlands suitable for carts). In this way, with the support of a few magazines in strategic locations, the English forces could move swiftly over comparatively long distances and yet still retain their full fighting strength. In the three-month campaign of 1654, Monck's army of about 6,000 men covered almost 1,600 kilometres in the uncharted Scottish Highlands and, thanks to their excellent supply system, pacified the area more completely than in any previous age. As one of those involved later recalled: 'Nothing is more certain than this: that in the late wars, both Scotland and Ireland were conquered by timely provisions of Cheshire cheese and biscuit'.[101]

But few armies were as professional as Cromwell's Ironsides. Most early modern forces, if ever they left their supply bases, courted catastrophe. Sometimes the problem was simply that too many troops were trying to exist in too small an area. Thus during the 1590s, while the armies of the Catholic League, their Spanish allies, and Henry IV struggled for control of Paris, some 10,000 soldiers tried to occupy, and live off, the Hurepoix (southwest of the city). Since the area's total population was only 80,000, it could not be done. Many villages paid contributions to keep the troops at bay, others hired defenders of their own and erected fortifications; but flight was cheaper, safer, and so more common. The troops, deprived of their source of sustenance, were therefore forced to leave also, or else starve.[102] Conditions were naturally far worse when an army was forced to traverse an area that had already been devastated. As Cardinal Richelieu noted in his *Testament politique*, 'One finds in the history books that many more armies perished through lack of food and lack of order than through enemy action'; and, almost as he wrote, the Swedish main army in Germany under Johan Baner was decimated by a retreat from Torgau on the middle Elbe to Pomerania in 1637; the French forces under the great Turenne lost two-thirds of their 16,000 men on the retreat from their defeat at Tuttlingen to the Rhine in 1643; and the Imperialists under Count Gallas reputedly lost 90 per cent of their 18,000 men when they withdrew from Holstein into Bohemia in 1644.[103] The culprit, in each case, was the inability of the commander to feed his men.

Of course, armies on the move did not consist only of military personnel. First there were the horses. Their numbers may have been less than in the Middle Ages, but the artillery, the cavalry, the officers, and the baggage wagons all nevertheless required them, so that a major field army might be accompanied by 20,000 beasts consuming between them some 90 tons of fodder, or 400 acres of grazing, daily. The baggage carts – up to 500 for an army of 15,000 men – also required carters; the horses required ostlers; while the troops required sutlers and servants (many of the latter being women who carried out a variety of functions in the army: prostitution, laundry, selling, sewing, stealing, nursing …) In all, the number of camp followers could sometimes equal and occasionally exceed the total of combatants.[104] When the Spanish Army of Flanders laid siege to Bergen-op-Zoom in 1622, the Calvinist pastors in the beleaguered town virtuously recorded in their diary that 'such a long tail on such a small body never was seen: … such a small army with so many carts, baggage horses, nags, sutlers, lackeys, women, children and a rabble which numbered far more than the army itself'. It may have been true, although the archives of the Army of Flanders (which kept meticulous records) suggest that camp followers only rarely attained even 50 per cent of its total troops.[105] But during the Thirty Years War in Germany, we find two Bavarian regiments in 1646 consisting of

480 infantrymen, 314 women and children, 74 servants and 3 sutlers; and 481 cavalry troopers accompanied by 236 servants, 102 women and children, and 9 sutlers. Between them, the 961 fighting men also brought along 1,072 horses.[106]

Such an escalation in the number of camp-followers, coming on top of the military manpower revolution, seriously exacerbated the difficulty of lodging an army. This problem was less serious for troops in garrisons – who, as suggested above, might account for up to one-half of a nation's armed forces – because they were normally accommodated either within a citadel or else in the households of local inhabitants. Contingents moving along an itinerary arranged in advance would also sometimes be quartered in private houses and inns along the way – provided there were not too many men and camp-followers travelling at the same time.[107] But an army of (say) 30,000 men on campaign, normally covering perhaps 20 kilometres a day on the march, could not be lodged in houses for much of the time. Instead they had to camp in the fields. Some armies marched with tents among their baggage, ready for use, but most did not. Instead they were expected to make shelters known as 'huts'. According to Roger Boyle in 1677:

In ancient times they used tents ... for then, the way of making war was in the field, and armies were daily in motion; ... but now that for the most part war is made in the besieging of strong places, or in standing camps, both soldiers and officers use to hutt, which is more warm and more lasting than tents.[108]

This was something of an over-simplification. Several military artists from the middle of the fourteenth to the middle of the seventeenth century depicted military camps containing both tents and 'huts' (in French *barraque* and in Spanish *barraca*: plate 19).[109] But, of course, on every expedition there was 'many a man weak in body who [in the words of a contemptuous Welsh soldier in 1523] preferred from sheer laziness to lie under a hedge rather than take the trouble to make a snug, warm hut' each night; and there were also nights when there was no time for anyone to make shelters, so that the entire army slept in battle order where it halted, as the Swedish army did before Breitenfeld in 1631 or the Imperialists did after Lützen in 1632.[110] Ultimately, the only solution to this problem was to carry along enough tents when an army travelled on campaign, and to build special barracks to house it in garrisons during winter. In the South Netherlands, stone and timber 'barraques' which accommodated eight men sprang up after 1609 in most garrison towns, so that at least some of the Army of Flanders were lodged away from the civilian population as a self-contained military community.[111] This innovation was soon followed by the other states of western Europe.

19 A *military camp* normally resembled a small town, with huts (or tents) arranged in streets, shops, pedlars and a 'wall'. The camp of a major army, which might number 30,000 'mouths', was in fact larger than most civilian settlements – Tudor England could only boast three cities of that size – and presented formidable problems of organization and supply. (Fronsperger, *Kriegsbuch*, I, fos. LV – LVI.)

V

In short, then, it would seem that eventually the Army of Flanders (at least) managed to solve all its supply problems. For most of the later seventeenth century, its commissariat provided each soldier – whether in barracks or on campaign – with a three-pound loaf every other day, thanks to the efforts of contractors who signed undertakings to provide millions of loaves at a time. Between 10 April 1678 and 12 February 1679, for example, the troops in the South Netherlands actually received (and consumed) 12,651,955 rations of bread from their victualling contractors – an average of 39,000 loaves each and every day.[112] At the same time, consignments of ready-made suits made from English cloth were regularly imported and distributed to the troops, and supplies of weapons and ammunition were guaranteed. Everything was paid for fairly punctually by the military treasury, which thus managed to avoid the great mutinies which had broken out in the days when governments had concentrated on trying to provide pay rather than provisions to their troops.[113]

Yet the Army of Flanders was, by this time, regarded as a broken force which could neither campaign effectively, nor defend the possessions it held, without foreign assistance. The armies of France, Austria, Brandenburg, the Dutch Republic and (a little later) Great Britain were far superior both in numbers and in logistical organization. Nevertheless, for all their refinements and professionalism, even the prodigious armies that so impressed Uncle Toby in the 1690s were still insufficient to achieve outright victory.[114] In the later conflicts of Louis XIV there were many spectacular battles – Blenheim, Turin, Oudenaarde, Denain – but none of them brought peace. Even with increased manpower, the political objectives of governments at war were still unattainable with the limited military strategies available. As before, most decisive wars were not big and most big wars were not decisive. The states of early modern Europe had discovered how to supply large armies but not how to lead them to victory.

That is one reason why, from the late sixteenth century onwards hostilities between the Great Powers came to be fought not only on the continent of Europe, but also at sea and even overseas. The more land warfare became a stalemate, the more the leading states sought a decision through naval power. This development may first be observed in the Low Countries' Wars. Although in the first phase (1572–1609) naval battles were relatively rare, once the struggle resumed in 1621 a powerful faction at the Court of Spain identified the strength of the Dutch by sea as their principal asset and argued that more funds should be directed away from the army and into the fleet. Spending on the 'Armada of Flanders' therefore tripled and the government of Philip IV kept its land forces in the Netherlands on the defensive for much of the 1620s, striving to gain an advantage over their adversaries by sea. Other states were not slow to follow suit. Gustavus Adolphus of Sweden also spent heavily on his navy during the 1620s, and the magnificent warship *Vasa*, recently recovered from the site where she sank on her maiden voyage, shows how powerful and well-equipped the Swedish navy had become (plate 27, p. 98). The French navy during the ministry of Richelieu grew to respectable size and, under the enlightened direction of Jean Baptiste Colbert (1661–83), became perhaps the most successful and powerful fleet in western Europe.[115] From the 1650s onwards, there was scarcely a war fought in Europe that did not overflow into a struggle for mastery of the seas and, beyond, into a contest for power and influence overseas. And there, too, the 'military revolution' made its mark.

3

Victory at sea

'In the present state of Europe,' wrote the duke of Choiseul, chief minister of France in the 1760s, 'it is colonies, trade and, in consequence, seapower which must determine the balance of power upon the continent.'[1] Some historians have argued that this had been true for at least a century, even perhaps since the defeat of the Spanish Armada in 1588. But such opinions beg the question of what, precisely, 'seapower' meant in the age of sail. Few at the time thought of it as more than the ability to send troops or trade-goods across the waters that separated a state (or its allies) from the place where they were required, and to prevent the enemies of the state (or its allies) from doing the same. No statesman in early modern Europe equated seapower with complete naval mastery in all areas, with 'that overbearing power on the sea which drives the enemy's flag from it, or allows it to appear only as a fugitive' – the influential definition offered in 1890 by A. T. Mahan in *The influence of seapower upon history, 1660–1783* – for the simple reason that no early modern state possessed the naval strength to achieve this. Mahan, after all, was primarily a naval theorist who sought to find and formulate 'universal rules' for the successful conduct of war at sea similar to those proposed by Jomini for land warfare. He was not a trained historian.[2] Indeed, Mahan, once stated that:[3]

Written history should consist of the 'artistic grouping of subordinate details around a central idea'; that some facts were 'not really worth the evident trouble' of searching them out; that the 'scholar's passion for certainty may lapse into incapacity for decision'; and that 'facts must be massed so well as troops' and kept subordinate to the 'central feature'.

It is worth remembering that *The influence of seapower upon history* contained no discussion of guns, sails or ship design, because the author did not believe that changes in these things could affect the application of strategic principles.

82

I

And yet Mahan addressed a major issue, which many previous historians had ignored: the period between the 'great discoveries' in the 1490s and the proliferation of railways in the 1840s was indeed the golden age of seapower, a time during which control of strategically important waters decided the balance of power both in Europe and beyond. And this was because a revolution in naval warfare occurred in early modern Europe which was no less important than that by land, for it opened the way to the exercise of European hegemony over most of the world's oceans for much of the modern period. At the centre of this revolution, too, lay the adoption of the gun, which the West used at sea with ruthless skill to control or destroy all its maritime rivals – starting with America, and moving through Africa and South Asia to Japan and China.

Herein lay a great irony, for it is now beyond dispute that the entire development of firearms was originally Chinese – from the first discovery of the correct formula for gunpowder (which is now thought to have occurred as early as the ninth century AD) to the perfection of the metal-barrelled cannon in the mid-thirteenth century. A hundred years later, when the first mention of iron artillery occurs in both Arabic and European sources, China already possessed a sophisticated arsenal of iron and bronze ordnance, and both pictorial and archaeological evidence proves that artillery was used (perhaps for the first time) during the ill-fated second seaborne invasion of Japan in 1281 by the forces of Kublai Khan.[4]

This early use should come as no surprise, for artillery was fully compatible with the traditions of Chinese warfare at sea. From the eighth century AD, at least, Chinese warships had preferred fighting from a distance with projectiles to close-combat and boarding, and war-junks with catapults and trebuchets became the staple of the navy in Sung times. Ship-borne artillery was noted aboard the fleet of the founder of the Ming dynasty, Chu Yuan-chang, in the 1350s; and the Peking military museum possesses a bombard with an inscription indicating that it was cast in the year 1372 for the 'Left naval station' near Nanking. It also bore the number '42' – which suggests that naval guns were by then standard issue.[5] In the early fifteenth century every Imperial warship was required to carry fifty firearms of various sorts, with 1,000 bullets, and this was probably the armament deployed some years later aboard the 7 great expeditions sent into the Indian Ocean under the command of the Muslim admiral Cheng Ho, which sailed as far as Mogadishu and Aden, and involved the Chinese invasion of Ceylon.[6] Guns were still in use aboard the ships of the Ming navy in the 1520s, and naval artillery helped to defeat a Portuguese flotilla off Tunmen in 1522, delivering the Europeans aboard to imprisonment and, eventually, execution.[7]

But to possess guns is one thing; to use them effectively is quite another.

Eventually, in the 1550s, the Chinese Imperial authorities decided that naval artillery was of little value against the pirate bands from Japan, known as *wakō* (literally: dwarf pirates), who terrorized the coasts of China. According to an illlustrated treatise of naval warfare, published in 1564 by a protege of the Chinese Grand Admiral, the pirates had been defeated, not by naval means, but by a combination of three things: intrigue designed to divide the Chinese from the Japanese groups among the invaders; diplomatic pressure on the pirates' supporters in Japan; and overwhelming military assaults on their land bases in China. And even the latter were conducted without firearms: the Ming commanders did not place their trust in muskets or cannon, whether by land or at sea, for they found them too difficult to supply with shot of standard calibre, and too prone to explode when fired. They also dismissed proposals for reinforced, shot-resistant junks on the grounds that they would be too cumbersome; and they deprecated ship-borne artillery as too inaccurate. Instead, they defeated the *wakō* in the traditional Chinese way: by concentrating vastly superior numbers of troops armed with bows, lances and swords.[8] And although Chinese war-junks continued to carry some guns, they were only light anti-personnel pieces (plate 20). The principal weapon of the Imperial navy remained, even in the 1630s, the fireship.[9]

So although ship-borne artillery was readily compatible with their naval traditions, the Chinese deliberately rejected it. In Europe, by contrast, the naval gun was adopted in spite of the fact that the standard technique of warfare at sea was ramming and boarding. But it was slow to make its mark. Firepower proved decisive at the battle of Sluys in 1340, the first major engagement of the Hundred Years War; but it was Edward III's archers, pouring their volleys into the crowded French decks, who won the day. Although some English ships may have carried gunpowder weapons, no authentic proof exists that they were used. And when (after the 1360s) credible reports of the use of artillery at sea appear, they clearly refer to anti-personnel rather than to ship-sinking weapons.[10] It is true that numerous fifteenth-century miniatures, which possess great beauty but little sense of proportion or perspective, do show seemingly large firearms in use both from 'fighting tops' on the masts and on the decks (plate 21); but in fact these can have been little more than light breech-loaders (pages 89–90 below). And the recoil from even a modest cannon mounted in the main top would inevitably have produced catastrophe![11]

But the Atlantic roundship was, at this time, not the principal European warship: that honour had been held, since at least the ninth century AD, by the Mediterranean galley. Thanks to the oars which made her sides vulnerable, the galley had to attack head-on rather than broadside-on and there was no possibility of mounting cannon along the sides. It proved simple, however, to add a small artillery platform at either the stem or the stern. By the middle of the fifteenth century, Christian galleys in the Mediterranean

20 *An armed Chinese junk*, pictured in the *Travels* of the Englishman Peter Mundy. The large warship 'A' was observed in the Pearl River, near Canton, in 1637 and Mundy noted that there were 'doores [sc. gunports] in their broadsides, furnished with Drakes [sc. Iight 3-pounders]'. Heavier guns could not be carried because the junk was so 'weakly plancked and timbred'. (Oxford, Bodleian Library, MS. Rawlinson A.315, plate no. 29.)

21 *The European art of war at sea*, c. 1470 made little use of firearms. Vasco de Lucena's
History of Alexander the Great, presented to the duke of Burgundy, showed the Macedonians
landing in Scythia, despite the fire of three breech-loaders (supplied with 'chambers' and
shot). But their ship carried three cannons, and only a few handguns were in use (in the
fighting tops). Although bombards were already in use on Burgundian galleys, and although
the design of roundships was already similar to that of the heavily gunned *Mary Rose* (plate
23), at the moment when Lucena illuminated his manuscript the two traditions had not
yet merged. (Paris, Bibliothèque Nationale, Fonds français 6440 fo. 173.)

were already carrying one or two small breech-loaders, on the poop-deck,
which were used both against other vessels and against fortifications built
close to water. In 1445, a galley sent by the duke of Burgundy to fight
the Turks even experimented with a 'great bombard' of iron during operations
on the lower Danube; but the gun became overheated and burst.[12] A century
later, however, Mediterranean war galleys regularly carried one heavy sixty-
pounder bronze cannon, two sixteen-pounders, and usually fifteen lesser guns
at the prow and the poop. This gave them impressive firepower: the sixteenth-
century sixty-pounders that survive in the Naval Museum of Venice were

175-millimetre calibre weapons, and the records of the Republic's test-firing programme show that they were highly effective up to 640 metres and that their maximum range was no less than three kilometres.[13] The centreline gun could be aimed, rather like those of a modern fighter aircraft, by correctly positioning the whole ship, and the massive recoil was absorbed by mounting it on a sledge which was allowed to slide back to the galley's mast (thus facilitating re-loading, if necessary). In the windless, calm waters that prevail in the Mediterranean for much of the summer, such oared fighting ships were easily able to hold their own against any sailing vessel, for they were far more mobile, and their main weapon had a longer range, delivered a much larger shot, and fired on a more dangerous trajectory.[14] Throughout the sixteenth and seventeenth centuries, sailing ships in the Mediterranean were regularly either captured or sunk by well-armed galleys. Even in the eighteenth century, oared fighting ships were still in use in the Baltic, where the skerries which fringed the coasts of Sweden and Finland complicated navigation by sail: the Russians used them for their raids on the Swedish coast in 1719–21; and the Swedes destroyed most of the Russian fleet at Svensksund in 1790 thanks to the imaginative use of heavily gunned galleys.

The real challenge to the galley in the sixteenth-century Mediterranean came not from the round ship, but from the galeass. The Venetian Republic, faced in the 1520s with a massive increase in piratical attacks on her merchant fleet, experimented with different ship types for better defence. In 1529, under the direction of a professor of Greek and with the aid of a rediscovered classical manuscript, the first quinquereme since the fall of the Roman empire was built. Measuring 74 metres long and 11 metres wide, it was possibly the largest wooden ship ever constructed; but unfortunately it was found to be too unwieldy to perform well in action. Then, in about 1540, the first galeass was laid down in the Arsenal: fifty metres long (as against the forty metres of most galleys) and nine metres wide. It was propelled by sails as well as by oars, and was far better armed: the standard galeass carried eight heavy guns at both stem and stern, and seven or more antipersonnel weapons along each side (plate 22).[15] It soon proved its worth. At the battle of Lepanto on 7 October 1571, for example, the Turkish fleet mistook six Venetian galeasses for merchant supply vessels and attacked them in force: they paid a high price for their error – no less than seventy galleys were said to have been sunk by the new warships, 'an incredible thing that only six galeasses should have caused such great destruction, for they had not [hitherto] been tried in the forefront of a naval battle'. The engagement lasted for only four hours, in part because of the excellence of the Spanish infantry (who also served aboard the Venetian vessels), but mainly because of the Christians' decisive superiority in firepower. It has been calculated that they deployed 1,815 guns, against only 750 on the

22 *A Mediterranean galeass* at sea in the English Channel, during the battle off Gravelines
which ensured the defeat of the Spanish Armada in 1588 . Four galeasses from Naples sailed
with Medina Sidonia and, although only one of them made it back to Spain, they proved
formidable in action – a fact which is reflected in the prominent place accorded to one in
this design for an English tapestry commemorating the battle. All the details, including the
number of oar-banks and guns, are confirmed by documentary sources.

Turkish side, and in the end the Turks ran out of ammunition even for
those.[16] But they did not immediately give up. A group of Janissaries was
seen to fight on, long after their defeat was clearly inevitable, 'and when
they had no more weapons with which to attack us, [they] collected up
oranges and lemons and started to throw them ... The melee reached such
a point that, in many places, one saw men laugh as often as cry'. But there
was little laughter once the fighting stopped. Broken and sinking ships lay
'scattered over about eight miles of water. The sea was entirely covered,
not just with masts, spars, oars and broken wood, but with an innumerable
quantity of corpses which turned the water red as blood'. And after the
battle, on the express orders of the Venetian government, all captured Turkish
veterans were executed in cold blood, while the rest of those taken were
condemned to servitude. In all, the Ottoman fleet lost 200 galleys, together
with their artillery, stores, and some 30,000 men. In addition, the Imperial

defeat sparked off several uprisings in Greece and Albania which seemed, for a time, to herald the collapse of Ottoman rule in the peninsula. It appeared to be one of the decisive battles of the century.[17]

And yet, to the horror of the victors, within seven months the Turks had replaced all their losses and were again able to send a major battlefleet to the West. There were, after all, many boat-builders working around the Mediterranean, men who were already fully experienced in the techniques of galley-construction, possessed the necessary shipyards, and probably also had stocks of raw material to hand. There may also have been some galleys held in reserve in the Imperial arsenals of Sinop and Istanbul.[18] But most of the new galleys were laid down in the Sultan's shipyards, where a massive building programme was initiated as soon as news of Lepanto became known, and it even proved possible to imitate the Venetians' 'secret weapon': by April 1572, some 200 galleys and five galeasses were ready for service.[19] However, it was more difficult to man them. Each galley required a crew of some 150 oarsmen, each galeass 250, but so many men had been lost at Lepanto that even the Ottoman empire experienced difficulties in replacing them. Conscription was not enough and, since most Christian captives had escaped, a large number of the oarsmen of the 1572 fleet were necessarily convicts.[20]

The size of the crew required was indeed the galley's crucial weakness: when troops were added, 400 men might be aboard each vessel. The 400 galleys which clashed at Lepanto therefore probably carried, between them, some 160,000 men, making that battle the largest ever fought in sixteenth-century Europe. There were, as a French galley captain wrote in the seventeenth century, 'an infinite number of villages that are far from having as large a number of inhabitants' as a single galley. 'When every man is at his post, only heads can be seen from prow to stern'.[21] Sufficient food and drink for so many men could not be carried for more than a few weeks at a time: galleys, however manoeuvrable, simply could not stay at sea for very long.

But between 1450 and 1650, the emergence of the heavily armed sailing ship transformed the situation. There were several distinct stages in the process. First, in the course of the fifteenth century, the merchant ships of several French, English, Portuguese and Hanseatic port-cities underwent a marked increase in size, but – thanks to improved sail-plans and better design – without a corresponding increase in crew. Then it was discovered that, when equipped with crossbows or handguns, the ships could be defended with fewer men. And from there it was a relatively short step to adding heavier guns to the larger vessels. At first, these were relatively small breech-loading cannons of wrought iron, capable of firing only 4-pounder shot. But just a few of these proved sufficient to keep boarders at bay and, since replacement charges could be prepared in advance, it was found that even a small crew could maintain a fairly rapid fire from several guns at once, whether mounted in the enormous 'castles' at the ship's bow and stern or along the main deck. From the late fifteenth century, however, two important inventions began to transform the nature of sea warfare. First, muzzle-loading bronze artillery joined wrought-iron breech-loaders aboard ships. Although muzzle-loading took more time and trouble, especially on a ship, the increased strength which resulted from casting the gun in a single piece more than compensated: with a breech-loader, a charge of more than 4 pounds often either burst the barrel or else blew the breechblock out; but a muzzle-loader could deliver an iron ball of 60 pounds or more (page 86 above). Here was a gun that could shoot straight through a ship's timbers. But the new artillery was too heavy to be carried safely in either the castles or along the main-deck: it had to be positioned lower down. Starting (according to tradition) around 1500 in the port of Brest in Brittany, and quickly spreading all over Atlantic Europe, hinged gun-ports were cut into the sides of the larger ships, making it possible to deploy artillery along their entire length on several levels (plate 23).[22]

It took some time before the full implications of these inventions were grasped. For example, the 1,000–ton *Henry Grace à Dieu*, one of several great ships built or purchased by Henry VIII of England after 1509 to rival those constructed by the kings of France and Scotland, carried 43 heavy and 141 light guns, with a combined weight of over 100 tons (the largest, a 300-millimetre weapon, was almost 6 metres long). But, as contemporary illustrations show, most of these weapons were still used from the castles, to fire down on potential borders, rather than near the waterline to sink ships. The *Great Harry*, like the Venetian quinquereme, was too cumbrous to be effective and, although she remained in service until 1553 (when she was destroyed by fire), a major rebuilding had to be carried out to 'slim her down' in 1540. The *Mary Rose*, another unwieldy 600-ton, 78-gun war-ship launched in 1511, suddenly keeled over and sank with all hands in 1545, as she sailed to prevent a French invasion fleet from capturing the Isle of Wight.[23] The history of Scotland's *Great Michael* was little better: although built in 1511 at the king's express request, she proved simply too expensive to operate – perhaps as much as one-half of James IV's total yearly receipts went on her construction and 10 per cent of his entire annual budget on wages for her crew. In 1514 she was sold to France and, under the name of the *Grand Nef d'Écosse*, appears to have been left in Brest harbour to rot.[24]

When Henry VIII embarked on his next major round of defence spending in England, after 1538, with the profits gained from the Dissolution of the Monasteries he bought or built ships that were somewhat smaller, with less superstructure (reduced 'castles') and more guns amidships. By 1547, the year of Henry's death, the Royal Navy consisted of fifty-three well-armed warships, with a total displacement of some 10,000 tons, a strength it would

23 *The Mary Rose*, c. 1545, pictured in an illustrated catalogue of Henry VIII's navy known as the Anthony Anthony Roll. The large number of guns carried both in the 'castles' and on the lower decks proves that the importance of guns at sea had been fully appreciated in England by this time. Unfortunately, however, the importance of keeping the lower gunports closed in rough seas had not: while moving down the Solent to thwart a French invasion of the Isle of Wight, the *Mary Rose* heeled over, flooded, and sank. (Cambridge, Magdalene College, Pepys Library MS. 2991.)

not regain for over a century. But it was a navy that England could not afford. Almost at once, without the windfall revenues from secularizing and selling church lands, it began to decline: by 1555, the fleet numbered only thirty vessels, and the great ships of 400 tons and upwards had declined from twelve to three.[25] But then came one of history's great ironies. In September 1555 Philip of Spain, king consort of England, appeared before the Privy Council to point out that 'England's chief defence depends upon the navy being always ready to defend the realm against invasion, so that it is right that the ships should not only be fit for sea but instantly available'.[26] Accordingly, a new generation of ships was added to the Royal Navy – the majority of which took part in the 1588 campaign against the man who had called for their construction!

These ships were both big and durable. The *Elizabeth Jonas* (begun in

1558 as the *Philip* but renamed after Elizabeth's accession later that year and launched in 1559) weighed 900 tons and carried sixty-four guns; it continued in service until 1618. The *Lion* of 600 tons, another of Philip and Mary's ships launched in 1557, carried sixty guns and, thanks to refits in 1582, 1609, 1640 and 1658, was still in service in the days of Samuel Pepys. Naval construction continued apace under Elizabeth so that, by the Armada year, there were three galleons of 800 tons or more, and eleven of 500 tons and upwards.[27] It is not true to say, as so many scholars have done, that the battles in the Channel in 1588 saw an articulated fleet of modern warships pitted against a random assembly of naval fossils. On the contrary, both the oldest and largest warships of the campaign were English; while the most modern men-of-war were the squadrons of Portuguese and Castilian galleons which, in normal times, policed successfully an empire on which the sun never set.[28]

For the problems of naval strategy that faced the Iberian powers in the sixteenth century were entirely different from those confronting England. The countries bordering on the North Sea and the Channel, where deep water ports were numerous and the theatre of operations relatively small, could rely upon their huge and unwieldy gun-ships for defence. But Portugal and Spain required men-of-war able to sail to distant oceans, through seas of unparalleled malignance, there both to trade and to destroy the ships of any other power operating without their permission. This called for a highly versatile vessel, and it took years before the small 'caravels' of Columbus and Vasco da Gama gave way to the purpose-built, ocean-going warship known as the galleon. Both the design – with its beak-shaped prow, its low lines, and shallow draft – and the very name 'galleon' reflect the fact that the new vessels owed much to the galley (plate 24). By the 1520s, when they are first found in Portugal, Spain and Italy, the average model weighed only 250 tons (which was about the same as a large galley); only after 1550 did displacement begin to rise until, by the 1580s, Iberian galleons of 400 to 500 tons were the norm. And yet in the battles with Elizabeth's navy in July and August 1588, these specialized warships were totally unsuccessful: although most of them managed (unlike many other vessels in the Armada) to return to Spain safely, they seem to have inflicted little or no damage on their adversaries.[29]

There are, of course, many explanations for the defeat of the Spanish Armada. In the first place, the Spaniards were operating far from their bases, in unfamiliar waters, whereas the English could at all times acquire replacements and reinforcements locally, and were fighting in the precise environment for which their ships had been designed. Second, although England's warships may have been old, they were in good shape. According to the (perhaps over-patriotic?) Navy Board, there was 'never a one of them that knows what a leak means'. Furthermore, two-thirds of the Queen's fighting

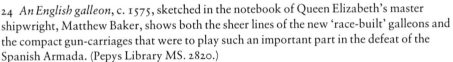

24 *An English galleon*, c. 1575, sketched in the notebook of Queen Elizabeth's master shipwright, Matthew Baker, shows both the sheer lines of the new 'race-built' galleons and the compact gun-carriages that were to play such an important part in the defeat of the Spanish Armada. (Pepys Library MS. 2820.)

ships had, by 1588, been either built or rebuilt as 'galleons' (with slimmer lines, more sail and less crew) so that they were able to sail faster and to carry more guns. The thirty-four ships of the Royal Navy, with a total displacement of 1,000 tons and a crew of 6,225, carried 678 guns. In the opinion of most contemporaries, it was the twin advantages of superior speed and firepower that gave England the edge. According to Sir Arthur Gorgas, who had been there, the Queen's ships were able to weave in and out among the Spanish fleet 'discharging our broadsides of ordnance double for their single, we carrying as good and great artillery as they do and to better proof'. A captured Spanish colonel, Don Diego Pimentel, agreed: to his Dutch interrogators he admitted his surprise at the ability of the English ships 'to be able to tack four or five times in the time it took us to go about once', so that they had been able to come close to the Spaniards and fire their guns with maximum effect, and with far greater frequency.[30]

Many modern scholars have given their full support to this explanation of Spain's defeat;[31] and yet it by no means fits all of the evidence. In the first place, the Portuguese and Castilian galleons had long been familiar with — and had often successfully employed — the tactic of stand-off gunnery. For instance, the *Instructions* given by King Manuel of Portugal to Pedro

Alvares Cabral in 1500 for his voyage to India specified that, if he met any Muslim ships, 'you are not to come to close quarters with them if you can avoid it, but you are to compel them with your artillery alone to strike sail' so that 'this war may be waged with greater safety, and ... less loss may result to the people of your ships'. The next fleet, sent under the command of Vasco da Gama in 1502, defeated a large Muslim fleet in pitched battle off the Malabar coast by sailing 'one astern of the other in a line', and keeping up rapid artillery fire, the gunners making 'such haste to load again that they recharged the guns with bags of powder which they had ready for this purpose, made to measure so that they could load again very speedily'. The technique was still in use in 1557, for when the English pirate William Towerson, and his partners, encountered a Portuguese squadron off Guinea the latter immediately adopted a line-ahead formation and drove off the interlopers with repeated broadsides.[32]

But this is clearly not what Philip II's fleet was doing in 1588. The eight Armada ships whose wrecks have now been investigated beneath the water, all of which were among the most heavily engaged vessels in the expedition, undoubtedly ended the desperate fights in the Channel with substantial stocks of roundshot still in hand – for all the excavated wrecks have produced large quantities of iron shot of 9-pounder size or above. Similarly, the administrative papers concerning the ships that returned safely to Spain usually noted the safe return of large stocks of powder and shot to the naval stores. This strange circumstance is explained by further entries in the same source, which recorded all the occasions on which each gun on most hired ships was fired throughout the campaign. Thus the 22-gun *Trinidad de Escala* was recorded as firing a grand total of thirty-five shots on 2 August (1.6 rounds per gun), twenty-one shots on 4 August (0.96 rounds per gun), and thirty-eight shots during the desperate Gravelines engagement on 8 August (1.7 rounds per gun). The 20-gun *Santa Bárbara* fired twenty-two shots on 31 July (1.1 rounds per gun), twenty-eight on 1 August (1.4 rounds per gun) and forty-seven on 2 August (2.35 rounds per gun). Finally, over the full period of fighting the Andalusian *San Francisco* fired 242 rounds from her twenty-one guns, and her two heaviest pieces, full cannons, discharged ten and twelve balls respectively – scarcely one round a day. These figures – and numerous others like them – come nowhere near to accounting for the fifty rounds with which each gun had originally been provided (although they certainly help to explain why the Armada was unable to make any impression on the English fleet).[33]

What, then, went wrong on the Spanish gundecks in the Channel? All the guns were, in accordance with the instructions of the commander-in-chief, the duke of Medina Sidonia, always kept loaded so that, when battle was joined, one salvo was available for immediate use. An operator holding a lighted linstock beside each gun was the only requirement for the first round. This is exactly how a galley was expected to loose off its close-range cannonade immediately before ramming its foe; in such a situation, there would be neither opportunity nor need for immediate reloading, and so no procedure for it as a battle-drill existed. But in the Channel, the English unchivalrously refused to be rammed or boarded. No doubt, as this became apparent, efforts were made to continue working some of the guns after the first round had been fired; and with the light, short-range breech-loaders this would have presented no problems. The bigger, muzzle-loading pieces, however, could only be recharged at sea in one of two ways. Either they could be brought inboard and the necessary operations carried out within the ship; or they could be left fully run-out and loaded outboard. Now both archival and archaeological evidence reveals that most of the bigger guns aboard the Spanish Armada were mounted upon large two-wheeled carriages, with trails so long that they could have been run back for reloading only with the greatest difficulty. Some carriages were almost as wide as the deck on which they stood. On the other hand, since outboard recharging required the loader to straddle a hot barrel outside the ship and carry out all the clearing and charging operations from this exposed and difficult position – perhaps under enemy fire – it is unlikely that it was often attempted with any degree of success. All the available evidence suggests that few of the Armada's ship-killing guns were able to apply a continuous close-range cannonade against the enemy, although this was the only way in which they might have achieved success.[34]

But the English navy did not suffer from this handicap because, for at least half a century, its guns had been mounted on a compact, four-wheeled truck carriage. The ill-fated *Mary Rose* carried them when she sank in 1545 (plate 25); the squadron sent to expel the Italian invaders from Smerwick in 1580 had them (plate 26); and the race-built galleons designed in the 1570s also used them (plate 24). The evidence suggests that they provided a decisive advantage. Sir Henry Mainwaring's *Seaman's dictionary* of about 1623 entertained no doubts: 'The fashion of those carriages we use at sea are much better than those of the land,' he wrote. 'Yet the Venetians and Spaniards and diverse others use the other in their shipping'. The design of the English truck carriages meant that the gun muzzles could protrude much further through the gun-ports, and ensured that there was no awkward trail or wide wheels to obstruct the sides and rear. Adequate working space was thus available for the crews to haul their guns back with tackles after firing, and reload inboard before heaving them into place for another round (plate 27). The truck carriage also allowed guns to be traversed and aimed far more easily and accurately in action. Broadsides could therefore be delivered consecutively during the course of a fight, the range being dictated by the superior sailing qualities of the English ships.[35]

It is customary to see the campaign of 1588 as causing a tactical revolution

25 *An English truck carriage*, c. 1540. England's 'secret weapon' in the sea-war against Spain was by no means new in 1588 . Among the wreckage of the *Mary Rose*, excavated in 1981, the unmistakable remains of a truck carriage were found beside one of the great guns. A modern replica was built, demonstrating the continuity of design between the Henrician model (dating from 1540 if not earlier) and that of Matthew Baker's day (plate 24) and beyond.

which turned the line ahead and stand-off artillery bombardment into the standard techniques of European naval warfare. But this was not so. In the first place, both tactics had been used in the Indian Ocean almost a century before – and Cabral's *Instructions* of 1500 (page 94 above) were so precise that clearly they were not new even then. In the second, the lessons of the English victory were slow to be drawn in Europe. In 1592, for example, the textbook of the Italian Eugenio Gentilini, *The perfect bombardier*, still claimed that 'to hit the enemy at long distance with artillery cannot be the purpose of a navy; the main object being ramming and boarding'. Even in England, there was no immediate change in warship design. The 'race-built' galleons had not been universally acclaimed, and various members of the Navy Board had objected that the removal of the fore- and aft-castles made 'the majestic ships of the Queen' look like mere merchantmen – a deep-seated conservatism which helps to explain why some of the great capital ships of 1588 were still in service twenty, thirty, even ninety years later. Admittedly,

26 *The siege of Smerwick*, 1580, provides a picture of the English truck carriage in action. The contemporary drawing of the action sent to lord Burghley in London showed two naval guns, secured by their anchors against recoil, bombarding the landward side of a small fortress (the Castello del Oro) built by Spanish and Italian invaders at Smerwick on the west coast of Ireland. The bombardment quickly led to the surrender (and massacre) of the defenders. (London, Public Record Office, MPF 75 [ex SP 64/1/8]. My thanks go to Dr Colin Martin and Dr Tom Glasgow for help in interpreting this document.)

27 *The lower gun-deck of the Vasa*, 1628, looking forward. The warship, intended as Gustavus Adolphus's flagship, was 62 metres long, with 4 decks, 64 guns and a displacement of some 1,300 tons. But she sank on her maiden voyage in 1628, in Stockholm harbour, and there she lay until her rediscovery in 1956. Over the next 30 years the *Vasa* has yielded almost 250,000 finds, of which the uniform set of 24 truck carriages lashed to the gunports are among the most impressive.

the lessons of the Armada campaign were not entirely lost. For instance, the Navy Board Commissioners in 1618 noted that:[36]

Experience teacheth how sea-fights in these days come seldome to boarding ... but are chiefly performed by the great artillery breaking down masts [and] yards, tearing, raking, and bilging the ships, wherein the great advantage of His Majesty's navy must carefully be maintained by appointing such a proportion of ordnance to each ship as the vessel will bear.

But there is little evidence of this advice being followed. On the contrary, the exploits of the Jacobean navy proved disastrous, largely because its principal warships were too unwieldy to operate outside the Narrow Seas. As the commander of the Cadiz expedition of 1625, Lord Wimbledon, perceptively (if bitterly) commented: 'I find that greate shipps (and especiallie the old ones) that are so over loaden with ordnance, are not for an offensive warre, but more fit for a defensive [one] at home'. His flagship, the *Anne Royal* (which, as the *Ark Royal*, had also been the English flagship in 1588) was 'rowling and making in the Spanish seas' so badly that they had to put 'much of the ordnance into the hould ... So that we are all of oppinion that shipps ... smaller stronglie built, without carving, are fitter for such journeyes'.[37] But again the government would not listen. The fleets sent to relieve La Rochelle in 1627 and 1628 were unequal to their assignment and Charles I's 'Ship Money' fleet, which was originally intended to be built with Spanish subsidies in order to keep the Channel open for Spanish shipping, likewise included veteran warships so massive that they were useless for service elsewhere. The 1,500-ton *Sovereign of the Seas*, launched as the Stuart flagship in 1637, was even less manoeuvrable than the Armada galleons, and her 104 guns (which weighed over 153 tons) later had to be reduced in number.[38]

It was in fact the Dutch, not the English, who first created a high-seas fleet capable of operating at long range. In their war against Spain, the three principal tasks of the Dutch navy were to protect their merchantmen at sea, to blockade those ports of the South Netherlands (above all Dunkirk) from which hostile privateers operated, and to intercept the fleets of warships and troop-transports which the Spaniards periodically sent into the North Sea.[39] These were difficult assignments, for the first two required ships that were swift, of shallow draft, and capable of remaining on station for months at a time, while the third called for powerful guns and great strength. Shortly after 1600, eight new 300-ton capital ships were built at Hoorn in North Holland: they were long in relation to their breadth, low in the water, yet shallow in draft. They came to be called frigates, and they soon became the mainstay of the fleet. In 1621 the Dutch navy included nine vessels of 500 tons or more, but by 1629 they had all been phased out of service. The forty-gun, 300-ton frigate had become the standard Dutch warship: only a few, such as the flagship of the Holland squadron, the *Aemilia* (fifty-six guns, built in 1632), now carried more. With these swift, efficiently armed vessels, aided by fireships, in October 1639 the Dutch destroyed a far larger Spanish fleet in the roadstead of the Downs off the Kent coast.[40]

It was at the Downs that the attack in line ahead was apparently first performed in European waters (plate 28). The Dutch admiral, Maarten Harpertszoon Tromp, led his squadron in among the Spaniards (despite the presence of Charles I's fleet, trying to keep the combatants apart) and sank forty of their fifty-three ships. It was an innovation that Holland's neighbours could not afford to ignore. But before anything could be done, the Civil Wars caused a seven-year hiatus in English warship-building. However, the vessels constructed thereafter were strikingly different from *The Sovereign of the Seas* and her like: whereas most of the galleons of Elizabeth had been built with a ratio of length to breadth of 2.5:1 and those of Charles I with a ratio of 3:1, the new vessels laid down in 1646–7 were 3.5:1.[41] They were indeed frigates. In the course of 1649, the Republican government ordered the construction of no less than seventy-seven vessels of this new design, and in 1651 it congratulated the shipwrights of England 'for their success in contriving and building of frigates'.[42]

The Republic's fleet, numbering 157 warships, was now expressly ordered to adopt in action the line-ahead formation favoured by the Dutch. The 'Instructions for the better ordering of the fleet in fighting', signed by Generals Blake, Monck and Deane on 29 March 1653, were quite specific:

As soon as they see the General engage, ... then each squadron shall take the best advantage they can to engage with the enemy next unto them; and in order thereunto the ships of every squadron shall endeavour to keep in a line with the chief.

Already the Republic was at war with the Dutch and a series of full-scale engagements took place in which the two battlefleets bombarded each other in parallel lines (much as land forces had been doing for the previous half century). Eventually the Dutch lost – or, in the terse message of Oliver Cromwell to one of their envoys: 'You have appealed to the judgement of heaven. The Lord has declared against you'.[43] So in the spring of 1654, after peace had been concluded with the Dutch, England possessed '160 sail of brave ships, well appointed, swimming at sea, and store of land forces, all of which required either to be lessened and laid down, or to be employed in some advantageous design'. After some discussion, the government opted for the latter. Before the year was out, with the aid of capital provided by London merchants, a fleet of thirty-eight ships was dispatched to the West Indies to carve out and defend a British empire in the Caribbean; then in 1656, after war had been declared on Spain, a further forty to fifty warships were maintained in the Mediterranean and in Spanish waters, with perhaps fifty more vessels permanently protecting England's shores.[44]

Here indeed was a high-seas fleet capable of operating at long-range, on a permanent basis, as an ocean-going force: it was arguably the first in

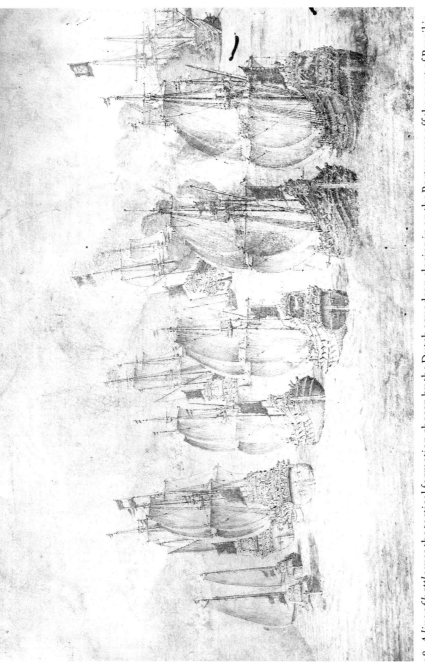

28 *A line of battle* was the tactical formation chosen by the Dutch squadron closing in on the Portuguese off the coast of Brazil in 1645. It is interesting to see that two of the Dutch ships – the second and fourth from the right – are in fact merchantmen. Until at least 1660 a large merchant ship carried much the same ordnance as a fourth-rate warship and could therefore join the line of battle. (A sketch by Willem van de Velde the elder.)

Euro-pean history. Part of the credit was due, of course, to the excellence of naval administration under the Republic, which kept the fleet properly supplied with men, munitions and stores in both war and peace; part was also due to the superior financial resources of the Republican navy, which attracted both tax-revenue and merchant capital on an unequalled scale; and part was due to the presence in the fleet of both gunners and soldiers who had acquired years of combat experience in the Civil Wars. But none of these factors would, by themselves, have allowed the navy to maintain permanent stations in the West Indies and the Mediterranean. The critical element was the change in ship-design, for only frigates could operate effectively for long periods at long range.[45]

Nevertheless, not all naval experts were convinced that 'the old-fashioned English ships of the biggest rate' (sc. 90–100 guns) should be abandoned. In 1656, for example, Admiral Sir George Ayscue argued that first-rate ships would soon come into their own again:

because they were stronger than the frigates, would endure the shaking of their own guns and the blows of the enemy's guns better than the frigates could, and were firm, like a castle in the sea, and not so easy to be boarded as the frigates, being higher built.

He was right. From 1659 onwards, when a new Anglo-Dutch war began to seem inevitable, both sides started once more to build bigger ships. Where Tromp had commanded only two warships armed with more than forty guns at the battle of Terheyden in 1653, de Ruyter twenty years later commanded sixty-two; and where Blake had led eighteen such vessels, his successors led seventy-four in 1672 and one hundred in 1689. The combined firepower of these fleets was awesome. At the battle of Kijkduin in 1673 the Dutch ships-of-the-line carried 4,233 guns, whereas the Christian fleet at Lepanto, a century before, had carried only 1,815 and the Spanish Armada only 2,431.[46]

The French, however, followed a different path. Although some of the ships laid down in the 1660s, as part of Louis XIV's 'floating fortress' plan, were 100-gun three-deckers, most of them were slim 74-gun two-deckers. And by the 1680s, from its bases at Dunkirk, Brest and Rochefort, the French battlefleet, 221 vessels strong (including 93 ships-of-the-line) was able to challenge both the English and the Dutch navies.[47] It might have been unable to stop William III from invading England in 1688, but it secured command of the sea the following year, permitting James II to land in Ireland with an army, and on 1 July 1690 it defeated the main Anglo-Dutch battlefleet off Beachy Head. But neither of these successes proved decisive: James and his supporters were routed at the Boyne on 12 July 1690 and, even after Beachy Head, the English still possessed formidable strength at sea. As the defeated admiral, Lord Torrington, observed: 'Most men were in fear that the French would invade, but I was always of another opinion, for I always said that whilst we had a fleet in being, they would not make the attempt'.[48]

A 'fleet in being' – that was, perhaps, the key to the naval stalemate in north European waters. With battlefleets of 100 vessels, even prolonged actions might fail to destroy the opponents' strength sufficiently since (as another defeated admiral, Sir Clowdesly Shovell observed disconsolately in 1690) 'at sea, if the fleets be near equal, there must be great success to win a great victory; for by the time one is beaten, the other generally is weary'. Even the defeat of the French at La Hogue in 1692 was not decisive: Louis XIV's navy stayed in port after the battle, it is true; but only because his ministers, led by the astute Vauban, convinced him that valuable resources could be saved if the battlefleet were 'put in moth-balls'. Instead, a few naval bases were heavily fortified and turned into highly effective centres of privateering. For the *guerre de course*, swift frigates armed with 32-pounder guns were ideal, so France placed all her trust in them – and not without results, for between 1689 and 1697 the French captured some 4,000 enemy vessels. Moreover, with her powerful yet mobile warships she could patrol and protect the sea-lanes to her colonies in America and Asia more effectively than her rivals because the frigate, as Cromwell's admirals had found, could sail to destinations far beyond the range of the battleship.[49]

Gradually, the same strategic truth dawned upon the other maritime powers of Europe: once the French abandoned fleet actions in favour of commerce raiding, her rivals' need for battleships diminished, while their own need for frigates grew. Thus although 24 British warships of 90 guns and above were built between 1660 and 1688, only 3 more were launched between then and 1697. Yet the overall size of the navy rose during these years from 173 ships (with 6,930 guns) to 323 ships (with 9,912. guns).[50]

II

The savage and prolonged naval rivalry of the Atlantic states of Europe in the century after 1588 had thus created battlefleets capable, both in number and design, of pursuing strategic objectives far from home. The new ships-of-the-line were able to operate by 1688 in the Caribbean, in the Indian Ocean, and in the Pacific, in order to gain both tactical and strategic superiority. But they were (of course) by no means the first European ships to sail those distant seas. In America, for example, seapower had been acquired by the Westerners from the days of Columbus, since the Amerindian peoples seem to have lacked any specialized warships of their own, whether in the Caribbean or on the inland seas. When, for example, on Lake Texcoco, Cortes and his troops encountered armed canoes in 1521, they simply constructed larger vessels of their own, which they called brigantines and equipped with firearms. Within a matter of hours the lake was theirs, making possible the conquest of the capital, Tenochtitlán. Protecting the riches of this empire from other European nations proved more difficult, however. For much of the sixteenth century, a flotilla of galleons was necessary to escort the convoys of merchantmen plying between Spain and the Caribbean, while dislodging French settlers from Florida in 1565–6 required the dispatch of a major expedition of warships from Spain. But Francis Drake's sustained piracy in American waters in the 1570s and 80s created a threat far beyond the capacity of the existing forces to resist.[51] On 25 October, 1586, the duke of Medina Sidonia, who was in overall charge of protecting the Indies trade, informed Philip II that, in his opinion, Elizabethan aggression overseas would be more cheaply and more effectively countered by mounting a major sea-borne attack on England, the pirates' base, than by improving the defences of the entire Caribbean.[52] It was not, of course, the duke's intention that, when his advice was accepted, he should be charged with leading the attack in person; but his strategic perception was undoubtedly correct – after the Armada, as the duke had predicted, no amount of effort expended on strengthening the fleets and fortresses of Spanish America sufficed to exclude interlopers.

The Armada also had important consequences for the defence of the Iberian empires in the Orient. On the one hand, the campaign itself absorbed resources that were ear-marked for further expansion – both an attack on Acheh and a plan to build a fort at Mombasa were called off, allegedly because of the need to concentrate all Philip II's efforts on the campaign against England.[53] On the other, having thus been forced off the offensive, the arrival in the Indian Ocean of first Dutch and then English ships in the 1590s presented the *Estado da India* with a new and intractable problem. The correspondence of the viceroys in Goa was thenceforth dominated by the deeds and threats of *os enemigos de Europa* in Asian waters.

Portuguese India was particularly vulnerable because it was essentially a trading network rather than a territorial enterprise: it was concerned with distribution rather than with production, and with relations between men rather than with control over land. The first Governor of Portuguese India, Francisco de Almeida, began by governing only his fleet; and even after bases like Goa, Malacca, Diu and Ormuz were conquered, control of the sea-lanes remained vital to the successful operation of the Portuguese system.[54] Until the arrival of the Dutch, this task proved relatively easy. Vasco da Gama destroyed the fleet of Calicut in 1502 with eighteen vessels, of which even the flagship carried only sixteen guns – none of them large. Twenty years later, the sixty ships and six fortresses of the Portuguese in and around the Indian Ocean possessed no more than 1,073 artillery pieces between them.[55] And, even in action, these guns were not always used effectively. At an encounter in 1510 between the 400-ton flagship of Viceroy Afonso de Albuquerque and a large Sumatran merchantman in the Straits of Malacca, for example, the entire Portuguese fleet closed in for the kill and started shooting at her; but this did not affect her in the least, and she went on sailing ... The Portuguese ships then shot at her masts ... and she dropped her sails. Because she was very tall ... our people did not dare to board her, and our artillery did not hurt her at all, for she had four layers of planking on her side, and our biggest cannon would not penetrate more than two.

In the end, after two days and nights of fruitless bombardment, the gallant and resourceful Albuquerque decided to pull off his adversary's two rudders; only then did she surrender.[56]

Such bully-boy conduct was only possible, of course, because the Sumatran *jong*, like all other native shipping in the Indian Ocean, was unprotected by guns. Once Asian vessels began to carry and use artillery, Portuguese domination of the sea-lanes came under serious threat. The rulers of Egypt, to begin with, occasionally managed to send a fleet from the Red Sea to challenge the Portuguese. In 1508 a fleet of six roundships and six large galleys sailed from Suez to Chaul and, together with some Gujarati warships, proceeded to destroy a Portuguese squadron there. But in February 1509 almost all the Portuguese vessels in Indian waters (nineteen of them) manned by almost all the Europeans in India (1,200 men) sailed to Diu and sank most of the Egyptian fleet at anchor. Subsequent attempts by the Ottoman rulers of Egypt to sweep away 'the ships of the evil-doing Portuguese' who had 'continually been causing damage to [Muslim] merchant ships coming by sea from the land of India' met with far less success. A fleet sent in 1538 captured Aden (at the entrance to the Red Sea) but was defeated decisively off Diu; a second, in 1552, captured Muscat (at the entrance to the Persian Gulf) but was then badly mauled by the Europeans and forced to retreat; a third, in 1559, never got out of the Persian Gulf. Indeed the latter's attack on Bahrain island failed so totally that the Ottoman commander had to pay the Portuguese 1,000 serafins in order to be ferried, with his men, back to the mainland.[57]

However, by this time, the disruption caused by the Iberian invasion of Asian waters had been partially contained by other means. In the west, the establishment of three great Islamic states adjoining the Indian Ocean – the Safavids, the Ottomans, and the Mughals – had by the 1550s created governments capable of resisting the *Estado da India*. At the same time, to the east, the Muslim states of Indonesia – especially Acheh – learned to produce great ships with sufficient armament to resist easy capture. There were furious naval encounters in the 1560s in the Red Sea and in the 1570s off Singapore between Portuguese galleons and Achinese ships equipped (in part) with Turkish guns and troops. Usually, it is true, the Europeans won, but at a terrible cost: in 1562 and 1565 Acheh's Red Sea carrack was sunk, but took a Portuguese great ship to the bottom with it. After that experience, some direct trade between Sumatra and Egypt by Muslim vessels was perforce permitted.[58] At the same time, small warships based on Calicut – referred to in the Portuguese sources as 'Malabar pirates' and in the Muslim chronicles as 'Islamic freedom fighters' – developed far better tactics for their light vessels of shallow draft: powered by oars and sails, they now operated in 'packs' and, rather like Mediterranean galleys, used their centreline gun against becalmed merchantmen.[59] In the seventeenth century, they were so effective that the Mughal port of Surat employed Malabar flotillas for defence against Portuguese attack; and, in the eighteenth, the 'pirates' even captured a British Eastindiaman at sea.[60]

It is often argued that the Portuguese empire was lost because of overextension; and its efforts to conquer territory in Mozambique and Ceylon after 1570 have been particularly criticized.[61] But it seems from the documents that these moves, which marked a clean break with the policies of Almeida and Albuquerque, were rather a response to the loss of the trading monopoly created earlier in the century than a prime cause of commercial decline. It was the resurgence of Muslim seapower that provoked the shift towards territorial conquest, and not vice versa. However, the enormous commitment of resources in Ceylon and Mozambique in the years around 1600 certainly facilitated the rise of English and Dutch power in the Indian Ocean. Portugal simply did not have the men, the ships or the guns to conquer Ceylon, keep the Muslim states in check *and* resist her European enemies; and although the Portuguese merchants in India urged the Lisbon government to suspend the conquests, the missionary establishment was simply not willing to abandon newly won souls to heretics.[62]

So the arrival of the Dutch and the English in Asia tipped an already adverse balance of power even further against the Portuguese. The 1590s were disruptive enough – with fifteen 'Voyages' by the Dutch, totalling sixty-five ships, and one by the English – but the pressure became far more intense after the creation of the Dutch United East India Company in 1602. The first fleet it sent comprised fourteen ships, of which nine were of 400 tons or more; the next, sent in 1603 and commanded by Stefan van der Hagen, numbered only ten vessels but was more heavily armed. Van der Hagen's flagship, the 900-ton *Dordrecht*, carried six 24-pounder and eighteen 8- or 9-pounder guns, and the Admiral was expressly directed to seek allies in Asia against the Portuguese and to destroy as much Portuguese trade as possible. The fleet of eleven ships sent out in 1605 under Cornelius Matelief was further instructed that the destruction of the Portuguese possessions must come first, even if it meant the neglect of the Company's own trade for a time. Eventually, by the end of 1619, the Company had spent perhaps 15 million florins (£1.5 million) on the war in Asia (and run up debts worth a further 6 million) in order to establish fortresses or major factories in 13 places, and to send out 246 ships to Asia.[63] But the trade of the Portuguese had effectively been ruined: between 1602 and 1619 only 79 ships from Lisbon, some of them very small, reached their destination in India.[64] Fewer still returned, partly because even the great carracks carried few heavy guns and, 'As for the gunners, they were mostly artisans, shoemakers, tailors and others who, when the time arrives, know not how to fire a gun'.[65]

All the same, it is possible to exaggerate the disparity between the two sides. The Dutch, after all, made little impression on Portuguese land bases until the 1640s: their attacks on Mozambique, Malacca, and Goa (despite nine costly blockades) all failed. And, even after that, although they captured the Portuguese bases along the coast of Ceylon in the 1650s, they repeatedly failed to conquer the kingdom of Kandy in the interior. Furthermore, their ships were not always invincible: of the forty Dutch vessels sent to the East Indies between 1603 and 1610, nine were lost through war.[66] The English record was little better. On the whole, they left the Iberian bases alone, but even their encounters with Portuguese ships in neutral waters did not always result in victory – as, for example, in the action of 23 December 1612 between two English ships under Thomas Best and four Portuguese galleons off Surat. Tactically, the English were clear winners. They steered straight for the enemy, passed 'from one to another, and gave them such bangs as maid their verie sides crack; for we neyther of us never shott, butt were so neere we could nott misse'. In all, the English fired over 600 rounds into the Portuguese who (according to Captain Best) scarcely fired back at all before retiring to lick their wounds like 'an armey of women ... Yf mine eyes had not seene, I could not [have] believed their baseness and cow-ardlyness'.[67] The English ships were undamaged. Nevertheless Best's victory was by no means complete, by no means decisive. His bombardment did not sink any of the galleons; nor did it even drive them off for long. In the end, in January 1613, the continued presence of the Portuguese ships, biding their time until the English made a mistake, forced Best to take his ships off to Indonesia before they were fully laden.[68]

The error made by the Portuguese in India was thus essentially the same as the error made by Philip II's Armada: they sought to fight as if they were aboard galleys, firing a preliminary salvo before closing in to board. But Best's smug sarcasm must not blind us to the fact that, outside European waters, a preliminary salvo ('shooting off one piece') was usually quite enough to compel the surrender of an unarmed merchantman. Recent research has shown that both the privateers of Elizabethan England and the buccaneers of the seventeenth-century Caribbean often carried no more than one or two guns; yet this was perfectly adequate for their prosperous operation.[69] And, except when other European warships were present in the area, the same was usually true in the Indian Ocean. For example, between 7 and 22 April 1612, some months before Captain Best arrived off Surat, six English ships already in the Indian Ocean congregated off the Arabian coast and hijacked, in succession, fifteen passing Muslim ships from India, culminating in the capture of the great 1,000-ton vessel *Rahimi*, which belonged to the mother of the Mughal emperor. The ship was at first reluctant to anchor, but three warning rounds convinced her master of the need to surrender. The other ships were taken without a shot being fired, and the English, 'havinge nowe as many shippes as wee could well tell whatt to doe withall', took their prizes to a nearby anchorage and plundered them at will.[70] The *Rahimi* was eventually ransomed for £4,000. Here was a prime example of what Professor K. N. Chaudhuri, in his fine study of the English East India Company, has termed 'redistributive enterprise' (and what others might call naked piracy).[71] But this is not yet the full story. The vessel, it must be remembered, belonged to the Mughal dowager empress, whose son was the overlord of Surat. Before long, the emperor decreed that, until the cargo was restored, no further English trade at Surat would be permitted. The Honourable East India Company soon came to terms. Then in 1613 the Rahimi was hijacked again, this time by the Portuguese. The enraged emperor at once declared war on the *Estado da India* and sent his armies to attack several Portuguese bases on his territories. Hostilities continued for two years until the Portuguese, too, restored their ill-gotten gains.[72] Similarly, in 1636, the English factory at Surat was seized by the Mughal authorities, and the factors imprisoned and threatened with torture, because English ships – not, in fact, East India Company vessels at all – had plundered some merchantmen from Surat in the Arabian Sea. The factors were released only when full compensation had been paid.[73]

For as long as the European powers lacked a military presence in Asia, the native rulers were able to counter the power of Western artillery with the permit and the prison. It is true that the *Rahimi* was armed with some fifteen pieces of artillery, and that the soldiers aboard her carried muskets; but these were merely anti-personnel weapons.[74] Western Indian vessels, which often relied on rope and treenails to hold their planks in place, lacked the strength either to suffer heavy artillery bombardment from without, or to absorb the recoil of large ordnance firing from within.[75] It was considered cheaper and more effective to pay protection money to the Europeans than to invest in new ship-designs and massive armament (which might, after all, fail to save the merchantman's cargo from damage); and to punish any who failed to honour the protection they had sold. The Mughals did not need navies or naval guns.[76]

Perhaps the maritime history of early modern Japan offers an even clearer example of the advantages of this policy. The crucial influence here appears to have been the abortive invasion of Korea in the 1590s by the forces of the warlord Toyotomi Hideyoshi, who had just completed the unification of Japan. Hideyoshi was of course fully aware of the need to control the seas during the invasion, and he tried (unsuccessfully) to hire two Portuguese galleons to help him. When this failed, he increased the size of his own fleet to 700 vessels, assuming that the Koreans would fight hand-to-hand

and be overwhelmed. In fact the invasion force landed at Pusan without meeting any Korean ships, and the Japanese forces began a lightening march north, reaching Seoul within twenty days on 2 May 1592. But the Korean navy was not idle. In May and June, in a series of actions, a small Korean fleet commanded by Yi Sun-sin destroyed several minor Japanese flotillas – in all perhaps seventy-two vessels were sunk. Then on 8 July, in a decisive battle, Admiral Yi destroyed the main enemy fleet in Hansan Bay; and on the following day he defeated a relief expedition sailing up from Japan. There were two main reasons for these victories. In the first place, the defeat of the *wakō* by the Chinese in the 1560s seems to have eliminated numerous experienced Japanese naval personnel who were not replaced. Certainly the sailors aboard the invasion fleet were mostly conscripts provided unwillingly by the lords of Kyushu and Shikoku, who had only recently been conquered by Hideyoshi's armies. The second decisive factor in Admiral Yi's victory was his use of the famous 'turtle ships', about 33 metres long and 8 metres broad, entirely encased in hexagonal metal plates so that they could neither be boarded nor holed (plate 29). They were armed with twelve gunports and twenty-two loopholes per side (for small-arms), plus four more ports at each end, together with fire-pots and toxic smoke. Sometimes the turtle-ships came up close, just like a modern torpedo boat, and fired broadsides; sometimes they used their metal ram to hole the enemy, leaving the other warships to close in for the kill. Their armament outweighed that of the Japanese by about 40 to 1.

But Hideyoshi and his commanders learned fast. The Japanese were not unfamiliar with the idea of proofing their ships with iron. In 1578 Oda Nobunaga, another powerful warlord, had deployed on the Inland Sea 'iron ships so arranged that guns would not penetrate them'. Probably they were ordinary ships plated with iron, for they keeled over and sank when the enemy tried to board at one side and everyone rushed over to repel them! Nevertheless, in 1592, Hideyoshi ordered his daimyo to supply him with iron plates, no doubt with the intention of creating ships equal to the turtle squadron. Meanwhile, at Pusan, the surviving Japanese warships took aboard some heavier guns, and clustered beneath the harbour's defences. Even Admiral Yi could not make any impression upon them.

There was a hiatus in the war between 1593 and 1597; but, when it resumed, the Japanese again failed to win command of the sea. After an initial success in July 1597, their fleet was lured by Yi Sun-sin into a tide-race and destroyed. The war continued for another year but, lacking naval support, the Japanese armies were unable to advance far beyond their base at Pusan. In August 1598 the survivors were ordered home. Yi tried once more to destroy the invaders at sea and, although his turtle ships inflicted heavy losses, the admiral was killed in the *mêlée*.[77]

The end of the Korean war, and the death of Hideyoshi the same year,

29 *A Korean Turtle ship*. Although one of these remarkable warships was reputedly still afloat in the 1790s, there are few authentic pictures or models of them. This later reconstruction however, gives some idea of both the compact design and the virtual impossibility of penetrating the hexagonal metal carapace which thwarted all Japanese attacks during the invasion of Korea in the 1590s.

was soon followed by a period of peace not only in Japan but in the surrounding seas. The *wakō* did not reappear, and the Korean turtle ships did not go into action again. Instead, a new form of maritime enterprise grew up in Japan: a fleet of large unarmed merchantmen, on average 300 tons each, was built locally. Many were entrusted by their merchant owners to European pilots and (often) European crews. By the 1600s, one or more of these great ships sailed annually to each of nineteen destinations in South-east Asia. They were known as *Shuinsen* – 'Red-seal ships' – because they were protected only by a passport bearing the shogun's *shuinjō* or red seal (plate 30). They carried no guns at all. At first this seems unnatural: after all, from 1531 onwards, every Portuguese vessel sailing southwards for Asia was required by law to carry artillery, and yet by contrast no Japanese merchantman was allowed by the shogun to arm itself. But that just shows how 'Eurocentric' naval history has become! The Japanese government, like the Mughals, considered it cheaper and more effective to persuade the Europeans to allow the safe passage of their unarmed merchantmen than to invest in expensive new ships

30 *A Japanese 'Red-seal' ship* of 1632 belonging to a Kyoto firm of merchants. Between the 1590s and 1635, when all long-distance overseas trade by Japanese nationals was terminated by order of the central government, a large number of these vessels traded with the other lands of East Asia under licence (the 'red seal') of the shogun. Note that the pilot and many of the crew in the rigging are European (distinguishable by their big noses and baggy breeches) even though the ship itself is Japanese. (From an 'emma', or votive plaque, placed by the ship's owners in the Kiyomisu temple in Kyoto in hope of securing a safe voyage.)

with massive armament, and to retaliate for any offence at sea by prohibiting the Europeans' access to Japanese markets.

Until the *Shuinsen* themselves ceased to trade in the 1630s, the system worked well. When a Red-seal ship arrived at Manila in 1610, for example, in the middle of a sea-battle between the Dutch and the Spaniards, hostilities were suspended while the Japanese neutral sailed serenely through.[78] On the rare occasions when a European ship – almost always Dutch – attacked or plundered a Red-seal vessel, the Japanese aboard made no attempt to defend themselves, but instead returned to Nagasaki and reported the incident to the magistrates. Thereupon *all* Dutch goods and ships in the port were impounded while the charge was investigated, restitution given, and punishment effected. The *Shuinsen* may have lacked heavy armament, but they were protected by legal remedies which were remarkably effective. Anyone who wished for a share of the lucrative Japanese trade was soon compelled to regard the shoguns' passport as sacrosanct.[79]

But if the Mughals and the shoguns did not have that direct interest in dominating the sea which might have prompted them to create an offensive fleet, many other Asian states did. Apart from the Samorins of Calicut and their 'Malabar pirates', several others powers tried to beat the Europeans at their own game. First, there was Acheh. In the sixteenth century, Sultan Ala al-Din Ri'ayat, who (according to the Portuguese chronicler Diego de Couto) 'never turned over in his bed without thinking how he could encompass the destruction of Malacca', tried a frontal attack in 1568; and his son tried again in 1573 and 1575. In 1629, Sultan Iskandar Muda launched yet another amphibious attack led by a flagship (called *The Terror of the World*) which weighed 2,000 tons. Although captured, along with the rest of the invasion fleet, the great vessel was considered so formidable that the victors sent it back to Europe as a showpiece.[80] Shortly afterwards, another maritime power began to challenge European shipping, this time with more success. Sultan Ibn Saif of Oman captured the Portuguese fortified port of Muscat in 1650, and immediately made the galleons sheltering in the harbour into the nucleus of a fleet of his own. New warships were ordered from the shipyards of Surat and Bombay until the Omani fleet in 1698, numbering twenty-four large ships – and including one 74-gun and two 60-gun frigates – was strong enough to force the surrender of Fort Jesus at Mombasa. Twenty years later, the Omanis also briefly captured Bahrain. Efforts by the Marathas of western India to construct Western-style warships were less successful. In the 1650s, their leader Shivaji created a battlefleet of some twenty vessels with the aid of some 300 Portuguese refugees; however, when, in 1659, the latter were all persuaded to desert, the Maratha navy crumbled.[81]

But these were just minor gadflies compared to the challenge offered to the Europeans by the Chinese pirate king, Chêng Ch'eng-kung, better known in Western sources as Coxinga. Coxinga grew up near the Dutch factory at Hirado in southern Japan, where his father was an interpreter for the Europeans. In the 1620s, his father also began to act as a pirate in Dutch service, modifying Chinese junks along European lines, with decks strengthened and adapted to carry heavy artillery and better sail-plans to improve monoeuvrability. Then, after 1644 and the collapse of Ming power before the Ch'ing onslaught, Coxinga established a powerful army and navy along the coasts of Fukien, dedicated to restoring the heirs of the Ming. But where the Cheng family commanded only three junks and a force of about 100 pirates in the 1620s, by 1655 Coxinga commanded some 2,000 warships and well over 100,000 troops, making admirable use of European-style weaponry – whether imitated, captured or purchased.[82]

The resources that underpinned this powerful military machine were derived from trade, and Coxinga's trading network by the 1650s was formidable. It alarmed even the Dutch. 'He is now the man who can spit much in our face in Eastern waters' the Dutch Governor-General reported from Batavia in 1654; and the next year he warned that 'Coxinga has become a terrible thorn in our flesh here'. These sentiments were by no means exaggerated. In 1655 Coxinga informed the Dutch that he regarded their trade as a threat: 'Such places as Batavia, Taiwan and Malacca are one inseparable market and I am master of this area. I will never allow you to usurp my position,' he told them; and in 1657 he sent forty-seven junks to Nagasaki alone, with cargoes that were worth more than twice as much as those of the eight Dutch ships of that year.[83] But Coxinga's commercial empire had a crucial weakness: it depended upon control of the Fukien coast and its offshore islands. Without them, his ships had no access either to the Chinese luxuries he exported or to the Chinese supplies on which his fleet and men depended. In 1656–8 his armies advanced triumphantly to the Yangtze, reclaiming almost all of southeast China for the Ming; but in 1659 his attempt to take the southern capital of Nanking failed disastrously, and the Ch'ing forces rolled forward to the coast of Fukien. The Ch'ing had eventually chosen to adopt the policies used against the *wakō* a century before: with irresistible force they subjugated the land bases of an adversary whom they could not defeat at sea. But Coxinga was resourceful. Early in 1661 he decided to shift his headquarters to the largest of the offshore islands: Taiwan.

Taiwan (or Formosa), however, was fast coming under European control. The Spaniards maintained forts in the north between 1626 and 1642, and the Dutch developed a colony around Fort Zeelandia in the southwest (on the site of modern Tainan) after 1624. By 1660, thanks to the labour of perhaps 50,000 mainland Chinese, whose immigration was encouraged by the Dutch, Taiwan had become one of the most prosperous parts of the Dutch overseas empire. But the colony was defended by only two small fortresses and, in April 1661, Coxinga led a major expedition to the island and called on the Dutch to surrender: he claimed that they had only been allowed to trade there under licence from the Ming, and that this licence he now hereby revoked. The Dutch, not surprisingly, rejected this line of argument and Fort Zeelandia was blockaded. After a nine-month siege, in which 28 Western artillery pieces were deployed by Coxinga, it fell; and Taiwan was organized as an 'imperial prefecture' under Ming rule.[84] Envoys demanding tribute were now sent out to the governor of the Philippines, in preparation for further expansion. Since there were less than 600 Spanish soldiers in Manila, and scarcely more in the rest of the archipelago, the governor panicked and ordered both the withdrawal of all troops from the southern island of Mindanao and the massacre of all Chinese residents in the vicinity of his capital.[85] But in the event Manila was saved, in June 1662 when death put an end to Coxinga's remarkable career. He was just thirty-seven.[86]

Although Coxinga's son carried on resistance for another twenty years, it was a hopeless task. Taiwan was not Fukien: it lacked the food supplies, the population and the shipbuilding facilities to sustain resistance to the Ch'ing on the mainland, and thereby to preserve access to the Chinese luxury goads essential for trade.[87] Gradually, the Ch'ing built up a navy of their own and, assisted from time to time by the Dutch, they began to challenge the Cheng forces. Coxinga's son suffered a catastrophic naval defeat in 1681, and Taiwan surrendered in 1683 . The Europeans could at least breathe again and the China Sea came back under the traditional system of Imperial control for the next 150 years. The equilibrium established in the later seventeenth century, with the Europeans ruling the waves around America, Africa and South Asia, but not in the Far East, was to endure until the Industrial Revolution, coupled with the conquest of much of India, created the resources that could 'open' East Asia by force in the nineteenth century and turn Western maritime superiority into global hegemony.[88]

4

The 'military revolution' abroad

In the Victoria and Albert Museum in London there is an ivory chess-set, made for Tipu Sultan of Mysore during the late eighteenth century (plate 3). One set of chessmen represents an Indian princely army, whose soldiers wield swords and hold shields; their adversaries, however, are the European officers and native infantry of the British East India Company – all in uniform, and all impressively equipped with firearms.[1] This contrast neatly symbolizes a central feature of European overseas expansion since the Middle Ages: namely, the absolute or relative superiority of Western weaponry and Western military organization over most others. Amid the wealth of statistics on Europe's import of Asian spices, on the silver production of colonial America, or on the export of African slaves, it is easy to forget that each of these lucrative economic enterprises rested in the last analysis upon force. Frederick C. Lane and Niels Steensgaard have insisted with good reason that the principal export of pre-industrial Europe to the rest of the world was violence and that the *fidalgos,* the *conquistadores,* the *vrijburghers* and the *nabobs* were (in effect) warrior nomads who differed little from the Mongols or the Mughals.[2] Even the contrasting styles of conquest, with the Europeans commanding from the quarterdeck while the Asians rode on horseback, was more apparent than real, for the major gains of both were all made on land; and to acquire and preserve a territorial base overseas required fortifications and armies as well as ships.

It follows that, if the dynamics of European overseas expansion are to be fully comprehended, a study of the changing military balance between the West and the rest is essential. But, almost immediately, a major paradox appears. In central America, small groups of Westerners in the first half of the sixteenth century caused the collapse of two mighty empires which (between them) had ruled over nearly one-fifth of the world's population; yet in India, until the mid-eighteenth century, the Europeans made virtually no impact on even the minor states of the subcontinent. Indeed, the sudden progress of Western military methods there after the 1740s was so rapid that it left many Europeans bewildered. When, for example, Edmund Burke

spoke in December 1783 in a debate in the British House of Commons on Fox's India Bill, he interrupted his tirade on the injustices and humiliations inflicted upon the Mughal emperor by officers of the Honourable East India Company to observe:

It is impossible, Mr Speaker, not to pause here for a moment to reflect on the inconsistency of human greatness and the stupendous revolutions that have happened in our age of wonders. Could it be believed, when I entered into existence or when you, a younger man, were born, that on this day, in this House, we should be employed in discussing the conduct of those British subjects who had disposed of the power and person of the Grand Mogul?[3]

No, indeed: in 1727, the year of Burke's birth, it *had* been unimaginable, for the Europeans in India were still confined to a handful of fortresses and factories huddled around the coasts of the subcontinent.

It used to be fashionable to attribute the rapid transformation of this situation either to the innate moral superiority of the White Man, or to the added strength afforded him by the Industrial Revolution. But unfortunately there is little evidence that Britons were more virtuous in 1800 (when they held much of India in their power) than in 1700 (when they held very little) or in 1600 (when they held none at all); while proof that the factory system played a major role in conquering the non-Western world before the nineteenth century is either ambiguous or absent. Although the Machine Age helps to explain how the Europeans extended their control over the total land area of the globe from 35 per cent in 1800 to 84 per cent in 1914, it cannot explain how they managed to acquire that initial 35 per cent.[4] By 1800, white colonists ruled all of Siberia, large parts of America and India, several enclaves in Southeast Asia, and a few outposts along the coasts of Africa; but in East Asia, by contrast, they had still scarcely made any impact. These striking differences can only be understood if the 'Rise of the West' is broken down into a number of distinct geographical and chronological components.

I

By 1650 the West had already achieved military mastery in four separate areas: Central and Northeast America; Siberia; some coastal areas of sub-

31 (opposite) *Tipu Sultan's chess set*, discovered in his ruined palace when the British army conquered Mysore in the 1790s, bears silent witness to the superiority of the forces of the English East India Company, whose arrogant officers (with their tricorn hats) ride on elephants and command sepoy 'pawns' armed with muskets. The men of Mysore, by contrast, are armed only with swords. The chessmen from Seringapatam, along with other plunder taken, were sent back to the Company's headquarters in London, whence they were transferred to the India Museum and finally (when that was dissolved) to the Victoria and Albert Museum. (London, Victoria and Albert Museum, I-M. 4 2–1910.)

Saharan Africa; and the islands of Southeast Asia. Different as these regions, and their inhabitants, undoubtedly were, their experience of the European invaders was, in one crucial respect, identical: the white men, they found, fought dirty and (what was worse) fought to kill. Thus the Narragansett Indians of New England strongly disapproved of the colonists' way of making war. 'It was too furious,' one brave told an English captain in 1638, 'and [it] slays too many men'. The captain did not deny it. The Indians, he speculated, 'might fight seven years and not kill seven men'. Roger Williams, a colonial governor, likewise admitted that the Indians' fighting 'was farre lesse bloudy and devouring than the cruell warres of Europe'.[5] Meanwhile, on the other side of the world, the peoples of Indonesia were equally appalled by the all-destructive fury of European warfare. The men of Java, for example, were 'very loth to fight if they can choose'. According to Edmund Scott, who lived among them between 1603 and 1606, the reason was simple: 'they say ... their wealth lyeth altogether in slaves; so that, if their slaves be killed, they are beggared'.[6]

Mr Scott had noted a vital and unusual feature of military organization in Southeast Asia which was shared (though he probably did not know it) with America and sub-Saharan Africa: native wars in these areas were almost always fought to enslave enemies rather than to exterminate them. In Guinea, according to an English visitor in 1788, the tribal chiefs freely admitted 'that the sole object of their wars was to procure slaves, as they could not obtain European goods without slaves, and they could not get slaves without fighting for them'.[7] On the Slave Coast and the Gold Coast, the same pattern of conflict had been noted almost three centuries before: wars were fought to control labour, not land; to gain men, not territory.[8] Of course there were exceptions. Some Amerindian tribes, such as the Algonquin, tortured their defeated enemies to death in an elaborate ritual; the Zulus in the nineteenth century killed their enemies indiscriminately; and the Igorots of central Luzon in the Philippines remained, until modern times, more interested in collecting heads than slaves.[9] Conversely, the Europeans, for their part, sometimes enslaved defeated enemies. Thus in the 1650s, the survivors of the Scottish armies captured by the English were condemned to permanent servitude (usually in Barbados, though sometimes at home: the members of a Parliamentary delegation sent to congratulate Oliver Cromwell on his victory at Worcester were each given a horse and two Scotsmen by the Lord General 'for a present' to do with as they pleased).[10] But the Scots were regarded as rebels and were treated accordingly; and, even in the case of this and other civil conflicts, the aim of making war in Europe was never to secure slaves, as it was in the non-European areas under consideration.

Another distinctive common feature of these regions lay in their settlement patterns. In America, although the Aztec and Inca empires possessed some walled cities, the less civilized peoples to the north and south of them did not. This dearth, of course, facilitated the initial conquest, because the natives lacked defensible bases to fall back on; but it complicated consolidation. As Increase Mather of New England complained in 1675: 'Every swamp is a castle to them, knowing where to find us; but we know not where to find them!' And there are innumerable examples of colonial soldiers marching out with drums beating and colours unfurled in order to destroy an Indian 'town' – only to find it gone. The logic of Western superiority in fixed encounters had been thoroughly digested by the Indians: after their costly initial defeats, they were scrupulously careful to avoid pitched battles - much to the fury of the Europeans – because they always lost them. 'They doe acts of hostility without proclaiming war; they don't appeare openly in the field to bid us battle', was the lament of another irate New England preacher.[11] Only gradually did the Europeans recognize that the only way to win was to adopt those same guerilla methods. The serious conflict of 1675 in New England, known as King Philip's War, only ended when the colonists followed the advice of Benjamin Church and fought in small units, armed with hatchets, dogs and knives as well as firearms, which operated in open formation rather than in lines or columns.[12]

But the Indians of New England were also learning fast. From the 1640s they managed to acquire an adequate supply of guns from the French, the English and (until the collapse of New Netherland in 1664) the Dutch; and they used them to deadly effect – soon realizing that a musket ball travelled with more force, and faster, than an arrow, and was less likely to be deflected by leaves or undergrowth. Furthermore, the Narragansetts in King Philip's War took refuge in 'the Great Swamp' behind the walls and bastions of a European-style fortress which claimed the lives of seventy colonists before it was taken. In the end the native Americans lost ground because their numbers dwindled throughout the seventeenth century (largely thanks to the inroads of European diseases), while those of the Westerners (largely thanks to immigration) relentlessly increased.[13]

Further south, the European colonists triumphed more rapidly. Indeed the vast, centrally organized empires ruled by the Aztecs and the Incas collapsed before the Iberian onslaught with a speed and finality that has few parallels: the former in 1519–21, to a force of some 2000 Spaniards (together with 14 cannons and only 16 horses) under Hernán Córtes; the latter in 1531–3, to only 168 Europeans (together with 4 guns and 67 horses) under Francisco Pizarro.[14] Naturally, such small forces would have achieved little without the divisions that paralyzed their enemies – both Cortés and Pizarro entered realms virtually in a state of civil war – yet they represented relatively *large* military concentrations by the standards of early colonial warfare. Areas without a well-organized central government were mostly brought under European control by 'bands' of under one hundred mounted warriors who killed or enslaved the Indians and plundered or destroyed their possessions.

Admittedly, on Mexico's northern frontier, against the tribes of the Great Plains which had acquired the horse (but not yet the gun), the Spaniards eventually had to build blockhouses and forts along strategic roads and near vulnerable settlements.[15] But to the south, in Chile, forts were backed up by terrorism. In what must rank as the first manual of guerilla warfare ever published – *The armed forces and description of the Indies* (Madrid, 1599) – Captain Bernardo de Vargas Machuca dismissed as irrelevant the entire pattern of European warfare, with its hierarchical tactical units, linear formations and permanent garrisons. Instead he advocated for the Americas the creation of commando groups to carry out search-and-destroy missions deep within enemy territory for up to two years at a time. The good leader, according to Vargas Machuca (who had a lifetime of experience to draw on), knew as much about planting survival crops and curing tropical ulcers as about laying ambushes and mounting surprise attacks.[16] And, thanks to the adoption of native methods, the colonial frontier in Chile was steadily consolidated, and warfare there became 'nothing but a manhunt' (in the phrase of a Jesuit contemporary) in which the settlers hunted down recalcitrant Indians with mastiffs and knives.[17]

The situation in Siberia, Southeast Asia and sub-Saharan Africa was not dissimilar. For most of the time, the Westerners held a decisive advantage thanks to their mastery of the gun. The Cossacks who crossed the Urals into Siberia in the 1580s made excellent use of both firearms and forts to expand eastwards, reaching the Pacific by the 1630s in their headlong search for furs. But their rapid progress was due also to the relative absence of concerted opposition: the native population of Siberia at the time was, after all, probably less than 200,000.[18] In this respect, Black Africa was very different. The Ottoman-trained Moroccan musketeers who crossed the Sahara in 1590–1 to attack the empire of Songhai were faced by numerous and determined adversaries, while the Portuguese who invaded the kingdom of Kongo in the 1660s were opposed by troops armed with Western muskets and reinforced by twenty-nine European renegades. But, nonetheless, the invaders triumphed: after the battles of Tondibi (1591) and Ambuila (1665), respectively, the states of Songhai and Kongo ceased to exist.[19]

However, it is misleading to relate the entire history of European expansion in Africa to the presence or absence of firearms. Until the machine-gun, Western armament may have proved adequate for winning battles, but it could seldom win wars. Until the nineteenth century, the Europeans remained largely confined to their numerous forts around the coasts.[20] In the east, attempts by the Portuguese to bring the upper Zambezi area under their control repeatedly failed, because the natives with their assegais were normally able to destroy the small groups of Portuguese musketeers as soon as they strayed outside their few fortified bases; while on the Swahili coast the Muslim princes always seemed able to secure copious firearms and ammunition from the Turks. In 1631 the sultan of Mombasa even captured the imposing Fort Jesus, whose bastions had long overlooked the town.[21] Meanwhile, further west, some native rulers proved able to amass Western weapons on an impressive scale, especially after the 1650s, when the Dutch began a direct exchange of guns for slaves. Some 8,000 muskets were sent to the Gold Coast for trade in the three years following July 1658, for example, exchanged at the rate of twelve per slave; whilst a century later, the total number of firearms exported every year was around 400,000, exchanged at the rate of 4, 5 or 6 per slave. And yet, in most areas, this inflow of Western technology scarcely affected most African military techniques.[22] As late as 1861 an English officer in Nigeria who observed the Yoruba at war noted that the native troops in battle still 'spread themselves out anyhow into open order, and skirmish away until their ammunition is exhausted, upon which they return to replenish'. He added that 'though thousands of rounds be fired, the killed may be counted by units and the wounded by tens'.[23] Tactics like these would clearly prove ineffective against highly trained European forces. But Black Africa did not import guns for this purpose. Its wars continued to be fought for slaves, not lands, and the irrelevance of musketry salvoes to operations aimed at securing fit and healthy slaves is obvious. Smoothbore weapons were far too inaccurate to be used with precision to wound rather than to kill; and, in any case, the injuries inflicted by lead shot, however slight, often smashed bones and created wounds that turned gangrenous and caused death. In the eighteenth century, the use of pellets rather than bullets overcame this problem in part – which perhaps explains the dramatic increase in musket imports – but this did nothing to facilitate the adoption of Western methods of musketry in warfare, for guns simply did not fit into most African military traditions at all.[24]

It was much the same story in the Indonesian archipelago. Sultan Iskandar Muda of Acheh, for example, had by 1620 accumulated some 2,000 artillery pieces from various Ottoman and European sources. But it led nowhere: the guns proved inferior in action against the Portuguese and almost all were lost at the unsuccessful siege of Malacca in 1629. In reality, firearms never fully replaced Acheh's 900 war-elephants as the front line of defence; and such cannon as remained after 1629 were reserved for ceremonial purposes.[25] In part this victory of tradition over innovation is explained, as in America, by the relative infrequency of walled towns. Indeed, in some cases, the boundary between town and country could be hard to find. A French visitor to the capital of Acheh in the 1620s claimed that it was despised by most Europeans 'because it is a town undefended by any wall, resembling more an open village in Normandy than a city.'[26]

In these areas, naturally, siege warfare was a new experience. Since wars had previously been fought to secure slaves or tribute, rather than to annex more territory or acquire new specific strategic bases, the best defence against attack was either immediate surrender (when the enemy appeared in over-whelming strength) or temporary flight (at all other times). Thus the last Muslim ruler of the thriving port-city of Malacca was not unduly alarmed by the arrival of a small Portuguese squadron in 1511. After some resistance, he and his men withdrew inland 'a day's journey' thinking (according to the *Commentaries* of Bras de Albuquerque) that the Portuguese 'simply meant to rob the city and then leave it and sail away with the spoil'. But instead, they built the powerful fort known as *A Famosa*, constructed (typically) on the ruins of the Great Mosque with stones gathered from the sacred hill where the sultan's ancestors lay buried. Eventually the walls of Portuguese Malacca stretched for two kilometres and withstood some ten sieges.[27] One of these, in 1629, was undertaken on a heroic scale: the sultan of Acheh (as already noted) led a besieging force of 20,000, supported by 236 boats and artillery. They erected siegeworks around Malacca so well that, according to a Portuguese account, 'not even the Romans could have made such works stronger or more quickly' (plate 32). But it was not enough to secure victory – on the contrary, the sultan eventually lost 19,000 men and his two senior commanders, as well as most of the ships and guns. In the same year, an equally formidable siege was begun by the ruler of Mataram against the Dutch fortified port of Batavia, which the sultan correctly identified as a 'thorn in the foot of Java' that had to be 'plucked out, for fear the whole body should be endangered'. The sultan's forces, like the troops of Acheh, managed to dig trenches in the European fashion; but they made no impression against the massive moat, wall and bastions of the new Dutch settlement.[28]

The Europeans erected many other fortifications in Southeast Asia: numer-ous small citadels in the 'Spice Islands' (as at Ternate, Tidore or Amboina) and the Philippines; Fort Zeelandia on Taiwan; the Monte fortress in Macao; defensible factories in other places – Ayutthia, Banten, Pegu.[29] But there was only one other fully fortified city to compare with Batavia and Malacca: Manila in the Philippines. Shortly before the arrival of the Spaniards in the 1560s, Muslims from Borneo and the Moluccas had introduced fortifications to the archipelago. They also imported Chinese firearms, founded bronze artillery and manufactured 'gunpowder and other munitions'. Although only one fort (near Puerta Galera on Mindoro island) was built of stone, and although the muskets were used 'more to frighten than to kill', the Spaniards took no chances. On the site of the Muslim stockade at Manila they built massive defences that defied all assaults for over two centuries. The citadel of Santiago itself was not much bigger than other forts (such as San Pedro at Cebu); but it was connected to the vast stone wall, three metres thick and studded with bastions, which surrounded the Spanish city (known as Intra-muros – figure 5) and dominated the finest natural harbour in East Asia.[30]

Impressed – or intimidated – by these developments, a few local rulers began to follow the European example: Banten, Pati, Japura and Surabaya

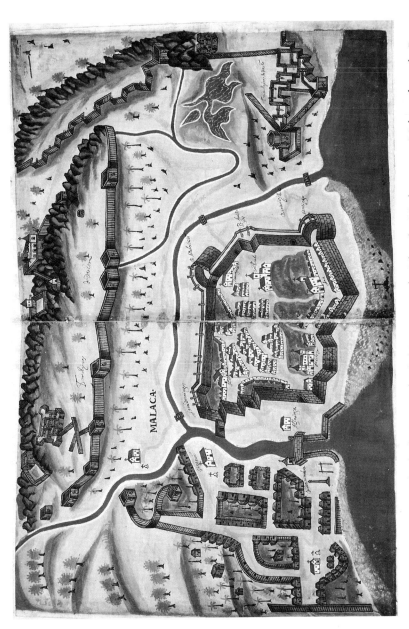

32 *The siege of Malacca*, 1629, was the final attempt of Acheh's greatest ruler Iskandar Muda to wrest Malacca from the Portuguese. The splendid illustration by Pedro Barreto de Resende (designed for Antonio Bocarro's manuscript *Livro do Estado da India* of 1635) shows the impressive Achinese fortifications around the sixteenth-century walls of Malacca (Albuquerque's original citadel, *A Famosa*, is at lower left within the walls) . . . But it failed. Instead, in 1641, Portuguese Malacca fell to the Dutch. (London, BL, Sloane MS. 197 fos. 381 v-2)

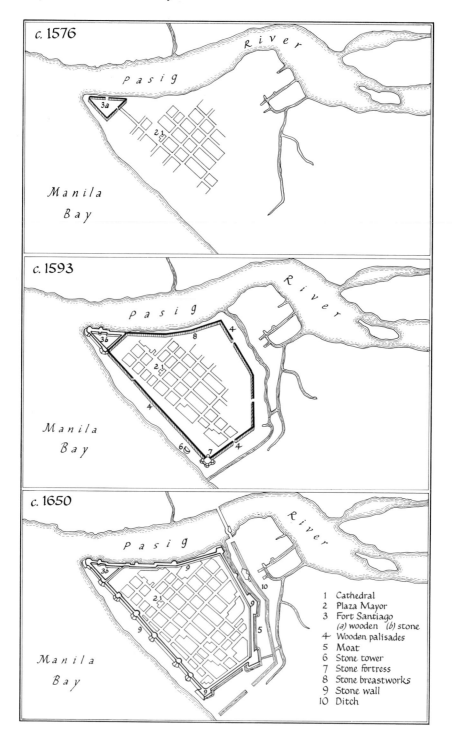

c. 1576

River

Pasig

3a

2 1

Manila Bay

c. 1593

River

Pasig

3b   8   4

2 1

4

6   7

Manila Bay

c. 1650

River

Pasig

3b   9

10

2 1   9

9   5

9

Manila Bay

1 Cathedral
2 Plaza Mayor
3 Fort Santiago
   (a) wooden *(b)* stone
4 Wooden palisades
5 Moat
6 Stone tower
7 Stone fortress
8 Stone breastworks
9 Stone wall
10 Ditch

all acquired brick or stone walls in the sixteenth century; the sultans of Makassar (in south Sulawesi) built a brick wall and three redoubts around their capital in the mid-seventeenth century.[31] But in vain: the keys to the long-distance trade of East Asia remained in European hands – Manila for the trans-Pacific link with America; Malacca and Batavia for commerce with India and beyond. All three quickly acquired large populations of both natives and Chinese, but they remained in Western hands (albeit not always in the same Western hands) until 1942; and with the wealth conferred by their possession, the Europeans could exercise a maritime hegemony over all other major ports in the region and prevent any rival state from mounting an effective challenge. They were also ideally placed to use the resources extracted from the area to extend that hegemony wherever an opportunity presented itself. Increasingly, their gaze was directed towards the territories, and the riches, of the Muslim rulers of India, Persia and the Levant.

II

Slaves also played an important role in determining the Muslim response to Europe's military challenge, for they were likewise central to Islamic warfare. In the early ninth century the Muslim states of North Africa, Spain and Egypt began to use slave soldiers to defend themselves; by the middle of the century, the Caliphs of Baghdad had followed suit; and the practice soon spread further. But the slave soldiers were not kidnapped and conscripted as adults: instead they were recruited while still children (often as a form of tribute paid by non-Muslims to their conquerors) and brought up in the ruler's household with his own children, so that they learned the ways of Islam as well as the art of war. The Mamluks of Egypt, mostly recruited in the Crimea, and the Ottoman Janissaries, mainly recruited in the Balkans, are merely the best known examples of these elite slave warriors. They were part of a military system that was unique to the world of Islam. Even the Muslim states of Indonesia had them: in the early seventeenth century the sultans of Acheh were served by 500 royal slaves born abroad and trained in warfare since their youth.[32] And although the Islamic states of India placed less reliance on slave soldiers, in compensation the sultans of

5 *The growth of Intramuros (Manila) the Philippines.* When the Spaniards under Legazpi first sailed into Manila Bay in 1572, there was only a bamboo stockade at the mouth of the Pasig river to defend the numerous small communities spread over the plain beyond. The conquerors soon expanded the fort – which they renamed Santiago (St James) – first in wood and then (after 1585) in stone, and surrounded the settlement which rapidly developed around it with a stockade. By the early seventeenth century, the Spanish town was encircled by a chain of bastions and walls as powerful as any in Europe, and Manila became by far the largest European city in Asia.

the Deccan made extensive use in the fifteenth and sixteenth centuries of foreign mercenaries, particularly those from the Ottoman empire and Persia (referred to in the Portuguese records as a *gente branca* [white men], because they looked pale in comparison with the native Indians).[33] The character of Islamic warfare was thus consistent and clear: the core of every major army was composed of men lacking any local ties, devoted entirely to fulfilling their government's wishes, and fighting in the traditional manner. It was not a system that necessarily favoured strategic or tactical innovation. In the memorable (though perhaps overstated) phrase of a historian of Islam: 'Mamluks were not supposed to think, but to ride horses; they were designed to be not a military elite, but military automata'.[34] And in 1517 the imperious knights of the Mamluk army – who tolerated the use of firearms for sieges but refused to deploy them in battle – were overthrown by the slave soldiers of the Ottoman Turks, whose commanders lacked such high principles.[35]

The Ottoman army, on the other hand, appears to have adopted and mastered Western military technology with remarkable speed and thoroughness. Handguns, field guns and siege guns were all rapidly developed by the Turks; advanced siege techniques of both offence and defence were evident from the 1520s; and for a century and a half following this, the Turks were clearly equal to all but the largest forces that the West could throw against them.[36] And yet in three important respects the military revolution was imperfectly practised by Europe's most dangerous neighbour. First, despite its abundant human and natural resources, and the services of some 'renegade' European experts, in 1602 the Turkish commander in Hungary complained that his troops could no longer match the firepower of their Christian adversaries. 'In the field or during a siege we are in a distressed position, because the greater part of the enemy forces are infantry armed with muskets, while the majority of our forces are horsemen, and we have very few specialists armed with muskets.' Western improvements in volley fire and the multiplication of field guns (p. 23 above) widened the gap. This proved particularly important in the Hungarian campaigns between 1683 and 1697, where fifteen major battles occurred. The well-equipped Christians repeatedly defeated their Turkish adversaries, starting with the striking victory scored by the Christian relief army, its field artillery at the ready, against the Turkish forces besieging Vienna.[37] But the Turkish defeat before Vienna resulted from other factors, the chief of which was the failure to fortify their siege-camp. It had become standard military practice in the West to build two sets of siege-works: one against the beleaguered town, the second around the siegeworks to guard against any attempt at relief (plate 33). That the Turks did not trouble with this elementary precaution in 1683 may have been mere carelessness by their commander on that occasion, the ill-fated Grand Vizier 'Black Mustafa'; but it fits in with other evidence that by the later seventeenth

33 *The siege of Vienna*, 1683. There were many prints made to commemorate the deliverance of the Austrian capital from its second siege by the Turks, but the most unusual was surely Nicholas Meldemann's fish-eye view, dedicated to the victorious commandant, Count Starhemberg. Like all the surviving illustrations, it shows the notable absence of defensive fortifications around the Turkish camp which led to their defeat. (Vienna, Kriegsarchiv, H. III. C. 172.)

century Ottoman troops had become expert imitators, but poor innovators. Contemporaries began to note that, although Turkish craftsmen could copy any new Western weapon that they found on a battlefield or that a renegade brought to them, it usually took them a long time; and that, even then, they only seemed able to deploy them within the traditional military framework.[38] The Turks never learned to change their thick columns to thin lines in pitched battle, just as they never fully mastered the complexities of siege warfare.

Even in the late eighteenth century, their Austrian opponents noted that the Turkish army still fought exactly as it had done 'in the days of Suleiman the Magnificent', two hundred years before. The Maréchal de Saxe in 1732 offered the following explanation:[39]

It is hard for one nation to learn from another, either from pride, idleness or stupidity. Inventions take a long time to be accepted (and sometimes, even though everyone accepts their usefulness, in spite of everything they are abandoned in favour of tradition and routine) . . . The Turks today are in this situation. It is not valour, numbers or wealth that they lack; it is order, discipline and technique.

The more the European forces improved these qualities, the greater their superiority over Islamic armies, until the great victory of Napoleon Bonaparte at the battle of the Pyramids in 1798 heralded the opening of the entire Levant to Western exploitation.

But there was also a third source of Ottoman inadequacy in the military sphere: metallurgical inferiority. There are two sorts of evidence for this phenomenon. Contemporary sources, on the one hand, almost invariably claimed that arms and armour taken from Islamic forces were of no use to Westerners. Thus, after the victory at Lepanto in 1571, some 225 bronze guns were captured by the Venetians alone, but almost all were melted down and recast (with reinforcement) because, according to the Council of Ten, 'the metal is of such poor quality'. That is, Ottoman naval artillery was found to be too brittle for safe and effective use.[40] This was apparently not mere chauvinism, for it is supported by a recent chemical analysis of the composition of some other Muslim weapons and armour from the Middle East which showed that Western iron and steel was also notably stronger than the Islamic equivalents. Admittedly the sample submitted to analysis was somewhat small – since few museums will consent to the mutilation of their exhibits in the cause of science – but the results were both consistent and convincing.[41]

Much the same technological inferiority was reported from India. Artillery had been in use in the north of the subcontinent from about 1440 and in the Deccan from about 1470 and yet, in the late eighteenth century, the Europeans still considered all 'country' artillery (as they called it) to be unserviceable for their needs.[42] Although the native rulers had plenty of guns, these were found to be poorly cast (even in the eighteenth century, some Indian guns were still made of iron strips held together with metal bands), poorly maintained, and too heavy to move. According to an Indian writer in the 1780s, the native artillery was as 'cumbrous, ill-mounted and ill-served as was the artillery of Europe three hundred years ago'. Many European sources bear him out. A report on the copious brass ordnance of the pro-British nawab of Oudh in 1777, for example, ruled ninety per cent of the guns to be unfit for service, due either to metal fatigue or to rotten carriages; while the artillery captured from Tipu Sultan of Mysore in the 1790s was likewise reckoned by Sir Arthur Wellesley, later duke of Wellington, to be suitable only for scrap. It was much the same with 'country' small arms, which were normally of limited usefulness, either because they wore out quickly and could not easily be replaced; or because they did not conform to a single size, so that the shot often failed to fit the barrel; or because they had a shorter range than European muskets.[43]

Before the eighteenth century, however, the Europeans were not always so contemptuous. As the Portuguese in India never tired of pointing out, Asia was not like America: adversaries there were armed with firearms and steel swords, not with wooden clubs and obsidian knives. It was simply not possible for 168 men with 67 horses to destroy the Mughal empire, as Pizarro and his Spanish companions had brought down the Incas, for the Mughal army numbered over a million men, many of them armed with muskets.[44] Moreover the Indian rulers (including the Mughals) were often advised by foreign experts – at first by Turks (particularly among the Muslim rulers) but later also by Europeans. As early as 1499, two Portuguese deserted from Vasco da Gama's fleet in order to serve native rulers for higher wages, and the number of 'renegades' remained high throughout the sixteenth century – two Milanese gunfounders to Calicut in 1503; four Venetians to Malabar in 1505; and so on.[45] After the arrival of other, rival European groups in South Asia in the seventeenth century, this trickle of Western weaponry, and of the experts to use them, became a flood. Some firearms were captured or confiscated; but most seem to have changed hands as a present, designed to win or keep a friendship that seemed in danger of wavering. Thus in 1663 the Dutch East India Company had to lend the nawab of the Carnatic four bronze field-guns for his next campaign, and the Portuguese on the Malabar coast regularly supplied their native allies with presents of artillery, munitions and gunners (plate 34).[46] Most of the European military personnel in Indian service, by contrast, continued to come independently and as individuals. Willem Verstegen, for example, a member of the Dutch Council in Batavia on his way home to Holland, entered the service of Prince Dara, one of the claimants to the Mughal throne, in 1658. There he met Niccolo Manucci, an Italian stranded in Delhi (by the death of his itinerant patron) who was already earning his living in Prince Dara's service along with perhaps 200 other Europeans and Turks.[47]

But, in spite of all the efforts of these foreign experts, Dara lost every battle that he fought and was at length captured and executed by his rival, Aurangzebe, who eventually became emperor and took most of the Europeans into his service. But Aurangzebe, too, seems to have derived little direct benefit from their presence. There are two obvious explanations for this.

34 *Europeans aim Indian guns* in this unfinished Mughal miniature from the early eighteenth century. It purports to show Ala-ud-din's siege of the fortress of Rathambor in 1301, but the uniform battery of guns and the presence of a European dressed in black clearly indicate a date four centuries later, when Western gunnery experts regularly supervised the artillery parks of Indian rulers.

In the first place, as in Southeast Asia, field artillery and musketry volleys simply did not fit easily into local traditions of warfare. As Manucci perceptively observed of a battle between Dara and Aurangzebe in 1658:[48]

Be it known to the reader that these two armies were not ordered in the disposition obtaining in Europe. But one division was close to another, as the trees of a pinewood ... I saw in this action, as in so many others where I was afterwards present, that the only soldiers who fought were those well to the front. Of those more to the rear, although holding their bared swords in their hands, the Moguls did nothing but shout *Bakush, bakush* and the Indians *Mar, mar* – 'Kill, kill'. If those in front advanced, those behind followed the example; and if the former retired, the others fled – a custom of Hindustan quite contrary to that of Europe.

Manucci was right: Indian armies may have been huge but they remained, essentially, aggregations of individual heroic warriors. Their principal ambition was to close with as many enemies as possible in single combat and, unless they achieved this quickly, their corporate strength soon disintegrated. The second reason for the failure of Mughal armies to adopt the European battle techniques extolled by Manucci was more prosaic: at that time, few Europeans in India actually used them! For example, the leading Portuguese chronicles of the age – those of Couto, Bocarro, Faria e Sousa – all bristle, like their predecessors, with the brutal and furious deeds of the *fidalgos* in the Far East. Attacks were conducted like guerilla actions, with all the reckless indiscipline of the street gang, because, for the *fidalgos* too, man-to-man duels were seen as the highest form of combat. It is true that, in the early seventeenth century, the Portuguese Crown tried to introduce European organization and discipline into its colonial units; but it met with little success.[49] The Crown likewise tried to introduce better weaponry for its overseas forces but, here too, success was limited: spare guns, powder and shot were simply not to be had. Although successive viceroys tried to manufacture their own – powder in Goa, cannon in Macao – hardly a year passed without the officers of the *Estado da Índia* pleading with the Lisbon government for the urgent dispatch of munitions from home. As for the numerous weapons sent by the Dutch, English and other East India companies for trade in the Orient, quality and reliability were seldom high: indeed some had a special category known as 'trade guns' which were (and long remained) far below the standard required for the European market.[50]

So there were good reasons why the European military revolution in field warfare failed to inspire imitation in early modern India; but the case for siege warfare at first sight seems different. Here, the superiority of Western techniques of both offence and defence was proved time and again, even against the most powerful adversaries – as with, for example, the sultan of Ahmadnagar's siege of Portuguese Chaul in 1571. No fewer than 140,000 Indian troops were pitted against no more than 1,100 European defenders, whose chances of relief were diminished by the simultaneous attack of other Muslim rulers against several other outposts of the *Estado da Índia*. The odds seemed impossible: the garrison held a perimeter of no more than 600 by 450 metres, covered by improvised walls and bastions and ill-protected by guns. Not surprisingly, the besiegers steadily took all the outworks until at last, after six months, they were close enough to launch a full-scale assault. But it was beaten back and, in the furious counter-attack that followed, the Portuguese captured or spiked all the enemy's artillery. The siege was over.[51]

As in Africa and Southeast Asia, remarkably few European strongholds in India fell to a native siege. Yet they fell easily enough to other Europeans after 1600. The Portuguese forts in Ceylon and on the Malabar coast, for example, all resisted numerous attacks by various native rulers; but every one of them surrendered between 1638 and 1663 to the Dutch. The Dutch, however, fortified their gains on a far more impressive scale: the walls of Galle, with twelve bastions (some of them thirty metres thick), ran for almost two kilometres; those of Colombo, with eight, and those of Negapatam, with twelve, were larger still.[52] They could resist even a full European siege.

It may at first sight seem curious that, despite these impressive examples, the native rulers of India and Ceylon never tried to imitate the *trace italienne*.

But it must be remembered that many of the major Indian fortresses were already so huge that even the heaviest early modern artillery bombardment could make little impression on them: thus the fourteenth-century walls of Gulbarga in the Deccan were seventeen metres thick, and those of the Purana Qila at Delhi, built between 1530 and 1545, were the same; the walls of Agra, rebuilt between 1564 and 1574, consisted of two revetments of dressed red sandstone blocks ten metres apart, filled in with sand and rubble. They lacked bastions because, on such a scale, they scarcely needed them: sieges in early modern India were decided by blockade and mines rather than by cannonade. Even in the late eighteenth century, the Europeans could not take any of these strongholds by bombardment.[53]

But until the late eighteenth century, the Europeans – for the most part – did not even try. Recent research has stressed how anachronistic it is to see the West as bent upon world domination from the voyage of Vasco da Gama onwards.[54] In fact, the Europeans originally came to Asia to trade, not to conquer, and most of them only undertook military expenditure either to coerce reluctant buyers or in order to safeguard themselves against attack from their European rivals; the cost of defence would otherwise have eaten up all trading profits. The Dutch were, however, an exception to this rule: they were already fighting a bitter war in Europe, and they therefore aimed straight for the overseas bases of their Spanish and Portuguese enemies, trying to destroy them, as well as usurping their trade. Heavy military spending was therefore, for them, essential and (according to an official investigation in 1613) even the 'voorcompagniëen' (the rival associations of Dutch merchants who traded in Asia before the foundation of the United East India Company) spent over 30 per cent of the running costs of each voyage on war-related items. After the formation of the United Company in 1602, the annual figure rose to 50, 60 and even 70 per cent. Indeed the total cost of building Dutch forts on the principal islands of the Moluccas between 1605 and 1612 amounted to no less than 1.72 million florins, almost one-third of the Company's initial capital.[55] This was because most Dutchmen in the East were utterly convinced that no profit was to be had without power, and no trade without war. In the terse (and oft-quoted) letter of Governor-General Jan Pieterszoon Coen to his Directors in 1614:[56]

You gentlemen ought to know from experience that trade in Asia should be conducted and maintained under the protection and with the aid of your own weapons, and that those weapons must be wielded with the profits gained by the trade. So trade cannot be maintained without war, nor war without trade.

Some of the British in the Far East during the seventeenth century thought that their East India Company should follow the Dutch model. Dr John Fryer, for example, a Company surgeon in Surat during the 1670s, observed that the Dutch were 'as powerful for men, riches and shipping in Batavia, as in Europe'; and continued:[57]

[Their strategy] is grounded on a different principle from our East India Company, who are for the present profit, not future emolument. These [the Dutch], as they gain ground, secure it by vast expences, raising forts and maintaining souldiers: ours are for raising auctions and retrenching charges, bidding the next age grow rich as they have done, but not affording them the means.

But the comparison was unjust. The British, after some initial failures, preferred to concentrate their trade in areas where the native Indian states were relatively small and weak, and European competitors were not deeply entrenched – Golconda, the Carnatic, Bengal.[58] The Directors of the Company could therefore take pride in their ability to avoid hefty military expenditure. 'All war is so contrary to our constitution as well as [to] our interest,' they informed their officials in 1681, 'that we cannot too often inculcate to you an aversion thereto.' Or, in a rather more succinct message sent in 1677: 'Our business is trade, not war'.

As late as 1750, the Directors still reproached their officials in the field for seeming 'to look upon yourselves rather as a military colony than [as] the factors and agents of a body of merchants'; and in 1759 they dismissed the strategic designs of the governor of Madras on the grounds that 'Were we to adopt your several plans for fortifying, half our capital would be buried in stone walls.'[59] But, by then, the Directors were seriously out of date. The arrival of the French on their doorsteps – at Pondichéry, close to Madras, in 1674; at Chandernagore, upstream from Calcutta, in 1686 – was bad enough. But after the reorganization of the *Compagnie des Indes* in 1719 these modest toeholds on the subcontinent suddenly became threatening bridgeheads from which French territorial influence in India might be extended. It became inevitable that, whenever Britain and France went to war in Europe, the conflict would now spread to their colonies. But still the Directors of the East India Company failed to see the need for change. As late as 1740, when the war of the Austrian Succession broke out, British forces in India totalled less than 2,000 men, widely distributed over the subcontinent in decrepit, poorly defended fortresses. And so, when the French in the Carnatic launched an attack on Madras in 1746, the 200 guns of Fort St George still had only 100 men to serve them and the chief gunner, Mr Smith, died of a heart attack when he saw the French approaching. The fortress fell. Then, later that same year, the victorious French went on to defeat a superior army of Britain's Indian allies at the battle of Adyar river with the classic European technique of the musketry salvo: 300 Europeans and 700 native troops, drawn up in three ranks, moved forward against their 10,000 adversaries firing successive volleys of shot. Almost immediately, they were masters of the field.[60]

The battle of Adyar river proved a turning-point in Indian history. Admittedly, the combination of a core of European soldiers with a larger number of European-trained Indian troops was not new. All the Western powers in the Orient, from the Portuguese onwards, had tried to compensate for their great numerical weakness by recruiting members of the 'martial races' of Asia, such as the Ambonese in Indonesia or the Pampangas in the Philippines They also made use of native converts to Christianity (often descended from a European father), such as the 'topazes' in British India and the 'mardijkers' in Dutch Java.[61] But these various recruits served as auxiliaries, not regulars: they fought in their traditional fashion, with their traditional weapons, and in their traditional formations. The French, however, trained native troops to fight in the European fashion with European weapons and European uniforms; and after 1751 they supplied them with European officers and N.C.O.s too.[62] In that same year, the French governor in Pondichéry informed his superiors in Europe that: 'All my efforts are directed towards attaining for you vast revenues from this part of India, and consequently placing the [French] nation in a position to maintain itself here even when it may lack support from Europe.'[63]

His British rival was well aware of the threat. 'Since the French have put themselves in possession of extensive domains', Governor Saunders wrote to his superiors in February 1751, 'and have raised their flag at the bounds of our territory and have striven to constrain our settlements to such an extent that they can neither receive supplies nor goods, it has been judged essential to thwart their designs, lest their success render our situation worse during peace than in time of war ... We shall therefore oppose them to the greatest extent of which we are capable.' In this, the British held one decisive advantage: their superior financial resources in the sub-continent. It was not merely that the volume of British trade in Asia by 1750 was roughly four times that of France; there was also the fact that, from the 1680s onwards, the Company's agents in Madras accepted substantial deposits in cash from both Indian and European merchants and officials. In normal times, most of this was remitted back to London in bills of exchange, but when war threatened, or erupted, these deposits provided a useful capital fund from which to finance military expenditure. And as the trade and population of Madras grew, so the capital on deposit increased.[64] By the 1750s it was sufficient to allow the Company to follow the French example and raise their own companies, battalions, and, eventually, regiments of 'sepoys' (as these troops were known, from *sipahi*, the Persian word for soldier). There were two sepoy battalions in the Company's service by 1758, five by 1759, and ten – some 9,000 men – by 1765. With numerical strength such as this, enhanced by the new, more reliable flintlock muskets and the quick-firing field artillery exported from Europe, it was now possible for the Company to challenge not only its French rivals, but also the smaller native states of India with some chance of success.[65]

The first major opportunity occurred in Bengal in 1757. The Mughal empire in its prime could call upon the services of 4 million warriors but, after the death of Aurangzebe in 1707, a number of satraps on the imperial frontier had broken away and created their own separate states.[66] Nevertheless the military strength of these rulers remained formidable, compared with the Europeans. The decision to send an army of sepoys and British troops to Bengal in 1757, under the command of Robert Clive, was something of a wild gesture. Admittedly the new nawab of Bengal had given provocation by taking Calcutta, and demanding increased payments from the Company in return for trade; but his army was ten times the size of Clive's 2,000 sepoys and 900 Europeans, and was assisted by French military advisers.

But, at the battle of Plassey, Clive won. The nawab, Siraj-ud-Daulah, was executed and a replacement more acceptable to the British set up in his place. After some years of further hostilities and negotiation, in 1765 the Mughal emperor and the new nawab finally recognized the right of the British Company to collect all state revenues in the provinces of Bihar, Orissa and Bengal. It was wealth beyond the dreams of avarice: the 'net amount of territorial revenues and customs, clear of charges of collection' received officially by the Company leapt from nothing before 1757 to almost £2 million in 1761–64, and to almost £7.5 million in 1766–69. With the aid of these funds (all paid in silver), it proved possible to build impregnable fortifications and to raise armies large enough to intervene effectively in the Deccan, in Mysore – indeed, anywhere in the subcontinent.[67] By 1782 the British were able to maintain 115,000 men in India (90 per cent of them sepoys) and reduce the odds against them in battle from the 10 to 1 of Plassey to only 2 to 1 against states such as Mysore. The prospect of the European domination of India, to match the European domination of America, now became a real possibility.[68]

And then, at the eleventh hour (as it were), some native rulers adopted Western military techniques with such success that the British were stopped in their tracks. Under the direction of over 100 European experts (mostly French), excellent bronze artillery was cast for the Maratha confederation which even Sir Arthur Wellesley (later duke of Wellington) found 'answers for our service'; and the new field guns were supplied to the Maratha sepoys, also directed by Europeans, on a more generous scale than the British – each Maratha battalion had five field pieces against the British two. Indeed, Wellesley considered himself lucky to win at Assaye in 1803: 'The battle was the most severe that, I believe, was ever fought in India,' he wrote. Two years later General Lake, after another hard-won victory over the Marathas at Laswari, wrote that 'Had we not made a disposition for attack in a style that we should have done against the most formidable enemy … we might have failed'; while Major Thorne, a survivor of both battles, wrote a lengthy *Memoir* some years later to warn the people of Europe of 'the changes that have taken place among the warlike tribes of India, through the introduction of European tactics and French discipline which, combined with their natural courage often bordering on enthusiastic frenzy, and their numerical superiority, has rendered our conflicts with them sanguinary in the extreme'.[69]

But in the end, the greater experience of the European forces told. The Marathas may have possessed an impressive field artillery, but by the 1800s they had still not fully mastered the correct method of deploying it – for almost all the guns were lost after their defeats (71 pieces at Laswari, 98 at Assaye, 164 at Agra). Likewise, the Marathas may have started out with European and Eurasian officers to train their sepoys but, before the crucial battles, most of them were lured away by bribes, leaving the rank-and-file to fight on alone. It seems like another case of routine mimesis: princely India only adopted Western inventions – whether in art, in clothing or in war – reluctantly and, when she did so, imitated too little and too late. But, whatever the reason, the military resources of India, once under European control, were to prove decisive for the further rise of the West. As early as 1762, a detachment of 650 sepoys was sent to assist the British to capture Manila; and after the defeat of the Marathas, such foreign service became more common – in Burma, in East Africa, above all in East Asia. For the Europeans now possessed the means to challenge even their most powerful opponents. The Western armies that invaded China in 1839–42, 1859–60 and 1900 all included important Indian contingents. Immediately after the Boxer Rising, even the traffic of Peking was directed by Sikhs. In the words of the distinguished Sinologist Louis Dermigny: 'It was as if the British had subjugated the Indian peninsula simply in order to use its resources against China'.[70]

III

If, therefore, the native peoples of America, Siberia, Black Africa and the Philippines lost their independence to the Europeans because they had no time to adopt Western military technology, those of the Muslim world apparently succumbed because they saw no need to integrate it into their existing military system. But the peoples of East Asia, by contrast, were able to keep the West at bay throughout the early modern period because, as it were, they already knew the rules of the game. Firearms, fortresses, standing armies and warships had long been part of the military tradition of China, Korea and Japan. Indeed it may be recalled that both bronze and iron artillery were fully developed in China before they spread westwards to Europe (page 83 above). However, after the mid-fourteenth century, contact between the Far East and the Far West diminished, and the subsequent evolution of firearms in the two areas took a somewhat different course. By 1500, the iron and bronze guns of Western manufacture – whether made by Turkish or

Christian founders – proved to be both more powerful and more mobile than those of the East, so that when they were brought to the Orient in the sixteenth century they attracted both attention and imitation. They may have arrived in China as early as the 1520s, perhaps with one of the numerous Ottoman diplomatic missions to the Ming Court; but, if so, knowledge of them seems to have remained confined to government circles. For most Chinese, Western-style firearms were first encountered in the hands of pirates operating from Japan against Fukien in the late 1540s.[71]

Although guns were not widely employed by Ming forces against the *wakō* (page 84 above), they were introduced shortly afterwards on China's northern frontier for use against the nomads of the steppe. In 1564, for example, the Peking garrison replaced their clay-cased cannonballs with lead; and in 1568 these too were abandoned in favour of iron. Then, in the 1570s, under the direction of Ch'i Chi-kuang (who had masterminded the defeat of the pirates), the Great Wall was rebuilt with pill-boxes to shelter musketeers, and the reserve units of the northern army were strengthened with small carts (known as 'battle wagons') each carrying breech-loading light artillery and served by twenty men.[72]

A remarkable source which illustrates the degree to which European weaponry had been adopted on China's northern frontier under the late Ming is the illustrated *Veritable records of the Great Ancestor (Tai-tsu shih-lu)*, compiled in 1635 to record the deeds of Nurhaci, founder of the Ch'ing dynasty (plates 35–36). It is significant that in the pictures of the 'Great Ancestor's' early victories all the guns are on the side of the Ming: the Imperial armies are shown deploying field-guns, mounted either on trestles or on two-wheeled 'battle wagons', while the northern warriors seem to rely on their horse-archers.[73] But in 1629, the Ch'ing attacked and annexed four Chinese cities south of the Great Wall: in one of them, Yung-p'ing, a Chinese artillery crew 'familiar with the techniques of casting Portuguese artillery' was also captured. By 1631, some forty of the new European-style artillery pieces had been made by the captives and, directed by men who had received either first- or second-hand training from Portuguese gunners, they were soon in action against Ming positions. Gradually, as shown in later illustrations from the *Tai-tsu shih-lu*, they appeared on the Ch'ing side.

But firearms remained only a minor part of the armament of Chinese armies. After all, the Ming supported (in theory at least) some 500,000 men and 100,000 horses on the northern frontier, while the Ch'ing army that entered Peking in 1644 probably numbered 280,000 warriors: it would have been almost impossible to equip all these troops with Western-style firearms.[74] So the soldiers of the new dynasty continued to fight in the traditional manner until the nineteenth century. It is true that, in 1675, the Chinese Imperial army was supported by 150 heavy guns and numerous batteries of field artillery, cast under the direction of Jesuit missionaries in Peking; but this

35–36 *Firearms in the battles between the Ming and Ch'ing* for control of China all appeared, at first, on the side of the Ming. However, in the later 1620s and in the 1630s the northerners began to use artillery as well as archery to defeat their foe. These pictures from the *Tai-tsu shih-lu* ('Veritable records of the Great Ancestor', sc. Nurhaci), with captions in both Chinese

and Manchu, were originally prepared around 1635 and suggest that, although the Ming possessed numerous types of firearms and gun-carriages, they seemed unable to use them effectively.

was a specific campaign against dangerous domestic enemies (the 'Three Feudatories' and their supporters).[75] At other times, the main strength of the Ch'ing lay in the overwhelming numbers of their armed forces.[76]

The Japanese, however, whose armies in the mid-sixteenth century were considerably smaller than those of their great continental neighbour (even though much larger as a percentage of the total population), made far more use of Western firearms. It is generally accepted that they were first introduced by some Portuguese castaways in 1543, on the island of Tanegashima south of Kyushu, and that they were quickly copied by Japanese metalsmiths.[77] Muskets were used effectively in battle by the army of Takeda Shingen in 1555 and a spectacular demonstration of the power of Japanese musketry occurred on 21 May 1575 at the battle of Nagashino. The warlord Oda Nobunaga deployed 3,000 musketeers in ranks in this action, having trained them to fire in volleys so as to maintain a constant barrage (plate 37). The opposing cavalry – ironically of the same Takeda clan which had pioneered the use of the gun – was annihilated. The battle-scene in Kurosawa's film *Kagemusha (The Shadow Warrior)* offers a credible reconstruction, for the action is intended to represent Nagashino.[78]

The originality of Japan's rapid adoption of the gun has perhaps not always been fully appreciated. In the first place, whereas Europe concentrated on increasing the speed of reloading, the Japanese were more interested in improving accuracy. So Western military manuals explained primarily how a soldier could recharge his weapon more rapidly, while Japanese treatises – from the 1550s onwards – gave instruction on how he could take better aim. The *Tanegashima* were, for their day, remarkably accurate. But this in fact accentuated the crucial defect of the muzzle-loading musket: the length of time required to recharge it. As noted above (pages 18–19), the only way to overcome this disadvantage was to draw up the musketeers in ranks, firing in sequence, so that the front file could reload while the others behind fired. This solution was not even suggested in Europe until 1594, and it did not pass into general use there until the 1630s. Yet Oda Nobunaga had experimented with musketry salvoes in the 1560s, and he achieved his first major victory with the technique in 1575, twenty years before the European innovation.[79]

By the time Nobunaga was assassinated, in 1582, he had conquered about half of the provinces of Japan; after a brief hiatus of disorder, the work was continued by two of his most brilliant generals, first Toyotomi Hideyoshi and then Tokugawa Ieyasu. As further provinces were brought under central authority, the size of the main army was swollen by contingents from Hideyoshi's new vassals and allies. In 1587, when he decided to invade the island of Kyushu, almost 300,000 troops were mobilized. The island was conquered in a matter of weeks. The reunification of Japan might perhaps have been achieved without the gun, but the ability to turn large numbers of peasants

37 *The battle of Nagashino,* 1575, marked a decisive stage in the reunification of Japan
after almost a century of civil war. The troops of Oda Nobunaga, on the left, used volley-fire
from their Western-style muskets to destroy the charges of the Takeda cavalry. It was a
striking demonstration of the power of firearms, which now assumed a prominent (if
transient) place in Japanese warfare.

into effective musketeers certainly accelerated the process. As Ieyasu informed the king of Siam in 1610: 'guns and gunpowder are ... what I desire more than gold'.[80]

Nobunaga and his successors also saw the usefulness of the heavier guns used by the Westerners, and they seem to have realized immediately that artillery would render indefensible almost every existing castle and fortress in Japan, since (as in Europe) any wall that was built high, in order to keep besiegers out, was thereby rendered vulnerable to the impact of artillery bombardment. A new sort of defensive fortification therefore emerged, situated on a ridge which was surrounded by stone walls in such a way that they could be backed by solid rock and soil. A prototype was built by Nobunaga himself beside Lake Biwa at Azuchi, between 1576 and 1579, using the combination of hilltop and thick stone walls to produce a virtually solid bailey, surrounding a seven-storey keep of unparalleled beauty.[81] But Azuchi was almost totally destroyed after its creator's murder (although the ruins of the outer walls and the surviving foundations of the keep are still impressive). Even less remains of another massive fortress of this period: Odawara, the stronghold of the Hojo clan, large enough to shelter 40,000 warriors and surrounded by twenty outlying forts. It required an army of over 100,000 men to starve it out in the summer of 1590 and was destroyed after its capture by Toyotomi Hideyoshi – giving rise to a popular doggerel the following year:

So what's the use of hauling rocks and building castles?
Just look at Azuchi and Odawara![82]

Rather more exists today of the even larger citadels built by Hideyoshi and his followers, who preferred to fortify isolated hills on the plain. There is a remarkable homogeneity about the sixty or so surviving castles built in Japan between 1580 and 1630 from Sendai in the north to Kagoshima in the south, even though some were bigger than others. Kato Kiyomasa's castle at Kumamoto, for example, was twelve kilometres in circumference (with forty-nine turrets and two keeps); Ikeda Terumasa's beautiful 'White Heron castle' at Himeji, almost as large, was constructed with an estimated 103,000 tons of stone (plate 38); while the walls of Tokugawa Hidetada's vast citadel at Osaka extended for over thirteen kilometres. Some of the individual stones used to build the defences of Osaka weighed 120 and 130 tons each and were brought to the site from all over Japan by feudatories anxious to prove their loyalty to the regime; even today each daimyo's mark can still be seen, affixed to 'their' rocks (which were also given special auspicious names). With such blocks, more appropriate to a pyramid than to a castle, walls were built that were in places nineteen metres thick.[83] Quite possibly (as Professor J. W. Hall pointed out some years ago) these Japanese castles had 'no peers in terms of size and impregnability' anywhere else in the early modern world.[84]

38 *The castle of Himeji*, known as the 'White Heron' because from a distance it seemed
like a great bird about to take off from the plain on which it stood, was just one of the
sixty or so massive fortresses built in Japan in the half-century after 1580. They were all
given solid foundations, and employed bastions much as the *trace italienne* did. They were,
to all intents and purposes, impregnable until the age of aerial bombardment.

Once again we find that, although the Japanese leaders were perfectly
prepared to take over Western military innovations, they always adapted
them to local conditions in a distinctive way.[85] Early modern China, however,
had no need of Western examples in the art of defensive construction: her
rulers had already been living with gunpowder for centuries, and the massive
fortifications erected under the Ming dynasty had been designed to resist
both artillery bombardment and mining. It is true that the Chinese had no
castles, preferring to fortify whole towns – indeed the Chinese character most
often translated as 'wall' (*cheng*) is also the character most often translated
as 'city' – but these towns were surrounded by massive walls (fifteen
metres thick in places) that could withstand even modern shells. Thus
in 1841, during the Opium Wars, a two-hour battery from a 74-gun
Royal Navy warship on a fort outside Canton 'produced no effect
whatever', according to an eye-witness. 'The principle of their construction was such as to render them almost impervious to the efforts of
horizontal fire, even from the 32-pounders'. Likewise, the British expeditionary force sent to China in 1860 found the walls of Peking impregnable.
According to the British commander, General Grant:

Ancient history tells us the walls of Babylon were so broad that several chariots
could be driven abreast on top of them; but I really think those of Peking must
have exceeded them. They were upwards of 50 feet in breadth, very nearly the
same in height, and paved on the top where, I am sure, five coaches-and-four could
with a little management have been driven abreast.[86]

Thus the scale of fortification in East Asia in effect rendered siege-guns useless. That may be why indigenous heavy artillery never really developed there: in Japan, it was only seriously deployed against Osaka in 1615 and against a rebellion at Shimabara in 1636–7 (and on both occasions it proved indecisive); in China, it was seldom used offensively except during the 1670s. In both empires, sieges were usually decided by mass assaults, mining or blockades rather than by bombardment.[87] Heavy guns, both of traditional and of Western manufacture, were certainly employed to defend the massive walls; but, otherwise, the use of artillery in the land warfare of East Asia was confined to the field.

Even so, the great states of East Asia paid more attention to the military innovations of the Europeans than to any other aspect of Western culture (except, perhaps, for astronomy and the clock). But this paradox may easily be explained when it is remembered that the seaborne arrival of the Europeans in the Far East coincided with a period of sustained political disintegration in both China and Japan. In the former, instability lasted roughly from the renewal of pirate attacks on Fukien in the 1540s to the suppression of the last of the Ming loyalists in the 1680s; in the latter, the era of civil war lasted from the start of the Onin war in 1467 to the fall of Odawara in 1590. Throughout this long period, every military innovation was naturally accorded close attention; but once stability was restored, the value of such things as firearms diminished. In China, they were largely confined to the frontiers; in Japan, most remained in government arsenals, and throughout the century the production of guns (which could only be made under licence) was steadily reduced.[88]

But Japan did not merely 'give up' the gun. After 1580, successive central governments carried out a series of 'sword hunts' aimed at removing *all* weapons from the temples, the peasants, the townsmen – from anyone who might try to resist the administration's taxes or policies. Some of the confiscated swords were melted down to make a great metal Buddha at Kyoto, while others were kept in state arsenals for use in emergencies (for instance during the invasions of Korea during the 1590s), until in the end wearing the sword became largely confined to the hereditary arms-bearing class (the samurai). However, although the samurai might be left with their swords, they were deprived of most of their castles: starting (again) in 1580, the central government commenced a systematic destruction of the fortifications belonging to its defeated enemies. Then, in 1615, the shogun decreed that each lord could thenceforth maintain only one castle: all the rest should be destroyed. Thus in the western province of Bizen, for example, where there had been over 200 fortified places at the end of the fifteenth century, there were only ten by the 1590s, and after 1615 only one – the great 'Raven Castle' at Okayama. This 'demilitarization' of Japan even affected literature. For some decades after 1671, the importation of all foreign books concerning military matters (and Christianity) was forbidden; and the *Honcho Gunki-ko (On the military equipment of our country)*, completed in 1722 and published in 1737, contained only one chapter on firearms, and that was brief.[89]

But by that time the West had also largely lost interest in Japan, for the European presence in East Asia had changed substantially. The Dutch had been expelled from Taiwan in the 1660s (page 113 above) and their factory in Japan no longer yielded vast profits; the Iberian powers had lost much of their trading empire in the Orient; and the English East India Company still traded relatively little in the Far East. So China and Japan remained largely unchallenged by the Europeans during the eighteenth century; nor did they threaten each other.[90] The distinctive 'world order' of both China and Japan endured intact until the Industrial nations of the West deployed steamships, steel artillery and sepoys against them in the mid-nineteenth century. They did not fall before the military revolution.

5

Beyond the revolution

The tools of empire used to overthrow the Marathas, the Ch'ing and the Tokugawa were totally different from those used to subjugate the Aztecs or the Incas. Clearly, in the three intervening centuries, a major transformation in European military and naval power had taken place, a transformation so profound that it must surely rank as a 'revolution'. But one of the greatest problems in writing the history of revolutions is to establish the true dates at which they began and ended. The separation of preconditions from precipitants, and of continuity from change, sometimes seems to promote more controversy than the details of the phenomenon itself. Thus, to take an extreme example, a vigorous debate continues amongst historians concerning the origins of the 'English Revolution' (as the revolts against the Stuarts in Scotland, Ireland and England between 1642 and 1660 are somewhat misleadingly known). Some have traced the process back to the introduction of the Reformation into England in the 1530s; others have seen a significant break with the past either during the 1620s, when the government lost the confidence of its Parliaments in the three kingdoms, or in the 1630s, when the king tried to rule the three kingdoms without Parliaments. But, more recently, claims to detect a long 'high road to Civil War' have been challenged on the grounds that, although relations between government and governed had certainly reached crisis-point by 1640, the situation then was not much worse than in some similar confrontations of earlier years. For the revisionists, the road to revolution only began with the failure of the English 'Short Parliament' in May 1640.[1] In much the same way, the precise point at which the revolution ceased has been hotly disputed. The 'Restoration' has been successively back-dated – from the return of Charles II in 1660 to the death of Cromwell in 1658, to the presentation of the Humble Petition and Advice in 1657, even to the creation of more conservative regimes in Scotland and Ireland in 1654–5.[2]

Fixing the chronology of the military revolution of early modern Europe is no easier; indeed it is at first sight rendered more difficult by the fact that the various changes in the scale and nature of war described in the preceding chapters were accompanied by changes in the structure and nature of the states which fought them. This should not surprise us for, as noted in chapter 2 above, the growth of an effective bureaucracy was an essential prerequisite for the creation, control and supply of larger and better-equipped armies. Thus the great leap in army size in the 1530s and 40s was accompanied by a major reorganization of government in most Western states in which the inherited administrative system (based on the household) gave way to a more complex bureaucratic edifice; while the further period of rapid increase in manpower between 1672 and 1710 was associated with the rise of absolutism – especially in the states that had been prominent in the Thirty Years War and had experienced a collapse in the pyramid of command during it (France, Sweden, Austria and Prussia). By the time of Louis XIV's death in 1715, the nature of government in most European countries had assumed a form that was to last until the 1790s.[3] Perhaps this broad administrative chronology offers a useful clue as to the date at which the military revolution came to an end. Michael Roberts originally proposed a transitional date of 1660, just before the prodigious armies and absolute states of Louis XIV and his contemporaries. However, the military methods, aims and problems of – say – Marlborough and Prince Eugene resemble those of Cromwell and Turenne too closely to permit a firm line to be drawn between them. And the same could be said of their successors: the campaigns of the Maréchal de Saxe or Frederick the Great in the mid-eighteenth century were not very different from those of Marlborough and his contemporaries either.

Categorizing Frederick II of Prussia (1740–86) as an exponent of the traditional art of war, rather than as the initiator of a new one, is controversial. When Hans Delbrück argued the case in *The strategy of Pericles illuminated by the strategy of Frederick the Great* (published in 1890), he sparked off a furious debate that lasted for twenty years. But he was surely right, for Frederick's wars were still dynastic rather than national, and his strategy aimed at attrition rather than annihilation (because the king lacked the resources either to destroy his enemies or otherwise to impose his will on them).[4] Furthermore, the size and composition of Frederick's armies were not much different from those of earlier rulers. During the Seven Years War (1756–63), Prussia's armed forces totalled about 150,000 men, rising to perhaps 200,000 in 1786; and, as in the continental armies of the seventeenth century, one-third of the men were normally foreigners. In few of Frederick's battles – which were numerous – did the king command more than 40,000 men, of whom up to 40 per cent might become casualties, even in victory.[5] This appalling wastage was due to further improvements in firepower since the days of Marlborough. Speed, not accuracy, remained the supreme goal and so the length of musket barrels was reduced and drill was intensified until Frederick's musketeers, drawn up in three ranks, were able to equal the continuous fire once achieved by Maurice of Nassau's army drawn up in ten. At the battle of Leuthen, in 1757, some of the Prussian musketeers fired off 180 rounds at the enemy. But at such speed, and with such weapons, accuracy was impossible. The drill-books of the Prussian army contained no command for 'take aim' (the troops just fired straight ahead) and their guns, like the English 'Brown Bess', possessed no sights.[6]

But these tactics of rapid fire at close range, with the consequent heavy losses of men, called for a far better supply of war materials than previous armies had enjoyed. In this lay Frederick's major military achievement. The Splitgerber and Daum arms factory at Potsdam, for example, turned out 15,000 muskets a year in the 1740s, while the annual powder production of Prussia rose from 448,000 pounds in 1746 to 560,000 pounds in 1756. The commissariat placed contracts for munitions supply two years ahead so that, according to Frederick himself, 'the army never ran short of what it needed, even though we had some campaigns which cost us 40,000 muskets and 20,000 horses'. Food rations were also accumulated on a massive scale: by 1776 the military magazines of Berlin and Breslau alone contained 76,000 bushels of grain or flour – enough to feed an army of 60,000 men for two years. And finally, new uniforms of standard design were issued annually to every regiment by its own individual manufacturers, whose blue cloth 'though coarser, wears better and has a more decent appearance, when long worn, than the finest cloth manufactured in England or France'.[7]

But the cost of all this was crippling. In human terms, the wars consumed too many men. The Prussian army may have been the fourth or fifth largest in Europe, and the largest of any European state *per capita*, but the Prussian population was only the thirteenth largest: almost a quarter of its young men were conscripted into the army, and the death of almost 180,000 of them during the Seven Years War – equivalent to a survival rate of only one in fifteen for those in the ranks when hostilities began in 1756 – was as deleterious in demographic terms as the slaughter of the Thirty Years War had been to Sweden (page 53 above). In financial terms, too, the cost was unacceptably high: 90 per cent of Frederick the Great's receipts were spent on war. It was enough to support an army of almost 200,000, but only by cutting corners: the currency was debased; contributions and plunder were ruthlessly extracted; no money was spent on curing wounded troops; and officers were not allowed to marry because Frederick could not afford to pay pensions to military widows.[8]

The originality of Frederick's military system thus lay principally in his improvements in supply, which allowed him to move his armies relatively swiftly and in relatively good order (provided they did not stray too far from Prussian territory); and in the superior discipline of his troops, which allowed the king to direct surprise attacks under the noses of his enemies (manoeuvres which, in other armies, would have produced chaos). But it was still not enough to secure decisive victories. Frederick's only substantial gain by war was the capture of Silesia in 1741; after that, he became a staunch defender of the military status quo. In 1775 he wrote:[9]

The ambitious should consider above all that armaments and military discipline being much the same throughout Europe, and alliances as a rule producing an equality of force between belligerent parties, all that princes can expect from the greatest advantages at present is to acquire, by accumulation of successes, either some small city on the frontier, or some territory which will not pay interest on the expenses of the war, and whose population does not even approach the number of citizens who perished in the campaigns.

Precisely the same sentiments, albeit less elegantly expressed, could have been written by almost any early modern statesman, for Frederick's Prussia (like its principal enemies) was not very different from the states of seventeenth-century Europe. Society was still rigidly hierarchical, with most wealth and power concentrated in the hands of the aristocracy; and armies naturally reflected this state of affairs – the officers of Frederick II, as of Louis XV, were all (or almost all) noblemen; the rank and file were all commoners; and up to half of them were foreigners, some of them even enlisted prisoners of war. Likewise the resources for financing war remained, for most eighteenth-century governments, similar to those of Philip II or Charles V; while the roads and transport available were also little better in most parts of Europe in 1750 than in 1550.[10] Just as the middle decades of the eighteenth century represented the apogee of the *ancien régime*, so the same period saw the culmination of 'the military revolution'.

By the time of Frederick's death in 1786, however, the military system of early modern Europe was clearly changing. In the first place, new varieties of regular troops appeared: the light infantry and light cavalry. They first achieved prominence in 1740–1, when Frederick of Prussia's surprise attack on the Habsburg empire was halted with the aid of some 20,000 veterans from the military border with the Turks, in Hungary and Croatia. These lightly armed skirmishers, few of whom wore uniforms, were described by an English observer as:

fierce, undisciplined and subject to scarcely any military laws. They were attached to the house of Austria by prejudices and predilections of religion, manners and education, peculiar to themselves ... A degree of primeval rudeness and simplicity characterizes them, totally unlike the spirit which animates the mercenary stipendiary of modern armies.

Their success against the best-trained regular troops in Europe came as a surprise (despite the fact that they had just withstood the Turks in 1737–9) and it caught the attention of other military leaders.[11] In 1742–3 the king of Savoy, defending his mountainous state against the Bourbons, also made extensive use of irregular forces in the Alps; and in 1743 the maréchal de

Saxe, who had once served in Hungary, introduced light infantry to the French army. Later, when the war was over and military commentators began to pick over the lessons and achievements to be digested, several reported favourably on the light troops and their tactics: the lord of La Croix in his *Treatise on small wars* of 1752, Turpin de Crissé in his *Essay on the art of war* of 1754, and the fifty or so other volumes on 'small wars' published in Europe between 1750 and 1800 all praised the 'light troops'.[12] Some of these works were read attentively by British army officers and, when regular battalions went to America after 1755 to fight against the French and their Indian allies, they adopted in part the techniques of irregular warfare recommended by La Croix and Turpin. According to one officer in the colonies, troops there:

> require no exercise but to be perfectly acquainted with the use of their arms, that is to load quick and hit the mark, and for military discipline but this one rule: if they are attacked by French and Indians to rush to all parts from where their fire comes.[13]

Admittedly, not all the experts were convinced of the need for light troops. Even after Austrian hussars made a raid deep into Prussian territory in 1757 and (briefly) captured Berlin, Frederick the Great refused to follow suit. Instead, obsessed by the fear that his expensively trained infantry would seize every available opportunity to desert, he surrounded his camps with fences, avoided marches through forests, and even forbore to send out scouting parties more than 200 metres ahead of the army for fear that his men would run away. He viewed organized skirmishing merely as a licence to escape. But he was wrong: the 'light' infantry and cavalry had come to stay.[14]

Another innovation of the War of the Austrian Succession (1740–8) was the organization of large armies into a number of self-suffficient units called divisions. Pierre de Bourcet's *Principles of mountain warfare*, composed in the 1760s, proposed that the ideal army should be made up of three separate columns, each of them one day's march (or less) distant from the others, so that the enemy should never know the point at which the force would concentrate and attack. The technique had worked well in the Franco-Spanish Alpine campaigns against Savoy in 1744–8 (in which Bourcet served as a staff engineer officer), but it met with considerable opposition from the army establishment. Only in 1787–8 did the French adopt the division as the basic administrative unit, so that up to 12,000 infantry, cavalry and artillery units, together with engineers and other ancillary groups, were organized under a single commander and his staff. Divisional organization in the field, however, was harder to achieve (and did not become standard in France until 1796) because of the relative scarcity of the roads and maps which would allow a large army to disperse, coordinate its movements, and reassemble swiftly.[15] Even in the Seven Years War, armies had managed to march off their maps, and suffered defeats through ignorance of topography. Not until the 1780s, with the enormous Josephine survey of all lands of the Austrian Habsburgs (in 5,400 sheets) and Cassini's massive cartographic survey of France, was the continental road network full surveyed and thus made available to military planners and generals. And that road network was now more extensive and better maintained than ever before: bridges were regularly repaired and road surfaces were often paved; and if strategy called for a road where none existed, the expanding corps of engineers and pioneers in the service of most governments could soon build one, as the British army did in Scotland in the mid-eighteenth century – 1,500 kilometres were constructed at a cost of £50 per kilometre (plate 39). In some areas of the continent there was also a programme of canal-building specifically to carry vital war materials swiftly from the centres of production to the army's magazines.[16]

These changes in the art of war in the later eighteenth century were accompanied by the creation, for the first time, of a powerful yet fully mobile field artillery. The guns of Louis XIV's day had been cast with the possibility in mind that they might, in case of need, be used against fortresses in sieges as well as against troops in battle: so their barrels were relatively long and thick, in order to withstand a heavy powder charge. But under Louis XV, attempts were made to produce shorter, lighter pieces that, although less useful in sieges, would be equally effective in the field. Under the enlightened direction of Jean Baptiste de Gribeauval, the calibres, carriages and equipment of the French artillery were standardized, and their parts were made interchangeable (thanks to the ability of industrial plants to mass-produce identical, precise and highly durable metalwork). At the same time, gunfounders in French service demonstrated that, with more accurate casting, the powder required for effective firing of cannon could be reduced by 50 per cent, making it possible to slim down gun barrels considerably, since the concussion was less. In the course of the 1750s and 60s, the weight of a French four-pounder field gun dropped from 1,300 pounds to only 600. At this weight, it could easily be drawn by only three horses (and handled by a mere eight men) and so could keep up even with the more mobile armies and divisions of the day.[17]

These three transformations – the use of light troops and skirmishers; the introduction of divisions and a more mobile strategy; and the creation of a swift and powerful field artillery – were associated after 1793 with a further revolution in military manpower. Once again, the French led the way. The royal army in 1788–9, on the eve of the Revolution, stood at some 150,000 men. By August 1793 its paper strength had reached 645,000 and the celebrated *levée en masse* probably doubled this figure. By September 1794, the army of the Republic numbered, at least in theory, 1,169,000 men.[18] Needless to say, reality lagged somewhat behind expectation. There

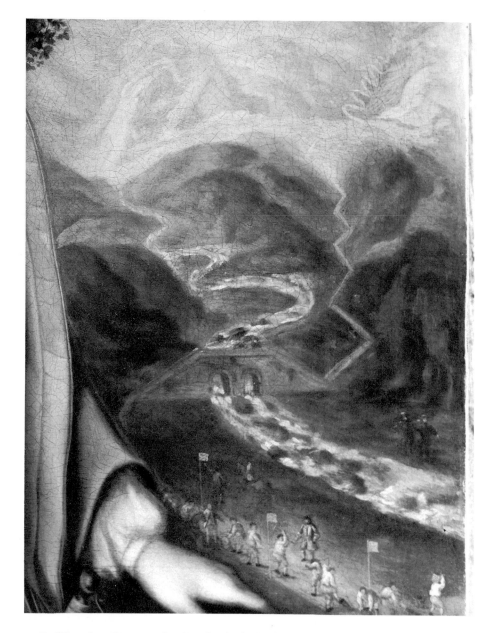

39 *Building the military roads of Scotland.* The background to a portrait of General George Wade shows the achievement for which he is best-known: road building in the Scottish Highlands. In the decades following the Jacobite rebellion of 1715, Wade's engineers surveyed, levelled and paved roads, bridged rivers, and crossed mountains (the switchback shown in the picture is probably the pass of Corrieyairick, 800 metres high, between Speyside and the Great Glen, where Wade built a road; and the bridge is probably that at either Perth or Aberfeldy). Roads, however, are neutral and, in the 1745 rebellion, the Jacobites made excellent use of Wade's roads in their lightning march towards the Lowlands. (Detail from a 'Portrait of General George Wade'.)

was very high wastage among the recruits – probably only 730,000 men were actually with the colours in September 1794 – and their equipment was often far inferior to that of the old royal army. For example, at first it proved impossible to clothe all the men in the same uniform, and some local authorities in 1793–4 were forced to order 'coats and trousers of the material that most closely resembles the "national blue"'; while others revived the pike for their recruits 'because it is the only appropriate weapon, given the short time available for instruction'. But such temporary problems were only to be expected, for no European state had ever attempted – let alone managed – to raise, equip and maintain an army of 730,000 men. In all, perhaps 3 million soldiers served in the armies of France between 1792 and 1815, providing her rulers with an almost irresistible concentration of force. In 1805, 176,000 French troops, with 286 field guns, moved through Germany on a 400-kilometre front; in 1812, the *Grande Armée* of 600,000 men, with 1,146 field guns, invaded Russia on a 400-kilometre front.[19]

Here at last was an army large enough to break the stranglehold of the *trace italienne*. The French did not sweep aside the problems posed by bastioned fortifications; indeed, as at Torres Vedras in Portugal in 1810, a well-defended position could still paralyse a mighty army. But, for most of the time, the armies were now so mighty that there were enough men to allow commanders to encircle the enemy's strategic fortresses, to defend their own, and yet still be able to lead forces of unprecedented size into the field. This was clearly warfare on a totally different plane to anything previously seen in Europe. Napoleon's armies may have fought in much the same way as those of Frederick, Marlborough or Gustavus Adolphus; and Napoleon, marooned in Egypt in 1798–9, may have asked the Paris government to send him military histories of the Thirty Years War to read. But the scale of warfare was by then so totally transformed that it might be said that another 'military revolution' had occurred.

The evolution of naval warfare was roughly similar. The near-equilibrium of the three navies of north-west Europe in the later seventeenth century (page 103 above) was shattered in the later eighteenth because Britain forged ahead while the others did not. In 1789, there were perhaps 440 ships-of-the-line in Europe's navies, of which almost one-third (153) were British, all of them equipped with standard, mass-produced steel cannon. But by 1810, after almost twenty years of continuous war at sea, the Royal Navy comprised over 1,000 purpose-built warships (243 of them ships-of-the-line) with a total displacement of 861,000 tons and a complement of 142,000 men. These, too, represented an almost irresistible concentration of force, which could be applied anywhere in the world. It was from this position of overwhelming strength that Britannia could, and did, rule the waves.[20]

However, these achievements in land and sea warfare represented another threshold beyond which, for several decades, European states could not pass.

The concentration of such large armies and fleets strained to the limit the expanded economic, political and technological resources which had permitted their creation. Even the system of command and supply that had served to conquer Italy and Germany for *La Grande Nation* failed when it was applied to the larger armies required to invade Spain and Russia. Telegraph, railways, and breech-loading firearms were needed before armies larger than those favoured by Napoleon could operate effectively; and it required the iron-clad steamship to challenge effectively the supremacy of the Nelsonian ship-of-the-line.[21] Not until then did the Europeans at last possess the means to subjugate those peoples who had so far escaped their embrace. In February 1841, on her way to Canton during the first Opium War, for example, the two pivot-mounted 32 pounders of the iron built steamship *Nemesis* destroyed, in just one day, nine war-junks, five forts, two military stations and one shore battery. In 1853, at Sinop, the destruction of the Turkish navy by Russian steamships opened the Ottoman empire to Western exploitation. And in 1863, a belated attempt by the Tokugawa government to exclude western warships from Japanese waters ended in catastrophic failure, with the Royal Navy closing in (despite a typhoon) to destroy all shipping (and large parts of the town) at Kagoshima, while the French, Netherlands, American and British navies combined to silence the modern gun batteries in the straits of Shimonoseki.[22] Meanwhile, at much the same time, the rapid-firing guns of the White Men swiftly and brutally overcame all resistance by the nativetribes and nations of the American plains and the African interior.

The West had now indeed risen. In a way that few could have foreseen, the sustained preoccupation of the European states with fighting each other by land and sea had at length paid handsome dividends. Thanks above all to their military superiority, founded upon the military revolution of the sixteenth and seventeenth centuries, the Western nations had managed to create the first global hegemony in History.

6

Afterword: in defence of The military revolution

Although *The military revolution* is a relatively small book, it took twenty years to write.[1] I had read and enjoyed Michael Roberts's seminal article before starting work on my dissertation and, while studying the Spanish Army of Flanders for my Ph.D. between 1965 and 1968, I looked for evidence that would support his model of a backward, benighted, ineffectual force. But I failed to find it. Instead at the battle of Nördlingen in 1634, Habsburg troops fighting in traditional fashion inflicted a crushing and decisive defeat on the masters of the new military science, forcing Sweden and her allies to abandon all their conquests in south Germany. It was most puzzling and the last chapter of my dissertation, entitled 'A military revolution?', expressed my doubts. With that grim humour for which academics are famous, the History Faculty Board of Cambridge University appointed Michael Roberts to serve as my external examiner; I walked to my oral defence with heavy heart. Much to my relief, however, that generous and gracious man told me that he found my critique convincing and advised me to publish it separately as an article, instead of tucking it away at the back of a book. In the event, I transferred some of the material to the front, to form the introductory chapter of *The Army of Flanders and the Spanish Road* (1972), and published the rest in 1976 as 'The military revolution, 1550–1660 – a myth?'.

And there the matter rested until the summer of 1982 when, while beginning research at the archives of Simancas for a book on the Spanish Armada, I received an invitation from the Master and Fellows of Trinity College Cambridge to deliver four lectures on a topic – any topic – concerning Military History. Simon Adams, then also working at Simancas, suggested that I might take the opportunity to develop the theme advanced in that first chapter of *The Army of Flanders and the Spanish Road*: namely that early modern warfare involved far more sieges than battles, and that 'actions' between men with firearms in and around the trenches proved far more common than full-scale encounters decided by sabre and lance in the field.

It sounded so simple, but it turned into something that took me around the world in search of material. I decided to begin by arguing that the emergence around 1520 of new techniques of artillery-resistant fortification – the most successful of which was known in Italy as *alla moderna* (in the modern style) and elsewhere as the *trace italienne* – led not only to the predominance of protracted sieges in Western warfare, but also to substantial increases in the size and dramatic changes in the composition of armies. For to capture a town or city defended by bastions required large numbers of disciplined infantry, not an elite force of knightly cavalry; while to defend one's own expanding stock of new-style fortresses also called for unprecedented numbers of men and guns. These related developments presented the states of early modern Europe with two new sets of problems: how best to deploy the new infantry in action, and how to maintain them. Solutions to both came but slowly. The first problem gave rise to a succession of experiments to maximize the firepower of the troops and to increase the proportion of an army able to engage the enemy directly in action. The second produced a whole range of logistical challenges, for if armies now needed to be substantially larger and better armed, how could they be recruited and kept up to strength, clothed and fed, equipped and paid? And how were the expensive new defences to be financed? Moreover the sixteenth century also saw a revolution in naval warfare, with the invention of the immensely expensive ship-of-the-line, which defeated its foes by artillery broadsides instead of by ramming or boarding. Over a century elapsed before the European states had expanded their administrative apparatus sufficiently to cope with all the logistical and financial consequences of the military revolution.

These innovations proved highly significant for non-Europeans as well. On the one hand, the technique of gunnery bombardment at sea (and of building ships sturdy enough to deploy heavy cannon effectively) was unknown to most other societies, and so conferred an instant advantage on the Europeans as they sought to expand; on the other, thanks to the *trace italienne*, the small European enclaves perched around the coasts of Asia and Africa could defend themselves efficiently against their powerful neighbours until help arrived. The whole thrust of the enterprise therefore changed from a reconsideration of the military history of early modern Europe to an attempt to explain the rise of the West.

Researching all this took me to libraries, archives and museums not only in Europe, but also in India and Ceylon, in east and south Africa, and in east and southeast Asia. In Japan I found a remarkable parallel, for warfare there in the sixteenth century evolved in almost exactly the same sequence as in Europe: the introduction of firearms seemed to produce massive new artillery fortresses, huge armies and rapid state-building, culminating in vigorous overseas expansion (the Korean campaigns of Toyotomi Hideyoshi in the 1590s).[2] Encouraged by this unexpected corroboration, I delivered the four Lees Knowles lectures at Cambridge in 1984 and, after substantial revision and expansion, plus a visit to consult with Michael Roberts, published them in 1988.

On the whole, *The military revolution* received a good press. Translations appeared in Spanish, French, German, Italian and Japanese; and a lively debate ensued.[3] Even Islamic fundamentalists welcomed it (at least until the Gulf War). 'The lessons for Muslims of today are obvious', claimed a long review in the journal *Crescent*: 'To ensure freedom from and victory against the adversaries [i.e. the West], military adaptation and innovation are imperative.'[4] So far, the only substantial critical notice remains a seven-page 'essay review' by Bert S. Hall and Kelly R. DeVries, published in *Technology and Culture*. The scale, however, is deceptive for 90 per cent of their critique consisted of attacks on my dates,[5] my facts[6] and my *apparatus criticus*.[7]

The sole substantive issue raised by Drs Hall and DeVries was to deny the link I posited between technological innovation and military growth in early modern Europe: 'Like a whole generation of economic historians,' they announced, 'Parker uses technology as a "black box", a primary *explanans* whose nature is itself inexplicable.'[8] Although this important point unfortunately remained tucked away in the final paragraph of their 'essay review', and remained undeveloped, it nevertheless constitutes one of four general criticisms – conceptual, chronological and geographical as well as technological – levelled since 1988 against my analysis of the military revolution of early modern Europe. Each deserves separate consideration.

I Concepts

The most fundamental criticism of the book concerns the use – or misuse – of the term 'revolution' for a process that lasted three centuries. According to Clifford Rogers,

The length of the time involved [in a revolution] can range from a year to a century, depending on the scope of the revolution – depending on whether it is a government, a social structure, an idea or an economy which is overturned – but in none of these cases does the time-frame during which the reversal takes places exceed a single (maximum) human life span.[9]

Now clearly not all 'revolutions' in History are alike. In the political sphere, one expects a 'sharp, sudden change or attempted change in the location of political power which involved either the use or the threat of violence and, if successful, expressed itself in the manifest and perhaps radical transformation of the process of government, the accepted foundations of sovereignty or legitimacy, and the conception of the political and/or social order'.[10] Dramatic changes in other spheres, however, take far longer and present more complexity because they affect, almost by definition, more than one country. One might disqualify the 'agricultural revolution' – the deliberate alteration of natural systems to promote the abundance of exploited plant

and animal species, which occurred independently in three or four different
locations world-wide and took over a millennium in each of them – on the
grounds that it occurred in prehistoric times. However both the scientific
and the industrial revolutions lasted well over a century; and, in the case
of the latter, no sooner had one aspect of the process (harnessing water and
coal to provide energy) been mastered than other sources of power (elec-
tricity and petroleum) superseded it, creating the so-called 'second industrial revolution.'

Attempts have also been made to divide the military revolution into discrete
phases. Jeremy Black has suggested that the 'major changes' in the military
emergence of the West occurred first, during the Renaissance, and again
during the reign of Louis XIV, leaving the 'Roberts century', 1560–1660, 'in
relative terms one of limited change between two periods of greater importance'. Others believe that many of the critical developments took place in
the later Middle Ages.[11] Perhaps it is more fruitful to view the military revolution of early modern Europe as part of a cyclical process. One need not
embrace crude determinism and assert the existence of either 'concentrations of warfare . . . in approximately fifty-year oscillations, each alternating
period of concentration being more severe' (Quincy Wright), or the 'defi-
nite tendency for a periodic increase in the level of violence about every
twenty-five years' (Frank Denton and Warren Philips).[12] Instead Clifford
Rogers has proposed an elegant and convincing 'punctuated equilibrium
model', with early modern 'punctuations' that include the birth of the capital
ship, the spread of the artillery fortress and a major manpower increase
between 1510 and 1560; the emergence of firepower as the dominant element
in warfare by both land and sea between 1580 and 1630; and a further rapid
increase in the size of both armies and navies between 1690 and 1715.[13]

A consequential conceptual difficulty lies in the link between armies navies,
on the one hand, and 'state formation' on the other, in each of these periods
of change. In *A military revolution? Military change and European society,
1550–1800* (London, 1991), Jeremy Black asserted that the rapid growth of
the armed forces of early modern Europe stemmed from political rather
than military factors. Basing his argument upon the dramatic expansion of
Louis XIV's army and navy, he suggested that enhanced state power formed
the critical precondition for military growth. Brian M. Downing, on the
other hand, argued in *The military revolution and political change. Origins
of democracy and autocracy in early modern Europe* (Princeton, 1992) that,
in terms of state-building, the formative stage of the military revolution was
in fact over by the reign of Louis XIV. By then, he claimed, it had already
created the decisive political changes (such as the growth of a powerful
bureaucracy) in several major states of continental Europe that eventually
produced absolutism. So where Black saw political change leading to military revolution, Downing perceived the reverse.

Perhaps both visions contain a measure of truth: clearly the two developments fed upon each other, and indeed required each other. The emergence of the 'Renaissance State', with its more efficient bureaucratic structure and its improved methods of raising money, constituted an essential precondition for the important military changes of the late fifteenth and early sixteenth centuries; while, conversely, the need to mobilize resources for war could enhance governments' power over their subjects. The same pattern recurred in the later seventeenth century. But not all wars produced the same effects. The celebrated formula of Charles Tilly that 'states made war but war also made states' is too simplistic.[14] As I. A. A. Thompson has perceptively noted:

Major hegemonic land wars, fought at a distance from their main resource base, because of their high borrowing requirements, tended to lead to the development of taxation and the fiscal-state; contrariwise, a permanent military establishment could in appropriate circumstances promote the privatization of military and administrative functions by means of the contracting out of funding, maintenance and supply; and protracted wars within the territory of the state could be sustained by a more primitive (from the statist point of view), local fiscality ... The development of the state as a fiscal entity was thus related to the type of military activity in which it was engaged.[15]

In the broad sense, however, Tilly was right: military activity and state formation have always been inextricably linked, and periods of rapid military change have usually coincided with major political innovations. Rather than trying to establish a simple model of causation, we should perhaps envisage something like the 'double helix' structure of the DNA molecule, with two complex spirals interacting at various discrete points over time.[16]

II Chronology

In spite of the doubts expressed by Jeremy Black and others concerning the concept and the precise chronology of the military revolution, the sixteenth century still seems of central importance because it witnessed the emergence of three key innovations: the capital ship with its broadside; the development of gunpowder weapons as the arbiter of battles and sieges; and, in direct response to this, the 'artillery fortress'.

Even contemporaries could see the 'revolutionary' nature of these changes. For example, Francesco Guicciardini – soldier, diplomat and historian – believed in 1509 that the mould of land warfare in his native Italy had been shattered for ever by the arrival in 1494 of modern siege trains. Previously,

When war broke out, the sides were so evenly balanced, the military methods so slow and the artillery so primitive, that the capture of a castle took up almost a whole campaign. Wars lasted a very long time, and battles ended with very few or no deaths. But the French came upon all this like a sudden tempest which turns everything upside down ... Wars became sudden and violent, conquering and capturing a state in less time than it used to take to occupy a village; cities were reduced with great speed, in a matter of days and hours rather than months; battles became savage and bloody in the extreme. In fact states now began to be saved or ruined, lost and captured, not according to plans made in a study as formerly but by feats of arms in the field.[17]

Many other military writers believed that gunpowder weapons distinguished 'Modern' from 'Classical' warfare; Francis Bacon ranked them, together with printing and the compass, as one of the three critical discoveries in the history of humankind; while Campbell Dalrymple, writing in 1761, noted that 'The effect of fire[arms] begins now to be disputed, at least, it is not believed so formidable, as it was; which in time may produce another military revolution, and send us back to the arms in use before the invention of gunpowder.'[18] The same 'revolutionary character' was ascribed by both contemporaries and subsequent generations to the broadside-firing warship and the artillery fortress. Each marked a turning-point after which warfare on sea and land (respectively) could never be the same again; each started an 'arms race' in which states strove first to equal and then to surpass the innovations that had defeated them; each, finally, provided the crucial instruments that enabled the Europeans to acquire trade and territory in Asia, Africa and the Americas.[19]

Admittedly not every part of these three developments occurred exclusively within this period. Writing in the first decade of the sixteenth century the Portuguese conquistador Duarte Pacheco Pereira could already boast that in 'fortresses surrounded by walls . . . Europe excels Asia and Africa; and she also excels them in her larger and better fleets, better equipped and armed than those of all other areas.'[20] And, indeed, gunpowder weapons came into effective use in Europe far earlier and far more widely than many previously thought. They first appeared in the West in the 1320s, and about a century later the crucial invention of 'corning' (turning loose powder into granules) and improvements in manufacture transformed their power and efficiency.[21] However, their effective use on board ships took somewhat longer. Thus some Western vessels – Mediterranean galleys – carried heavy artillery from the 1440s; and pictorial evidence indicates the appearance of gunports as early as the 1470s; but the first vessel capable of firing a broadside, the hallmark of European naval warfare ever since, appears to have been the 1,000-ton *Great Michael*, launched in Scotland in 1511, which carried twelve cannon on each side as well as three 'grete basilisks' at the bow and stern. English and French capital ships of similar design soon followed.[22]

The use of hand-held firearms in battle likewise originated in the fifteenth century, and some of the battles fought by Charles the Rash in the 1470s, and by both Castilian and Granadan troops in the 1480s, saw units equipped with firearms pitted against each other.[23] Given the technological limitations of the available weapons, however, optimum use of handguns in battle required a continuous barrage of fire; and that was only achieved in the later sixteenth century. The idea seems to have appeared first in a treatise written in 1579 by Thomas Digges which argued that, although untrained men should still be formed into squares, experienced soldiers armed with arquebus and musket should 'after the old Romane manner make three or four several fronts, with convenient spaces for the first to retire and unite himselfe with the second, and both these if occasion so require, with the third. The shot having their convenient lanes continually during the fight to discharge their peces.'[24] Martín de Eguiluz, a Spanish veteran with twenty-four years' service, in 1586 likewise advocated forming three files of five soldiers each, in order to maintain a constant fire during a skirmish.[25] In the revised edition of this *Stratioticos* (1590), Digges repeated that musketeers should be drawn up for action in 'three or four rankes at the utmost', but now suggested that when the enemy approached 'the first ranke shal give their volee, and presently deliver their peece to the second ranke to charge againe, taking theirs that are readie charged, with the which they may give another volee'. But, Digges admitted, it was all hypothetical: 'I know this opinion of mine, being different from common custome, will be of the common multitude of such men of warre as can brooke nothing but their owne customes, not onely disliked but derided and contemned.'[26] The origin of continuous volley fire in European warfare therefore seems to originate, as claimed at pp. 18–19 above, with William Louis of Nassau in 1594, who saw the critical link between the massed infantry firepower made available by sixteenth-century technology and the Roman close-order drill described by Aelian. It had become the standard tactic of the army of the Dutch Republic by 1610 at the latest.[27]

Discussion of the third sixteenth-century innovation, the evolution and impact of the artillery fortress, is complicated by its relationship to the contemporaneous rapid growth in army size. It is true that large – sometimes very large – forces had operated during the Middle Ages. For example during the First Crusade, 50,000 combatants may have marched eastwards in 1096–7 with some 35,000 men leaving Constantinople; and the force mustered for the Fourth Crusade in 1202 certainly exceeded 25,000 men, transported in a fleet of 200 Venetian ships.[28] On the eve of the Black Death, Philip VI of France maintained an army of almost 45,000 men in September 1340 while even Edward III of England, ruler of a far smaller state, commanded some 32,000 men at the siege of Calais in 1346–7 (with more in action in Brittany and Guienne and on the Scottish frontier). But these concentrations all proved exceptional and short-lived; moreover in the century 1350–1450 both field armies and total military establishments declined dramatically. However, by the 1480s the French crown once more on occasion maintained over 40,000 troops, with some 24,000 in its campaign armies, while the Catholic Kings subdued Granada with forces that frequently exceeded 60,000 and in the final campaign (1491–2) may have reached 80,000 men.[29]

This upward trend continued and even accelerated during the sixteenth century. French expeditionary forces steadily increased in size – 22,000–29,000 men marched to Italy under Charles VIII and Louis XII, but 36,000 went to Metz in 1552 and 40,000 mustered at Pierrepont in 1558 under Henry II – as did the total armed forces of the crown, at least on paper: 41,000 in 1515, 69,000 or more in 1544 and 80,000 by 1567–8.[30] Meanwhile the armies of France's great rival, the Habsburgs, grew even more: the Emperor Charles V led 42,000 men on his invasion of France in 1544, 56,000 to defeat the Schmalkaldic League in Germany in 1546 and 55,000 men to besiege Metz in 1552.[31] The total number of troops Charles commanded in 1552 approached 150,000 – twice the size of the armies of his grandparents, the Catholic Kings – and his son, grandson and great-grandson all maintained forces of similar dimensions for much of the following century.

But why did the armies of France and the Habsburgs increase in size so rapidly in the mid-sixteenth century? Three possible explanations have been advanced. First, the rise of the 'new monarchies' in the preceding half-century enabled several states to create military bureaucracies capable of raising and maintaining large armies. Events such as the 'Tudor Revolution in Government' occurred at precisely the time when England's armed forces and military expenditure reached unprecedented levels; indeed the latter is inconceivable without the former. But that is not to say that the one caused the other; merely that when it became necessary to increase military establishments, several (but not all) European states proved able to respond. Second, army sizes may also have risen in response to inter-state competition. The election of Charles V as Holy Roman Emperor in 1519 brought together under a single sceptre almost half the lands of Western Europe – Spain, much of Italy, the Netherlands, Franche-Comté, the Empire and even (from 1554 until 1558) England. France was encircled, and the contemporary Habsburg aphorism that 'The heart of the Spanish empire is France' did little to reassure the government in Paris. Francis I and his successor Henry II therefore did everything they could to defeat their more powerful enemy, even if it meant allying with the Turks and with the German Protestants.

According to David Parrott, the rapid increase in military manpower – however caused – produced strategic stagnation. 'The overriding need to pay and supply armies inflated beyond the capacities of their states', he wrote, 'reduced strategy to a crude concern with territorial occupation or its denial to the enemy' in this period.[32] But although examples of armies paralysed by logistics abound, imperfect execution did not always imply absence of planning.[33] In the autumn of 1552, for example, while the Emperor Charles V besieged the 5,800 man garrison of Metz in Lorraine, France's field army hovered in Champagne, in case Metz needed to be relieved and, if not, to invade Flanders (and indeed, in December it seized the fortress of Hesdin, forcing the emperor to abandon the siege of Metz).[34] Meanwhile another army operated in Italy, at first in defence of Parma and then to garrison the rebellious republic of Siena.[35] France thus fought on three fronts at once – four, if one counts the garrisons occupying Savoy and along the Pyrenees. Nor was this all: King Henry II had also arranged for both the German Protestants and the Turkish Sultan to attack Charles V at the same time, the former within the Empire and the latter in the Mediterranean.[36] The pressure of this Grand Alliance forced the Habsburgs to deploy armies on an unprecedented scale: in Germany and the Austro-Hungarian borderlands, around Metz; in the Netherlands; in Italy; along the coasts and frontiers of Spain; and in the isolated fortresses along the North African coast. According to the emperor's own advisors, a total of 148,000 men had been mobilized.[37]

So both strategy and politics enhanced the revolutionary growth in military manpower during the mid-sixteenth century, for no state had ever maintained armed forces in so many different theatres at the same time before – although many did so afterwards. However, a high proportion of the troops were required not for offence but for defence, and it is here that the third factor comes in: the creation, in the half-century before 1530, of what John Lynn has termed the 'artillery fortress,' which notably affected the military manpower requirements of most early modern states.

III Technology

No one has yet cast doubt on the chronological coincidence of the diffusion of the artillery fortress and the rise in army size in France, Italy and the Netherlands in the first half of the sixteenth century. Nor has the intrinsic importance of the *trace italienne* been questioned. According to Lynn White in 1967:

The early sixteenth century in Europe witnessed two revolutions, both of which altered habits of the previous thousand years and each of which, by the latter 1500's, had crystallized into patterns that remained nearly intact until the end of the nineteenth century. One was the Protestant Reformation and the defensive response to it in the regions still loyal to Rome. The other was a sudden and profound change in military technology, the chief element of which was the development of light, highly mobile cannon that shot iron balls in fairly flat trajectories. Since the older style of fortifications crumbled before such devices, an entirely new, and enormously costly, apparatus of defense was required. It would be hard to decide which of these simultaneous revolutions had the greater impact on European life, or the more lasting effects.[38]

The assessment of the doyen of the historians of the technology naturally carries enormous weight; but we must not fall into the trap of technological determinism. Once again we must study the medieval antecedents closely.[39] Cannon do not seem to have been used to batter down walls before the 1370s, and the practice remained rare until the 1420s.[40] Nevertheless, from the late fourteenth century onwards, a number of important innovations increased the capacity of fortifications to withstand gunpowder bombardment: first the addition of guns and gunports for offensive use as a counter-battery; then a variety of new structural designs, such as 'countersinking' the fort, to minimize the damage done by incoming fire; and later the introduction of polygonal defensive designs to maximize the opportunities for outgoing fire. But such innovations proved the exception: in most areas the traditional 'vertical system' remained the principal means of defence and, for a century after 1430, whenever good siege artillery bombarded vertical walls, the outcome was predictable.[41] The verdict of Andreas Bernaldez on the conquest of Granada in the 1480s – 'Great towns, which once would have held out a year against all foes but hunger, now fell within a month' – was echoed by Niccolo Machiavelli concerning the French invasion of Italy in the 1490s: 'No wall exists, however thick, that artillery cannot destroy in a few days.'[42] By 1530, however, this ceased to be true, thanks to the newly designed 'artillery fortress' with its low, thick walls and its angled bastions.

In a report commissioned by the government of Florence in 1526, Machiavelli suggested three distinct ways of turning a town into an artillery fortress. Two involved starting from scratch: tearing down the existing walls and either building a new defensive system beyond them, so as to include all the suburbs and all points (such as neighbouring high ground) from which an enemy might threaten; or else building a smaller circuit than before, abandoning (and levelling) all areas deemed indefensible. However, both these methods involved colossal expense: on the one hand, the cost of building the fortress itself; on the other, high social costs, because the new-style fortifications covered far larger areas than before – including the suburbs lying just beyond the medieval walls, often the site of important buildings such as hospitals, religious houses and industrial plant (mills and furnaces).

Machiavelli's report of 1526 therefore considered a third technique of installing modern defences which, although weaker than the others, proved both far quicker and far cheaper: a drastic modification of the existing fortifications, reducing the height and increasing the depth of the existing walls, redesigning the towers and gateways into bastions, and creating an escarpment to give a proper field of fire. Of course earthen ramparts, when unprotected by brick and stone, would not last for long (contemporary estimates ranged from four years, with minimal maintenance, up to ten) before the weather eroded them. But they proved relatively fast and cheap to erect;

they could absorb incoming fire effectively; and, with enough determined defenders, they could defy even the largest armies of the day.[43] Thus in 1552 the city of Metz in Lorraine managed to resist for three months a siege mounted by 55,000 men despite its lack of a full 'modern' defensive system. The French had captured the city in May, and the 5,800-man French garrison worked day and night to strengthen the existing fortifications, erecting 'boulevards' (sixteen feet thick in places) with 'flancs' on either side of them at precisely the most vulnerable area, and backing all walls with ramparts constructed of earth and bales of wool. Metz had become an artillery fortress by September, when Charles V's forces arrived to recapture it. So when, on 27 November, having fired over 7,000 rounds against a sector of the curtain wall, the besiegers finally brought some seventy feet of it crashing down, they dared not launch an assault because the defenders' guns on the flanks could not be silenced.[44]

Machiavelli's two other techniques of fortification, *alla moderna* large and small, of course maximized these strengths. John Lynn has provided an excellent account of all the novel aspects of the artillery fortress envisaged by Machiavelli, and of their remarkable constancy over time. However, some of his deductions seem open to question. First, it may be true that enlarging an artillery fortress three-fold would only increase the lines of circumvallation by 15 per cent, and that such a small increment seems insignificant.[45] But this misses the point: the critical development was not the 'upgrade' from one *trace* to another but the switch from a system of vertical defence, which could be rapidly demolished by gunfire and taken by storm, to a *trace italienne* with bastions that bristled with guns – because even a relatively modest artillery fortress, in a good state of repair and sufficiently garrisoned, could seldom be taken by assault and therefore required a full-dress siege, a large army, time and money to capture. Contemporaries seemed unanimous on this point. On the one hand, the French military expert Raymond de Beccarie, lord of Fouquevaux, held that only fortifications constructed since the year 1510 presented a serious threat to a well-armed aggressor:

Because those fortified before that date cannot be called strong, seeing that the art of making bastions came to light only a short while ago. But those which have received ramparts since then, or in our own day, must (provided they were constructed at leisure and not in haste) be held extremely difficult to capture.

On the other hand, as the engineer Francesco Laparelli noted in the 1560s, 'It is impossible to defend a place against an army with artillery without flanks.' On the tactical level, size as such did not enter into it: either one had the new defensive system, however small, or one did not.[46]

This is not to say that new bastions remained impregnable for ever. In 1672, in the wake of Louis XIV's lightning conquest of much of the Dutch

Republic, the king's chief engineer, Sébastien le Prestre de Vauban, noted the advanced state of neglect of the Dutch fortresses, most of which had fallen with scarcely a blow. Major expenditure, he warned, would be required to make them defensible.[47] Such an operation would take time, both because to build a new artillery fortress in the seventeenth century took at least twenty years, and because, for optimum effect, each fortification needed to form part of an overall defensive system.

Although relatively small states such as Mantua, Montferrat, Lucca and Geneva could concentrate on a single 'impregnable' superfortress, capable of holding out almost indefinitely, larger polities needed not one but many artillery fortresses in order to create a layered defence in depth.[48] Thus, soon after they gained control of the duchy of Lombardy in the 1530s, the Habsburgs began a comprehensive programme of fortifications: Cremona and Lodi against Venice in the east, Alessandria and Novara against Savoy in the west, with Pavia and above all Milan itself as a strategic reserve. At the same time the Venetian Republic also embarked upon a programme of defence in depth, constructing a network of refortified, mutually supporting cities both in the west and, slightly later, in the east – culminating with the magnificent stronghold of Palmanova in the 1590s.[49] Meanwhile, two similar systems were taking shape in the Low Countries. Already by 1572, when the Dutch Revolt began, twelve towns had been turned into artillery fortresses and the walls of eighteen more had been rebuilt in part – a total of 43 kilometres of new walls. By 1648, when the Revolt came to an end, the Spanish Netherlands alone boasted twenty-eight artillery fortresses and a further twenty-seven towns with partially modernized walls; and the provinces of Holland and Utrecht in the Dutch Republic, which in 1572 had possessed only one artillery fortress and three more towns with one or two bastions, by 1648 had thirteen of the former and fourteen of the latter.[50] An even more impressive 'defence in depth' using artillery fortresses went up around the French frontier between 1670 and 1702, under the direction of Louis XIV's superintendent of fortifications, Vauban. It eventually included almost 300 fortified (and garrisoned) strongholds, and proved capable of halting every attempt by the king's enemies to reach the heart of the kingdom: between 1702 and 1711, in spite of a string of catastrophic defeats (Blenheim, Turin, Ramillies, Oudenaarde, Malplaquet) and the loss of innumerable towns through siege, Vauban's succession of 'barriers' of artillery fortresses, each one arranged in a zig-zag of mutually supporting positions laid out like a giant *trace italienne* between the North Sea and the Meuse, kept France's enemies at bay until at the 'Ne Plus Ultra' line the war came to an end. Not for nothing did Vauban term it 'Le pré carré': the duelling field.[51]

When constructed as part of an integrated system, fortifications *alla moderna* dominated the conduct of warfare. As John Cruso, an English military writer, observed in 1632: 'The actions of the modern warres consist chiefly in sieges, assaults, sallies, skirmishes etc., and so affoard but few set battels.' According to Roger Boyle, Lord Orrery, in 1677, 'Battells do not now decide national quarrels, and expose countries to the pillage of conquerors, as formerly. For we make war more like foxes, than like lyons; and you will have twenty sieges for one battell'; while in exactly the same year Johann Behr stated that 'Field battles are in comparison scarcely a topic of conversation . . . Indeed at the present time the whole art of war seems to come down to shrewd attacks and artful fortification.'[52] The point was expressed most cogently by Vauban himself in a tract of *c.* 1670:

The attack on fortresses has with justice always been considered one of the most essential elements of the art of war. But since the number of strongholds has increased to the point where one can no longer enter enemy territory without encountering many fortified towns, its importance has increased to the point where one can say that today it alone offers the means of conquest and conservation. To be sure, winning a battle leaves the victor in control of the countryside for the time being, but only taking the fortresses will give him the entire country . . . One might say that a war waged by sieges exposes the state less and secures conquests far better. It is therefore today the commonest form of warfare in the Low Countries, Spain, and Italy, where wars are without doubt conducted with more sophistication and discipline than anywhere else in the world. In Germany battles play a greater role because the country is more open and there are fewer fortresses.[53]

The Marshal was right. Outside the 'duelling field', the destruction of a major field army did normally lead to the surrender of many if not all the fortresses that had depended upon it for relief: after Nördlingen (1634) during the Thirty Years War almost all Protestant garrisons in south Germany surrendered; after Naseby (1645) during the English Civil War almost all royalist garrisons in the Midlands came to terms. But in the Netherlands, where (as Vauban noted) few towns in his day lacked modern fortifications, in spite of 'over 60 battles and 200 sieges' the country had never been totally subdued.

The reason is obvious. A battle lost in the Low Countries normally has few consequences, for the pursuit of a defeated army continues for only two, three or four leagues, because the neighbouring fortresses of the enemy halt the victors and provide a refuge for the vanquished, saving them from being totally ruined.[54]

As the construction of artillery fortresses continued, in one region of Europe after another sieges eclipsed battles in importance and wars eternalized themselves.[55]

The underlying explanation of this stagnation is clear. In the nineteenth century, the perceptive military theorist Carl von Clausewitz, in his influential treatise *On War*, borrowed from physics the concept of a 'center of gravity' to explain what seemed to him the essential aim of strategy.

A theater of war, be it large or small, and the forces stationed there, no matter what their size, represent the sort of unity in which a single center of gravity can be identified. That is the place where the decision should be reached.

Clausewitz drew upon his direct experience of the spectacular French victories of the period 1792–1812, and his extensive reading of military history, to conclude that: 'For Alexander, Gustavus Adolphus, Charles XII, and Frederick the Great, the center of gravity was their army. If their army had been destroyed, they would all have gone down in history as failures.'[56] But his analysis ignored the fact that the army of Gustavus Adolphus did in fact meet with a major defeat, at Nördlingen in 1634 (two years after the king's death at the indecisive battle of Lützen), and yet this did not lead Sweden to 'fail'. On the contrary, when the war eventually ended with the Peace of Westphalia in 1648, she achieved all her major war aims: extensive gains, guarantees for future security and a substantial war indemnity.

The contradiction between the defeat at Nördlingen and the gains at Westphalia stemmed from Sweden's control of numerous artillery fortresses which held steady even after the defeat of the main army. In 1648 the Swedish forces in Germany still numbered 70,000 troops, of whom almost half were dispersed as garrisons in 127 strategically located strongpoints: they thus presented no 'centre of gravity' that an adversary could destroy with a single blow. Other theatres of war dominated by the *trace italienne* in the sixteenth and seventeenth centuries proved equally resistant to the knock-out blows advocated by Clausewitz.[57] The problem was memorably summarized by the commander of the Spanish forces striving to suppress the Dutch Revolt, Don Luis de Requeséns. 'There would not be time or money enough in the world', he warned Philip II in 1574, 'to reduce by force the twenty-four towns which have rebelled in Holland if we are to spend as long in reducing each one of them as we have taken over similar ones so far.' Or again, slightly later:

Many towns and a battle have been won, each of them a success enough in itself to bring peace and even to win an entire new kingdom elsewhere; but here they have been to no avail ... I believe that God for my sins has chosen to show me so many times the Promised Land here, as he did to Moses, but that someone else is to be the Joshua who will enter therein.[58]

But no Spanish Joshua appeared: instead, the artillery fortresses of Holland and Zeeland defied all of Philip II's efforts at reconquest until his treasury declared bankruptcy in 1575 and his army mutinied and abandoned its posts in 1576.

Simon Adams has suggested that the Spanish Habsburgs – whose territories lay at the centre of the military revolution – consciously decided to fight wars of sieges rather than of battles through political choice rather than through military necessity, but this flies in the face of the evidence.[59] First, it takes two to tango: if the enemy cannot be brought to battle, as was normally the case in the Low Countries' Wars, no battle can be fought.

Second, when an enemy offered to fight, the Spaniards usually accepted – and won: at Mühlberg (1547) against the German Protestants; at Pavia (1525), St Quentin (1557) and Gravelines (1558) against France; at Jemmingen (1568), Mook (1574) and Gembloux (1578) against the Dutch. Third, whenever possible, commanders sought to by-pass bastions in favour of an old-style thrust to the enemy's heart, as Charles V did during his dramatic invasion of France in 1544.[60] But successes like these ultimately proved counter-productive, because they demonstrated – as little else could – the advantage of the new artillery fortress. Italian or Italian-trained military architects soon spread knowledge of their art all over Europe.[61]

How, then, did the artillery fortress influence army size? First, the advent of the *trace italienne* and the increased frequency of long sieges expedited the transition from cavalry to infantry as the backbone of armies. Whereas in 1494 Charles VIII of France invaded Italy with 12,000 cavalry, which represented two-thirds of his total strength, in 1525 Francis I invaded with only 6,000, which constituted but one fifth of his army. The percentage of cavalry in Western field forces continued to fall for another century, and contemporaries saw a clear link between this development and the proliferation of artillery fortresses. In 1645 George Monck, an English officer, suggested that:

Where your service lieth in Campagnia [open country], the proportion of your army ought to be two footmen to one horseman . . . But where the service of your army shall be most in sieges, there you ought to have three footmen unto one horseman; and sometimes four footmen to one horseman.

Eight years before, a senior commander of the Spanish Army of Flanders had made much the same point: 'We need more infantry if we invade the rebel provinces and more cavalry if we campaign in France' he asserted, because the war on the northern frontier was almost entirely one of sieges, where horsemen could do little, whereas operations in the south afforded more opportunity for manoeuvre.[62]

The reduction of the mounted component of armies created a more 'elastic' workforce – since infantry is far easier to increase than cavalry and much simpler to supply. Moreover, the *trace italienne* actually forced up the number of footsoldiers in two distinct ways. To begin with, as already noted, an artillery fortress could, under normal circumstances, only be captured by a formal siege, often with elaborate walls of circum- and contravallation to guard against attacks from a relief army as well as sorties by the garrison. In these circumstances, success required very large concentrations of troops. John Lynn's denial of the correlation between fortification design and army size, although shedding much new light on the subject, rests upon some dubious data. A statistical table culled largely from entries in encyclopedias – in this case from those compiled by the Dupuys and by

Bodart – may prove reliable concerning the duration of sieges, on which most sources agree; but it provides a perilous guide to numbers, whether of besiegers or defenders, which varied dramatically as the siege proceeded. Thus, to take a single example, at Metz in 1552 Lynn's table shows 60,000 attackers, 10,000 defenders and no relief army (in this case he cites as sources a biography of King Henry II published in 1910 and a general history of France published in 1904).[63] However, Gaston Zeller's meticulous study of the siege, published in 1943 and including many relevant documents, showed some 55,000 attackers but only 5,800 defenders, together with a French relief army numbering 30,000 foot and 7,000 horse.[64] Clearly errors on this scale render generalization about the changing size of armies and the fluctuating proportions of garrisons to besiegers extremely hazardous.[65]

Lynn uses the Metz example to suggest that 'while modern fortifications claimed very real advantage over updated medieval walls, the effect on army size seems to have been much the same': and he buttresses his case with the siege of St Omer in 1638 where, he asserts, the Habsburg garrison 'kept at bay some 30,000 French for two months behind medieval walls.' A note informs us that 'Saint Omer's walls were still medieval in 1668.'[66] But this is quite untrue. The detailed cityscape published by Jan Blaeu in 1649, which also describes the siege, clearly shows eleven bastions, nine ravelins, two hornworks and a crownwork surrounding St Omer. Small wonder, then, that the French siege lasted two months – and in the end proved unsuccessful, because the Spaniards managed to relieve the town.[67]

Lynn's figures on – and deductions about – the numbers involved in capturing towns in the later seventeenth and eighteenth centuries seem particularly misleading because he includes only the forces directly involved in the siege works and deliberately excludes 'armies of observation'. Admittedly, Vauban boasted that, before his time, a ratio of at least ten besiegers to one defender prevailed, which his 'system' had cut back to six or seven to one; however, that reduction made necessary the creation of large armies of observation. In a treatise written *c.* 1704 he asserted that:

It is best to be stronger, and to have two armies whenever one can: that is to say one which besieges and one which observes. The siege army shuts itself off in its lines, as we shall later show; the army of observation simply covers and occupies the routes by which the enemy['s relief force] may arrive, or takes outlying positions.

'These two armies', he continued, 'must always keep within range of one another, especially in the initial stages, in order to offer mutual support and keep the enemy at a distance.'[68] The principal advantage of this division of forces, according to Vauban, lay in the fact that the troops manning the siegeworks no longer needed to face about when a relief army approached – and in many cases enemy troops waited nearby, in a camp protected by its own bastions, ready to exploit any weakness (see page 15 above).[69]

The available data thus flatly contradict Lynn's claim that 'Relief and observation forces were not involved in the actual defence or attack of fortresses. By definition they stood off miles, and often tens of miles, from the actual siege.'[70] On the contrary, according to Vauban himself, the 'observation forces' formed an integral part of the siege process. Lynn's 'Table of French sieges' – even if we admit his figure – should therefore show a rise in the 'total attacking force' from a maximum of 50,000–60,000 in the mid-sixteenth century (Metz, Renty, St Quentin) to 90,000–110,000 in the late seventeenth and early eighteenth centuries (Mons and Namur in 1691–2; Lille and Mons in 1708–9).[71] This marked increase in the size of the armies engaged in sieges seems entirely compatible with the argument advanced in chapter 1, above, that the development – and constant refinement – of defensive systems based upon the *trace italienne* helped to fuel an expansion in the armed forces of the major European states.

And of course attack represents only half the story, for the need to garrison artillery fortresses, especially when they formed part of a defence in depth, also drove up military establishments. Contemporary evidence suggests that garrisons tied down roughly half the armed forces of many Western states. In 1621 Cosimo del Monte, Venice's senior military advisor, neatly expressed the prevailing orthodoxy when he argued that the Republic would need a total of 25,000 infantry and 3,500 cavalry to withstand any attack on its mainland possessions – half of them in garrisons and the rest 'to serve on campaigns' and 'to assist in the defence of the cities'.[72] And the greater the number of fortresses, the greater the overall size of the garrisons. It may be true, as Mahinder S. Kingra has observed for the Dutch Republic, that individual 'garrison sizes . . . rarely exceeded one thousand soldiers, frequently hovering between two and five hundred, and sometimes totalling less than one hundred troops'. However, although the size of individual garrisons may indeed have been small, the cumulative totals were enormous.[73] Unfortunately, because of the decentralized system of government within the Dutch Republic, no detailed figures can be advanced with confidence; however, in 1639, the opposing Spanish Army of Flanders numbered 77,000 men, of whom over 33,000 were distributed in 208 separate garrisons, the largest of which numbered scarcely 1,000.[74] According to Vauban, the defence of France's fortresses already tied down 116,370 men in 1678, rising to 166,000 in 1688; while by 1705 no fewer than 173,000 men occupied 297 fortified positions. Each of these totals represented about 40 per cent of Louis XIV's army.[75] The rapid and sustained increase in French army size between 1670 and 1710 thus stemmed at least in part from Vauban's programme of fortress building, which dramatically expanded the number of strongpoints requiring garrisons.[76]

Attempts to diminish the impact of the new military architecture on the finances of early modern European states likewise seem unconvincing.[77]

I. A. A Thompson has noted the small share of the central budget of the Spanish Habsburgs devoted to fortifications, and deduced that defences therefore constituted a low priority. But this ignores two facts. First, protected by the Pyrenees until 1640 (when the revolts of Catalonia and Portugal opened up new theatres of operation within the peninsula), most of Spain had little need of artillery fortresses and therefore built few. Had Thompson included the money devoted by the Spanish monarchy to constructing and maintaining fortifications in North Africa, Italy and the Netherlands, the picture would have been very different. Second, even when new fortifications became necessary, the local community was expected to fund most of the cost (especially labour costs, probably the most expensive component). This had been the case in the Middle Ages – indeed in some states communities financed the entire operation.[78] Even in the sixteenth century a rich city like Antwerp could be forced to pay first for a full circuit of *trace italienne* defences and then for a vast citadel (although the loans taken out to finance these projects remained outstanding in the 1790s!).[79] But Antwerp proved the exception: throughout early modern Europe, the cost of fortifying was normally shared between the state, the regional government and the community itself. In the Venetian Republic, for example, 'central government funds' contributed only one-third to the total cost of fortifications, the rest being borne by the cities concerned and by their surrounding territories.[80] This devolved system of finance makes it almost impossible to quantify the total costs, except by examining all the relevant sources for a particular area; it thus invalidates any attempt (such as those by Kingra and Thompson) to estimate total spending on fortifications – and thus the fiscal impact of the artillery fortress – based solely on the records of a state's central treasury.[81]

IV Geography

The fourth and final substantive criticism of *The military revolution* concerns the diffusion of the military innovations discussed above. To begin with, some questions have been raised concerning their spread both to the British Isles and to Poland. Admittedly, documenting the precise mechanics of diffusion of new military methods sometimes proves difficult. On the one hand, many manuals on training were published in London on the subject between 1590 and 1640, sometimes in more than one edition, which argues that a market existed (presumably among militia officers); on the other hand, many young men served in continental armies – some on a regular basis and others 'swallowlike, for a summer or only for a siege' – and returned with some direct experience of the new ways in warfare.[82] The process of modernization began in Ireland and Scotland during the 1630s and accelerated in the 1640s with the return of many veterans from continental armies.[83] In 1646, at the battle of Benburb in Ireland, a commander trained in the Spanish Army of Flanders used the classic defensive tactics favoured by Habsburg armies in order to defeat a Scottish force under a general who had fought for Gustavus Adolphus.[84] By then, in England, the 'discontinuity in revenue totals, army and navy size, and the change in the nature of the armed forces' all reflected the profound military transformation that had taken place; so did the fact that Gregory King's statistical profile of England in 1688 already recognized the 'officer corps' as a distinct social group.[85]

If recent literature has confirmed the westward spread of the military revolution, its impact further east has been questioned. The case of Hungary seems clear enough. The medieval kingdom boasted a double line of fortifications in the south, running along the Danube and its tributaries from the Carpathian Mountains to the Adriatic. Between 1521 and 1566, the Turks captured almost all of them: only four fortresses held out. To make good these losses, a horde of Italian military architects came to Hungary to create a new defence in depth of 'artillery fortresses'. Although several of these new strongholds also fell during the next war, between 1593 and 1606, the line held.[86]

Other areas, however, proved less receptive to the new military doctrines. A nephew of the Dutch statesman Johan de Witt, visiting eastern Europe in 1656, felt tempted to participate in the conflict then raging between Sweden and Poland. His uncle sternly discouraged any involvement since 'in that war, which is so wild and savage, there is much less to learn than in others, where matters of fortification and siegecraft are practised better'. De Witt advised the young man to come home and acquire military experience more 'relevant' to the West.[87] But such dismissal seems excessive. The armed forces of Russia and Poland needed to fight two distinct types of opponent: the infantry-based troops of their western enemies, and the cavalry hosts of their neighbours to the south and east. On the whole, they responded well to this dual challenge until the late seventeenth century. Thus Polish troops soundly defeated Gustavus Adolphus of Sweden in the 1620s; and although Charles X's Polish campaign of 1655 succeeded triumphantly, the following year his forces failed to take the artillery fortress of Zamość and his reinforcements met with defeat at Warka. By 1659 the Polish army of 54,000 regulars included almost 11,000 infantry serving in Western-style regiments. Charles X never came back. To the south, although the Turks invaded the Polish Commonwealth in 1621 and imposed a humiliating peace, King John Sobieski and a large Polish contingent spearheaded the spectacular defeat of the Ottoman army outside Vienna in 1683. The Russians, too, through a combination of 'new formation' (i.e. Western-style) infantry regiments and traditional cavalry, defeated the Poles in the 1660s and took Azov from the Turks in the 1690s.[88]

The forces of Islam, however, did not always lose. The Turks conquered

Crete from the Venetians in the 1660s, and soundly defeated Russia in 1711 and Austria in 1737–9; the Omanis captured Muscat in 1650 and Mombasa in 1698 from the Portuguese; Spanish attacks on Algiers failed in 1775, 1783 and 1784; even Napoleon failed to take Acre in 1799. Strong and successful Muslim states possessed an extensive and sophisticated military tradition (both written and practical) of their own and rapidly adopted Western firearms into their military repertory – albeit often by a process of routine mimesis, of copying captured weapons and importing foreign specialists.[89]

Recent research has documented an interesting early transmission of the 'military revolution' of early modern Europe to a Muslim society: the case of Sa'adian Morocco in the sixteenth century. As early as 1541, in the wake of the successful siege of a Portuguese outpost, King John III observed:

We must recognize that warfare in Morocco has changed. The enemy is now very adept in the arts of war and siegecraft, due in part to the aid of many Turks and renegades, numerous military weapons, and the important materials of war.

His grandson, Sebastian, demonstrated the truth of this in spectacular fashion in 1578 when he and his army met defeat and death at the hands of Sa'adian forces in the battle of Alcazarquivir. The subsequent conquest of the sub-Saharan Songhay empire by Moroccan troops in 1590–1 offers a textbook 'gunpowder conquest', to rank with those of Cortés and Pizarro.[90]

But the process did not continue indefinitely. In most Islamic societies, the founding and management of artillery became the exclusive preserve of small cadres of foreign specialists, most of them renegades and adventurers with little training and less experience in their craft.[91] Once the industrial revolution began to transform the production of gunpowder weapons systems in Europe, the Muslim states' lack of the bureaucratic and financial institutions necessary to support capital-intensive and constantly changing military establishments, by land and sea, became critical. They could no longer meet and defeat the expanding repertory of innovations developed by their Christian adversaries, because the Westernization of war also required replication of the economic and social structures and infrastructures, in particular the machinery of resource-mobilization and modern finance, on which the new techniques depended. But until the late eighteenth century, thanks to their ability to mobilize and maintain enormous armies, the major Islamic states – like the empires of East Asia – proved able to keep the West at bay. Although the Europeans inflicted great defeats on Muslim forces during the seventeenth century, such as the rout of the Turks outside Vienna in 1683, it was still the Turks at the gates of Vienna and not the Europeans at the gates of Istanbul.[92]

One must not claim too much for the 'military revolution'. Before 1800, as Anthony Reid has argued, the expansion of the West came about through a combination of three factors: superior firepower (particularly on ships), the artillery fortress, and the ability to acquire local allies. William R. Thompson has objected that *The Military Revolution* devotes insufficient attention to the third factor: to 'the Europeans' ability to cultivate local allies and their ability to manipulate the weaknesses and vulnerabilities of indigenous political structures against their non-European opponents'. Without that, Thompson claims, 'military superiority alone would not have sufficed to bring about the regional supremacy of Western Europe'.[93] Ross Hassig agreed. After reviewing all available sources for Cortés's conquest of Mexico – Spanish, Nahua, ethnographic and archaeological – he concluded that:

> What made the conquest of Mexico possible was not the Spaniards' military might, which was always modest, but the assistance of tens and even hundreds of thousands of Indian allies – labourers, porters, cooks and especially soldiers ... Spanish technology was important, but the key to the success of the Conquest was acquiring native allies who magnified the impact of those arms ...

All this forms a welcome corrective to earlier Eurocentric accounts, yet we must remember that few major conquests have ever taken place without the cultivation of local allies and the manipulation of indigenous political structures. Gustavus Adolphus in Germany between 1630 and 1632, like Napoleon Bonaparte in Italy and Central Europe between 1794 and 1809, only achieved his spectacular successes with help from his enemy's enemies. Nonetheless, the forces of the invader played the decisive military role; the rest remained secondary. Cortés may only have commanded (at most) 2,000 Europeans during his campaigns against the Aztecs, but their weaponry and above all their unit cohesion and discipline served as a decisive force-multiplier.[94]

Thompson's 'alternative model' underplays another military factor in European expansion: the Europeans' artillery fortresses. These crucially extended their power in two ways. First, they offered advantages to indigenous rulers threatened by a more powerful neighbour: to the king of Malindi in East Africa, faced by the Sultan of Mombasa; to the king of Cochin in South India, threatened by the Samorin of Calicut; to the Mohawks in Northeast America, beset by the Iroquois. Second, their capacity to withstand even a prolonged siege offered obvious advantages to local merchants fearful that the wars endemic in most regions might destroy their goods. Many of them therefore chose to keep their trading stock inside fortified European bases, and sought to uphold Western power in the region. Thus the Portuguese relief of Diu in 1539 was financed largely by loans from Indian merchants living in Goa; and from the 1680s onwards the local Indian elite made substantial cash deposits with the English East India Company in Madras.[95]

Nevertheless, the Europeans' seaborne empires remained fragile, especially when compared with the power of Islam. In the course of the sixteenth century, the Mughals gained control of more than one million square miles of India, while the Ottoman empire – of scarcely smaller extent – made major inroads into the Balkans and Hungary. So many states and societies fell that the West's ability to resist the Islamic advance stands out as unusual. And it was a close-run thing: at Mohacs (1526) and Mezokeresztes (1596) in Hungary the Turks triumphed; and if they were routed at Lepanto in the Mediterranean in 1571, they nevertheless conquered Cyprus in 1570 and Tunis in 1574. Only military resilience and technological innovation – especially the capital ship, infantry firepower and the artillery fortress: the three vital components of the military revolution of the sixteenth century – allowed the West to make the most of its smaller resources in order to resist and, eventually, to expand to global dominance.

Notes

The following abbreviations are used in the notes:

AD   Archives Départmentales (France)
AGRB   Archives Générales du Royaume/Algemeen
            Rijksarchief, Brussels (Belgium)
AGS   Archivo General de Simancas (Spain)
AHN   Archivo Histórico Nacional, Madrid (Spain)
ARA   Algemeen Rijksarchief, The Hague (Netherlands)
BL   British Library, London (Great Britain)
BNM   Biblioteca Nacional, Madrid (Spain)
HAG   Historical Archive, Goa (India)

The names of Japanese and Chinese authors are given with the surname first.

INTRODUCTION

1 Testi quoted by J. M. Brown and J. H. Elliott, *A palace for a king. The Buen Retiro and the court of Philip IV* (New Haven, 1980), 225. Other details from K. Repgen, *Kriegslegitimationen in Alteuropa. Entwurf einer historischen Typologie* (Munich, 1985: Schriften des historischen Kollegs: Vorträge, IX), 7f; and G. N. Clark, *The seventeenth century* (2nd edn, Oxford, 1945), 98.

2 J. S. Levy, *War in the modern great power system, 1495–1975* (Lexington, 1983), 139–41. The calculations on which Levy based his generalizations are not always convincing (see, for example, pp. 172–5), but the magnitude of the changes he charts is so great that minor inaccuracies do not affect the overall conclusions. See also the calculations in A. Corvisier, 'Guerre et mentalités au XVIIe siècle', *XVIIe siècle*, XXXVIII (1985), 219–32, at pp. 220f; and P. Q. Wright, *A study of war* (2nd edn, Chicago, 1965), 52ff. J. R. Hale, *War and society in Renaissance Europe 1450–1620* (London, 1985), 21, goes even further: 'There was probably no single year throughout the period in which there was neither war nor occurrences that looked and felt remarkably like it.'

3 M. Roberts, *The military revolution, 1560–1660* (Belfast, 1956), reprinted with some amendments in M. Roberts, *Essays in Swedish history* (London, 1967), 195–225. Another essay (pp. 56–81) deals more particularly with the military practice of Imperial Sweden. For unqualified acceptance, see G. N. Clark, *War and society in the seventeenth century* (Cambridge, 1958), 73–5.

4 See G. Parker, 'The military revolution, 1550–1660 – a myth?', *Journal of modern history*, XLVII (1976), 195–314, reprinted in G. Parker, *Spain and the Netherlands 1559–1659: ten studies* (London, 1979), 86–103; K. J. V. Jespersen, 'Social change and military revolution in early modern Europe: some Danish evidence', *Historical journal*, XXVI (1983), 1–13; H. L. Zwitzer, 'The Dutch army during the *Ancien Régime*', *Revue internationale d'histoire militaire*, LVIII (1984), 15–36; J. A. Lynn, 'Tactical evolution in the French army, 1560–1660', *French historical studies*, XIV (1985), 176–91; and D. A. Parrott, 'Strategy and tactics in the Thirty Years War: the "military revolution"', *Militärgeschichtliche Mitteilungen*, XVIII, 2 (1985), 7–25.

5 See M. Duffy, ed., *The military revolution and the state 1500–1800* (Exeter, 1980: Exeter studies in history, I); and the three articles by Leon Jespersen, Jan Lindegren and Oystein Rian on the state and the military revolution in (respectively) seventeenth-century Denmark, Sweden and Norway in *Scandinavian journal of history*, X (1985), 271–363. See also pp. 158–9 above.

6 These remarkable figures are defended in the brilliant account of Hsu Cho-yun, *Ancient China in transition. An analysis of social mobility 722–222 BC* (Stanford, 1965), chap. 3, especially pp. 66–71. See also M. E. Lewis, *Sanctioned violence in early China* (New York, 1990), 53–96.

7 Details from Hsu, *Ancient China*, chaps. 4 and 5, and *The emperor's warriors* (Edinburgh, 1985: the catalogue of an exhibition of items recently excavated from the mausoleum of the first Ch'in emperor). It is true that the numbers included in classical Chinese sources were sometimes arbitrary 'pseudonumbers'. Thus 3 might mean 'several'; 9 might mean 'many'; and 3,000 might mean 'a lot' (see Yang Lien-shang, *Studies in Chinese institutional history* [Cambridge, Mass., 1961], 75–84: 'Numbers and units in Chinese economic history'). But Professor Hsu has confirmed to me that the size and military techniques of Chinese armies remained remarkably stable right down to our own day. For further information, and an explanation, see M. Elvin, *The pattern of the Chinese past* (Stanford, 1973).

8 See the masterly studies of Hale, *War and society in Renaissance Europe*; and W. H. McNeill, *The pursuit of power. Technology, armed force and society since AD 1000* (Oxford, 1982).

1 THE MILITARY REVOLUTION REVISITED

1 J. X. Evans, ed., *The works of Sir Roger Williams* (Oxford, 1972), 33.

2 Details in J. R. Hale, *Renaissance war studies* (London, 1983), *passim*. Concerning the Classical authority on war most respected by Renaissance writers, see W. Goffart, 'The date and purpose of Vegetius' *De re militari*', *Traditio*, XXXIII (1977), 65–100; on Lipsius, see note 40 below.

3 Machiavelli (and others) quoted in M. E. Mallett, *Mercenaries and their masters: warfare in Renaissance Italy* (London, 1974), 196. See also G. R. Potter, ed., *The new Cambridge modern history*, I (Cambridge, 1967), 274ff. Recent writers such as John Keegan, Michael Howard and Geoffrey Parker are rebuked for their misconceptions about medieval warfare by J. Gillingham, 'Richard I and the science of war in the Middle Ages' in J. Gillingham and J. C. Holt, eds., *War and government in the Middle Ages* (Woodbridge, 1984), 78–91, at p. 79.

4 The origins of a new style of warfare, in which stone-built castles were used to create a defence in depth, have been traced to Anjou in the early eleventh

century. See the important article of B. S. Bachrach, 'Early medieval fortifica-
tions in the "West" of France: a revised technical vocabulary', *Technology
and culture*, XVI (1975), 531–69; Bachrach, 'Fortifications and military tactics:
Fulk Nerra's strongholds *c.* 1000', *ibid.*, XX (1979), 531–49; and Bachrach, 'The
Angevin strategy of castle building in the reign of Fulk Nerra, 987–1040',
American historical review, LXXXVIII (1983), 533–60; and of R. J. Bartlett,
'Technique militaire et pouvoir politique, 900–1300', *Annales: Economies,
sociétés, civilizations*, XLI (1986), 1135–59.

5 R. C. Smail, *Crusading warfare 1097–1193* (Cambridge, 1956), 24. See also
pp. 21–5, 39, and 204–5.

6 For further information on strategic thinking in the 'High Middle Ages', see
A. Guillerm, *La Pierre et le vent. Fortifications et marine en occident* (Paris, 1985),
chap. 2; J. F. Verbruggen, *The art of war in western Europe during
the Middle Ages* (Amsterdam, 1977), especially chaps. 4 and 5; and J. Heers,
ed., *Fortifications, portes de ville, places publiques dans le monde méditerranéen*
(Paris, 1985). For the stalemate of the century 1350–1450, see H. J. Hewitt,
The Black Prince's expedition of 1355–7 (Manchester, 1958), 27–9, 71f, 107–
16; Hewitt, *The organization of war under Edward III (1338–1362)* (Manchester,
1966), 99–118; and R. A. Newhall, *The English conquest of Normandy,
1416–1424. A study in fifteenth-century warfare* (London, 1924), 143–268. The
best general study is P. Contamine, *War in the Middle Ages* (Oxford, 1984).

7 There is an excellent account of the development of firearms in Europe, starting
in the 1320s, in J. Needham, Ho Ping-Yü, Lu Gwei-Djen and Wang Ling,
*Science and civilization in China. Volume V part vii: military technology; the
gunpowder epic* (Cambridge, 1986), 39–51, 365–9. For the lack of influence of
early artillery on military architecture in the West, see E. Cooper, *Castillos
señoriales en la corona de Castilla* (2nd edn, Salamanca, 1991); D. H. Caldwell,
ed., *Scottish weapons and fortifications, 1100–1800* (Edinburgh, 1981), 21–54,
94–152, 491; A. M. T. Maxwell-Irving, 'Early firearms and their influence on
the military and domestic architecture of the Borders', *Proceedings of the Society
of Antiquaries of Scotland*, CII (1970–1), 192–224; and J. R. Kenyon, 'Early
artillery fortifications in England and Wales: a preliminary survey and reap-
praisal', *Archaeological journal*, CXXXVIII (1981), 205–40.

8 For the campaigns in France, see Guillerm, *La Pierre et le vent*, chap. 2;
Contamine, *War*, 148–9; and M. G. A. Vale, *War and chivalry. Warfare and
aristocratic culture in England, France and Burgundy at the end of the Middle
Ages* (London, 1981), 130–41. For those in Granada, see M. A. Ladero Quesada,
Castilla y la conquista del reino de Granada (Valladolid, 1967), 127.

9 This point, which is often overlooked, is well-made by J. B. Bury, 'Francisco
de Holanda: a little-known source for the history of fortifications in the sixteenth
century', *Arquivos do Centro Cultural Português*, XIV (1979), 163–202.

10 Quotation from M. E. Mallett, 'Diplomacy and war in later fifteenth-century
Italy', *Proceedings of the British Academy*, LXVII (1981), 267–88, at p. 270.

11 Guicciardini's *Counsels and reflections* (*c.* 1528) and *History of Italy* (*c.* 1537)
are quoted in S. Pepper and N. Adams, *Firearms and fortifications. Military
architecture and siege warfare in sixteenth-century Siena* (Chicago, 1986), 11. See
also the quotations on pp. 159f above.

12 Machiavelli's views are presented in several of his writings – *The prince* (1513;
published 1532); *The art of war* (1521); and *Discourses on the first decade of Titus
Livy* (completed 1515–17; published 1531). The quotation comes from *Discourses*,
book II, chap. 17. The most thorough study of Machiavelli's military writing

remains M. Hobohm, *Machiavelli's Renaissance der Kriegskunst* (Berlin, 1913); but see also Hale, *Renaissance war studies*, chap. 6. On the military crisis caused by the unexpected invasion of the French, and on how it was overcome between 1494 and 1530, see P. Pieri, *La crisi militare Italiana nel Renascimento* (Turin, 1952).

13 The claim that the fortifications of Civitavecchia, designed by Antonio da San Gallo the younger, were the 'first complete angle-bastioned enceinte' is made by Pepper and Adams, *Firearms and fortifications*, 28. Their fascinating, illustrated account of the spread of the new fortifications, in chap. I, updates J. R. Hale, 'The early development of the bastion: an Italian chronology, *c.* 1450–*c*.1534', in Hale, J. R. L. Highfield and B. Smalley, eds., *Europe in the late Middle Ages* (London, 1965), 466–94 (reprinted in Hale, *Renaissance war studies*, 1–29); and H. de la Croix, *Military considerations in city planning: fortifications* (New York, 1972), 39–55.

14 Details from J. Hook, 'Fortifications and the end of the Sienese state', *History*, LXII (1977), 372–87; Pepper and Adams, *Firearms and fortifications*, chaps. 2–7; and the eye-witness account of the bitter siege of 1554–5 written by the French commandant, Blaise de Monluc, *Commentaires* (ed. J. Giono, Paris, 1964), book III.

15 See the excellent study of E. Cooper, *Castillos señoriales de Castilla*, who stressed that defences tend to be built against the 'normal' form of attack, not against the worst conceivable threat. The medieval castles of Castile, often relatively inaccessible to siege guns, only became seriously outdated after *c.* 1550. On the subsequent evolution of fortifications in Italy, see M. E. Mallett and J. R. Hale, *The military organization of a Renaissance state: Venice c. 1400 to 1617* (Cambridge, 1984), chap. 14. Although I cannot accept the interesting suggestion of Philippe Contamine (*War*, 205) that the bastion idea evolved independently 'at about the same time in several countries', his overall account of why the bastion emerged is nevertheless admirable (*War*, 202–7).

16 Examples taken from P. Lavedan, *L'Histoire de l'urbanisme. II. Renaissance et temps modernes* (2nd edn, Paris, 1959), 76–87; La Croix, *Military considerations*, 39–55 and plates 62–86; and P. Contamine, 'Les Industries de guerre dans la France de la Renaissance: l'exemple de l'artillerie', *Revue historique*, CCLXXI (1984), 249–80. For an early assessment of the transformation wrought by these new fortifications, see G. Dickinson, ed., *The 'Instructions sur le faict de la Guerre' of Raymond de Beccarie de Pavie, sieur de Fourquevaux* (London, 1954), fos. 85f. See also the quotation on p. 165 above.

17 Details from M. van Hemelrijck, *De Vlaamse Krijgsbouwkunde* (Tielt, 1950), 131–95; and the richly documented article of W. Brulez, 'Het gewicht van de oorlog in de nieuwe tijden. Enkele aspekten', *Tijdschrift voor Geschiedenis*, XCI (1978), 386–406, at pp. 394ff. The financing of the fortification of Antwerp, directed by Donato Buoni from Bergamo, is brilliantly analysed by H. Soly, 'Fortificaties, belastingen en corruptie te Antwerpen in het midden der 16e eeuw', *Bijdragen tot de geschiedenis*, LIII (1970), 191–210. See also p. 160 above. For a clear statement from the 1580s that, north of the Alps too, the new fortifications were so expensive that only great states could afford them, see F. de la Noue, *Discours politiques et militaires* (ed. F. E. Sutliffe, Geneva, 1967), 384ff ('Discours XVIII: 4e paradoxe').

18 L. A. Maggiaroti, *L'opera del genio italiano all' estero. Seria IVa: Architetti e architetture militari*, II (Rome, 1936) and III (Rome 1939), provide much detail on the Italian military engineers in Hungary, Spain, Portugal and Latin America.

For the Italians in Britain, see M. H. Merriman, 'Italian military engineers in Britain in the 1540s' in S. Tyacke, ed., *English map-making 1500–1650. Historical essays* (London, 1983), 57–67. On the spread of bastions in Germany, see U. Schütte, ed., *Architekt und Ingenieur. Baumeister in Krieg und Frieden* (Wolfenbüttel, 1984: Ausstellungskatalog der Herzog August Bibliothek, XLII), 287–94 and 318–19; and H. W. Herrmann and F. Irsigler, eds., *Beiträge zur Geschichte der frühneuzeitlichen Garnisons- und Festungsstadt* (Saarbrücken, 1983: Veröffentlichungen der Commission für Saarländische Landesgeschichte und Volksforschung, XIII). Of course, Italian techniques did not spread only by personal contact: there were also numerous descriptive publications. See the invaluable bibliographical surveys of H. de la Croix, 'The literature of fortification in Renaissance Italy', *Technology and culture*, IV (1963), 30–50; and J. B. Bury, 'Early writings on fortifications and siegecraft, 1502–54', *Fort*, XIII (1985), 5–48. See also pages 169 and 173 above.

19 On the siege of Breda, see the splendid account of H. Hugo, *Obsidio Bredana* (Antwerp, 1626; English edn, Louvain, 1627); and the meticulous map based on it by Jacques Callot, *The siege of Breda* (Antwerp, 1628). The intimate connexion between these two works is demonstrated by S. Zurawski, 'A fresh look at Jacques Callot's map of the Siege of Breda', *The art bulletin*, LXX (1988), 621–39.

20 See the excellent contemporary chronicle of H. Haestens, *La Nouvelle Troye, ou mémorable histoire du siège d'Ostende, le plus signale qu'on ait veu en l'Europe* (Leiden, 1615); and the admirable more recent account of P. Henrard, *Histoire du siège d'Ostende 1601–4* (Brussels, 1890).

21 See J. I. Israel, *The Dutch Republic and the Hispanic world, 1606–1661* (Oxford, 1982), 176–9; and S. Groenveld and H. P. R. Leeuwenberg, *De bruid in de schuit. De consolidatie van de Republiek 1609–50* (Zutphen, 1985), 78–9. It is hard to grasp the effort involved in sinking mines, because normally the tunnels were destroyed by the eventual explosion. Much detail is offered, however, by J. B. Bury, 'The early history of the explosive mine', *Fort*, X (1982), 23–30; and S. Pepper, 'The underground siege', *ibid.*, 31–8. Both authors agree that the first spectacular use of an explosive mine occurred at the siege of Castel Nuovo in Naples in 1495. Some idea of the size of an early modern mine and countermine may be gathered from the unique surviving examples at St Andrews Castle in Scotland, dating from the siege of 1546–7: the mine is 1.8 metres wide and 2.1 metres high – large enough for ponies to be used for excavating the debris. See also the contemporary description of them, written before 1554, by G. Bellucci, *Nuova inventione de fabricar fortezze* (Venice, 1598), 80. The mine and countermine survived because, before they were completed, the besiegers suddenly brought up heavy guns which, after six hours' bombardment, made a breach in the castle walls. The defenders immediately surrendered.

22 A glance at the siege-plans included in J. Blaeu, *Toonneel der Steden van de Vereenighde Nederlanden met hare beschrijvingen* (Amsterdam, 1649), fos. dd3/ee (Rijnberg), and Blaeu, *Toonneel der steden van 's konings Nederlanden* (Amsterdam, 1649), fos. 1/12 (Breda) – or in J. P. Abelinus, *Theatrum Europaeum*, II (Frankfurt, 1637), 74–5 (Stralsund), 270–1 (Casale) – gives a clear idea of the extent of seventeenth-century siegeworks. See also plate 4.

23 See Israel, *Dutch Republic*, 176f; and the views of the Spanish general quoted in G. Parker, *The Army of Flanders and the Spanish Road, 1567–1659. The logistics of Spanish victory and defeat in The Low Countries' Wars* (Cambridge, 1972), 19.

24 J. D. Durange, *Des verirreten Hauptrisses der Regulair Fortifikation getreuer Wegweiser* (Frankfurt, 1722). Much the same complaint had been made two centuries before by Antonio da San Gallo, who advised Pope Paul III to ignore the plans of Michelangelo for a new fortress because 'his profession was sculpture and painting, and not fortification' (quoted, with other admirable material, by J. R. Hale, *Renaissance fortification: art or engineering?* [London, 1977], 36). Later in the century came the strictures of the French military writer, Blaise de Vigenère, *l'Art militaire d'Onosender, autheur grec* (Paris, 1605), fo. 629v: 'Everyone likes to get out his pencil and sketch a system of fortification, whether he is a painter, art-dealer, mason, cabinet-maker or architect ... They seem to imagine that it is enough to dream up a fortress design in one's head, and know how to draw a straight line'.

25 Roger Boyle, earl of Orrery, *A treatise on the art of war* (London, 1677), 15. See also his observation (pp. 148 and 179f) that the decisive battles were normally those in which a relief army was defeated by besiegers. The military career that lay behind this work is narrated by K. M. Lynch, *Roger Boyle, first earl of Orrery* (Knoxville, 1965): see chaps. 2–3, and p. 221 (about his 'war diaries').

26 The importance of the Ordinance is discussed in F. Lot and R. Fawtier, *Histoire des institutions françaises au Moyen Âge. II. Institutions royales* (Paris, 1958), chap. 5; and P. Contamine, *Guerre, état et société à la fin du Moyen Âge. Études sur les armées des rois de France 1337–1494* (Paris, 1972), part IV. The distinction between 'archers' and 'men-at-arms' must not be made too sharp however: the archers were mounted, and wore some armour, so that they might (if need arose) also serve as auxiliary cavalry.

27 Examples taken from J. B. Paul, ed., *Accounts of the Lord High Treasurer of Scotland, vol. IV 1507–1513* (Edinburgh, 1902), lxviiff. On the English attachment to archery, see C. Gaier, 'L'Invincibilité anglaise et le grand arc après la Guerre de Cent Ans: un mythe ténace', *Tijdschrift voor Geschiedenis*, XCI (1978), 379–85; and J. R. Hale, ed., *Certain discourses military by Sir John Smythe* (Ithaca, N.Y., 1964), l.

28 Details from Contamine, *War*, 129, 134; R. Taveneaux, ed., *Cinq-centième anniversaire de la bataille de Nancy (1477)* (Nancy, 1978), 365–73, 398; and Mallett and Hale, *The military organization of a Renaissance state*, 76, 167, 350–4. On the character of late medieval warfare before the gun, see C. T. Allmand, ed., *Society at war. The experience of England and France during the Hundred Years War* (Edinburgh, 1973), 6–9 and 104–5, as well as the interesting documentary extracts appended.

29 J. F. Guilmartin, Jr, *Gunpowder and galleys. Changing technology and Mediterranean warfare at sea in the sixteenth century* (Cambridge, 1974), 150–5. Much the same verdict on the superior speed and accuracy of the archer over the musketeer was given by a French traveller in seventeenth-century India who noted that the Mughal horse archers could fire six times to the European musketeer's twice, and to greater effect: see F. Bernier, *Travels in the Mogul empire AD 1656–1668* (ed. A. Constable, London, 1891), 48. For a further discussion of Indian warfare, see pp. 128–36 above.

30 See the useful calculations reported in Pepper and Adams, *Firearms and fortifications*, 15f, 199 n. 27. See also p. 237 n. 6 below.

31 Machiavelli quoted by F. L. Taylor, *The art of war in Italy 1494–1521* (Cambridge, 1921), 61f; Barret's dialogue quoted in Hale, ed., *Certain discourses military*, l.

32 For full studies of two Swiss victories, see Taveneaux, *Nancy*; and *Revue internationale d'histoire militaire*, XL (1978): 'Grandson, 1476: essai d'approche pluridisciplinaire d'une action militaire du XVe siècle'. For imitation of Swiss methods by Florence (after 1495) see Taylor, *Art of War*, 36; and by the Germans see E. von Frauenhoz, *Entwicklungsgeschichte des deutschen Heerwesens*, II.2: *Das Heerwesen des Reiches in der Landsknechtszeit* (Munich, 1937).

33 The detailed account of C. W. C. Oman, *A history of the art of war in the sixteenth century* (London, 1937), chap. 2, is still the most convenient and reliable available.

34 There is a good discussion of the different types of gun used in the sixteenth century in J. D. Lavin, *A history of Spanish firearms* (London, 1965), 44ff.

35 The Spanish infantry, it is true, normally included a high proportion of pikes – 1:1; but the South Netherlands ('Walloon') infantry, after 1636, included three times as many 'shot' as pikes; while the Dutch, as early as the 1570s, included four times as many. See the detailed analyses in Parker, *Army of Flanders*, 274–6; R. Quatrefages, *Los tercios españoles 1567–1577* (Madrid, 1979), 113–22, 198f; J. W. Wijn, 'Het Noordhollandse regiment in de eerst jaren van de Opstand tegen Spanje', *Tijdschrift voor Geschiedenis*, LXII (1949), 235–61, at p. 259; and F. J. G. ten Raa and F. de Bas, *Het Staatsche Leger 1568–1798*, I (Breda, 1911), 54. For the proportions in some other armies, see C. H. Firth, *Cromwell's army. A history of the English soldier during the Civil Wars, the Commonwealth and the Protectorate* (4th edn, London, 1962), 69ff; M. Roberts, *Gustavus Adolphus. A history of Sweden, 1611–1632*, II (London, 1958), 173ff; and A. de Mosto, 'Ordinamenti militari delle soldatesche dello stato romano nel secolo XVI', *Quellen und Forschungen aus italienische Archiven und Bibliotheken*, VI (1904), 72–133, at pp. 74f.

36 See Roberts, *Gustavus Adolphus*, II, 177 for speculation on a musket's rate of fire. For that of bigger guns, see Pepper and Adams, *Firearms and fortifications*, 198f.

37 G. Davies, ed., 'The autobiography of Thomas Raymond', *Camden Society Publications*, 3rd series XXVIII (1917), 19–66, at p. 39. For other examples, see Firth, *Cromwell's army*, 90; and Roberts, *Gustavus Adolphus*, II, 227 n.6. Most of the doubts concern the high cost of rifles, their extremely slow rate of fire, and the speed with which their barrels became fouled. But one accurate round from a sniper could justify much inconvenience. For the general problems presented by muzzle-loading weapons, see the discussion (and illustrations) in B. P. Hughes, *Firepower weapons' effectiveness on the battlefield 1630–1850* (London, 1974).

38 See the admirable discussion of W. Reinhard, 'Humanismus und Militarismus. Antike-Rezeption und Kriegshandwerk in der oranischen Heeresreform' in *Krieg und Frieden im Horizont der Renaissancehumanismus* (Wernheim, 1986), 185–204, at p. 195f (which points out that Aelian described no less than three varieties of countermarch in his *Tactics*!). See also W. Hahlweg, 'Aspekte und probleme der Reform des niederländischen Kriegswesens unter Prinz Moritz von Oranien', *Bijdragen en Mededelingen betreffende de geschiedenis der Nederlanden*, LXXXVI (1971), 161–77 (the letter of 8 December 1594 – plate 5 in this volume – is discussed at pp. 171–2). In fact, as noted on p. 140 above, the Japanese had perfected the salvo thirty years earlier, but there is no evidence that this was known to the Nassau cousins in 1594: they acknowledged only Roman precedents. The coincidence is thus an interesting example of simultaneous but independent invention. See also p. 161 above.

39 See the brilliant analysis of M. D. Feld, 'Middle-class society and the rise of military professionalism. The Dutch army 1559–1609', *Armed forces and society*, I (1975), 419–42 (reprinted with additions in Feld, *The structure of violence: armed forces as social systems* [London, 1977], 169–203).

40 L. Mulder, ed., *Journaal van Anthonis Duyck, advocaat-fiskaal van den Raad van State 1591–1602*, I (The Hague and Arnhem, 1862), 636, records the Dutch army 'exercising' at a siege in Drenthe in August 1595, some time before Lipsius published his book on the Roman army. However, the philosopher's influence on Count Maurice is not in doubt: see G. Oestreich, *Neostoicism and the early modern state* (Cambridge, 1982), Part I, and chaps. 5 and 13; and Reinhard, 'Humanismus und militarismus', *passim*. It is interesting to find that some observers felt that both Lipsius and the Dutch were rash to place so much trust in Classical precedents when military circumstances had changed so radically since Roman times: see A. Grafton, 'Rhetoric, philology and Egyptomania in the 1570s. J. J. Scaliger's invective against M. Guilandinus's Papyrus', *Journal of the Warburg and Courtauld Institutes*, XLII (1979), 167–94, at pp. 193f. On Dutch military practice in general at this time, the standard work remains J. W. Wijn, *Het krijgswezen in den tijd van Prins Maurits* (Utrecht, 1934).

41 See J. B. Kist, ed., *Jacob de Gheyn: the exercise of arms* (New York, 1971), 'A commentary', pp. 6–7; and the pertinent remarks of Feld, *Structure of Violence*, 174–8; and of W. Schulze in J. Kunisch, ed., *Staatsverfassung und Heeresverfassung in der europäischen Geschichte der früher Neuzeit* (Berlin, 1986), 142f. On the first English edition see Anna E. C. Simoni, 'A present for a prince' in J. A. van Dorsten, ed., *Ten studies in Anglo-Dutch relations* (Leiden, 1974), 51–71. On John of Nassau's earlier version see W. Hahlweg, *Die Heeresreform der Oranien: das 'Kriegsbuch' des Grafen Johann von Nassau-Siegen* (Wiesbaden, 1973: Veröffentlichungen der historischen Kommission für Nassau, XX).

42 Bingham and others quoted by W. Hahlweg, *Die Heeresreform der Oranien und die Antike* (Berlin, 1941), 176. There were many other literary ways in which the new techniques might be propagated. Numerous newspaper reports circulated from 1618 onwards – by the 1630s some papers even had a regular 'war correspondent' – and some armies published annual campaign reports (such as those of J. A. Vincart for the Spanish Army of Flanders). The victorious Spanish siege of Breda was celebrated in plays, books, paintings – including Velásquez's magnificent *Las Lanzas* – as well as in the vast map prepared by Jacques Callot on the orders of the Brussels government, which was sent (together with a description and 'index' in four languages) to some 200 distinguished personages. (See Zurawski, 'A fresh look'; and S. A. Vosters, *La rendición de Bredá en la literatura y el arte de España* [London, 1973]). There were also letters and memoranda written by various ambassadors and other government officials which discussed the new ways in warfare – even when fought by others – and, since many of these have survived in multiple copies, it is clear that they too circulated widely. Finally, there were even plays which popularized the military techniques of the Dutch. Thus London theatre-goers in 1599 could watch a play 'full of quips' called 'The overthrow of Turnholt' (*sc.* Turnhout: a battle fought in the Netherlands two years before: see C. L. Kingsford and W. A. Shaw, eds., *Report on the manuscripts of the Lord de L'Isle and Dudley preserved at Penshurst Place*, II [London, 1934: Historical Manuscripts Commission Report, LXXVII], 406–8: Rowland Whyte to Robert Sydney, who featured in the play, 26–7 October 1599). Of course the Spaniards also wrote plays about the Low

Countries' Wars – see E. Gossart, *Les Espagnols en Flandre. Histoire et Poésie* (Brussels, 1914), *passim*, and J. Loftis, *Renaissance drama in England and Spain. Topical allusion and history plays* (Princeton, 1987) – but, understandably, these had little to say about Dutch military superiority.

43 Details from E. von Frauenholz, *Das Heerwesen in der Zeit des dreissigjährigen Krieges*, II (Munich, 1939), 30; and F. Redlich, *The German military enterpriser and his workforce, 13th to 17th centuries*, I (Wiesbaden, 1964: Vierteljahrschrift für Sozial- und Wirtschaftsgeschichte, Beiheft XLVII), 157ff. Redlich also noted the large number of senior commanders in the Thirty Years War who learned the trade of war either fighting for or against the Dutch.

44 See L. Plathner, *Graf Johann von Nassau und die erste Kriegsschule. Ein Beitrag zur Kenntnis des Kriegswesens um die Wende des 16. Jahrhunderts* (Berlin, 1913). It was certainly an exclusive school. Classes began at Easter 1619, but only 20 students had attended when the Academy closed its doors in 1623. On other 'military schools' see H. M. Scott and C. Storrs, 'The military revolution and the European nobility, c. 1600–1800', *War in History*, III (1996), 1–41, at pp. 24–7.

45 The way in which Dutch methods and models reached Switzerland are well set out in F. Walter, *Niederländische Einflüsse auf das eidgenössische Staatsdenken im späten 16. und frühen 17. Jahrhundert: Neue Aspekte der Zürcher und Berner Geschichte im Zeitalter des werdenden Absolutismus* (Zürich, 1979), chaps. 1, 3. In his article, 'Tactical evolution in the French army, 1560–1660', J. A. Lynn argued that an 'alteration of French tactics ... occurred at roughly the same time as, or even predated, the Dutch reforms'. But none of his evidence came from the years before 1600; and he did not discuss 'volley fire' which was surely the crucial development. For a further discussion of Professor Lynn's work on the military revolution, see pp. 165 and 169–71 above.

46 On the growing complexity, see H. Eichberg, 'Geometrie als barocke Verhaltensnorm. Fortifikation und Exerzitien', *Zeitschrift für historische Forschung*, IV (1977), 17–50. The example given is J. F. von Fleming, *Der volkommene teutsche Soldat* (Leipzig, 1726).

47 William Louis discussed Cannae with Maurice by letter in 1595, and then wrote a short treatise on it, entitled *Annibal et Scipion ou les Grands Capitains*, which enjoyed considerable circulation: see W. Hahlweg, 'Wilhelm Ludwig von Nassau und das Cannae-problem', *Nassauische Annalen*, LXXI (1960), 237–42. On Turnhout see A. Koyen, 'De slag op Tielenheide (1597) in het kader van de 80-jarige oorlog', *Taxandria*, new series LV (1983), 5–136, at p. 42; on Nieuwpoort, see B. Cox, *Van den tocht in Vlaenderen. De logistiek van Nieuwpoort, 1600* (Zutphen, 1986), and the interesting account in Haestens, *La nouvelle Troye*, 20–61. At p. 22 Haestens mentions an early use of 'grapeshot': 'nostre artillerie, chargé de balles de mousquets, ioua sur l'ennemy'. On Nieuwpoort see J. P. Puype, 'Victory at Nieuwpoort, 2 July 1600', in M. van der Hoeven, ed., *Exercise of arms. Warfare in the Netherlands, 1568–1648* (Leiden, 1997), 69–112; and p. 240 n. 27 below.

48 Roberts, *Gustavus Adolphus*, II, 229–34. For further details on rates of fire, see the sources quoted in Pepper and Adams, *Firearms and fortifications*, 198 n. 20 and 211 n. 18. The use of 'cartridges' dates back to the mid-sixteenth century (see Pepper and Adams, *Firearms*, 199 n. 21) although they were still described in 1677 by Orrery, *Treatise*, 31f, as some rare novelty.

49 Monro, quoted in Roberts, *Gustavus Adolphus*, II, 258. Curiously, Orrery, *Treatise*, 38, did not favour volley fire, on the grounds that 'the first rank cannot have loaded their muskets again by that time the fourth rank has done

firing'. Instead he urged that all ranks should load their muskets with pistol balls and fire one salvo in unison and at point-blank range. But Orrery had never seen the Swedish army in action.

50 Lynn, 'Tactical evolution', 182f, offers an important corrective here to Roberts: he points out that the 'caracole' had already been abandoned in favour of the full cavalry charge under Henry IV in the 1580s and 90s; and that Henry also added musketeer formations among his squadrons of horse in order to enhance their impact, as Gustavus was also later to do.

51 Account based on [Swedish Army General Staff], *Sveriges Krig 1611–1632*, IV (Stockholm, 1937), 472–86; T. M. Barker, *The military intellectual and battle: Raimundo Montecuccoli and the Thirty Years War* (Albany, N.Y., 1975), 174–81; and W. S. Brockington, ed., *Monro his expedition with the worthy Scots regiment called Mackays* (1637; Westport, CT, 1999), 190–8. Several of Tilly's captured standards may still be seen in Stockholm, in the Army museum's 'State Trophy Collection'.

52 See the calculations in C. M. Cipolla, *Guns and sails in the early phase of European expansion 1400–1700* (London, 1965), 55–7.

53 Army sizes from Parker, *Spain and the Netherlands*, 96, and sources there quoted; artillery figures from Contamine, 'Les Industries de guerre', 278.

54 In fact most of Spain also resisted the military revolution. There were very few bastions before 1640, except along the frontier with France in Catalonia and Guipúzcoa: see Cooper, *Castillos*. See also the remarks of Bartlett, 'Technique militaire', 1152f.

55 Detailed examples from G. Parker, *The Thirty Years War* (London, 1984), 12f. See also the general theory of E. Ennen, 'Die Festungsstadt als Forschungsgegenstand: die Herausbildung der Festungs- und Garnisonsstadt als Stadttyp' in Herrmann and Irsigler, *Beiträge zur Geschichte*, 19–34; and the numerous studies of the slow pace of fortification in individual strategic centres, such as H. Kessler, *Die Stadmauer der freien Reichsstadt Nördlingen* (Nördlingen, 1982: Schwäbische Geschichtsquellen und Forschungen, XII); Pepper and Adams, *Firearms and fortifications*, chaps. 3–4; H. A. van Oerle, *Leiden binnen en buiten de Stadsvesten. De Geschiedenis van de Stedebouwkundige ontwikkeling binnen het Leidse rechtsgebied tot het einde van de gouden eeuw* (2 vols., Leiden, 1975), I, 274–92; and B. Roosens, 'De stadsomwalling van Breda: de eerste toepassing van het gabastioneerd vestingsbouw in de Nederlanden (1531–47)', *Bijdragen tot de geschiedenis*, LXIII (1980), 87–120. See also Merian's splendid engravings in J. P. Abelinus, ed., *Theatrum Europaeum* (6 vols., Frankfurt, 1639–63; 2nd edn, Frankfurt, 1670); and compare them with the city plans from the 1570s published by G. Braun and F. Hogenburg, *Civitates orbis terrarum* (3 vols., ed. R. A. Skelton, Amsterdam, 1965).

56 The distances marched in 1626–33 were carefully calculated in *Monro his expedition* 117–23: 1677 Dutch miles. Those of 1645–8 are discussed in [Försvarstabens Krigshistoriska Avdelning], *Från Femern och Jankow till Westfaliska Freden. En minnesskrift år 1948* (Stockholm, 1948), *passim*.

57 Sir Thomas Wilson quoted in Parker, *Spain and the Netherlands*, 139. For a clear survey of Henry VIII's fortress-building, see H. M. Colvin, ed., *The history of the king's works*, IV (London, 1982), 367–401 (by J. R. Hale, reprinted in Hale, *Renaissance war studies*, 63–97). See also C. Platt, *The castle in medieval England* (London, 1982), chap. 9; Merriman, 'Italian military engineers'; Guillerm, *La Pierre et le vent*, 110–17; B. H. St J. O'Neil, *Castles and cannon: a study of early artillery fortifications in England* (Oxford, 1960), 65–79; and J. A. Donnelly, 'A study of the coastal forts built by Henry VIII', *Fort*, X (1982), 105–26.

58 See details in W. G. Ross, 'Military engineering during the Great Civil War, 1642–1649', in F. J. Day, ed., *Professional papers of the corps of Royal Engineers* (London, 1887: Royal Engineers Institute Occasional Papers, XIII), 86–205; and I. Roy, 'England turned Germany? The aftermath of the Civil War in its European context', *Transactions of the Royal Historical Society*, 5th series XXVIII (1978), 127–44, at p. 132.

59 The surviving traces of this important complex are described in [Ancient Monuments Commission], *Newark-on-Trent: the Civil War siegeworks* (London, 1964). For details on the siege, see D. E. Lewis, 'The use of ordnance in early modern warfare, with particular reference to the English Civil War' (Manchester University M.A. thesis, 1971), 200, 219.

60 Details from P. R. Newman, 'The Royalist army in Northern England, 1642–1645' (York University Ph.D. thesis, 1978), chaps. 8 and 11; and Lewis, 'The use of ordnance' chap. 7.

61 Dr Newman suggests that one reason why many commanders preferred to storm a town was the fear that their inexperienced troops would never withstand the rigours of a blockade; but Lewis seems more convincing when he points to the lack of siege guns as the main reason – medieval walls were no less vulnerable to artillery bombardment in England than anywhere else after the advent of gunpowder; but one still needed guns to fire!

62 On the limited diffusion of the *trace italienne* in early modern Scotland, see D. H. Caldwell, 'A sixteenth-century group of gun towers in Scotland', *Fort*, XII (1984), 15–24.

63 Details in H. G. Leask, 'Castles and their place in Irish history', *The Irish sword*, X (1971–2), 235–43; B. de Breffny, *Castles of Ireland* (London, 1977), *passim*; J. G. Simms, 'Cromwell at Drogheda, 1649', *The Irish sword*, XI (1973–4) 212–21; and (a source not used by Simms) B. Whitelocke, *Memorials of the English affairs*, III (Oxford, 1853), 110–12. See also p. 244 n. 83 below.

64 Details from E. M. Jope, 'Scottish influence in the north of Ireland: castles with Scottish features', *Ulster journal of archaeology*, 3rd series XIV (1951), 31–47; R. Gillespie, *Colonial Ulster. The settlement of East Ulster 1600–1641* (Cork, 1985: Studies in Irish History, 3rd series I), 117f, 231; and T. W. Moody and W. E. Vaughan, eds., *A new history of Ireland. IV: The eighteenth century, 1691–1800* (Oxford, 1986), 472–5.

65 See the list, and map, of 148 fortifications built or rebuilt in seventeenth-century Ireland provided by P. M. Kerrigan, 'Seventeenth-century forts, fortifications and garrisons in Ireland: a preliminary list', *The Irish sword*, XIV (1980), 3–24 and 135–56. On the men who built them, see R. Loeber, 'Biographical dictionary of engineers in Ireland, 1600–1730', *The Irish sword*, XIII (1977–9), 30–44, 106–22, 230–55 and 283–314.

66 On Kinsale, see P. M. Kerrigan, 'Charles Fort, Kinsale', *The Irish sword*, XIII (1977–9), 322–38; Phillips's report, presented to James II in Council in March 1686, is in the National Library of Ireland, Dublin, MS. 3137, 'Survey of all forts in Ireland' (quotation from part I, fo. 20). See also P. A. Lucas, 'Irish armies in the 17th century' (University of Manchester Ph.D. thesis, 1982), 190, 254, 381–2.

67 Five bastioned citadels were built in Scotland in the 1650s (at Inverlochy, Inverness, Ayr, Perth and Leith: see plans of the first three in C. H. Firth, ed., *Scotland and the Protectorate: letters and papers relating to the military government of Scotland from January 1654 to June 1659* [Edinburgh, 1899: Publications of the Scottish History Society, XXXI], xxxviii, xliv, xlviii). More were

constructed in the 1690s (for example at Fort William) and in the 1720s (such as the still surviving Fort Augustus in the Great Glen). But none could match the massive proportions of Fort George. See B. P. Lenman, *The Jacobite clans of the Great Glen 1650–1784* (London, 1984), 31–5 and 97–8. For the eighteenth-century defences of Ireland, see Public Record Office of Northern Ireland, MS. D 2778/8: 'Plans of the principal towns ... in Ireland for Mr Tindal's continuation of Mr Rapin's History'.

68 Froissart quoted, together with other sources, by K. Simms, 'Warfare in the medieval Gaelic lordships', *The Irish sword*, XII (1975–6), 98–108. See also S. de Hóir, 'Guns in medieval and Tudor Ireland', *ibid.*, XV (1982–3), 76–88. Complaints similar to Froissart's about the unchivalrous Irish were also made, in the seventeenth century, about the reluctance of the American Indians to stand and fight: see p. 119 above.

69 Details from T. Churchyard, *A Generall rehearsall of warres* (London, 1579), sig. Q. ii; A. O'Rahilly, *The massacre at Smerwick (1580)* (Cork, 1938: Cork Historical and Archaeological Papers, I), 21f; and J. S. Brewer and W. Bullen, eds., *Calendar of the Carew manuscripts*, II (London, 1868), 470: Carew to Walsingham, 18 September 1588 – modern research bears out his estimate of both Spanish ships (16) and men (3,000) lost in Ireland. See also H. C. Hamilton, ed., *Calendar of state papers relating to Ireland, ... Elizabeth: 1586–1588* (London, 1877), 161, for a chilling account of how English troops massacred some 1,500 Scottish invaders in 1586: 'Truly I was, never since I was a man of war, so weary with killing of men ... '.

70 On the 'Nine Years War' see G. A. Hayes-McCoy, 'Strategy and tactics in Irish warfare, 1593–1601', *Irish historical studies*, II (1940–1), 255–79; G. A. Hayes-McCoy, 'The army of Ulster, 1593–1601', *The Irish sword*, I (1949–53), 105–17; G. A. Hayes-McCoy, *Ulster and other Irish maps circa 1600* (Dublin, 1964: these include twelve maps by Richard Barthelet, Mountjoy's military cartographer during the war); J. J. Silke, *Kinsale. The Spanish intervention in Ireland at the end of the Elizabethan Wars* (Liverpool, 1970); and T. W. Moody, F. X. Martin and F. J. Byrne, eds., *A new history of Ireland*, III (Oxford, 1976), 115–41.

71 Lewis, 'Use of ordnance', 166–76.

72 Details from D. Stevenson and D. H. Caldwell, 'Leather guns and other light artillery in mid-seventeenth-century Scotland', *Proceedings of the Society of Antiquaries of Scotland*, CVIII (1976–77), 300–17. In Ireland, attempts to use leather guns proved even less successful. In 1642, the Protestant defenders of Ballynally castle in County Clare watched with interest as the besiegers brought up a 'great lethern piece of ordnance' fastened to a timber sledge. But when it was fired 'shee gave only a great report, having 3 pounds of powthar in her, but lett fly backwarde the bullet remaining within'. The Irish seem to have been deluded by all the talk of 'leather guns' into omitting to place a metal barrel inside the leather casing (Moody, *A new history of Ireland*, III, 305). However, it should be remembered that 'leather guns' had never been intended for use at sieges (and had in any case been abandoned by Sweden as useless before 1630).

73 Mackay quoted by J. M. Hill, *Celtic warfare 1595–1763* (Edinburgh, 1986), 65; and Hawley by D. Stevenson, *Alastair MacColla and the Highland problem in the seventeenth century* (Edinburgh, 1980), 82.

74 D. Stevenson, 'The Highland Charge', *History today*, XXXII (August, 1982), 3–8; D. Stevenson, *Alastair MacColla*, 82–4, 127–8, 133–4, 156, 200, 251, 261–2, 267; and Hill, *Celtic warfare*, *passim*.

75 See the description in Lenman, *Jacobite clans*, 189. Of course there were other reasons for the success of the 'Highland Charge', such as the careful selection of terrain and opportunity. But the crucial elements were speed, determination, and courage.

76 J. T. Lappalainen, *Elämää suomen sotaväessä Kaarle X Kustaan aikana* [Life in the Finnish army in the time of Charles X] (Jyväskylä, 1975), 83–4, 211.

77 P. F. Sugar, 'The Ottoman "professional prisoner" on the Western borders of the empire in the sixteenth and seventeenth centuries', *Études balkaniques*, VII(2) (1971), 82–91; and G. Agoston, 'Habsburgs and Ottomans: defense, military change and shifts in power', *Turkish Studies Association Bulletin*, XXII (1998), 126–41.

78 See quotations from Franciszek Malkot (1624), Sebastian Zakrzewski (1627) and Kasper Twardowski (1626) in J. Nowak-Dłużewski, *Okolicznościowa poezja polityczna w Polsce. Zygmunt III* (Warsaw, 1971), 300, 312, 315. I am grateful to Dr R. I. Frost for help in interpreting the Polish reaction to Western military techniques.

79 The full title of Freitag's book made the Dutch connexion clear: *Architectura militaris nova et aucta, oder newe vermehrte Fortification ... auff die neweste Niederländische Praxin gerichtet*. It was dedicated to Prince Władisław. New-style defences built in Poland at this time are noted by E. Malachowicz, 'Fortification in Poland', *Fort*, III (1977), 25–30; and A. P. Hryckiewicz, 'Warownie miasta magnakie na Bialorusi i Litwie', *Przegląd Historyczny*, LXI (1970), 428–44.

80 T. M. Nowak, 'Polish warfare technique in the seventeenth century. Theoretical conceptions and their practical applications' in W. Biegański, ed., *Military technique, policy and strategy in history* (Warsaw, 1976), 11–95 (see pp. 17–18 for Polish gunnery manuals – the first published in 1624, the second, by Andrea dell'Acqua, working at Zamość, in 1630); W. Majewski, 'The Polish art of war in the 16th and 17th centuries' in J. K. Fedorowicz, ed., *A republic of nobles. Studies in Polish history to 1864* (Cambridge, 1982), 179–97; and J. Teodorczyck, 'L'Armée polonaise dans la première moitié du XVIIe siècle' in W. Biegański, ed., *Histoire militaire de la Pologne: problèmes choisis* (Warsaw, 1970), 95–113. On Kirchholm and Klushino, see M. Roberts, *The early Vasas. A history of Sweden 1523–1611* (Cambridge, 1968), 400–3 and 455.

81 On later developments, see T. Nowak, *Polska technika wojenna, XVI–XVII wieku* (Warsaw, 1970), 262–3; T. Nowak, 'Polish warfare technique', 32–8 (on guns), 83–90 (on Getkant's Atlas of fourteen maps), and 54–5 (on fortification literature). It was still not enough to secure victory against Western powers, however: the Polish commanders during the Swedish invasion of the 1650s constantly called on the government to provide both more firearms and more men capable of withstanding firearms (see R. I. Frost, *After the deluge. Poland–Lithuania and the second northern war 1655–1660* [Cambridge, 1993]).

82 See R. M. Hellie, *Enserfment and military change in Muscovy* (Chicago, 1971), 166. It should be noted that, although Hellie's analysis of the changes in Russian warfare is admirable, his unfortunate tendency to rely on Russian sources for military developments in the West gives rise to some questionable statements and dubious comparisons.

83 Details drawn from Hellie, *Enserfment*, chaps. 10–12; and the excellent survey of J. L. H. Keep, *Soldiers of the Tsar. Army and society in Russia, 1462–1874* (Oxford, 1985), part 1. See, in particular, Keep's map of Muscovy's fortified southern border at p. 17. See also P. Dukes, 'The Leslie family in the Swedish period (1630–5) of the Thirty Years War', *European studies review*, XII (1982),

401–24, at pp. 405–12; and C. Duffy, *Russia's military way to the west: origins and nature of Russian military power* (London, 1981), 6–7, 15–17.

84 The 'houten redouten' are described by P. Giustiniano, *Delle guerre di Fiandra, libri VI* (Antwerp, 1609), 228f and figures 14 and 25 (see plate 14 above); and by T. Coryate, *Coryat's crudities* (London, 1611), 640f. A similar 'Maginot line' along the Isonzo, built by the Venetian Republic in the 1590s is noted by Pepper and Adams, *Firearms and fortifications*, 206 n. 47.

85 In an interesting essay, Gerhard Oestreich argued that early modern German states moved towards militarism in two distinct stages: the first, in the 1580s and 90s, involved the creation of defensive militias and forts; the second, in the 1620s and 30s, produced aggressive standing armies. There is much truth in this view, but it overlooks the facts that (a) relatively few states ever raised a standing army and (b) after 1648 many states demobilized all except their self-defence forces. See Oestreich, *Neostoicism and the early modern state*, 228–34. For an alternative view, see Parker, *Thirty Years War*, 12f.

86 Details on 1632 from *Sveriges Krig*, III, 397, 569–71, and VI, 392f, 488. Details on 1648 from *Från Femern och Jankow*, 383 (40,000 Swedish-paid troops in the field and 30,000 more in garrisons); and from Krigsarkivet, Stockholm, *Historiska planscher 1648*, 24 folio, 'Amore pacis: geographische Carten von gantz Teutschland'.

87 AGS, *Estado* 2247 unfol., 'Relación de la gente que es menester para las guarniciones', sent by the Cardinal-Infante to Philip IV, 31 December 1639. Other figures are given in Parker, *Army of Flanders*, 272, and Israel, *The Dutch Republic*, 163–5. Of course garrisons were not only maintained for defensive purposes: there might also be domestic considerations such as the need to nip local rebellion and disorder in the bud.

88 See Israel, *The Dutch Republic*, 167f, and the figures on page 14 above. For an example of a town where soldiers regularly outnumbered civilians see V. A. M. Beerman, *Geschiedenis van Breda: II 1568–1795* (Schiedam, 1978), *passim*. Many of the soldiers of Louis XIII of France also spent most of their time in garrisons. In 1636, for example, 360 companies – almost 30,000 men – were assigned to permanent garrison duties. See D. A. Parrott, 'The administration of the French army during the ministry of Cardinal Richelieu' (Oxford University D.Phil. thesis, 1985), 94.

89 R. Williams, *The actions of the Low Countries* (London, 1618: there are two modern editions – one by D. W. Davies [Ithaca, 1964]; the other by Evans, *The works of Sir Roger Williams*), covering his service in the Netherlands, first with the Dutch and then with the Spaniards, between April 1572 and January 1574; W. Dillingham, ed., *The commentaries of Sir Francis Vere* (Cambridge, 1657), covering the years 1589–1600; and A. L. Sells, *The memoirs of James II. His campaigns as duke of York 1652–1660* (London, 1962). See also Churchyard, *Generall rehearsall of warres*, whose subtitle was 'wherein is five hundred severall services of land and sea, as sieges, battailes, skirmishes and encounters', many of them in the Low Countries. Works by other English writers who served in the Netherlands are noted by M. J. D. Cockle, *A bibliography of military books up to 1642* (3rd edn, London, 1978), and H. J. Webb, *Elizabethan military science: the books and the practice* (Madison, 1965). Veterans of the Spanish Army of Flanders also filled their memoirs with details of small-scale 'actions'. See, for some representative examples, B. de Mendoza, *Comentarios de lo sucedido en las guerras de los Países Bajos* (Madrid, 1592), covering 1567–77; A. Vázquez, *Los sucesos de Flandes y Francia del tiempo de Alejandro Farnese*

(Madrid, 1879–80: *Colección de Documentos Inéditos para la historia de España*, LXXII–LXXIV), covering 1577–92; and C. Coloma, *Las guerras de los Estados Bajos* (Antwerp, 1625), covering 1588–99. Monluc, La Noue and other French military commentators of the sixteenth century also devoted the majority of their accounts to small encounters.

90 Schenck's operations are noted, along with other similar endeavours, in Parker, *Army of Flanders*, 17. On the 'forgotten army' in Friesland, see F. Verdugo, *Comentario de la guerra en Frisa* (Naples, 1610; ed. H. Lonchay, Brussels, 1899): the ten-man company appears on p. 141. Verdugo's memoirs cover the years 1581–94.

91 Monluc, who died in 1577 and whose book was referred to by Henry IV as 'the soldier's Bible', quoted in Parker, *Army of Flanders*, 12. See the identical, cynical views of Eustache Piémond, a notary from Dauphiné who kept a diary during the Religious Wars, quoted in the admirable article of M. Greengrass, 'The later wars of religion in the French Midi' in P. Clark, ed., *The European crisis of the 1590s* (London, 1985), 106–34, at pp. 106–8.

92 H. Drouot, *Mayenne et la Bourgogne: contribution à l'histoire des provinces françaises pendant la Ligue 1587–1596*, I (Paris, 1937), 300ff, offers the best account of a 'dirty war' in early modern times. He shows that it was the departure of the Catholic regional leader, Mayenne, and his major local followers in 1589 that opened Burgundy to the *guerre aux vaches* directed by castellans and barons with old scores to settle or new wealth to win. Within six years their activities had devastated the province, and thereby destroyed Mayenne's power-base and contributed to his fall. Although this example comes from a civil war, in which political and military factors were equally important, the same story could be told for the Thirty Years War in (for example) the Rhineland or Westphalia. It must be remembered, however, that many local communities managed to 'buy' themselves out of these local wars, either by securing letters of protection (as in the Low Countries: see Parker, *Army of Flanders*, 18f); or through individual treaties of neutrality (see, for France, Drouot, *Mayenne et la Bourgogne*, I, 310–15, and Clark, *European crisis of the 1590s*, 116; and for England, J. S. Morrill, *The revolt of the provinces* [London, 1976], 36–9 and 159–67); or, finally, through a 'contributions system' (see pp. 65–71 above).

93 Details from P. R. Newman, *Atlas of the English Civil War* (London, 1985), 21, 53; R. E. Sherwood, *Civil strife in the Midlands 1642–1651* (London, 1974), chap. 4, and especially the map at p. 43; Firth, *Cromwell's army*, 26–9; and P. Young, *Naseby 1645: the campaign and the battle* (London, 1985), 228–37. The character of these local wars is, once again, graphically displayed in some of the memoirs written by participants: see, above all, C. H. Firth, ed., *The memoirs of Edmund Ludlow ... 1625–1672* (2 vols., Oxford, 1894).

94 The Royalist garrisons in June 1645, and the dates of their surrender, are listed in Young, *Naseby*, 284–7; while Parliamentary ones are reviewed by H. M. Reece, 'The military presence in England, 1649–60' (Oxford University D.Phil. thesis, 1982), chap 6. For some individual exploits of garrison commanders, see I. Roy, 'England turned Germany', 134–44; I. Roy, 'The English Civil War and English society' in B. Bond and I. Roy, eds, *War and society*, I (London, 1975), 24–43; Newman, 'The royalist army', *passim*; M. D. G. Wanklyn, 'The king's armies in the West of England 1642–1646' (Manchester University M.A. thesis, 1966), *passim*; and R. Hutton, *The Royalist war effort 1642–1646* (London, 1982),

102–4. Although seldom coordinated by the High Command or influenced by the movements of the main armies, the military exploits of commanders in these 'dark corners of the land' were widely reported, so that wartime newspaper readers in London and the Home Counties came to be as knowledgeable about the topography of distant shires as, for example, their descendants became in 1982 about the geography of the Falkland Islands.

95 For early modern 'small wars' in general see P. Paret, *Yorck and the era of Prussian Reform 1807–1815* (Princeton, 1966), 21–8. See also the stimulating study, based on nineteenth-century examples, by C. Callwell, *Small wars: their principles and practice* (3rd edn, London, 1906).

96 Details in R. R. Harding, *Anatomy of a power elite: the provincial governors of early modern France* (New Haven, 1978), 200; and C. Tilly, *The contentious French. Four centuries of popular struggle* (Cambridge, Mass., 1986), 130f. Of course this aspect of demilitarization was paralleled, as both authors note, by Richelieu's more famous attempts to ban duelling. For an earlier phase of French 'demilitarization', in the mid-fifteenth century, see Contamine, *Guerre, état et société*, 550f.

97 See Lewis, 'Use of ordnance', 198–202; and Reece, 'Military presence', 128–34.

98 On the defective defence of the Baltic provinces, see H. Eichberg, *Militär und Technik. Schwedenfestungen des 17. Jahrhunderts in der Herzogtümern Bremen und Verden* (Düsseldorf, 1976: Geschichte und Gesellschaft. Bochumer Historische Studien, VII). On the costs of garrisoning the overseas provinces, see Roberts, *Sweden's age of greatness*, 22–4 and 27–9. The castles of the Spanish interior were also regularly razed: thus orders were issued to destroy 180 between 1454 and 1474, and 84 more between 1474 and 1504.

99 Vauban to Louvois, 20 January 1673, quoted in H. Guerlac, 'Vauban' in P. Paret, ed., *Makers of modern strategy from Machiavelli to the nuclear age* (Princeton, 1986), 64–90, at p. 86. See, however, a different view – denying that Vauban meant a 'straight line' by *pré carré* – in C. J. Ekberg, *The failure of Louis XIV's Dutch war* (Chapel Hill, 1979), 116–19. See also pp. 166–71 above.

100 See G. Livet and B. Vogler, eds., *Pouvoir, ville et société en Europe, 1650–1750* (Paris, 1983), 13–16; and Guillerm, *La Pierre et le vent*, 124–33.

101 There is apparently no full-length work on irregular warfare before the eighteenth century. The general survey by W. Laqueur, *Guerrilla: a historical and critical study* (London, 1977), for example, covers the period between the Hittites and the American Revolution in seventeen pages. There is, however, an interesting study of one earlier guerilla conflict by C. Ingrao, 'Guerilla warfare in early modern Europe: the *Kuruc* war (1703–1711)', in B. K. Király and G. E. Rothenberg, eds., *War and society in east central Europe*, I (New York, 1979), 47–66; and a useful survey of the light infantry of the eighteenth-century Austrian army by J. Kunisch, *Der kleine Krieg. Studien zum Heerwesen des Absolutismus* (Wiesbaden, 1973: Frankfurter historische Abhandlungen, IV).

102 See Roberts, *Gustavus Adolphus*, II, 265; Roberts, *Essays in Swedish history*, 202; and the excellent article of I. A. A. Thompson, 'The impact of war' in Clark, *The European crisis of the 1590s*, 261–84, at pp. 275f. For a suggestion that Calvinism may have favoured a disposition to seek battles, see H. H. Rowen and A. Lossky, *Political ideas and institutions in the Dutch Republic* (Los Angeles, 1985), 45 (about William III); and J. A. Aho, *Religious mythology and the art of war. Comparative religious symbolisms of military violence*

(Westport, 1981), 194–217 – an interesting study, though marred by numerous factual errors.

103   It is notable that in the excellent collection of essays recently edited by Peter Paret, *Makers of modern strategy from Machiavelli to the nuclear age*, the only 'strategists' before Frederick the Great to be discussed are Machiavelli, Maurice of Nassau, Gustavus Adolphus, Montecuccoli and Vauban – and even they take up only three chapters out of twenty-eight. Similarly, R. A. Preston and S. F. Wise, *Men in arms: a history of warfare and its interrelationships with western society* (4th edn, New York, 1979), devote only 20 of their 450 pages to the period 1525–1700.

2   SUPPLYING WAR

1   J. de Guibert, *Essai général de tactique* (Paris, 1772; revised edn, 2 vols., Paris, 1802), I, lv; Laurence Sterne, *The life and opinions of Tristram Shandy, gentleman*, I (London, 1760), chap. 24. On Guibert's ideas, see Paret, ed., *Makers of modern strategy*, 105–13; and R. A. Quimby, *The background of Napoleonic warfare: the theory of military tactics in eighteenth-century France* (New York, 1957: Columbia University Studies in the Social Sciences DXCVI), 106–74.

2   AGS, *Estado* 1199 fos. 1–2, bishop of Palencia to Prince Philip, Pavia, 4 August 1552, enclosing a 'Copia del exército que tiene su magestad en Flandes y en Alemaña'; and 1201 fo. 112, *Relación* of the Army of Lombardy, September 1552.

3   'Resumen que hizó el Rey Don Felipe IV ... al consejo de Castilla (1627)', in J. H. Elliott and J. F. de la Peña, *Memoriales y cartas del Conde Duque de Olivares*, I (Madrid, 1978), 244: 'Este año pasado de 1625 se pudieron contar cerca de 300 mil hombres de infantería pagada, y mas de 500 mil de milicia'. However, I cannot account for more than 70,000 men in the Army of Flanders, 30,000 in Italy, at most 20,000 in Spain and the same again in Germany, plus perhaps 10,000 in Portugal. There were, of course, more troops defending the overseas empires of both Portugal and Castile, but it seems unlikely that the king was including them. Rather, the phrase '300,000' was probably meant to imply 'a very large number': this is certainly how it was used by others at the time – see J. Correia-Afonso, ed., *Indo-Portuguese History: sources and problems* (Oxford, 1981), 139 ('the figure of 300,000 seems to have exercised a peculiar fascination for many missionary writers and editors').

4   Figures from J. A. Lynn, 'The growth of the French army during the seventeenth century', *Armed forces and society*, VI (1980), 568–85, at pp. 575–7; A. Corvisier, *Louvois* (Paris, 1983), 330, 349, 514–16; and A. Corvisier, 'Guerre et mentalités au XVIIe siècle', 221. Contamine, *War in the Middle Ages*, undoubtedly the best book currently available on medieval European warfare, suggests (pp. 306–7) that 100,000 men may have been mobilized briefly by France in 1340, just before the Black Death. But at other times in the Middle Ages, European armies were far smaller (see *ibid.*, pp. 11, 28, 64, and so on).

5   A. Corvisier, *L'Armée française de la fin du XVIIe siècle au ministère de Choiseul. Le Soldat*, I (Paris, 1964), 316–27: Villars and the musicians both quoted on p. 317.

6   R. Chaboche, 'Les soldats français de la guerre de Trente Ans: une tentative d'approche', *Revue d'histoire moderne et contemporaine*, XX (1973), 10–24.

7   See Corvisier, *L'Armée française*, I, 387–448 (especially the table at p. 406 and

the maps at 430f); and J. Chagniot, *Paris et l'armée au XVIIIe siècle. Étude politique et sociale* (Paris, 1985), 313–62. Chagniot points out, however, that only about 15 per cent of the troops recruited in Paris were actually born there: most of the rest were provincial immigrants (or the children of provincial immigrants) who could not make a living in the capital. But in the 1790s there is no doubt about the urban preponderance: see J. A. Lynn, *The bayonets of the Republic. Motivation and tactics in the army of revolutionary France* (Urbana, 1984), 44–8. I have learned much on all this from discussions with Professor Lynn, to whom I am most grateful. The same preponderance of urban recruits has been noted in other armies: see Parker, *Army of Flanders*, 40 (although reservations are expressed in note 1); and, less equivocally, J. Ruwet, *Soldats et régiments nationaux au XVIIIe siècle. Notes et documents* (Brussels, 1962), 30f, 41f: almost three-quarters of the troops raised by the government in the Austrian Netherlands in the mid-eighteenth century seem to have come from the towns.

8 Excellent extended accounts of the various motives for enlistment are to be found in Hale, *War and society in Renaissance Europe*, chap. 3 (Savorgnan quoted at p. 109); A. Corvisier, *Armies and societies in Europe 1494–1789* (Bloomington, 1979), 131–48; M. S. Anderson, *War and society in Europe, 1620–1789* (London, 1988), 122; and Chagniot, *Paris et l'armée*, 347–56.

9 Before the composition of detailed dossiers on each new recruit in the eighteenth century, it is impossible to offer more precision on soldiers' backgrounds. See, however, the individual motives for enlistment given in the handful of autobiographies that have come down to us, such as those discussed in P. Delaney, *British autobiography in the seventeenth century* (London, 1969), chap. 8 – Sydnam Poyntz, runaway apprentice; Thomas Raymond, unemployed...; or printed in J. M. de Cossio, ed., *Autobiografías de soldados (siglo XVII)* (Madrid, 1956: Biblioteca de Autores Españoles, XC) – Jerónimo de Pasamonte, runaway orphan; Alonso de Contreras, joined up after stabbing a school friend... The role of ecclesiastical discipline in driving errant youths into the army varied according to the power of the church in a given area. In Scotland, for example, where the kirk was very strong, numerous church courts had to abandon their search for many a suspected malefactor when they 'went for a soldier'. See, by way of example, William MacPherson, 'adulteror and thereafter fornicator in Inverness' who in 1677, after 'having appeared several yeares' in sackcloth and ashes at the church door, preferred possible death in the Dutch army to certain humiliation at home (W. Mackay, ed., *Records of the presbyteries of Inverness and Dingwall, 1643–88* [Edinburgh, 1896: Scottish History Society, XXIV], 60, 84). For an example of a recruit who enlisted in return for payment of his debts with the enlistment bounty, see Ruwet, *Soldats et régiments nationaux*, 254f.

10 Turner's motives were recorded in his autobiography: J. Turner, *Memoirs of his own life and times (1632–1670)* (Edinburgh, 1829: Bannatyne Club, XXVIII), 3; those of Monro in *Monro his Expedition*, 2, 190, 202. For some other English volunteers who wished to include a siege or two in their Grand Tour, see J. W. Stoye, *English travellers abroad 1604–1667. Their influence in English society and politics* (London, 1952), 239–67 – including John Evelyn, Thomas Fairfax and William Brereton. The Spanish Armada campaign of 1588 attracted volunteers from all over Catholic Europe, some serving aboard the fleet and others coming to join the Army of Flanders (which was to assist in the invasion of England). When it became clear that the campaign had failed, most of the latter went home: see, for example, AGRB *Secrétairerie d'Etat et de Guerre*

II fos. 40 (permit to Captain Juan de Anaya Solís to go home, 12 September, 1588) and 46v (same to Marquis of Favara, who had raised a company of Italian light horse specifically for England, 27 October 1588). No less than 122 *adventureros* and 214 *entretenidos* joined the Armada in Spain and were individually listed in Medina Sidonia's *Order of Battle* (Lisbon, 9 May 1588).

11 See H. L. Rubinstein, *Captain Luckless. James, first duke of Hamilton 1606–1649* (Edinburgh, 1975), 26–37; I. Grimble, *Chief of Mackay* (London, 1965), 81–105; and Dukes, 'The Leslie family in the Swedish period (1630–5) of the Thirty Years War', 401–24. There was, of course, nothing new in clan warriors serving abroad. Those daughters of clan chiefs from the west of Scotland who married their Ulster relatives in the sixteenth century normally brought soldiers for their new husbands in their retinue. Thus when Lady Agnes Campbell of Kintyre married the O'Neil of Ulster in 1569, her dowry consisted of 500 Campbell and 700 MacDonald swordsmen. See G. A. Hayes-McCoy, *Scots mercenary forces in Ireland 1565–1603* (Dublin, 1937), chap. 3 ('The dowry of a Scottish wife') especially pp. 98–109. I am grateful for this reference to Dr Jane Dawson.

12 See A. Corvisier, 'Clientèles et fidélités dans l'armée française aux 17e et 18e siècles', in Y. Durand, ed., *Hommage à Roland Mousnier. Clientèles et fidélités en Europe à l'époque moderne* (Paris, 1981), 213–36. The same was true in England where many regiments were commanded by officers from the same family. For example, during the Civil War, the Royalist infantry regiment raised by Colonel Thomas Forster was 'a singular example of what might be called a family concern since all the officers, ... save one, were Forsters'. (See Newman, 'Royalist Army', II, 335f.) There are many other (albeit less comprehensive) examples in Dr Newman's list of units in the marquis of Newcastle's Northern Army between 1642 and 1645. An excellent earlier case of (in effect) a feudal levy is well described by S. Adams, 'The gentry of north Wales and the earl of Leicester's expedition to the Netherlands 1585–6', *The Welsh history review*, VII(2) (1974), 129–47. For a similar Austrian example, see F. Hausmann, 'Das Regiment hochdeutscher Knechte des Grafens Julius von Hardegg' in *Der dreissigjähriger Krieg. Beiträge zu seiner Geschichte* (Vienna, 1976: Schriften des Heeresgeschichtlichen Museums in Wien, VII), 79–167 – a splendidly informative regimental history of Wallenstein's Life-Guards, 1630–6, largely raised in (and supplied from) Hardegg's lands in Lower Austria. For examples of Spanish regiments recruited through feudal ties in the 1630s, see C. J. Jago, 'Aristocracy, war and finance in Castile 1621–1665: the titled nobility and the house of Béjar during the reign of Philip IV' (Cambridge University Ph.D. thesis, 1969), chap. 2.

13 For warrior families in Renaissance Italy, see G. Hanlon, *The twilight of a military tradition. Italian aristocrats and European conflicts, 1560–1800* (London, 1998) chap. 6. The records of almost any European elite group offer similar examples of families who provided one soldier after another, generation after generation. But after about 1600, permanent armies began to breed their own recruits: soldiers settled in garrisons often married the daughters of other soldiers, and raised sons to carry on their work. See the details on over 4,000 Scottish soldiers who settled in the Netherlands, patiently collected and published by J. Maclean, *De huwelijksintekeningen van Schotse militairen in Nederland 1574–1665* (Zutphen, 1976); and, for a later period: 'Huwelijken van militairen behorende tot ... de Schotse Brigade ... 1674–1713', *De Brabantse Leeuw*, XVII (1968), 97–124, XX (1971), 140–59, and XXI (1972), 90–113; and, during the eighteenth century, in articles published in the *Jaarboek van het centraal bureau*

The same exercise could be carried out for the Spanish Army of Flanders, which was numerous enough to support its own garrison churches. The Antwerp citadel church kept a parish register from 1599 onwards: Stadsarchief, Antwerp, *Parochieregisters* 167–168, 'Registro de los que se baptizan, casan y entierran en esta yglesia parochial de S. Phelipe del Castillo de Amberes'. See the discussion of this and other sources in G. Parker, 'New light on an old theme: Spain and the Netherlands 1550–1650', *European History Quarterly*, XV (1985), 219–36, at pp. 220 and 232 n.9.

14 It is customary to portray the life of Spanish troops serving abroad in the sixteenth century as attractive and easy: see, most recently, Quatrefages, *Los tercios españoles*, and R. Puddu, *Il soldato gentiluomo. Autoritratto d'una società guerriera: la Spagna del '500* (Bologna, 1982). But both works rely mainly upon the printed testimony of a few veterans, written in retirement; documents composed at the time tend to tell a different story. Admittedly the 10,000 troops led from Italy to the Netherlands by the duke of Alva in 1567 were, according to one eye-witness, 'so well equipped in dress and weapons (most of them gilded and the rest engraved) that one would have thought them captains rather than soldiers ... One would have said they were so many princes ...' (L. Lalanne, ed., *Oeuvres complètes de Pierre de Bourdeille, seigneur de Brantôme*, I [Paris, 1874], 103f). But later expeditions fell far short of this standard. In 1586, the duke of Parma complained that a newly raised Spanish tercio came overland from Italy 'not only without arms but also without proper clothes. They are badly treated [along the way] so that it is a shame to see them' (AGS *Estado* 592 fo. 141, Parma to Philip II, 14 November 1587). And in 1620 one of the last contingents of recruits to march along the 'Spanish Road' was dismissed by an observer in Turin as 'not men to be reckoned with: those in the first two ranks were good enough, with a martial spirit about them, but the rest were poor boys between 16 and 20 years old, sickly and ill-clothed, the majority without hats or shoes. Their carts are already full of sick men, although they have only been on the march five days, and I firmly believe that ... before they reach Burgundy half of them will fall by the wayside' (Archives de l'État, Geneva, *P.H.* 2651, unfol., Dr Isaac Wake to the council of Geneva, 4 July 1620).

15 Details in Parker, *Army of Flanders*, chaps. 1–3.

16 A.-J. du Plessis, cardinal-duke of Richelieu, *Testament politique* (ed. L. André, Paris, 1947), 394–5. Of the 1,429 French veterans studied by Chaboche ('Les Soldats français', 17), one-fifth were born outside France. For the Irish see P. Gouhier, 'Mercenaires irlandais au service de la France (1635–64)', *The Irish sword*, VII (1965–6), 58–75. For the troops of Louis XIV and Louis XV see Corvisier, *L'Armée française*, I, 259–74.

17 Among the foreign troops in the Dutch army, the Scots Brigade has been particularly well studied. See ten Raa and de Bas, *Het staatsche leger*, II, 161–3 and *passim*; J. Ferguson, *Papers illustrating the history of the Scots Brigade in the service of the United Netherlands 1572–1782*, I (Edinburgh, 1899: Scottish History Society Publications, XXXII); and the works of Dr J. Maclean listed in note 13 above. The origins of the Scots Brigade are noted in J. H. Burton, ed., *Register of the Privy Council of Scotland*, II (Edinburgh, 1878), 148: in view of 'the present hunger, derth and scarcitie of viveris', all unemployed Scotsmen were invited to take ship at Leith and go to the Netherlands 'quhair they may haif sufficient interteniment' (Order of 21 June 1572).

18 On the Scots, see J. Dow, *Ruthven's army in Sweden and Esthonia* (Stockholm,

voor Genealogie, XIX (1965) – XXVI (1972). The same exercise could be carried out for the Spanish Army of Flanders, which was numerous enough to support its own garrison churches. The Antwerp citadel church kept a parish register from 1599 onwards: Stadsarchief, Antwerp, *Parochieregisters* 167–168, 'Registro de los que se baptizan, casan y entierran en esta yglesia parochial de S. Phelipe del Castillo de Amberes'. See the discussion of this and other sources in G. Parker, 'New light on an old theme: Spain and the Netherlands 1550–1650', *European History Quarterly*, XV (1985), 219–36, at pp. 220 and 232 n.9.

19 On the Grahams, see C. M. F. Ferguson, 'The Anglo-Scottish border in the seventeenth century' (St Andrews University Ph.D. thesis, 1981), 117, 125.

20 For Spynie's and Mackay's regiments see D. Masson, ed., *Register of the Privy Council of Scotland. Second series I (1625–7)* (Edinburgh, 1899), 385, 542–3. For Spens's criminals see J. Bruce, ed., *Calendar of State Papers. Domestic Series 1628–9* (London, 1859), 395, 568. The female felon was not unique: a number of women voluntarily joined up, disguised as men, in early modern armies and navies. See, for numerous Dutch examples, R. Dekker and L. van de Pol, *The tradition of female cross-dressing in early modern Europe* (London, 1989).

21 The services of the three English writers are conveniently noted in Webb, *Elizabethan military science*, 44–50 (Williams served under Julián Romero); Romero's service during 'the Rough Wooing' is described in the admirable biography of A. Marichalar, *Julián Romero* (Madrid, 1952). On Henry VIII's other foreign soldiers during the war of 1544–6, see G. J. Millar, *Tudor mercenaries and auxiliaries, 1485–1547* (Charlottesville, 1980), chaps. 3–7.

22 See Parker, *Army of Flanders*, 213–15, for details on the 1590s. The picture in the 1640s is less clear. It is known that a number of officers returned to Britain from the continent to fight, but how many fully trained NCOs and veterans came too? Judging by the speed with which the Civil War armies picked up continental military practice, they must have been numerous. Edmund Ludlow, who rose to be colonel in the Parliamentary service, was 17 when the Civil War began and had no military knowledge. So he and some fellow-students at the Inns of Court 'procured a person experienced in military affairs to instruct us in the use of arms'; but to little avail. In September 1642, Ludlow and his regiment were thrown into total panic by rumours of the enemy's approach, until rallied by 'an old souldier (a generation of men much cried up at that time)'. At the battle of Edgehill the next month, they managed to fire the artillery at the cavalry of their own side, and disaster was only averted because the inexperienced gunners aimed their pieces badly and packed the wrong charge. Incidents like this, in which Ludlow's fascinating account abounds, help to explain the desperate hunger of all armies for veterans. See Firth, *The Memoirs of Edmund Ludlow*, 38–42. For some further details see Roy, 'England turned Germany?', 130f; and P. Young, *Edgehill 1642. The campaign and the battle* (Kineton, 1967), 52 and 63–9.

23 Robert Baillie and the Scots Commissioners in London, quoted in D. Stevenson, *Revolution and counter-revolution in Scotland* (London, 1977), 32. For a list of the troops and an assessment of their achievements see C. O Danachair, 'Montrose's Irish regiments', *The Irish sword*, IV (1959–60), 61–7; and J. Lowe, 'The earl of Antrim and Irish aid to Montrose in 1644', *ibid.*, 191–8.

24 Stevenson, *Alastair MacColla*, 106f, has argued that the troops were probably not from Flanders, largely on the basis of the account in T. Carte, *The life of James, duke of Ormond*, III (2nd edn, Oxford, 1851), 58. But Carte was extremely hostile to Antrim (cf. *ibid.*, 53, 57, 508 etc.); and he did not have access to

Antrim's own papers. Compare the account of the better-informed secretary to Owen Roe O'Neill (Antrim's ally and himself a Flanders veteran) in J. T. Gilbert, ed., *A contemporary history of affairs in Ireland from 1641 to 1652*, I.i (Dublin, 1879), 89f. See also D. Laing, ed., *The letters and journals of Robert Baillie ... 1637–1662*, II (Edinburgh, 1842: Bannatyne Club, LXXIII.2), 233; J. Spalding, *Memorialls of the trubles in Scotland and in England AD 1624–AD 1645*, II (ed., J. Stuart, Aberdeen, 1851: Spalding Club, XXIII), 385; B. Jennings, *Wild Geese in Spanish Flanders 1582–1700. Documents relating chiefly to Irish regiments from the Archives Générales du Royaume, Brussels, and other sources* (Dublin, 1964), 361f, 593f; and R. D. Fitzsimon, 'Irish swordsmen in the Imperial service in the Thirty Years War', *The Irish sword*, IX (1969–70), 22–31. I am grateful to Jane Ohlmeyer for drawing these sources to my attention. For further examples of continental veterans among Irish forces in the Civil Wars see T. W. Moody, F. X. Martin and F. J. Byrne, eds., *A new history of Ireland. III: Early modern Ireland, 1534–1691* (Oxford, 1976), 293; and p. 245 n.83 below.

25 See Roy, 'Royalist army', 206; and Firth, *Cromwell's army*, 37.

26 Parker, *Thirty Years War*, 204; Parker, *Army of Flanders*, 213 n.4; and B. Kroener, 'Soldat oder Soldateska', in M. Messerschmidt, ed., *Militärgeschichte. Probleme-Thesen-Wege* (Frankfurt, 1982), 100–23, at p. 119. The number of veterans in the Army of Flanders was also very high. For example in the nominal lists of mutineers compiled in the 1590s, men were noted whose service stretched back for decades and covered most of the Habsburg empire – from the Indies Guard Squadron and the Armada campaign to Lepanto and Lombardy. See AGS, *Contaduría Mayor de Cuentas* 2a época, 29 and 47.

27 Turner, *Memoirs*, 14. These lines were written as a comment on his behaviour in 1640 when he left Sweden for Scotland: there were two ships in the harbour, one going to the Royalists and the other to the Covenanters. Turner realized he did not care which one he boarded. See similar examples of troops from the same nation showing reluctance to fight each other in Hale, *War and society*, 70f.

28 Copious details are provided by C. G. Cruickshank, *Elizabeth's Army* (2nd edn, Oxford, 1966), chap. 2; L. Boynton, *The Elizabethan militia 1558–1638* (London, 1967), chap. 5; and S. J. Stearns, 'Conscription and English society in the 1620s', *Journal of British Studies*, XI (1972), 1–23. 'Impressment' was used by both sides during the English Civil War from 1643 onwards (see Roy, 'The Royalist army', 186–9; and Firth, *Cromwell's Army*, 21 and n.4); and afterwards – see, for example, R. E. Scouller, *The armies of Queen Anne* (Oxford, 1966), chap. 3.

29 S. Reid, *Scots armies of the civil war 1639–1651* (Leigh-on-sea, 1982), 12, quoting a contemporary description. The Scots may have been unique in their obsession with punishing sexual transgressions, but the idea of sending secular offenders off to the wars was accepted by most continental governments: for some examples see Parker, *Army of Flanders*, chap. 1.

30 On the *indelningsverk*, see Roberts, *Gustavus Adolphus*, II, 207–11; C. Nordmann, 'L'Armée suédoise au XVIIe siècle', *Revue du Nord*, LIV (1972), 133–47; and A. Åberg, 'The Swedish army from Lützen to Narva', in Roberts, ed., *Sweden's age of greatness 1632–1718* (London, 1972), 265–87. Information on its costs from J. Lindegren, *Utskrivning och utsugning. Produktion och reproduktion i Bygdeå 1620–1640* (Uppsala, 1980: Studia Historica Upsaliensia, CXVII), 159, 168, 175, and 256–7; J. Lindegren, 'The Swedish military state, 1560–1720', *Scandinavian Journal of History*, X (1985), 305–27, especially pp. 317ff; and from further details kindly supplied to me by Dr Lindegren in January 1980, and by

Dr Jan Sundin and his colleagues at the Demographic Database at Umeå. Dr Lindegren was at pains to discourage scholars from generalizing from the experience of Bygdeå until other parishes had been studied; but the Database team has confirmed that Bygdeå was by no means unique. The drain in manpower did not, of course, cease in 1640. Considerable numbers of Swedish troops were sent to Germany in 1642 (7,000 under Torstensson), in 1646 (a further 6,630 men) and in 1648 (7,100 under Prince Karl Gustav). See these and other figures in L. Tingsten, *Fältmarskalkarna Johan Baner och Lennart Torstensson såsom härförare* (Stockholm, 1932) part II, chap. 1; *Från Femern och Jankow till Westfaliska Freden*, 80; and F. Asgaard, *Kampen om Ostersjön på Carl X Gustafs tid. Ett bidrag till nordisk Sjökrigshistoria* (Haderslev, 1974: Carl X Gustav Studier, VI), *passim*. It should be noted that the *indelningsverk* system was overhauled under Charles XI and worked thereafter with exemplary efficiency for domestic defence; but for overseas campaigns it still proved inadequate (see Roberts, ed., *Sweden's age of greatness*, 248 and 268). Denmark also introduced permanent conscription in 1627, but only for defence: see E. L. Petersen, 'Defence, war and finance: Christian IV and the Council of the Realm', *Scandinavian journal of history*, VII (1982), 309.

31 Lord Mountjoy to the Privy Council, 1 May 1601, quoted in Fitzsimon, 'Irish Swordsmen', 22. For loss ratios, see Corvisier, 'Guerre et mentalités', 222. He suggests a total military mortality of 600,000 (or 20,000 a year) during the Thirty Years War (1618–48) and of 700,000 (or 64,000 a year) during the War of the Spanish Succession (1702–13).

32 Apart from the data in figure 3, see Parker, *Army of Flanders*, 209f (details on Spanish, Italian, German and Walloon units, 1574–1630); and J. W. Wijn, 'Het Noordhollandse regiment in de eerste jaren van de opstand tegen Spanje', *Tijdschrift voor Geschiedenis*, LXII (1949), 235–61 (deaths ran at 1.5 per cent per month 1572–7); and Corvisier, *L'Armée française*, II, 682 and 737.

33 See P. Newman, *The battle of Marston Moor, 1644* (Chichester, 1981), 126; H. H. Schaufler, *Die Schlacht bei Freiburg-im-Breisgau* (Freiburg, 1979), 7, 86, and *passim*; and D. S. Chandler, *The art of war in the age of Marlborough* (London, 1976), 304.

34 Details from *Monro his Expedition*, 75, 78, 94; E. de la Barre Duparcq, *L'Art militaire des guerres de religion* (Paris, 1864), 59f; and D. Dymond, *Captain John Mason and the duke of Buckingham* (Portsmouth, 1972: the Portsmouth Papers, XVII), 10. Another English example of heavy losses is offered by the 20 volunteers recruited in 1642 for King Charles I in the parish of Middle, Shropshire: 13 were killed, 'And if soe many dyed' from Middle, noted its chronicler in 1700, 'wee may reasonably guesse that many thousands dyed in Englande in that warre' (R. Gough, *The history of Myddle* [ed. D. Hey, Harmondsworth, 1981], 71f. See also the estimates of C. Carlton, *Going to the wars. The experience of the British civil wars, 1638–1651* (London, 1992), 204–6.

35 Quotation from C. A. Campan, ed., *Bergues sur le Soom assiégée* (Brussels, 1867, reprinting an original tract of 1623), 407. For a further example of troops deserting '50 by 50 and 100 by 100' from the Spanish siege of Leiden in 1574, see Parker, *Army of Flanders*, 212n; and for desertion by 'scores and half scores at a time' from the same army thirty years later, see *De L'Isle and Dudley Mss.*, III, 205–6 (Sergeant Throckmorton to Robert Sydney, 22 September 1605) and 302–3 (Sir William Browne to *idem*, 12 August 1606).

36 See E. G. Friedman, *Spanish captives in North Africa in the early modern age* (Madison, 1983), chap. 2.

37 See Parker, *Army of Flanders*, 207, 210; and L. G. White, 'War and government in a Castilian province: Estremadura, 1640–1668' (University of East Anglia Ph.D. thesis, 1985), 257: in September 1657, the four tercios of the army of Extremadura, with a paper strength of 9,900 men, actually numbered (according to their commander-in-chief) less than 1,000.

38 Details from Parrott, 'The administration of the French army,' chap. 2; B. Kroener, *Les Routes et les étapes. Die Versorgung der französischen Armeen in Nordostfrankreich 1635–1661* (2 vols., Münster, 1980: Schriftenreihe der Vereinigung zur Erforschung der neueren Geschichte, XI), 4, 177–8; and idem, 'Die Entwicklung der Truppenstärken in den französichen Armeen zwischen 1635 und 1661' in K. Repgen, ed., *Forschungen und Quellen zur Geschichte des dreissigjährigen Krieges* (Münster, 1981: Schriftenreihe der Vereinigung zur Erforschung der neueren Geschichte, XII), 163–220.

39 See Parrott, *The administration of the French army*; and Corvisier, *Armée française*, II, 682 and 737.

40 A. Zysberg, 'Galley and hard labor convicts in France (1550–1850)' in P. Spierenburg, ed., *The emergence of carceral institutions: prisons, galleys and lunatic asylums 1550–1900* (Rotterdam, 1984), 78–124, at pp. 82–4; and Corvisier, *Armée française*, II, 693–747. For the treatment of deserters in the Spanish army (often execution or outlawry), see Parker, *Army of Flanders*, 216 and n. 3; and Parker, *Thirty Years War*, 277 n.26. No early modern state, however, adopted the stringent methods of the Roman Imperial Army, which *branded* its recruits on enlistment in order to facilitate recapture if they tried to desert. See A. H. M. Jones, *The later Roman Empire, 284–602. A social, economic and administrative survey*, II (Oxford, 1964), chap. 17 ('The army'), at p. 618.

41 The whole question of looting is admirably covered in F. Redlich, *De Praeda militari: looting and booty, 1500–1815* (Wiesbaden, 1956: Vierteljahrschrift für Sozial- und Wirtschaftsgeschichte, Beiheft XXXIX). For a selection of harrowing incidents arising from the plundering of armies see: W. Crowne, *A true relation* (London, 1637) in F. C. Springell, *connoisseur and diplomat. The earl of Arundel's embassy to Germany in 1636* (London, 1963), 54–135; A. T. van Deursen, 'Holland's experience of war during the revolt of the Netherlands' in A. C. Duke and C. A. Tamse, eds., *Britain and the Netherlands. VI: War and society* (The Hague, 1977), 19–53; S. Gaber, *La Lorraine meutrie: les malheurs de la Guerre de Trente Ans* (Nancy, 1979), 83–98; G. Franz, *Der dreissigjährige Krieg und das deutsche Volk* (4th edn, Stuttgart, 1979), 104–15; and H. Langer, *The Thirty Years War* (Poole, 1980), *passim*.

42 Details from A. Ernstberger, 'Plünderung des Leipziger Messegeleites Nürnberger und Augsburger Kaufleute am 26. Januar 1638 bei Neustadt an der Heid', *Jahrbuch für fränkische Landesforschung*, XXII (1962), 101–20.

43 Naturally the ransoms varied according to the status of the captive. King Francis I, captured at the battle of Pavia in 1525, was ransomed for 2 million escudos (£500,000), probably the largest ransom ever paid: see the fascinating study of R. Carande, 'Solimán no llega a Viena (1532) y de España sale un tesoro recibido de Francisco I' in *Studi in onore di Amintore Fanfani*, IV (Milan, 1962), 185–218. On the tariffs established in the seventeenth century for the exchange or ransom of prisoners, see: Parker, *Army of Flanders*, 169f; Parker, *Thirty Years War*, 203f; and the references there cited.

44 On the 'rules' of war that governed such actions as plunder and sack, see T. Meron, *Henry's wars and Shakespeare's laws. Perspectives on the law of war in the later Middle Ages* (Oxford, 1994); G. Parker, 'Early modern Europe' in M.

Howard, G. J. Andreopoulos and M. R. Shulman, *The laws of war. Constraints on warfare in the Western world* (New Haven, 1994), 40–58 and 233–40; B. Donagan, 'Codes and conduct in the English Civil War', *Past and Present*, CXVIII (1988), 65–95; and Redlich, *De Praeda Militari*.

45 On the spoils of Antwerp see P. Genard, 'La Furie espagnole. Documents pour servir à l'histoire du sac d'Anvers en 1576', *Annales de l'Académie royale d'archéologie de Belgique*, XXXII (1876), 471ff; and Parker, *Army of Flanders*, 181f. On the Scottish plunder – much of it from Dundee, which was sacked for two weeks – see H. Cary, *Memorials of the Great Civil War in England from 1646 to 1652*, II (London, 1842), 351: Monck to Lenthall, 1 September 1651. Among other contemporaries, John Nicoll in Aberdeen (*A diary of public transactions* [Aberdeen, 1836: Bannatyne Club, LII], 58), thought the booty taken at Dundee was worth £200,000 sterling; while Bulstrode Whitelocke in London (*Memorials*, III, 351) heard that the soldiers got spoil worth £500 each, so that 'a private soldier [was] hardly to be known from an officer'. Further examples of plunder at this time are recorded in Firth, *Cromwell's army*, 189–94.

46 Emeric Crucé, *Le nouveau Cynée* (1623), quoted (with sundry early modern examples of impoverishment through war), by Parker, *Army of Flanders*, 120. See, for an earlier period, the masterly essay of M. M. Postan, 'The costs of the Hundred Years War', *Past and present*, XXVII (1964), 34–53; and, more recently, P. Contamine, *La France aux XIVe et XVe siècles. Hommes, mentalités, guerre et paix* (London, 1981), chap. 8.

47 The Spanish mutinies during the Low Countries' Wars are discussed at length in Parker, *Army of Flanders*, chap. 8, and Parker, *Spain and the Netherlands*, chap. 5 (references to works concerning mutinies in other early modern armies are given at pp. 242–3, notes 22–4 and 26). But see also the subsequent studies of R. Baumann, *Das Söldnerwesen im 16. Jahrhundert im bayerischen und süddeutschen Beispiel. Eine gesellschafts-geschichtliche Untersuchung* (Munich, 1978), 185–201; M. A. Kishlansky, *The rise of the New Model Army* (Cambridge, 1979), 179–222; and H. Valentinitsch, *Die meuterei der Kaiserlichen Söldner in Kärntern und Steiermark, 1656* (Vienna, 1975: Militärhistorische Schriftenreihe, XXIX).

48 Sanuto quoted by Hale, *War and society*, 70.

49 Redlich, *The German military enterpriser*, I, 456. The largest groups were Germans (534 soldiers) and Italians (217), with smaller numbers of Poles, Slovenes, Croats, Hungarians, Greeks, Dalmatians, Lorrainers, Burgundians, Turks, French, Czechs, Spaniards, Scots and Irish.

50 AGRB, *Secrétairerie d'État et de Guerre* 36 fo. 29v, Order of 20 March 1636; and *ibid.* 43 fo. 128v, Order of 3 February 1643. The fact was confirmed by a sharp-eyed English soldier in the Netherlands who noted that the surrendered Spanish garrison of Rijnberg in 1633 included 'foote companies very thin and many of them mere boys carrying small fierlocks' (G. Davies, ed., 'The autobiography of Thomas Raymond', 37).

51 Corvisier, *Louvois*, 347; Corvisier, *Armée française*, 637–52; Ruwet, *Soldats et régiments nationaux*, 67–99. 'Measuring soldiers' in the eighteenth century is complicated by two facts: (i) the records clearly show that males in this period continued to grow until at least age 24 (soldiers were measured each year: each year the younger men had grown a little taller); (ii) the 'feet and inches' of each country were somewhat different, making comparison hazardous (thus 1.83 metres corresponds to 6 feet for England, 5 *pieds* 10 *pouces* in the Austrian Netherlands but only 5 *pieds* 8 *pouces* in France). The problem of finding suffi-

cient tall soldiers was not confined to early modern times. 'Tall fellows' had also been hard to recruit during the Middle Ages (A. Goodman, *The Wars of the Roses. Military activity and English society 1452–1497* [London, 1981], 137); and continued to be so in the early nineteenth century (J. P. Aron, P. Dumont and E. Le Roy Ladurie, *Anthropologie du conscrit français d'après les comptes numériques et sommaires du recrutement de l'armée 1819–26* [Paris, 1972], 193ff). In the First World War short men enlisted into 'Bantam regiments', where heights ranged from 5 feet to 5 feet 3 inches (see J. Keegan, *The face of battle* [London, 1976], 219).

52 BL, *Additional Ms.* 28,373 fos. 129–30, Memorial of Esteban de Ibarra to Philip II, 15 December 1596. Other armies shared the experience. According to Wijn, 'Het Noordhollandse regiment', 245 and n. 19, the cost to the States-General of a 150-man company almost doubled between 1576 and 1623.

53 G. Botero, *Relatione della Republica Venitiana* (Venice, 1605), fo. 19v (part of a section entitled 'Si il denaro sia, o non sia, neruo della guerra'); Aytona quoted in Parker, *Army of Flanders*, 18; Mendoza, *Teoría y práctica de la guerra* (Madrid, 1595), quoted in G. Parker, *The Dutch Revolt* (London, 1977), 309 n. 15. In 1695, Charles Davenant wrote that 'the whole art of war is in a manner reduced to money; and nowadays that prince who can best find money to feed, clothe and pay his army ... is surest of success' (quoted in A. Cobban, *The eighteenth century* [London, 1969], 181).

54 1982 figures from International Institute for Strategic Studies, *The military balance 1983–1984*; 1700s figures from P. Goubert, *L'Ancien régime*, II (Paris, 1973), 126–39. On England in the 1650s, see M. Ashley, *Financial and commercial policy under the Cromwellian protectorate* (2nd edn, London, 1962), 48, 104–5. It could be argued that such comparisons are misleading, because the governments of early modern Europe absorbed a far smaller proportion of the Gross National Product than their present-day successors; but in the preindustrial economy the surplus of goods and services beyond those needed for mere subsistence was so small that meeting the cost of war required economic and social adjustments wholly disproportionate (by our standards) to the size of the resources involved.

55 See, for some examples, P. Contamine, 'Les Fortifications urbaines en France à la fin du Moyen Âge: aspects financiers et économiques', *Revue historique*, CCLX (1978), 23–47; R. Endres, 'Der dreissigjährige Krieg in Franken', *Jahrbuch des historischen Vereins für Mittelfranken*, XCI (1983), 65–77, at pp. 76f; and C. R. Friedrichs, *Urban society in an age of war: Nördlingen 1580–1720* (Princeton, 1979), 25ff.

56 Details from M. Merriman, *The rough wooing: Scotland, England, France 1543–1550* (forthcoming); and F. C. Dietz, *English public finance, 1485–1641*, I (2nd edn, London, 1964), 144–58.

57 Details from R. Carande, *Carlos V y sus banqueros*, III (Madrid, 1967), 16–21.

58 Figures from C. M. Cipolla, ed., *The Fontana economic history of Europe*, II (London, 1974), 568–70.

59 See Parker, *Dutch revolt*, 168–78, for 1575–6; and Israel, *The Dutch Republic*, 170–81, for 1627–9.

60 See J. D. Tracy, *A financial revolution in the Habsburg Netherlands. Renten and Renteniers in the county of Holland 1515–1565* (Berkeley, 1985); and M. 't Hart, *The making of a bourgeois state. War, politics and finance during the Dutch Republic* (Manchester, 1993).

61 Details from Cipolla, *Fontana economic history*, 573–4 and 579–81; and

Groenveld and Leeuwenberg, *De bruid in de schuit*, 146. It is true that the Dutch, in particular, were able to finance part of their war-effort by prizes and by 'convoy and licence money', but the costs of collection were high and the returns uncertain. See the salutary remarks by F. Snapper, *Oorlogsinvloeden op de overzeese handel van Holland 1551–1719* (Amsterdam, 1959), 41f, 52ff, 76f.

62 There are two outstanding studies on the rise of the military enterprisers: Redlich, *Military enterpriser*; and I. A. A. Thompson, *War and government in Habsburg Spain 1560–1620* (London, 1976). Both are essential reading.

63 For the singularly unsuccessful careers of Mansfeld and Knyphausen see (respectively), W. Brünink, *Der Graf von Mansfeld in Ostfriesland (1622–1624)* (Aurich, 1957: Abhandlungen und Vorträge zur Geschichte Ostfrieslands, XXXIV); and C. Sattler, *Reichsfreiherr Dodo zu Innhausen und Knyphausen, königliche schwedischen Feltmarshall* (Norden, 1891). For the personal fortunes of some others, see Redlich, *Military enterpriser*, I, 420–6; and K. R. Böhme, *Bremisch-Verdische Staatsfinanzen 1645–76* (Uppsala, 1976), 34. The splendid palaces of generals such as Wrangel (at Skokloster, north of Stockholm) or Wallenstein (in Prague, Mnichovo Hradiště and Jičín) testify even today to the wealth that could be gained through war. The wealthy generals brought with them a style of expenditure that few had seen before in northern Europe: when Sir James Turner revisited Stockholm in the 1650s he noted it was 'much beautified ... with these sumptuous and magnificent palaces which the Suedish generals have built, as monuments of these riches they acquired in the long German warre' (*Memoirs*, 12).

64 Wallenstein to Count Harrach, 28 January 1626: quoted A. Ernstberger, *Hans de Witte, Finanzmann Wallensteins* (Wiesbaden, 1954: Vierteljahrschrift für Sozial- und Wirtschaftsgeschichte, Beiheft XXXVIII), 166.

65 H. J. C. von Grimmelshausen, *Der abenteurliche Simplicissimus Teutsch* (Montbéliard, 1669), Book I, chap. 16.

66 The best description of *Brandschatzung* is to be found in Redlich, *De praeda militari*, 45–8. On the spread of 'protection' in the Dutch wars see Parker, *Army of Flanders*, 17f. However, not all commanders favoured the selling of indiscriminate protection. In 1640 a Spanish general complained that 'The majority of the villages in the "contribution land" [North Flanders and North Brabant] contain enemy "protection troops" ... [This] gives rise to many inconveniences for His Majesty's service. One is that our own men cannot go there to collect information about the enemy, because they are immediately arrested as spies by the protection troops. And, thanks to their presence, the peasants are able to bring their crops in safely and provide full aid and assistance to the enemy' (AHN, *Estado libro* 972, Sfondrato to Salamanca, 4 June 1640).

67 On contributions see Parker, *Army of Flanders*, 142f; F. Redlich, 'Contributions in the Thirty Years War', *Economic history review*, XII (1959–60), 247–54; I. Bog, *Die bäuerliche Wirtschaft im Zeitalten des Dreissigjährigen Krieges. Die Bewegungsvorgänge in der Kriegswirtschaft nach der Quellen des Klosterverwalteramtes Heilsbronn* (Coburg, 1952), 142–54; G. Benecke, 'Labour relations and peasant society in north-west Germany, c. 1600', *History*, LVIII (1973), 350–9; and J. A. Lynn, 'How war fed war: the tax of violence and contributions during the *Grand siècle*', *Journal of Modern History*, LXV (1993), 286–310.

68 L. André, *Michel le Tellier et l'organisation de l'armée monarchique* (Paris, 1906), 64. In general, see M. van Creveld, *Supplying war: logistics from Wallenstein to Patton* (Cambridge, 1977), 34ff, and Kroener, *Les Routes et les étapes, passim*.

69 Hale, *War and society*, 47. Some idea of the total cost of artillery may be

gained from an admirable study of the foundry at Mechelen in the Habsburg Netherlands: B. Roosens, 'Het arsenaal van Mechelen en de wapenhandel 1551–1567', *Bijdragen tot de geschiedenis*, LX (1977), 175–247. Vigenère, *L'Art militaire d'Onosender*, 675v–723v, reckoned that, when the cost of ammunition, transport, manufacture and wages was added in, each cannon ball fired represented an outlay of between 200 and 300 escudos (about £50). Normally transport was the most expensive item: the hire of a team of 80 horses, drivers and carts for each cannon of the Army of Flanders cost, in 1579, 25 escudos a day (AGRB *Audience* 1818/2, unfol., 'Estimation' of Peter-Ernest of Mansfelt and Alfonso Dávalos).

70 For the problems of arming the troops fighting Tyrone, see Huntington Library, MS. HA 4151, 4160 and 4162–4164 (references kindly supplied from the Lieutenancy Papers among the Hastings Manuscripts by Dr Simon Adams); and R. W. Stewart, 'Arms and politics: the supply of arms in England 1585–1625' (Yale University Ph.D. thesis, 1986), chapter 6 part ii. Essex's lament is from E. G. Atkinson, ed., *Calendar of state papers relating to Ireland ... 1599–1600* (London, 1899), 29 (the earl to the Privy Council, 9 May 1599).

71 Orrery, *Treatise*, 29. In 1621, a Bill to standardize all calibres and bores for firearms was defeated in the English Parliament: see Stewart *Arms and politics*, chap. 7.

72 Clarendon and Bulstrode quoted by Roy, 'Royalist army', 50.

73 Quotation from Wanklyn, 'The king's armies in the west', 98. Bristol's arms production is given at p. 100. See also further details at pp. 95–102.

74 Hopton to Prince Rupert, September 1643, quoted *ibid.*, 95. Both Roy and Wanklyn offer convincing evidence that the king's armies were not defeated through any defect in their supply, but by bad leadership. Neither do Charles's enemies seem to have experienced difficulties in securing arms: the Scottish factor at Vere in Zeeland, Thomas Cuningham, dispatched no less than 31,673 muskets, 29,000 swords, 8,000 pikes, 500 pairs of pistols, 12 field pieces and 50,000 pounds of shot to the Covenanting armies between 1639 and 1644 (E. S. Courthope, ed., *The journal of Thomas Cuningham of Campvere, 1640–1654* [Edinburgh 1928: Scottish History Society, 3rd series XI], *passim*).

75 See the important and provocative essay of R. H. C. Davis, 'The medieval warhorse' in F. M. L. Thompson, ed., *Horses in European economic history: a preliminary canter* (Reading, 1983), 4–20.

76 Allmand, *Society at war*, 6–8, argued that the place of cavalry in the French army declined from Agincourt onwards. But Vale, *War and chivalry*, chap. 4.i, demonstrated that, although the loss of several thousand knights in the battle created a temporary shortage of cavalry, it was soon made good.

77 See F. Lot, *Recherches sur les effectifs des armées françaises des guerres d'Italie aux guerres de religion (1494–1562)* (Paris, 1962), 16–21 and 53–6.

78 French army strengths noted in D. L. M. Avenel, ed., *Lettres, instructions diplomatiques et papiers d'État du Cardinal de Richelieu*, IV (Paris, 1861), 688–9: Richelieu to Servien, 23 March 1635; and V (Paris, 1863), 3–6: 'Abrégé du Controole générale', May 1635. Monck's *Observations* (1645), quoted in Firth, *Cromwell's army*, 110n, advocated an infantry to cavalry ratio of 2:1 on campaign and of 3 or 4:1 in sieges. Admittedly, at Naseby (1645) the king's army contained almost as many cavalry as infantry (Firth, *Cromwell's army*, 111); and, in the same year, the Swedish *Hauptarmee* in Germany included 8,500 horse to 6,100 infantry (Tingsten, *Fältmarskalkarna Johan Baner och Lennart Torstensson såsom härförare* 258ff). But these were exhausted armies,

operating in exhausted terrain, for whom mobility was imperative.

79 Details from Vale, *War and chivalry*, 121–6; Giorgio Basta, *Gobierno de la Cavallería ligera* (Brussels, 1624), 68; Barker, *The military intellectual and battle*, 182ff; and A. T. S. Goodrick, ed., *The relation of Sydnam Poyntz* (London, 1980: Camden Society Publications, 3rd series XIV), 127f.

80 The problems of the Army of Flanders were only overcome when 1,500 remounts arrived from Germany: AGRB, *Secrétairerie d'État et de Guerre* 14 fos. 53–4, Order of 4 August 1592. For England, see Hutton, *The Royalist war effort*, 97; J. S. Morrill, ed., *Reactions to the English Civil War, 1642–1649* (London, 1982), 118–20; for Spain, R. A. Stradling, 'Spain's military failure and the supply of horses, 1600–1660', *History*, LXIX (1984), 213.

81 Details from Ian Roy, 'The Royalist army in the First Civil War' (Oxford University D.Phil. thesis, 1963), chap. 3; and Newman, 'The Royalist army in Northern England 1642–5', chap. 11.

82 Joan Thirsk, *Horses in early modern England: for service, for pleasure, for power* (Reading, 1978), 27. Unfortunately Dr Thirsk provides no information on horses for war during the 1640s. See, however, P. R. Edwards, 'The horse trade of the Midlands in the seventeenth century', *Agricultural history review*, XXVII (1979), 90–100; Firth, *Cromwell's army*, 241–7; and C. A. Holmes, *The Eastern Association in the English Civil War* (Cambridge, 1974), 149f.

83 See Stradling, 'Spain's military failure'; and White, 'War and government', 253 and 494–500 (see also p. 298 on horse losses). For the increasing cavalry component in Louis XIV's wars, see Chandler, *The art of war*, part I. But equestrian supply problems could recur even in the late eighteenth century: see Lynn, *Bayonets of the Republic*, 195–9.

84 Davies, 'Autobiography of Thomas Raymond', 40. Sir James Turner noted that it was always hard for new recruits 'who knew not before what it was [like] not to have tuo or three meals a day, and goe to bed at a seasonable houre at night ... to ly constantly in the fields with little or no shelter, to march allways a foot and drinke water' (*Memoirs*, 4, 6). Similar hardship stories are to be found in the annals of all armies. See a selection in Firth, *Cromwell's army*, 247–50 and, for an earlier period, in Hale, *War and society*, 171–8.

85 Details from Roy, 'Royalist army', 252; and Reid, *Scots armies*, 18.

86 André, *Michel le Tellier*, 339. In the 1620s the Swedish army planned to supply its troops from a central depot with clothes of only two sizes, two-thirds large and one-third small; but there is no evidence that this scheme was ever implemented (Roberts, *Gustavus Adolphus*, II, 237f; and Nordmann, 'L'Armée suédoise', 137).

87 In the 1470s duke Charles the Rash of Burgundy issued his infantry with a special ribbon of blue and white, and his cavalry with a red St Andrew's cross (which remained the badge of troops fighting for the House of Burgundy, and its Spanish Habsburg descendents, until 1700). See M. de la Chauvelays, *Les Armées de Charles le Téméraire dans les deux Bourgognes* (Paris, 1879), 126. The idea of coloured 'scarves' as distinguishing marks is found as early as the fourteenth century: see Contamine, *Guerre, état et société*, 667ff. Later, the 'scarf' was combined with a coloured token worn in the hat. See, for example, the description of a group of Spanish mutineers in 1603 who, at a given moment, 'all tooke out of their hatts the king's colours and putt off their red skarfes, and putt orange coloured feathers and other skarfes instead of them', to show they would sooner fight for the Dutch than for Spain (*De L'Isle and Dudley Mss*, III, 31: Sir William Browne to Robert Sydney, 25 May 1603).

88 Whitelocke, *Memorials of the English affairs*, III, 345–6. This was a cunning device, for white had been the 'token' used when Parliamentary and Scottish forces fought on the same side in the 1640s! Orrery, *Treatise*, 183f, gives a number of examples to show how easily a mark could be replaced when the fortunes of battle left men temporarily in the midst of their enemies (*inter alia*, Sir Thomas Fairfax at Marston Moor).

89 M. Roberts, ed., *Swedish diplomats at Cromwell's court 1655–1656: the missions of Peter Julius Coyet and Christer Bonde* (London, 1988: Camden Society, 4th series XXXVI), 125, Christer Bonde to Charles X, 23 August 1655 o.s. The view that the New Model Army wore red coats is repeatedly stated by Firth, *Cromwells army*, 231–5; but his evidence all concerns how units were supplied for a new campaign, never how they were equipped once it got underway.

90 For Gallas, see Parker, *Thirty Years War*, 192. For the permanence of regiments see Roberts, *Gustavus Adolphus*, 220f; P. Hoyos, 'Die Kaiserliche Armee 1648–50' in *Der dreissigjährige Krieg*, 170–232; and J. Childs, *The army of Charles II* (London, 1976), chap. 1.

91 On the first hospital see E. van Autenboer, 'De eerste stichting van het spaansche gasthuis, 1567–8', *Mechelse Bijdragen*, X (1943), 99–103; on complaints about the absence of such facilities in 1574 see the documents quoted in Parker, *Spain and the Netherlands*, 109f, and 156ff.

92 See L. van Meerbeck, 'Le service sanitaire de l'armée espagnole des Pays-Bas à la fin du XVIe et au XVIIe siècle', *Revue internationale d'histoire militaire*, XX (1959), 479–93; L. van Meerbeeck, 'L'Hôpital royale de l'armée espagnole à Malines en l'an 1637', *Bulletin du cercle archéologique de Malines*, LIV (1950), 81–125; Parker, *Army of Flanders*, 167–9; and – a document overlooked by all of the above – AGRB, *Secrétairerie d'État et de Guerre* 175 bis fos. 1–16. Between 1614 and 1629, the hospital's administrator spent almost 1 million florins (£100,000) on the cure of sick and wounded soldiers. It is interesting to note that a substantial annual payment was made to the hospital in the 1640s specifically to cure those afflicted with *el mal gálico* (syphilis) by a course of steambaths and cauterization (Parker, *Army of Flanders*, 169 n.2).

93 These services are discussed in Parker, *Army of Flanders*, 168–72. For the pensions see also AGRB, *Secrétairerie d'État et de Guerre* 175 bis fos. 20–45; for payments to ransomed troops, see *ibid.*, fos. 46–169 (this 486-folio register, which appears to have belonged to the army's *Contaduria del Sueldo*, contains 32 sections, each one full of important government orders on different aspects of military administration). For payment of free bread rations even to the wives of Spanish troops captured at Rocroi and the Dunes, see *Secrétairerie d'État et de Guerre* 43 fo. 186v (19 November 1643) and 57 fo. 2 (10 March 1659). For a general survey of the records of the Army of Flanders – probably the richest for any early modern army – see G. Parker, *Guide to the archives of the Spanish institutions in or concerned with the Netherlands 1556–1706* (Brussels, 1971); and L. van Meerbeck, *Les Sources de l'histoire administrative de l'armée espagnole des Pays-Bas aux XVIe et XVIIe siècles* (Brussels, 1948: Collection d'histoire militaire belge, X).

94 On care for the sick, the wounded and the old in some other armies see, for France: L. André, *Michel le Tellier et Louvois* (Paris, 1943), 379–83; André, *Michel le Tellier et l'organisation de l'armée*, 469–95; C. Jones, 'The welfare of the French footsoldier', *History*, LXV (1980), 193–213 (containing a splendidly apposite quotation from Cardinal Richelieu on p. 194: '2000 men leaving hospital cured, and in some sense broken in to the profession, are far more valuable than even 6000 new recruits'). For the ancillary services of the English army,

see Webb, *Elizabethan military science*, 213f (for details on a military hospital in Dublin after 1600, run and financed on lines similar to the Spanish); Firth, *Cromwell's army*, chap. 11; Childs, *Army of Charles II*, 53–6, 72–4; and V. Neuburg, *Popular literature: a history and a guide* (London, 1977), 249–51 (on *The souldier's pocket Bible*, a 16-page pamphlet issued to Parliamentary troops after 1643, and *The souldier's monitor*, of which 15,500 copies were distributed to the English army in 1701). See, for further examples of military philanthropy, Corvisier, *Armies and societies*, 82–6.

95 See some detailed representative figures in Firth, *Cromwell's army*, 208–12; J. Hogan, ed., *Négociations de M. le Comte d'Avaux en Irlande 1689–90* (Dublin, 1934), 705–11 (Avaux was attached to the army of James II for the campaign in Ireland in 1690 and his correspondence is full of military detail); and, from the other end of Europe, G. Benaglia, *Relazione del viaggio fatto a Constantinopli, e ritorno in Germania dell'illmo. Sig. Conte Alberto Caprara* (Bologna, 1684), 136–41 (with details on provisioning the Turkish army on its march along the Danube in 1683); and *Encyclopaedia of Islam*, III (Leiden, 1971), 191.

96 The arithmetic was daunting, as the following table (based on contemporary calculations) shows.

Livestock Yields

Date	Number of animals slaughtered	Average Dead Weight (in lbs.)	Total weight of meat (in lbs.)
1573	26 bullocks	254	6,596
	132 sheep	20	2,581
1577	8 bullocks	298	2,368
	56 sheep	22	1,212
1578	27 bullocks	300	6,800
	200 sheep	20	4,000
1580	25 bullocks	328	8,218
	159 sheep	28	4,654
1596	104 bullocks	163	17,013

The sources all come from areas along the Spanish Road: 1573 = AD Doubs (Besançon) B 1956; 1577 = AGRB *Chambre des Comptes* 25,775 (Arlon); 1578 = AGRB *Audience* 1690/2 (Luxembourg); 1580 = AGRB CC 25,805 (Arlon again); 1596 = AD Meurthe-et-Moselle B 5415 (Lorraine). Similar calculations of an average sheep-weight of between 20 and 30 pounds, and an average bullock weight of between 200 and 300 pounds (with an occasional *gras boeuf* of 500), are found in numerous other documents: e.g. AD Meurthe-et-Moselle G 79 fos. 8–10 (Toul, 1577); AGRB *Audience* 1733/2, fo. 130 (Luxembourg, 1573); and *ibid.*, 1818/4 folder 2 (mémoire of 1582). See further detail in: G. Parker, 'The Spanish Road and the army of Flanders. A study of the formation and disintegration of a European army 1567–1647' (Cambridge University Ph.D. thesis, 1968), 68; and BNM MS 8695 fo. 94, 'Estado de lo que es menester ... de un exército de 30,000 hombres'.

97 There is a good collection of material on quartering and its attendant evils in Holmes, *Eastern Association*, 153f, and Firth, *Cromwell's army*, 209–21.

98 See Parker, *Army of Flanders*, chaps. 2–3.

99 See the calculations in the important article of G. Perjés, 'Army provisioning, logistics and strategy in the second half of the seventeenth century', *Acta Historica*, XVI (1970), 1–51.

100 Davies, 'Autobiography of Thomas Raymond', 41.

101 Details from Firth, *Cromwell's army*, 222–5; and F. Dow, *Cromwellian Scotland 1651–1660* (Edinburgh, 1979), 123–35 (and map at p. 116). Monck's strategy was remarkably similar to that of Alexander the Great, who also used pack-horses instead of carts, and always tried either to campaign close to a sea or river, or else to create forward magazines. Both generals also exploited their superior supply system in order to force their worse-provisioned enemies to attack in unfavourable circumstances. See D. W. Engels, *Alexander the Great and the logistics of the Macedonian army* (Berkeley, 1978), 12–28, 45–61, and *passim*.

102 Examples taken from J. Jacquart, *La Crise rurale en Île-de-France, 1550–1670* (Paris, 1974), 186–99.

103 Richelieu, *Testament politique*, 480; and Parker, *Thirty Years War*, 163 (Baner) and 175 (Turenne and Gallas).

104 For some specific examples, see Parker, *Army of Flanders*, 176f, 288f; Parker, *Thirty Years War*, 199; and C. J. Gudde, *Vier eeuwen geschiedenis van het garnizoen 's Hertogenbosch* ('s Hertogenbosch, 1958), 29 – 3,000 soldiers with 2,219 camp-followers and family. J. J. Wallhausen, writing in 1621, estimated that a regiment of 3,000 soldiers normally travelled with 2,000 camp-followers and 300 carts (quoted by von Frauenholz, *Heerwesen*, I, 99). The figure of 500 carts per 15,000 men is given in Avenel, ed., *Lettres ... de Richelieu*, V, 3–6: 'Abrégé du controole générale', May 1635. For some interesting general remarks on camp-followers, see B. C. Hacker, 'Women and military institutions in early modern Europe: a reconnaisance', *Signs: the journal of women in culture and society*, VI (1980–1), 643–71; and H. M. Möller, *Das Regiment der Landsknechte. Untersuchungen zu Verfassung, Recht und Selbstverständnis in deutschen Söldnerheeren des 16. Jahrhunderts* (Wiesbaden, 1976: Frankfurter historische Abhandlungen, XII), 177–82.

105 Campan, ed., *Bergues sur le Soom*, 247; Parker, *Army of Flanders*, 176–7 and 288–9. But see the inflated estimates of 'mouths' given by some military commanders to those responsible for feeding the troops cited in *ibid.*, 87.

106 Redlich, *Military enterpriser*, I, 521–2. For further details on the 'civilian penumbra' which surrounded every early modern army, see Hale, *War and society*, chap. 6.

107 Numerous examples of the various methods of lodging troops in early modern times are given by Holmes, *Eastern Association*, 152–4; Hutton, *Royalist war effort*, 96–8; Firth, *Cromwell's army*, 216–19; Parker, *Army of Flanders*, 87–90; André, *Michel le Tellier*, 359–414; and André, *Michel le Tellier et Louvois*, 358–68.

108 Orrery, *Treatise*, 86. For examples of armies at this time which certainly marched with tents, see Firth, *Cromwell's army*, 247–50.

109 Compare, for example, Mallett, *Mercenaries*, plates 3a (a detail from Simone Martini's *Fogliano* fresco) and 13a (Giovanni Bettini circa 1449); G. and A. Parker, *European soldiers 1550–1650* (Cambridge, 1977), 28–9 (engravings of camps from 1544 and 1573); and A. Freitag, *Architectura militaris nova et aucta* (2nd edn, Leiden, 1665), figs. 111–12.

110 Elis Gruffudd, quoted by C. G. Cruickshank, *Army royal: an account of Henry VIII's invasion of France, 1513* (Oxford, 1969), 42; Monro, *Expedition*, II, 61f; Goodrick, *Poyntz*, 126. At the other end of the scale, see the luxurious campaign tent of Francis I in 1525, captured at Pavia and currently displayed in the Armería Real in Madrid, and the prefabricated wooden 'campaign house' and tent made of cloth of gold, taken to France by Henry VIII in 1513 and described in Cruickshank, *Army royal*, 43f.

111 Details and further references in Parker, *Army of Flanders*, 166f.
112 ARGB, *Secrétairerie d'État et de Guerre* 97, unfol., 'Resumen sucinto ... del pan de munición' (1678–9). Cfr. *ibid.*, 27 fos. 127–8, quittances for bread supplied by Proveedor-General Robertin to 'troops outside garrisons' in 1613 and 1614: on average, 350,000 rations of bread were supplied every month. Even in the 1570s and 80s, the army's contractors had succeeded in delivering heroic quantities of bread to the troops: between 11 October 1577 and 31 March 1580, Adam d'Odrimont provided 3,913,628 loaves to the army (AGRB, *Chambre des Comptes* 25,767). See also Antwerp, Plantijn Archief, no. 1263: accounts concerning the food supplied to the Antwerp garrison during the 1620s, including numerous testimonials from the troops concerning the high quality and commendable reliability of the daily bread provided to them by the local contractor (e.g. fos. 156–65).
113 See Parker, *Army of Flanders*, chaps. 7 and 8, for further detail.
114 For an interesting discussion of what constitutes a 'decisive' war, see G. Blainey, *The causes of war* (Melbourne and London, 1973), 112ff; J. S. Levy, 'Theories of general war', *World Politics*, XXXVII (1985), 344–74 and J. M. Black, *European Warfare 1660–1815* (London, 1994), 67–86.
115 Details from Israel, *The Dutch Republic*, 109–17, 190–7, and 263–71; Roberts, *Gustavus Adolphus*, II, 272–304; Guillerm, *La pierre et le vent*, 151ff.

3 VICTORY AT SEA

1 Choiseul quoted by Paul M. Kennedy, *The rise and fall of British naval mastery* (London, 1976), 53.
2 Kennedy, *ibid.*, 1–9; P. A. Crowl, 'Alfred Thayer Mahan: the naval historian' in Paret, ed., *Makers of modern strategy* 444–77; Guilmartin, *Gunpowder and galleys*, 16–41; G. Symcox, *The crisis of French sea power, 1688–1697* (The Hague, 1974), 227–30; and C. F. Richmond, 'The war at sea' in K. E. Fowler, ed., *The Hundred Years War* (London, 1971), chap. 4, all offer a devastating critique of A. T. Mahan, *The influence of seapower on history 1660–1783* (Boston, 1890).
3 See Crowl, 'Alfred Thayer Mahan', 454, quoting Captain Mahan's presidential address to the American Historical Association in 1902 (*sic*). Mahan was such a passionate disciple of the Swiss military theorist that he even named his favourite dog 'Jomini'.
4 See Needham, *The gunpowder epic*, *passim* (especially pp. 3f and 277–341, copiously illustrated).
5 See the fascinating discussion in Needham, *Science and civilization in China, Volume IV part iii: civil engineering and nautics* (Cambridge, 1971), 425ff and 682–95; and also L. C. Goodrich and C. Feng, 'The early development of firearms in China', *Isis*, XXXVI.1 (1946), 114–23 and 250.
6 Goodrich and Feng, 'The early development of firearms', 121–2; and a personal communication from Dr Clayton Bredt (July 1984).
7 See Needham, *Science and civilization*, IV. iii, 516 n.6, and sources there quoted for Cheng Ho; for the 1522 incident, see D. Ferguson, *Letters from Portuguese captives at Canton* (Bombay, 1902), and T.-T. Chang, *Sino-Portuguese trade from 1514 to 1644* (Leiden, 1934), 51, 57–9. It should be noted, however, that the Chinese themselves recognized that their artillery was far inferior to the Europeans' weapons. 'The Franks', said one, 'use guns with great skill. The

Chinese, on the other hand, blow off their fingers, their hands and even their arms' (quoted by Cipolla, *Guns and sails*, 116n).

8 Details in K. W. So, *Japanese piracy in Ming China during the sixteenth century* (East Lansing, 1975), 148ff; and Lea Williams, 'Notes on Ming policy and shipping as related to early Portuguese activities in the Far East' in L. Albuquerque and I. Guerreiro, eds., *Il seminário internacional de história indo-portuguesa* (Lisbon, 1985: Estudos de história e cartografia antiga, Memorias XXV), 137–45; R. Huang, *1587: a year of no significance. The Ming dynasty in decline* (New Haven, 1981), 163–74; and L. C. Goodrich and C. Feng, *Dictionary of Ming Biography*, I (New York, 1976), 204–8 (Cheng Jo-tseng, author of the *Ch'ou-hai t'u pien*) and 631–8 (Hu Tsung-hsien). The information and date concerning the *Ch'ou-hai t'u pien* given in Cipolla, *Guns and Sails*, 125f, seem to be incorrect.

9 See the excellent illustrated description of both war-junk and fireship in R. C. Temple, ed., *The travels of Peter Mundy*, III (London, 1919: Hakluyt Society, XLV–XLVI), 203, 228–30, and plate 29 (reproduced here as plate 20). Of course the Europeans also used fireships to good effect on numerous occasions – for example, by the English against the Spanish Armada in 1588, or by the Dutch in the Medway in 1667. Fireships were only abandoned in the later seventeenth century because they could not keep up with the faster, more streamlined ships-of-the-line.

10 Cipolla, *Guns and sails*, 75, notes 1–3 suggests that naval firearms before the 1380s were probably 'Greek fire' launchers. However the careful discussion of F. C. van Oosten and P. M. Bosscher, 'Taktiek: het taktisch gebruik van het zeilschip', *Marineblad*, LXXX (1970), 997–1035, at pp. 1015–20, and LXXXI (1971), 863–89, at p. 867, demonstrates that they were indeed proper guns. See also K. DeVries, 'The effectiveness of 15th-century shipboard artillery', *Mariner's Mirror*, LXXXIV (1998), 389–99 – although unfortunately the author fails to distinguish examples that concern galleys from those that concern round ships!

11 See, for example, plate 21 above and the illustrations in G. Asaert, J. van Beylen and H. P. H. Jansen, eds., *Maritieme geschiedenis der Nederlanden*, I (Bussum, 1976), 50, 118, 257, 306. See also the references in Contamine, *War in the Middle Ages*, 206.

12 Jehan de Wavrin, *Recueil des chroniques et anchiennes istories de la Grant Bretaigne, à present nommé Engleterre*, v (ed. W. and E. Hardy, London, 1891), 35f, 95f. The account, composed by Walerin de Wavrin *circa* 1446, specifically noted that the 'deux canons que chascune gallée a en poupe' were of uniform breech-block design 'car toutes les cambres des canons servoient aussi bien à l'un comme à l'autre' and fired as fast as a crossbow (35f). The bombard must have been made of bound iron strips like a barrel because Wavrin reports that first it burst 'deux cercles', and then two more 'cercles et ure douve' (a stave) – p. 96.

13 Details from the richly documented article of M. Morin, 'La battaglia di Lepanto: il determinante apporto dell' artiglieria Veneziana', *Diana: Armi*, IX.1 (January, 1975), 54–61; and J. R. Hale, 'Men and weapons: the fighting potential of sixteenth-century Venetian galleys' in B. Bond and I. Roy, eds., *War and society. A yearbook of military history*, I (London, 1975), 1–23. Centreline guns, for use on galleys, able to fire 100- and 120-pound shot are noted in the Venetian records, but none seem to have survived. I have derived great benefit from conversations with both Dr Morin and Sir John Hale on this matter.

14 The standard account of the galley as a naval dinosaur is offered by Guilmartin, *Gunpowder and galleys*. Although this volume provides much invaluable new

information on Spanish galley warfare and artillery, it neglects Ottoman and (to some extent) Venetian sources. Neither confirm Guilmartin's findings. See, for Venice, the articles by Morin and Hale noted above; and, for the Ottoman side, C. J. Heywood, in *Bulletin of the School of Oriental and African Studies*, XXXVIII (1975), 643–6.

15 Details form Guillerm, *La Pierre et le vent*, 44–8; and Morin, 'La battaglia di Lepanto', 57. Later on, reports of the distinguished part played in the Armada campaign by the four galeasses of Naples much impressed the English naval writer John Mountgomerie: see Houghton Library (Harvard), MS Typ 16: J. Mountgomerie, 'A Treatice concerning the navie of England' – 'Addicione' of 1589. Later still, in the early seventeenth century the English naval expert, Sir Robert Dudley, designed an even larger version for the Tuscan navy: the 'countergaleass' (see A. G. Lee, *The son of Leicester. A biography of Sir Robert Dudley* [London, 1964], 166ff).

16 K. M. Setton, *The Papacy and the Levant, 1204–1571*, IV (Philadelphia, 1984), 1056, quoting the vivid *Historia* of Gianpietro Contarini, who wrote only a few months after the battle. Various estimates of the size of the opposing fleets, and of their weaponry, are given in M. Lesure, *Lépante: la crise de l'empire Ottomane* (Paris, 1971), 115f.

17 Quotations from the eye-witness account of Girolamo Diedo in Lesure, *Lépante*, 141f. The order of the Council of Ten to execute all prisoners with marine experience is printed in *ibid.*, 151f; and the aftermath of the battle in the Ottoman empire is discussed at 179ff. It is true that, in spite of all this, Cyprus was lost to the Turks, and some have therefore denied that Lepanto was a major Christian victory. But this is to miss the point. By October 1571, Cyprus was already lost; and had Lepanto not been won, the Turks would certainly have gone on to attack Crete or the Christian outposts in Albania. See C. H. Imber, 'The reconstruction of the Ottoman fleet after the battle of Lepanto', in Imber, *Studies in Ottoman history and law* (Istanbul, 1996), 85–101.

18 This was certainly the case in the West. In 1570, when it became clear that the Turks were about to attack, Venice began to assemble and launch the galleys stored in the Arsenal at the rate of roughly two per day. In a matter of weeks, the size of the Republic's fleet at sea increased from 45 to 155 galleys (see F. C. Lane, 'Wages and recruitment of Venetian galeotti, 1470–1580', *Studi veneziani*, new series VI [1982], 15–43, at p. 41).

19 Details from Imber, 'Reconstruction'. I am very grateful to Dr Imber for letting me see a copy of his important article in advance of publication. See also the information in M. Cizakça, 'Ottomans and the Mediterranean. An analysis of the Ottoman shipbuilding industry as reflected by the Arsenal registers of Istanbul, 1529–1650' in R. Ragosta, ed., *Le genti del mar mediterraneo*, II (Naples, 1981), 773–87; Lesure, *Lépante*, 213–33; and H. Inalcik, 'Lepanto in the Ottoman documents' in G. Benzoni, ed., *Il Mediterraneo nella seconda metà del '500 alla luce di Lepanto* (Florence, 1974: Civiltà veneziani, studi, XXX), 185–92.

20 The same problem afflicted the galleys of the Western powers from the 1560s, and the same solution – to use convicts – was adopted. See details for Spain in Thompson, *War and government in Habsburg Spain*, chapter 6; for Italy in Lane, 'Wages and recruitment', and M. Aymard, 'Chiourmes et galères dans la Méditerranée du XVIe siècle' in *Mélanges en honneur de Fernand Braudel: histoire économique du monde méditerranéen 1450–1650*, I (Paris, 1973), 51–64; and for France, at a slightly later period, in Zysberg, 'Galley and hard labor convicts

in France 1550–1850'. At p. 85, Zysberg notes that between 1680 and 1715, some 38,000 persons were sentenced to the galleys in France, of whom over 16,000 were army deserters.

21 Quoted by Zysberg, 'Galley and hard labor convicts', 96. Forces at Lepanto estimated by Lesure, *Lépante*, 115f.

22 See F. C. Lane, 'The crossbow in the nautical revolution of the Middle Ages', *Explorations in economic history*, VII (1969–70), 161–71; R. W. Unger, *The ship in the medieval economy 600–1600* (London, 1980), chap. 6 ('Warships, cargo ships and cannon, 1550–1600'); and R. W. Unger, 'Warships and cargo ships in medieval Europe', *Technology and culture*, XXII (1981), 233–52.

23 L. G. Carr Laughton, 'Early Tudor ship-guns', *Mariner's mirror*, XLVI (1960), 242–85. For the *Mary Rose*, see M. Rule, *The Mary Rose* (London, 1983).

24 Details on the *Great Michael* from Paul, ed., *Accounts of the Lord High Treasurer of Scotland*, IV, li–lviii; and from N. A. T. Macdougall, '"The greatest schipp that ewer saillit in Ingland or France": James IV's "Great Michael"', in Macdougall, ed., *Scotland and War AD 79–1991* (Edinburgh, 1991), 36–60. See also p. 238 n. 22 below. On the 'great ship' in general, see the excellent survey by W. A. Baker, 'Ships, weapons and protection, 1400–1900' in D. Howse, ed., *Five hundred years of nautical science 1400–1900* (Greenwich, 1971), 12–22.

25 Details from T. Glasgow, Jr, 'List of ships in the Royal Navy from 1539 to 1588', *Mariner's mirror*, LVI (1970), 299–307. See also Dr Glasgow's important series of articles on 'The Royal Navy in the French wars of Mary and early Elizabeth I, 1557–1564' (under various titles) in *Mariner's mirror*, LIII (1967), 321–42; LIV (1968), 23–36 and 281–96; and LVI (1970), 3–26.

26 Quoted by Glasgow, 'The navy in Philip and Mary's war, 1557–8', *Mariner's mirror*, LIII (1967), 322.

27 Details from R. C. Anderson, *List of English men-of-war, 1509–1649* (London, 1959: Society for Nautical Research Occasional Papers, VII); and BL, *Egerton Ms.* 2541, fos. 1–4, 'Queen Elizabeth's whole army at sea agaynst the Spanish forces, anno 1588'.

28 Glasgow, 'List', 306–7; and 'Maturing of Naval administration 1556–1564', *Mariner's mirror*, LVI (1970), 25. See also his article 'The shape of the ships that defeated the Spanish Armada', *Mariner's mirror*, L (1964), 177–87; and R. Pollitt, 'Bureaucracy and the Armada: the administrator's battle', *Mariner's mirror*, LX (1974), 119–32.

29 For the early evolution of the galleon, see J. da G. Pimentel-Barata, 'The Portuguese galleon (1519–1625)' in Howse, *Five hundred years of nautical science*, 181–91; for its later history see C. R. Boxer, *From Lisbon to Goa, 1500–1750* (London, 1984), chaps. 8 ('Admiral João Pereira Corte-Real and the construction of Portuguese East-Indiamen') and 9 ('The naval and colonial papers of Dom António de Ataíde'). F. C. Lane, *Venetian ships and shipbuilders of the Renaissance* (Baltimore, 1934), 50f, 63, noted galleons in Venetian yards from about 1525; and C. R. Phillips, *Six galleons for the king of Spain. Imperial defence in the early seventeenth century* (Baltimore, 1986), chap. 2, provides convincing evidence that they emerged in Spain at much the same time (she does not include Portugal in her survey). Her 'six galleons' were built in Vizcaya between 1620 and 1628. For the Armada's lack of impact against the Royal Navy, see the detailed surveys of Elizabeth's ships after the campaign, which record virtually no damage. See the discussion in G. Parker, 'The *Dreadnought* revolution of Tudor England', *Mariner's Mirror*, LXXXII (1996), 269–300; and C. Martin and G. Parker, *The Spanish Armada* (revised edn, Manchester, 1999), chap. 11.

30 T. Glasgow, Jr, 'Gorgas' seafight', *Mariner's mirror*, LIX (1973), 179–88, at pp. 180–1; P. Bor, *Vervolch der Nederlantsche Oorloghen*, III part 2 (Amsterdam, 1626), fos. 10–12: Interrogation of Don Diego Pimentel, taken from the contemporary pamphlet which printed the questions and answers verbatim: *Breeder verclaringhe van de vloote van Spaegnien* (Knuttel Pamphlet Collection, nos. 847–8).

31 M. Lewis, *Armada guns: a comparative study of English and Spanish armaments* (London, 1961); I. A. A. Thompson, 'Spanish Armada guns', *The Mariner's mirror*, LXI (1975), 355–71; D. B. Quinn and A. N. Ryan, *England's sea empire 1550–1642* (London, 1983), 102–8; and K. R. Andrews, *Drake's voyages. A reassessment of their place in Elizabethan maritime expansion* (London, 1967), chap. 8.

32 Details from P. Padfield, *Tide of empires. Decisive naval campaigns in the rise of the West. I: 1481–1654* (London, 1979), 43, 51–2; P. Padfield, *Guns at sea* (London, 1973), 25–7; and Guilmartin, *Gunpowder and galleys*, 89–93 ('William Towerson's fight'). Other sources mentioning the use of cartridge cases in the sixteenth century are noted by Pepper and Adams, *Firearms and fortifications*, 198 n. 21.

33 This account is based upon Colin J. M. Martin, 'The equipment and fighting potential of the Spanish Armada' (St Andrews University Ph.D. thesis, 1983), chaps. 3, 4, 5, 7; upon Dr Martin's underwater excavation of several wrecked Armada vessels; and upon documents concerning the fleet from AGS, *Contaduria del Sueldo*, 2a serie, and *Contaduria Mayor de Cuentas*, 2a and 3a épocas. These sources, and others, form the basis of the new edition of Martin and Parker, *The Spanish Armada*.

34 Information from Martin and Parker, *The Spanish Armada*, chap. 11. It should not be assumed, however, that inboard reloading was hazard-free. Gunners still faced the risk that a new charge would be ignited prematurely by smouldering remnants from the previous round. See the moving account of Jón Olafsson, a gunner in Danish service, injured in such an accident in 1623: R. Temple and L. M. Anstey, eds., *The life of the Icelander Jón Olafsson, traveller to India*, II (London, 1931: Hakluyt Society, 2nd series LXVIII), 197f.

35 See G. E. Manwaring and W. G. Perrin, eds., *The life and works of Sir Henry Mainwaring*, II (London, 21: Navy Records Society, LVI), 119. See also M. Oppenheim, ed., *The naval tracts of Sir William Monson*, V (London, 1914: Navy Records Society, XLVII), 147: Monson further noted that the Spaniards 'carry their great ordnance upon field carriages, which make them the more dangerous and unserviceable', for they could not be reloaded, could not be aimed, and could not be properly secured in rough weather. In their detailed consideration of how the English fought in 1588, both L. G. Carr Laughton, 'Gunnery, frigates and the line of battle', *Mariner's mirror*, XIV (1928), 339–63, and Padfield, *Guns at sea*, chap. 12, concluded that inboard loading only became standard practice in the Royal Navy during the 1620s. For example, they note that the 'Fighting Instructions' issued to the fleet sent to Cadiz in 1625 still ordered the ships to close in by threes, fire, and then fall away to reload, rather like a caracole; which suggests that reloading may have been performed outboard (see J. S. Corbett, *Fighting instructions 1530–1816* [London, 1905: Navy Records Society, XXIX], 65). However, Lord Wimbledon's fleet in 1625 included only 3 royal warships, as against 34 in 1588, so different procedures would have been appropriate. Most of the examples of outboard loading quoted from this period by Carr Laughton and Padfield concern merchantmen. For the Navy, I am convinced

by the arguments in favour of inboard loading advanced by Martin, 'Equipment and fighting potential', chap. 9, and especially pp. 377–9.

36 Quotations from Cipolla, *Guns and sails*, 86 n.2, and A. P. McGowan, ed., *The Jacobean commissions of enquiry of 1608 and 1618* (London, 1971: Navy Records Society, CXVI), 258–9, 286–8. The age of ships continued to rise in the seventeenth century. Ten ships built in 1619–23 were still in service in the 1650s and two were still in service in the 1680s! (McGowan, p. xxvi n.4). See also Padfield, *Tide of Empires*, I, 126–8.

37 Sir Edward Cecil to Sir John Coke, 27 February 1626, in A. B. Grosart, ed., *The voyage to Cadiz in 1625. Being a journal written by Sir John Glanville* (London, 1883: Camden Society Publications, New Series, XXXII), xliii. See the similar strategic assessment of the Navy Commissioners in 1618 in McGowan, *Jacobean commissions*, 286f. Even in Elizabeth's reign, five of her warships were considered too large to operate outside home waters, while both George Waymouth (*The Jewell of arts*, 1604) and Sir Walter Raleigh ('Observations on the navy', *c.* 1610) considered that English warships generally tended to be too large and carried too much ordnance for their own good. See the material cited in M. Oppenheim, *A history of the administration of the Royal Navy and of merchant shipping in relation to the navy from MDIX to MDCLX* (London, 1896), 121f and 186. I am not convinced by the claim of K. R. Andrews, *Elizabethan privateering. English privateering during the Spanish war, 1585–1603* (Cambridge, 1964), 18, that, under Elizabeth, 'The greater part of the Queen's navy was transformed from a short-range, Narrow Seas, almost coastal defence, force into a high-seas fleet capable of operating at long-range as an ocean going force'.

38 The Spanish origins of Charles I's 'Ship-Money Fleet', and its initial purpose, are well set out by Simon Adams, 'Spain or the Netherlands? The dilemmas of early Stuart foreign policy' in H. Tomlinson, ed., *Before the English Civil War. Essays on early Stuart politics and government* (London, 1983), 79–101, at pp. 84f; and J. H. Elliott, *The Count-Duke of Olivares. The statesman in an age of decline* (New Haven, 1986), 508.

39 The maritime expeditions from Spain are listed in Parker, *Army of Flanders*, 77f and 278f; the Dunkirk frigates are described by R. Baetens, 'The organization and effects of Flemish privateering in the seventeenth century', *Acta Historiae Neerlandicae*, IX (1977), 48–75, at pp. 56–9; and in R. A. Stradling, *The Armada of Flanders. Spanish maritime policy and European war, 1568–1668* (Cambridge, 1992).

40 L. M. Akveld, S. Hart, and W. J. van Hoboken, eds., *Maritieme geschiedenis der Nederlanden*, II (Bussum, 1977), 58–65; J. E. Elias, *De vlootbouw in Nederland in de eerste helft der 17e eeuw, 1596–1655* (Amsterdam, 1933); R. E. J. Weber, *De seinboeken voor nederlandse vloten en konvooien tot 1690* (Amsterdam, 1982: Verhandelingen der Koninklijke Nederlandse Akademie van Wetenschappen. Afdeling Letterkunde, n.r. CXII); Carr Laughton, 'Gunnery, frigates and the line of battle', 357f. On the Downs, see C. R. Boxer, *The Journal of Maarten Harpertszoon Tromp, Anno 1639* (Cambridge, 1939); and, more recently, J. Alcalá-Zamora y Queipo de Llano, *España, los Países Bajos y la mar del Norte* (Madrid, 1975), 402–64. The changing designs of Spanish ships are illustrated in G. de Artiñano, *La arquitectura naval española (en madera)* (Madrid, 1920); in the first illustrated manual of ship-building, D. García de Paredes, *Instrucción náutica para navegar* (Mexico, 1587: reprinted Madrid, 1944), fos. 88–128; and in the useful 'dialogue' of T. Cano, *Arte para fabricar, fortificar y aparejar naos de guerra y merchante* (Seville, 1611; reprinted Seville, 1964).

My thanks to Professor William S. Maltby for bringing several of these items to my attention, and for sharing with me his knowledge of the subject.

41 Details in Oppenheim, *History*, 253–7. In fact some ships of Charles I's navy approached a ratio of 3.5:1. The *Providence* and *Expedition* of 1637 were both 27.5 metres long but only 8 metres wide, and carried 30 guns (*ibid.*, 276f).

42 See *ibid.*, 330–8; and H. C. Junge, *Flottenpolitik und Revolution. Die Entstehung der englischen Seemacht während der Herrschaft Cromwells* (Stuttgart, 1980: Publications of the German Historical Institute in London, VI), 130–2, 202.

43 Corbett, *Fighting instructions*, 100. On the battles of 1652–3, see van Oosten and Bosscher, 'Taktiek', *Marineblad*, LXXXI (1971), 607–17; and A. H. Taylor, 'Galleon into ship of the line', *Mariner's mirror*, XLIV (1958), 267–85. Cromwell quoted by Junge, *Flottenpolitik*, 225. See also R. E. J. Weber, 'The introduction of the single line ahead as a battle formation by the Dutch, 1665–6', *Mariner's Mirror*, LXXIII (1987), 5–19.

44 Details from Oppenheim, *History*, 302f; and Junge, *Flottenpolitik*, 248, 255ff, 274, 311ff. For further detail see B. Capp, *Cromwell's Navy. The fleet and the English Revolution, 1648–60* (Oxford, 1989), and N. A. M. Rodger, *The safeguard of the sea. A naval history of Great Britain, 660–1649* (London, 1997). Of course the Spaniards, the Portuguese and the Dutch had all sent war-fleets into American waters before 1650, but none kept them there on a permanent basis. Rather, fleets were sent out for a specific purpose and then withdrawn. See E. Sluiter, 'Dutch-Spanish rivalry in the Caribbean area, 1594–1609', *Hispanic-American historical review*, XXVIII (1948), 165–96; R. H. Boulind, 'The strength and weakness of Spanish control of the Caribbean 1520–1650: the case for the Armada de Barlovento' (Cambridge University Ph.D. thesis, 1965), especially chap. 9; C. R. Boxer, *The Dutch in Brazil 1624–1654* (Oxford, 1957), *passim*; Phillips, *Six galleons*, chaps. 5, 8; and J. F. Guilmartin, 'The guns of the *Santissimo Sacramento*', *Technology and Culture*, xxiv (1983), 559–601 (especially p. 562).

45 The change in design is apparent from the dimensions of ships recorded in Oppenheim, *History*, 300–7, and revised in R. C. Anderson, *Lists of men-of-war 1650–1700. Part I: English ships, 1649–1702* (London, 1935: Society for Nautical Research, Occasional Papers V). The importance of design is also demonstrated by the one and only success of Charles I's navy: the Sallee raid of 1637, which prospered because of the presence of two newly built frigates in the blockading fleet (see the important discussion in Oppenheim, *History*, 276f). My argument here owes much to discussions with Professor Paul M. Kennedy, to whom I am most grateful.

46 Whitelocke, *Memorials of the English affairs*, IV, 271, quoting an after-dinner debate between Admiral Sir George Ayscue and the Swedish ambassador, Christer Bonde. See also Nathaniel Butler's earlier (1635) discussion of the ideal size and design for ships in W. G. Perrin, ed., *Boteler's dialogues* (London, 1929: Navy Records Society, LXV), 247–59.

47 Figures from J. Ehrman, *The navy in the war of William III (1689–1697). Its state and direction* (Cambridge, 1953), chap. 1; C. R. Boxer, *The Anglo-Dutch Wars of the seventeenth century* (Greenwich, 1974), 4, 6, 47; J. P. Cooper, ed., *The new Cambridge modern history*, IV (Cambridge, 1970), chap. 7: 'Sea-power'; Quinn and Ryan, *England's sea-empire*, chap. 8; and F. Fox, *Great ships. The battlefleet of King Charles II* (Greenwich, 1980), 21 (and *passim*).

48 Quoted by Erhman, *The navy*, 350.

49 Symcox, *The crisis of French sea power*, 32–4 and 55–71 (Shovell quoted p. 56); A. H. Taylor, 'Galleon into ship of the line: part III', *Mariner's mirror*, XLV

(1959), 100–14; and Guillerm, *La Pierre et le vent*, 149–69 (with important new data on the role of Vauban in the decision to shift from a *forteresse flottante* to a *forteresse mobile*).

50 Details from M. Duffy, 'The foundations of British naval power' in Duffy, ed., *The military revolution and the state*, 49–85; and van Oosten and Bosscher, 'Taktiek', *Marineblad*, LXXX (1970), 997–1035 and LXXXI (1971), 593–651. Eventually, battleships were also able to operate in Far Eastern waters, but only when they had vastly increased the amount of sail they carried. Thus where the 100-gun *Sovereign of the Seas* after a refit in 1652 weighed 2,072 tons but carried only 5,513 yards of sail, an equivalent ship-of-the-line in the 1840s would carry almost 13,000 yards. (See Oppenheim, *History*, 338f.)

51 See C. H. Gardiner, *Naval power in the conquest of Mexico* (Austin, 1956), on Cortés; and E. Lyon, *The enterprise of Florida. Pedro Menéndez de Avilés and the Spanish conquest of 1565–1568* (Gainesville, 1976), on operations against the French. For the English Challenge see K. R. Andrews, *Trade, plunder and settlement. Maritime enterprise and the genesis of the British empire 1480–1630* (Cambridge, 1984), chaps. 6 and 7.

52 The little-known proposal of Medina Sidonia, dated 25 October 1586, is quoted in H. P. Kraus, *Sir Francis Drake. A pictorial biography* (Amsterdam, 1970), 129f and 189f.

53 Philip II to the viceroy of India, 23 February and 14 March 1588, in J. H. de Cunha Rivara, ed., *Arquivo Português Oriental*, III (Nova Goa, 1861), 130–1 (cancelling the Acheh attack); and 146 (abandoning plans to fortify Mombasa).

54 L. F. F. R. Thomaz, *De Malaca a Pegu. Viagens de um feitor português (1512–15)* (Lisbon, 1966), 11–18, offers a most valuable reinterpretation of the nature of Portuguese power in Asia. A useful up-to-date survey of Portuguese India and its neighbours at this time is offered by K. S. Mathew, *Portuguese trade with India in the sixteenth century* (New Delhi, 1983).

55 R. J. de Lima Felner, ed., *Subsídios para a história de Índia portuguesa* (Lisbon, 1868), part III, 11–25 prints a contemporary survey of artillery in India in 1525. A century later, the Portuguese warships which still sought to regulate the coastal trade of western India remained surprisingly lightly armed. According to one source 'greater pieces [of artillery] than falcons [3-pounders] these ships carry not': see E. Grey, ed., *The travels of Pietro della Valle in India*, II (London, 1892: Hakluyt Society, LXXXV), 389. But the same was also true of both the Dunkirk privateers and the Caribbean buccaneers: see note 69 below.

56 G. Correa, *Lendas da India*, I. 1 (Lisbon, 1858), 216–18. However, at the battle of Diu in 1509, the Portuguese flagship sank one of her adversaries with a single waterline shot from 'hũa bombarda grosa': see L. de Albuquerque, ed., *Cronica do descobrimento e conquista da Índia pelos Portugueses* (Lourenço Marques, 1974), 181. Other ships were destroyed by fire as well as by bombardment (see various individual encounters narrated in *ibid.*, 180–7).

57 See the detailed accounts of J. Aubin, 'Albuquerque et les négociations de Cambaye', *Mare Luso-Indicium*, I (Paris, 1971), 3–63; Albuquerque, ed., *Cronica*, 180–2; C. H. Imber, 'The navy of Suleiman the Magnificent', *Archivum Ottomanicum*, VI (1980), 211–82, at pp. 224–5; and S. Özbaran, 'The Ottoman Turks and the Portuguese in the Persian Gulf 1534–1581', *Journal of Asian History*, VI. 1 (1972), 45–87.

58 See I. A. Macgregor, 'A sea-fight near Singapore in the 1570s', *Journal of the Malayan branch of the Royal Asiatic Society*, XXIX.3 (1956), 5–21; and C. R. Boxer, 'A note on Portuguese reactions to the revival of the Red Sea spice

trade and the rise of Atjeh, 1540–1600', *Journal of south-east Asian history*, X (1969), 415–28 (reprinted in Boxer, *Portuguese conquest and commerce in southern Asia, 1500–1750* [London, 1985], chap. 2).

59 On the phenomenon of one man's pirates being another man's patriots cf. M. N. Pearson, *Coastal Western India* (New Delhi, 1981), chap. 2; and S. F. Dale, *Islamic society on the south Asian frontier. The Mappilas of Malabar 1498–1922* (Oxford, 1980), chaps. 1–2. Malabar 'grabs' are well described and illustrated in Temple, ed., *Travels of Peter Mundy*, II, 316f and plate 25, and III, 109.

60 On the assistance offered by the 'Malabar pirates' to Surat (and, after 1610, to the English) see W. Foster, ed., *The voyage of Nicholas Downton to the East Indies 1614–1615* (London, 1938: Hakluyt Society, 2nd series LXXXII), 25, 29, 33; and W. Foster, *The journal of John Jourdain* (London, 1905: Hakluyt society, 2nd series XVI), 191–2. On their capture in 1735 of the Eastindiaman *Derby*, by keeping astern of her and shooting her rigging to pieces, see P. J. Marshall, 'Western arms in maritime Asia in the early phases of expansion', *Modern Asian Studies*, XIV (1980), 13–28, at p. 22. For a similar example, this time of the ship *Lion* taken by Portuguese galliots in 1625, see Boxer, *Portuguese conquest and commerce*, chap. 1 (at pp. 104f).

61 See, for example, the criticisms of João Ribeiro, *Fatalidade historica da Ilha de Ceilão* (1685): 'From the Cape of Good Hope onwards, we were unwilling to leave anything outside our control. We were anxious to lay hands on everything in that huge stretch of over 5,000 leagues from Sofala to Japan. And what was worse, was that we set about this without calculating our strength, or thinking that even with the natives themselves, this conquest could not last for ever ...' (translation from C. R. Boxer, 'Captain João Ribeiro and his history of Ceylon' in Boxer, *Portuguese conquest and commerce*, chap. 11, p. 11).

62 See the ingenious and convincing explanation advanced by G. D. Winius, *The fatal history of Portuguese Ceylon* (Cambridge, Mass., 1971), 121–70.

63 Details from N. Steensgaard, 'The Dutch East India Company as an institutional innovation' in M. Aymard, ed., *Dutch capitalism and world capitalism* (Cambridge, 1982), 244–50; and N. Macleod, *De Oostindische Compagnie als Zeemogendheid in Azië*, I (Rijswijk, 1927), 10, 17–19, 57, 80, 294.

64 Dutch totals from I. Schöffer, J. R. Bruijn and F. S. Gaastra, eds., *Dutch-Asiatic shipping in the 17th and 18th centuries*, II (The Hague, 1979), 1–44; Portuguese totals from A. Botelho de Sousa, *Subsídios para a história militar marítima da Índia* I (Lisbon, 1930), 656–7; II (Lisbon, 1948), 639–50; and III (Lisbon, 1953), 628–30.

65 On the Portuguese lack of guns, see C. R. Boxer, 'The *Carreira da Índia* 1650–1750', *Mariner's mirror*, XLVI (1960), 35–54, at pp. 53–4; on the poor gunners see A. Gray and H. C. P. Bell, eds., *The voyage of François Pirard of Laval* (London, 1888: Hakluyt Society, LXXVII), II part 1, 193.

66 See S. Arasaratnam, *Dutch power in Ceylon, 1658–87* (Amsterdam, 1958). Nonetheless, large forces were committed against Kandy by the Dutch and the annual deficit of the Company's Ceylon *kantoor* rose from 200,000 florins in the 1660s to 731,000 in 1673–74. In 1676 the Dutch handed back all the conquests they had made from Kandy since 1659, in return for peace. Dutch shipping losses calculated from Schöffer *et al., Dutch-Asiatic shipping*, II, 18–27.

67 W. Foster, ed., *The voyage of Thomas Best to the East Indies, 1612–1614* (London, 1934: Hakluyt Society, 2nd series LXXV), 39, 135, 136, 243–4. The Portuguese version of the action notes that the smaller of the English boats lured three Portuguese galleons on to a sandbank by sailing safely across it, thanks to her

shallower draft. It was when the galleons were stuck on the sand that Captain Best closed in for the kill (cf. Bocarro's account, p. 221). At the same time, the Portuguese themselves freely admitted that the northerners could shoot faster. See, for example, the account of the battle between a Dutch and Portuguese squadron of Goa in 1637, which estimated that the former fired three times as often as the latter: A. da Silva Rego, ed., *Documentação Ultramarina Portuguesa*, I (Lisbon, 1960), 21–8 (at p. 27; Dutch and Portuguese accounts of the action are printed in Temple, ed., *Travels of Peter Mundy*, III, 467–74 – one source claimed that the *Vlissinghen* fired 355 rounds at the Portuguese). The same figure of 'three for one' is given in an English account of the naval action off Surat in February 1625: see W. Foster, ed., *The English factories in India 1624–1629* (Oxford, 1909), 47 (on p. 51f another patriotic account claimed the English and Dutch 'ware not answered above one in tenn' by the Portuguese).

68 Several similar engagements between the English and the Portuguese in the Indian Ocean, in almost all of which the English were tactically victorious but strategically thwarted, are chronicled by C. R. Boxer, 'Anglo-Portuguese rivalry in the Persian Gulf, 1615–1635' in Boxer, *Portuguese conquest and commerce*, chap. 1. See, for example, p. 70, where four English ships in January 1621 claimed to have fired no less than 4,021 'great shot' into the opposing Portuguese galleons, but without sinking any of them. See also pp. 97 and 99.

69 On the light armament of the buccaneers, see O. H. K. Spate, *The Pacific since Magellan. II. Monopolists and freebooters* (London, 1983), chap. 6 (especially pp. 151–2); for that of the privateers, see Andrews, *Trade, plunder and settlement*, 246. See also note 55 above.

70 See Foster, ed., *Journal of John Jourdain*, 205–18. This was the typical pattern of Indian overseas trade at the time – one or two large princely vessels, and a host of smaller ones. See A. Das Gupta, 'Indian merchants and the Western Indian Ocean: the early seventeenth century', *Modern Asian Studies*, XIX (1985), 481–99. Some European sources estimated the *Rahimi* at 1,000 tons, others at 1,500. According to John Saris, she was 52 metres long and 15 metres broad – a very large ship: see A. J. Qaisar, 'Shipbuilding in the Mughal empire during the seventeenth century', *Indian economic and social history review*, V (1968), 149–70. For another eye-witness account of how a large Indian ship might be stopped and searched by the Portuguese on the high seas, see J. Mocquet, *Voyages en Afrique, Asie, Indes orientales et occidentales* (2nd edn, Rouen, 1645), 280f (an incident from 1609).

71 See K. N. Chaudhuri, *The trading world of Asia and the English East India Company 1660–1760* (Cambridge, 1978), 114. For the cost to native merchants and rulers of the Europeans' 'redistributive enterprise', see R. B. Serjeant, *The Portuguese off the South Arabian coast. Hadrami chronicles* (Oxford, 1963), 115–29.

72 See Foster, ed., *Journal of John Jourdain*, 218ff; and Foster, ed., *Voyage of Nicholas Downton*, xxff.

73 See W. Foster, ed., *The English factories in India 1634–1636* (Oxford, 1911), xxiiff and 232–3. For similar sequences of events somewhat earlier, see *ibid.*, 1622–3 (Oxford, 1909), 27–9; and Grey, ed., *The travels of Pietro della Valle in India*, 417–19. Also in the 1630s, the Sultan of Bijapur retaliated for the Portuguese capture of one of his ships by arresting Portuguese officials, closing his ports to Portuguese shipping, threatening to capture Salsete and flirting with the Dutch: see P. S. S. Pissurlencar, ed., *Assentos do Conselho do Estado da India*, I (Nova Goa, 1953), 233–43. Even in the 1690s, the same technique was

employed by Aurangzebe when the English seized one of his ships: see R. Ritchie, *Captain Kidd and the war against the pirates* (Cambridge, Mass., 1986), 131f.

74 HAG, MS. 1043, 'Register of Cartazes 1618–1623', regularly notes that the annual ship of the 'Great Mughal' was allowed to carry 15 'versos e falconetes' – but these were breech-loading weapons of low penetrating power. Dr John Fryer, who visited India during the 1670s, observed that although 'some of their ships carry 30 or 40 pieces of cannon [they were] more for show than service'. (Quoted with other pertinent material by A. J. Qaisar, *The Indian response to European technology and culture, AD 1498–1707* [Oxford, 1982], 43–6.) In T. Raychaudhuri and I. Habib, eds., *The Cambridge economic history of India*, I (Cambridge, 1982), 150–1, Dr Simon Digby stressed that the use of firearms was spreading fast around the Indian Ocean shortly before the arrival of the Portuguese; but it should be noted that they were neither used at sea by non-Europeans nor often used effectively ashore by anyone (see pages 128–32 above).

75 The classic account of W. H. Moreland, 'The ships of the Arabian Sea about AD 1500', *Journal of the Royal Asiatic Society*, (1939), 63–74 and 173–92, is now rather outdated. See the penetrating remarks of K. N. Chaudhuri, *Trade and civilization in the Indian Ocean. An economic history from the rise of Islam to 1750* (Cambridge, 1985), chap. 7; R. R. di Meglio, 'Arab trade with Indonesia and the Malay peninsula from the 8th to the 16th century' in D. S. Richards, ed., *Islam and the trade of Asia: a colloquium* (Oxford, 1970), 105–35; S. Gopal, 'Gujarati shipping in the seventeenth century', *Indian economic and social history review*, VIII (1971), 31–40; and, best of all, P. Y. Manguin, 'Late medieval Asian shipbuilding in the Indian Ocean', *Môyen Orient et Océan Indien*, II.2 (1985), 1–30.

76 During the invasion of Assam in the 1660s, the Mughals used warships built and manned by Portuguese, French, Dutch, English and even Russian renegades (see J. N. Sarkar, *The life of Mir Jumla, the general of Aurangzeb* [2nd edn, New Delhi, 1979], 279f). But this appears to have been unique. Several explanations have been advanced for the failure of the Mughals (and of other great Indian princes) to create a permanent navy. The best survey by far may be found in J. N. Sarkar, *The art of war in medieval India* (New Delhi, 1984), 267–70. Briefly stated, M. N. Pearson, *Merchants and rulers in Gujarat. The response to the Portuguese in the sixteenth century* (Berkeley, 1976), chap. 6, argued that the land powers were content to let the merchants get on with their overseas trade, since they had no interest in controlling the seas beyond assuring their profits from customs and licences. But the studies of A. Das Gupta, *Indian merchants and the decline of Surat 1700–1750* (Wiesbaden, 1979), and H. W. van Santen, *De Verenigde Oost-Indische Compagnie in Gujarat en Hindustan 1620–1660* (Leiden, 1983), argue that in fact the Indian princes showed rather more concern for the protection of local trade and merchants than Pearson believed. Nevertheless, this stopped short of the provision of convoy escorts and confrontations with the Portuguese. I am very grateful to Michael Pearson for discussing these matters with me and for providing much bibliographical assistance.

77 Watanabe Yosuke, 'Chōseneki to waga zōsen no hattatsu' [The invasion of Korea and the development of shipbuilding], *Shigaku zasshi*, XLVI (1935), 574–97. Details on the use of firearms at sea during the Korean War may be gleaned from S. W. Jeon, *Science and technology in Korea. Traditional instruments and techniques* (Cambridge, Mass., 1974), 215–18; H. H. Underwood, 'Korean boats

and ships', *Journal of the Royal Asiatic Society: Korean branch*, XXIII (1933), 1–99, at pp. 71–84; A. L. Sadler, 'The naval campaign in the Korean war of Hideyoshi (1592–8)', *Transactions of the Asiatic society of Japan*, 2nd series XIV (1937), 177–208; Needham, *Science and civilization*, IV.iii, 683–5; Park Yune-Hee, *Admiral Yi Sung-Shin and the turtle-boat Armada* (2nd edn, Seoul, 1978); and S. R. Turnbull, *The samurai: a military history* (London, 1977), 161–2. It must be said that none of these works on the subject are definitive. Underwood and Park have interesting illustrations, and Needham and Jeon are clear and incisive; but without question Sadler offers the best synthesis, which was largely repeated by A. J. Marder, 'From Jimmu Tennō to Perry: sea power in early Japanese history', *American historical review*, LI (1945), 1–34, at pp. 20–31. The campaign was also recorded in the magnificent Ming 'Korean Invasion Scroll', of which selections are reproduced in B. Smith and W. G. Weng, *China: a history in art* (New York, 1972), 234–7.

78 Details of the incident are given in the 'Relation' of Philippine affairs in 1609–10 sent by Gregorio López, S.J., to the Jesuit General: see E. H. Blair and J. A. Robertson, *The Philippine Islands 1493–1898*, XV (Cleveland, Ohio, 1909), 103–43. He noted that the Japanese ship was searched by the Dutch (to see if any Spaniards were aboard) before being allowed through; but his claim that 300 pesos were exacted from the Japanese was probably wrong, since the Dutch commander had given strict orders for a search only (see Algemeen Rijksarchief, The Hague, 1e *Afdeling: VOC 550*, General Orders of Admiral Wittert, 22 March 1610). I am grateful for these references to Mr P. J. N. Willman.

79 Iwao Seiichi, *Shuinsen bōekishi no kenkyū [A study of the trade by Japanese merchant ships licensed by the Shogun]* (2nd edn, Tokyo, 1987). Of 356 known licences issued, 38 went to Europeans, 43 to Chinese, and the rest to Japanese merchants. Professor Iwao discovered that, although no documentation exists in Japan on disregard of the *shuinjō*, the Algemeen Rijksarchief in The Hague contains translations of now-lost Japanese legal documents on the subject. There is a picture of a *Shuinsen*, from a votive plaque dated 1634 donated to the Kiyomisu temple of Kyoto in the hope of a prosperous voyage, in M. Cooper, ed., *The southern Barbarians: the first Europeans in Japan* (Tokyo, 1971), 191, plate 105. The original, and three more, may still be seen in the Kiyomisu-dera; see plate 30 above.

80 C. R. Boxer, 'The Achinese attack on Malacca in 1629' in J. Bastin and R. Roolvink, eds., *Malayan and Indonesian Studies: essays presented to Sir Richard Winstedt* (Oxford, 1964), chap. 5 (reprinted in Boxer, *Portuguese conquest and commerce*, chap. 4).

81 Literature on the Omani fleet is surprisingly thin, but see J. Strandes, *The Portuguese period in East Africa* (2nd edn, Nairobi, 1961), chap. 16; R. D. Bathurst, 'Maritime trade and Imamate government: two principal themes in the history of Oman to 1728' in D. Hopwood, ed., *The Arabian peninsula. Society and politics* (London, 1972), 89–106; and P. Risso, *Oman and Muscat: an early modern history* (London, 1986), 12ff. For the short-lived Maratha navy, see S. N. Sen, *The military system of the Marathas* (2nd edn, Calcutta, 1979), chaps. 10–13; and Afzal Ahmad, 'Portuguese trade on the Western coast of India in the seventeenth century (1600–1663)' (Baroda University Ph.D. thesis, 1984).

82 Iwao Seiichi, 'Li Tan, chief of the Chinese residents at Hirado, Japan, in the last days of the Ming dynasty', *Memoirs of the Research Department of the Toyo Bunko*, XVII (1958); and J. D. Spence and J. E. Wills, eds., *From Ming to Ch'ing*.

conquest, region and continuity in seventeenth-century China (New Haven, 1979), 216–28.

83 Quotations from the excellent article of Yamawaki Teijiro, 'The great trading merchants, Cocksinja and his son', *Acta Asiatica*, XXX (1976), 106–16.

84 Coxinga's father had, in fact, handled the negotiations by which the Dutch were allowed by Ming officials to move from the Pescadores to Taiwan in 1624 (the year of Coxinga's birth): see Spence and Wills, eds., *Ming to Ch'ing*, 216f. On the final campaign there, see C. R. Boxer, 'The siege of Fort Zeelandia and the capture of Formosa from the Dutch, 1661–2', *Transactions and proceedings of the Japan Society of London*, XXIV (1926–7), 16–47. Coxinga's twenty-eight guns included 30- and 36-pounders under the direction of Dutch renegades. My thanks go to Leonard Blussé for this information.

85 On the Spanish position in the Philippines in 1661–62, see N. P. Cushner, *Landed estates in the colonial Philippines* (New Haven, 1976), 36ff; J. E. Wills, *Pepper, guns and parleys. The Dutch East India Company and China 1622–1681* (Cambridge, Mass., 1974), chaps. 22–4; C. J. McCarthy, 'On the Koxinga threat of 1662', *Philippine Studies*, XVIII (1970), 187–96; and D. Abella, 'Koxinga nearly ended Spanish rule in the Philippines in 1662', *Philippine historical review*, II (1969), 295–347.

86 There is currently no proper biography of Coxinga in a Western language; see, however, the material in J. E. Wills, *Mountain of fame. Portraits in Chinese history* (Princeton, 1994), 216–30; A. W. Hummel, ed., *Eminent Chinese of the Ch'ing period 1644–1912* (Washington, D. C., 1943), 108–12; and F. Wakeman, *The great enterprise. The Manchu reconstruction of Imperial order in seventeenth-century China*, II (Berkeley, 1985), 994f, 1003–5; 1042–9. There is a detailed description of Coxinga's campaigns, and of their political setting, in Lynn A. Struve, *The southern Ming 1644–1662* (New Haven, 1984), 109–17, 154–66 and 178–93 (the maps on pp. 155 and 184 are particularly useful).

87 On the generally backward state of Taiwan at this time, see R. G. Knapp, ed., *China's island frontier: studies in the historical geography of Taiwan* (Honolulu, 1980), 3–29; and J. L. Oosterhoff, 'Zeelandia: a Dutch colonial city on Formosa (1624–62)' in R. Ross and G. J. Telkamp, eds., *Colonial cities: essays on urbanism in a colonial context* (Leiden, 1985: Comparative studies in overseas history, V), 52–63.

88 For a brilliant study of a later phase of the 'traditional' equilibrium see C. N. Parkinson, *War in the eastern seas, 1793–1815* (London, 1954).

4 THE 'MILITARY REVOLUTION' ABROAD

1 Victoria and Albert Museum (London, Catalogue no. I.M. 42–1910. See plate 31.

2 F. C. Lane, *Venice and History* (Baltimore, 1966), chaps. 23 and 24; N. Steensgaard, 'Violence and the rise of capitalism: F. C. Lane's theory of protection and tribute', *Review*, V (1981), 247–73. See also the perceptive socio-historical analysis of G. B. Ness and W. Stahl, 'Western Imperialist armies in Asia', *Comparative studies in society and history*, XIX (1977), 2–29.

3 P. J. Marshall, ed., *The writings and speeches of Edmund Burke*, V (Oxford, 1981), 392.

4 D. R. Headrick, *The tools of empire: technology and European imperialism in the nineteenth century* (Oxford, 1981), *passim*.

5 Quotations from J. L. Axtell, *The European and the Indian. Essays in the ethno-history of colonial North America* (Oxford, 1981), 139; and F. Jennings, *The invasion of America* (New York, 1976), 150. Admittedly in some Mesoamerican societies those spared in battle were later slaughtered in religious rituals. The 'Flower Wars' of the later Aztec empire, for example, involved no deaths precisely because all those captured were required for sacrifice. See C. M. Maclachlan and J. E. Rodríguez O, *Forging of the cosmic race. A reinterpreta-tion of colonial Mexico* (Berkeley, 1980), 38ff; and I. Clendinnen, 'The cost of courage in Aztec society', *Past and Present*, CVII (1985), 44–89.

6 Edmund Scott, 'An exact discourse of the Subtilties of the East Indies' in W. Foster, ed., *The voyage of Sir Henry Middleton to the Moluccas, 1604–1606* (London, 1943: Hakluyt Society, 2nd series LXXXVIII), 142. Of course, all testi-mony by Europeans on the *motives* of people from different cultures must be treated with some caution: the Europeans' view of the 'savages' was often insen-sitive and not infrequently confused. Take, for example, the assertion of the French missionary in seventeenth-century Canada, Louis Hennepin, who claimed that when the Indians went to war ''tis commonly to recovery satisfaction for some injury that they pretend has been done to them. Sometimes they engage in it upon arrival of a dram; and often as Fancy takes 'em ...' (quoted by C. J. Jaenen, *Friend and foe: aspects of Franco-Amerindian cultural contact in the sixteenth and seventeenth centuries* [Ottawa, 1976], 129).

7 W. Rodney, *A history of the Upper Guinea Coast 1545–1800* (Oxford, 1970), 237. The source (John Matthews) continued, 'their Religion affords them an apology for this horrible injustice, by permitting them to destroy all infidels, a term which seems to include all their neighbours'. Dr Rodney concluded (p. 238) that 'although these wars failed to increase the number of believers, they certainly reduced the numbers of unbelievers'! Even in the 1860s wars in West Africa were still fought for slaves: see J. F. Ade Ajayi and R. Smith, *Yoruba warfare in the nineteenth century* (Cambridge, 1964), 51–2.

8 A. F. C. Ryder, *Benin and the Europeans, 1485–1897* (London, 1969), chaps. 1–2.

9 Jaenen, *Friend and foe,* 138–41; D. R. Morris, *The washing of the spears. The rise and fall of the great Zulu nation* (London, 1966), 47, 108, 389; and W. H. Scott, *The discovery of the Igorots. Spanish contacts with the pagans of northern Luzon* (Quezon City, 1974), 48–50, 52. A. Reid, *Europe and South-East Asia: the military balance* (James Cook University of North Queensland, South-East Asian Studies Committee: occasional paper XVI [1982]), 1–2, notes that some Indonesian battles ended with a suicidal charge by a few of the defeated; but this practice, known as 'running amok', was merely a token of the mettle of the vanquished before the rest became slaves. It did not herald a mass-slaughter.

10 Whitelocke, *Memorials of the English affairs*, III, 351. The author claimed to have set his Scotsmen free at once.

11 Quotations from Axtell, *The European and the Indian*, 142, 145. For the Indians' guerilla tactics, see K. F. Otterbein, 'Why the Iroquois won: an analysis of Iroquois military tactics', *Ethnohistory*, XI (1964), 56–63; and F. R. Secoy, *changing military patterns on the Great Plains (17th through early 19th century)* (New York, 1953: Monographs of the American Ethnological Society, XXI), 52ff.

12 For Benjamin Church, see Axtell, *The European and the Indian*, 146f; and R. Slotkin and J. K. Flosom, eds., *So dreadfull a judgment. Puritan responses to King Philip's War 1676–7* (Middletown, 1978), 370–470 (which provides a crit-ical edition of Church's *Entertaining passages relating to Philip's War*).

13 Details from Secoy, *Changing military patterns*, 68; P. M. Malone, 'Changing

military technology among the Indians of southern New England 1600–77', *The American Quarterly*, XXV (1973), 48–63; H. Lamar and L. Thompson, eds., *The frontier in history: north America and southern Africa compared* (New Haven, 1981), chaps. 5 and 7; and F. Jennings, *The ambiguous Iroquois empire. The Covenant chain confederation of Indian tribes with English colonies from its beginning to the Lancaster Treaty of 1744* (New York, 1984), 80ff.

14 On the Spanish conquerors, see the prosopographical studies of B. Grunberg, *L'univers des conquistadores: les hommes et leur conquête dans le Méxique du XVIe siècle* (Paris, 1993), and J. Lockhart, *The men of Cajamarca. A social and biographical study of the first conquerors of Peru* (Austin, 1972). See also biographies of Cortés and his companions by an eye-witness: Bernal Díaz del Castillo, *Historia verdadera de la conquista de la Nueva España* (Madrid, 1984), chaps. 205–6.

15 See, once more, Secoy, *Changing military patterns*, chap. 2, for the Apache; and, for their Spanish opponents, P. W. Powell, *Soldiers, Indians and silver. The northward advance of New Spain 1550–1600* (2nd edn, Berkeley, 1969), chap. 7.

16 B. de Vargas Machuca, *Milicia y descripción de las Indias* (Madrid, 1599), fos. 1–100. See also A. Jara, *Guerre et société au Chili: essai de sociologie coloniale* (Paris, 1961), 127ff; G. Guarda, *Flandes Indiano. Las fortificaciones del reino de Chile, 1541–1826* (Santiago, 1990); and E. Cabral de Mello, *Olinda restaurada. Guerra e açúcar no Nordeste 1630/1654* (Rio de Janeiro, 1975), chap. 7: 'Guerra de Flandes e Guerra do Brasil'.

17 Fr. André Richard, about Canada in 1661–2, quoted by Jennings, *Invasion*, 155. Cf. the very similar view of Alonso González de Nájera concerning the other end of the continent; 'This war in Chile is nothing other than a chase – a great chase for game' (his book, appropriately called *Desengaño* – 'Disillusion' – is quoted with other interesting materials by Jara, *Guerre et Société*, 141).

18 Details from D. W. Treadgold, *The great Siberian migration* (Princeton, 1957); and G. V. Lantzeff and R. A. Pierce, *Eastward to empire: exploration and conquest on the Russian open frontier to 1750* (London, 1973).

19 The daring march of the Moroccans (most of them, including their leader, in fact European renegades or mercenaries) is well described by E. W. Bovill, *The golden trade of the Moors* (London, 1958), 145–78. For the Ambuila campaign, see the admirable brief account of D. Birmingham, *The Portuguese conquest of Angola* (London, 1965), chap. 4. The presence of musketeers among the Congolese army should come as no surprise: the Portuguese had been offering military advice to the kings of Congo since the early sixteenth century. See A. Brásio, *Monumenta missionaria Africana. Africa ocidental, 1471–1531*, I (Lisbon, 1952), 233–4, 241 (from the *Regimento* for Simão da Silva, 1512).

20 A. W. Lawrence, *Trade castles and forts of West Africa* (Stanford, 1964), part I, lists forty-three fortified stations maintained in early modern times by nine European nations along the African coast from Arguim to Whydah. The first – São Jorge da Minha, built at Elmina in 1482 – was also the first European building ever constructed in the Tropics.

21 On Fort Jesus, built in the 1590s to a full bastion plan upon solid coral (which made it almost impossible to mine), see G. S. P. Freeman-Grenville, ed., *The Mombasa rising against the Portuguese 1631. From sworn evidence* (London, 1980); and J. Kirkman, *Fort Jesus. A Portuguese fortress on the East African coast* (Oxford, 1974). On the abortive Portuguese attempts to conquer the High Veldt between 1571 and 1695, see R. Gray, 'Portuguese musketeers on the Zambezi', *Journal of African history*, XII (1972), 531–3; and M. D. D. Newitt, *Portuguese settlement on the Zambezi* (London, 1973), 1–73.

22 However the possession of firearms certainly influenced the rise and fall of such west African states as the Asante, whose expansion from the late seventeenth century onwards seems to have been based on the gun. See I. Wilks, *The Asante in the nineteenth century* (Cambridge, 1975), 20, 110ff. But this is a highly controversial subject, for which much conflicting evidence has been unearthed. See R. Kea, *Settlements, trade and politics in the seventeenth-century Gold Coast* (Baltimore, 1982), 158f; R. Kea, 'Firearms and warfare on the Gold and Slave coasts from the sixteenth to the nineteenth centuries', *Journal of African history*, XII (1971), 185–213; K. Y. Daaku, *Trade and politics on the Gold Coast 1600–1720* (Oxford, 1970), 149–53; J. E. Inikori, 'The import of firearms into West Africa, 1750–1807: a quantitative analysis', *Journal of African history*, XVIII (1977), 339–68; W. Richards, 'The import of firearms in West Africa in the eighteenth century', *ibid.*, XXI (1980), 43–59; and R. Elphick, *Kraal and castle. Khoikhoi and the founding of white South Africa* (New Haven, 1977), 53ff.

23 Ade Ajayi and Smith, *Yoruba warfare*, 31 and 50. In East Africa, wars in the immediate pre-colonial period became largely ritualized for lack of manpower; see J. de V. Allen, 'Traditional history and African literature: the Swahili case', *Journal of African history*, XXIII (1982), 227–36, at p. 234.

24 On the muted impact of the gun, which was repeatedly introduced into African societies only to fall out of use again, see (apart from the sources quoted above): H. J. Fisher and V. Rowland, 'Firearms in the central Sudan', *Journal of African history*, XII (1971), 215–39; G. White, 'Firearms in Africa: an introduction', *ibid.*, 173–84; R. Oliver, ed., *The Cambridge History of Africa*, III (Cambridge, 1977), 305–12; and H. A. Gemery and J. S. Hogendorn, 'Technological change, slavery and the slave trade' in C. Dewey and A. G. Hopkins, eds., *The Imperial Impact: studies in the economic history of Africa and India* (London, 1978), 243–58.

25 See D. Lombard, *Le Sultanat d'Atjeh au temps d'Iskandar Muda (1607–1636)* (Paris, 1967), 83–100; C. R. Boxer, 'The Achinese attack on Malacca in 1629'; D. K. Bassett, 'Changes in the pattern of Malay politics 1629–c. 1655', *Journal of south-east Asian history*, X.3 (1969), 429–52; and A. R. Reid, 'Sixteenth-century Turkish influence in western Indonesia', *Journal of south-east Asian history*, X.3 (1969), 395–414. For similar evidence of poor use of Western guns and military techniques by another Malayan native state, see I. A. Macgregor, 'Johore Lama in the 16th century', *Journal of the Malayan branch of the Royal Asiatic Society*, XXVIII.2 (1955), 48–125.

26 On the typology of towns in south-east Asia, see the excellent studies of A. R. Reid, 'The structure of cities in south-east Asia, 15–17th centuries', *Journal of south-east Asian studies*, X.2 (1980), 235–50; A. R. Reid, 'Southeast Asian cities before colonialism', *Hemisphere*, XXVIII.3 (1983), 144–9; and R. Reed, *Colonial Manila: the context of Hispanic urbanism and process of morphogenesis* (Berkeley, 1978), 1–3. The Philippines on the eve of Spanish conquest in the 1560s possessed no towns at all. Beaulieu's contempt for Acheh is quoted by Lombard, *Sultanat*, 45 n.2.

27 Bras de Albuquerque, *The Commentaries of the great Alfonso Dalboquerque* III (London, 1880: Hakluyt Society, LXII), 129. See also G. Irwin, 'Malacca fort', *Journal of south-east Asian history*, III.2 (1962), 19–44. The article is reprinted, with some additional material, In K. S. Sandhu and P. Wheatley, eds., *Melaka. The transformation of a Malay capital c. 1400–1980*, I (Oxford, 1983), 782–805. This admirable two-volume work contains much else on the subject, although unfortunately there is no chapter on Portuguese Malacca. Today only one gate

(the so-called Porto de Santiago, which is in fact Dutch) and some rubble on the site of *A Famosa* remains.

28 See the sources quoted in note 25 above, and C. R. Boxer, 'Asian potentiates and European artillery in the 16th–18th centuries', *Journal of the Malayan branch of the Royal Asiatic Society*, XXVII.2 (1965), 156–72 (reprinted in Boxer, *Portuguese conquest and commerce*, chap. 7). There is a fine painting of the siege of 1629 in the Museum 'Old Batavia' in Jakarta. See also the description in H. J. de Graff, *De regering van Sultan Agung, vorst van Mataram 1613–1645* (The Hague, 1958), 144–63; and the similar conclusion (reached more than a century ago!) of R. Maclagen, 'On early Asiatic fire-weapons', *Journal of the Asiatic Society (Bengal)*, XLV.1 (1876), 30–71.

29 Excavations of the fort at Cebu and the factory at Ayutthia reveal a great deal about sixteenth-century European construction techniques in the tropics: see M. Maceda, 'Preliminary report on the excavation at Fort San Pedro, in Cebu City, Philippines', *Fu-Jen Studies* (Taipei, 1973), 45–59; and *The Portuguese and Ayutthaya* (Exhibition catalogue: Bangkok, Portuguese embassy, 1985). It seems clear that the Iberians intended to create a fourth fortified port-city, at Nagasaki, but the Japanese government refused to allow bastions to be built: see D. Pacheco, 'The founding of the port of Nagasaki and its cession to the Society of Jesus', *Monumenta Nipponica*, XXV (1970), 303–23; and G. Elison, *Deus destroyed. The image of Christianity in early modern Japan* (Cambridge, Mass., 1973: Harvard East Asian Series, LXXII), 133f. The Dutch, for their part, created a 'colonial city' at Zeelandia after 1624, with its own town hall, weigh-house, hospital, orphanage and even a house of correction for fallen women; but they only fortified the citadel and one outlying redoubt. The city itself was not provided with walls, and so it was captured in 1662 by the Chinese warlord Coxinga: see Oosterhoff, 'Zeelandia: a Dutch colonial city'; and pp. 112–14 above.

30 Details taken from Archivo de Indias, *Filipinas* 6/1/5 and 12, Legazpi to Prince Carlos, 15 July 1567, and to Philip II, 25 July 1570; Reed, *Colonial Manila*, chap. 5; and Blair and Robertson, eds., *The Philippine Islands 1493–1898*, III, 141–72 ('Relation of the conquest of ... Luzón'). Not everyone, however, was impressed by Intramuros. One Spanish official in Manila told the king in 1588 that the fortifications then being built were 'a disgrace' and 'a waste of time and money, because ... they are made with round bulwarks in the old fashion'; while the military commandant three years later regretted that, because the Spanish architect who designed them had remained in Europe, the defences were 'somewhat out of proportion, being made without architect, advice or plan'. (Quotations from the excellent study of M. L. Díaz-Trechuelo Spinola, *Arquitectura española en Filipinas (1565–1800)* [Seville, 1959], 43f.) The walls built in the 1650s, however, were more formidable.

31 See A. Reid, 'The rise of Makassar', *Review of Indonesian and Malaysian affairs*, XVII (1983), 117–80; L. Andaya, *The heritage of Arung Palakka: a history of South Sulawesi (Celebes) in the seventeenth century* (The Hague, 1981), chap. 3; J. A. J. Villiers, 'Makassar and the Portuguese connexion 1540–1670' (Paper given at the *Symposium on south-east Asian responses to European intrusions* [Singapore, 1981]); and D. de Iongh, *Het krijgswezen onder de Oostindische Compagnie* (The Hague, 1950), 36f and 102–13.

32 See P. Crone, *Slaves on horses: the evolution of the Islamic policy* (Cambridge, 1980); D. Pipes, *Slave soldiers and Islam: the genesis of a military system* (New Haven, 1981); and R. Irwin, *The Middle East in the Middle Ages. The early*

Mamluk Sultanate 1250–1382 (London, 1986). On the slave soldiers of Acheh see Reid, *Europe and Southeast Asia* 7.

33 See details in J. Aubin, 'Le Royaume d'Ormuz au début du XVIe siècle' in *Mare Luso-Indicum*, II (Paris, 1972), 77–179, at pp. 175–9. For the pre-European period, see S. Digby, *War-horse and elephant in the Delhi Sultanate: a study of military supplies* (Oxford, 1971); and M. Habib, *Politics and society during the early medieval period*, II (New Delhi, 1981), 144–8 ('Heritage of the slave kings') with the chronicle of Alauudin Khalji that follows (pp. 149–270).

34 Crone, *Slaves on horseback*, 79.

35 See the classic account of D. Ayalon, *Gunpowder and firearms in the Mamluk Kingdom. A challenge to medieval society* (London, 1956). See also the similar situation in North Africa described by A. C. Hess, 'Firearms and the decline of Ibn Khaldun's military elite', *Archivum Ottomanicum*, IV (1972), 173–99. Ayalon argued that Safavid Iran was defeated by the Turks at Chaldiran because her forces were unfamiliar with firearms; but it has recently been shown that this was not so. Rather, as with the Mamluks, the Persian army sometimes used guns – but only with reluctance, and (even then) only in siege warfare: see R. N. Savory, *Iran under the Safavids* (Cambridge, 1980), 42–4; and the observations (made in the 1620s) that the Persians long continued to 'detest the trouble of the cannon, and such field peeces as require carriage', in T. Herbert, *Some yeares' travels into divers parts of Asia and Afrique* (4th edn, London, 1677), 232, 298ff. Conversely, parts of the Ottoman army – the *sipahis* – refused to use the gun, or else used it unwillingly: see R. C. Jennings, 'Firearms, bandits and gun control: some evidence on Ottoman policy towards firearms in the possession of Reâya, from judicial records of Kayseri 1600–27', *Archivum Ottomanicum*, VI (1980), 339–80, at p. 340f.

36 See on all this the important articles of G. Káldy-Nagy, 'The first centuries of the Ottoman military organization', *Acta orientalia academiae scientiarum hungaricae*, XXXI.2 (1977), 147–84; D. Petrović, 'Firearms in the Balkans on the eve of and after the Ottoman conquests' in V. J. Parry and M. E. Yapp, eds., *War, technology and society in the Middle East* (Oxford, 1975), 164–94; G. Agoston, 'Ottoman artillery and European military technology in the 16th and 17th centuries', *Acta Orientalia Academiae Scientiarum Hungaricae*, XLVIII (1994), 15–48; and Agoston, 'Habsburgs and Ottomans'. Quotation from H. Inalcik, 'The socio-political effects of the diffusion of firearms in the Middle East', in Parry and Yapp *War, technology and society*, 195–217, at p. 199.

37 See P. Broucek, *Historischer Atlas zur zweiten Turkenbelagerung Wien 1683* (Vienna, 1983) – in which all the prints and maps show the Turkish camp undefended against attack by a relief army; and J. Stoye, *The siege of Vienna* (London, 1964), 157–9 and 255–7.

38 *Encyclopaedia of Islam*, I (2nd edn, Leiden and London, 1960), 1055–69 (article on 'barūd' – gunpowder – by D. Ayalon, V. J. Parry and R. N. Savory) notes, *inter alia*, that the Turks still had no pistols by the 1590s, were slow to adopt new siege techniques and, even in the 1600s, had no 'good powder but that whyche they gett from overthrone Christians, or els is broughte them out of England'. See also G. Agoston, 'Ottoman gunpowder production in Hungary in the 16th century', in G. David and P. Fodor, eds., *Hungarian–Ottoman military and diplomatic relations in the age of Suleyman the Magnificent* (Budapest, 1994), 149–59.

39 Saxe, *Rêveries*, (written, 1732), quoted by V. J. Parry, 'La Manière de combattre' in Parry and Yapp, *War, technology and society*, 218–56, at p. 256.

40 Council of Ten order of 27 November 1572, quoted Mallett and Hale, *Military*

organization of a Renaissance state, 400; and Luis Collado, *Manual de artillería* (Milan, 1592), fo. 8v. (guns 'founded by the Turks are usually poor and flawed, even though the alloy is good'). Of course a slight technical inferiority did not normally matter to the Turks: the Ottoman fleet dominated the Mediterranean neither by virtue of superior commanders (most of their admirals were relatively inexperienced graduates of the palace school) nor through superior organization. They won thanks to greater resources. Their empire had more men, more ships and more equipment at its disposal than any enemy, and all were directed by a unified supreme command. Minor defects in individual items scarcely mattered when the Turks could send 250 galleys against Christian adversaries who possessed only 100. See Chapter 3 above.

41 See A. Williams, *The metallurgy of muslim armour* (Manchester, 1978: Seminar on early Islamic science, monograph III), 4, 5, 11.

42 On the introduction of ordnance to India see B. Rathgen, 'Die Pulverwaffe in Indien', *Ostasiatische Zeitschrift*, XII (1925), 11–30 and 196–217; I. A. Khan, 'Early use of cannon and musket in India, AD 1442–1526', *Journal of the economic and social history of the Orient*, XXIV (1981), 146–64; and I. A. Khan, 'Origin and development of gunpowder technology in India AD 1250–1500', *Indian historical review*, IV.1 (1977), 20–9. But the quality was often poor. When, for example, in 1525 the government of Portuguese India was computing the total quantity of ordnance available for defence, they noted: 'We make little mention of moorish guns, because they are no good on our ships; however if the metal is melted down, better guns can be cast'. See Lima Felner, ed., *Subsídios para a história da Índia portuguesa*, part III, 12. See the admirable general discussion in Sarkar, *Art of war*, 126–42.

43 Details from W. Irvine, *The army of the Indian Moghuls. Its organization and administration* (London, 1903), 114–17; B. P. Lenman, 'The weapons of war in eighteenth-century India', *Journal of the Society for Army Historical Research*, XLVI (1968), 33–43; and Sen, *Military system of the Marathas*, 103.

44 See references in Boxer, 'Asian potentates', 161. On the difficulty of estimating accurately the size of Indian armies, see D. H. A. Kolff, *Naukar, Rajput and Sepoy. The ethnohistory of the military labour market in Hindustan 1450–1850* (Cambridge, 1990), 2–17; and R. K. Phul, *Armies of the great Mughals (1526–1707)* (New Delhi, 1978), 125–34. Phul estimates Akbar's campaign army in the later sixteenth century at some 50,000 men, and Prince Dara's in 1653 at 90,000. But with provincial armies and feudal levies, the total manpower available for Akbar's army in the 1590s was estimated by one expert at 342,696 cavalry and 4,039,097 infantry (Kolff, *op. cit.*, 3).

45 Irvine, *Army*, 152ff; Boxer, 'Asian potentates', 158; and Cipolla, *Guns and sails*, 111–14. Further detail in M. A. Lima Cruz, 'Exiles and renegades in early sixteenth-century Portuguese Asia', *Indian economic and social history review*, XXIII (1986), 249–62; and S. Subrahmanyam, 'The *Kagemusha* effect: the Portuguese, firearms and the state in early modern South Asia', *Moyen Age et Océan Indien*, IV (1987), 97–123.

46 For captured guns see P. Baldaeus, *Naauwkeurige Beschrijvinge van Malabar en Choromandel*, I (Amsterdam, 1672), 3; for guns given as presents see Cipolla, *Guns and sails*, 109f, and Boxer, 'Asian potentates', 160; for munitions supplied by the Portuguese to Indian princes in order to preserve the balance of power between them, see HAG, *Livro das Monções* 21A fo. 52, king to viceroy, 18 February 1640; for the same technique practised by the Dutch, see Bernier, *Travels*, 31. For the use made by one notable Mughal commander of European technology see Sarkar, *The life of Mir Jumla*, 96, 279f.

47 Both Verstegen and Manucci have left interesting accounts of their foreign service: see P. H. Pott, 'Willem Verstegen, een extra-ordinaris Raad van Indië, als avonturier in India in 1659', *Bijdragen tot de Taal-, Land- en Volkenkunde*, CXII (1956), 355–82; and N. Manucci, *Storia do Mogor, or Mogul India 1653–1708* (4 vols., ed. W. Irvine, London, 1906–8). There are also numerous references to European military experts in Mughal service in Bernier, *Travels* (e.g. 31, 47–56, 93). On p. 55 Bernier, writing in the 1660s, ventured the opinion that 'I could never see these [Mughal] soldiers, destitute of order, and marching with the irregularity of a herd of animals, without reflecting upon the ease with which 25,000 of our veterans from the [French] Army of Flanders, commanded by the Prince of Condé or Marshal Turenne, would overcome these armies, however numerous'. The problem, however, was to get so many Europeans (to say nothing of Condé or Turenne) to India at the same time.

48 Manucci, *Storia*, I, 276, 278.

49 Of course, 'street gang' tactics continued to characterize European colonial warfare until the twentieth century: see, for a classic example, R. Meinertzhagen, *Kenya Diary 1902–1906* (Edinburgh, 1957), e.g. pp. 74, 143f, 152, and most of Part II. For the introduction of regular European military practice to Portuguese India see, for example, clause 53 of the royal Instructions to Viceroy Redondo, going to India in 1617: 'We have tried many times to reorganize our troops in India according to the European manner, since experience has shown that without it we have suffered several important losses, and now that we are at war with the Dutch, who are disciplined soldiers, it is more important than ever' (R. A. Bulhão Pato, ed., *Documentos remetidos da India ou Livros das Monções*, IV, [Lisbon, 1893], 168–9). See also pp. 287–8 (royal letter of 1618) and others in later years on the same subject. An interesting insight into Portuguese military practice in India in the early seventeenth century is offered by G. D. Winius, 'Francisco Rodrigues de Silveira: the forgotten "soldado pratico"' in Albuquerque and Guerreiro, eds., *II seminário internacional de histório Indo-Portuguesa*, 773–86.

50 For examples, see HAG, *Livro das Monções* 22 fos. 322–4, viceroy to king, 7 December 1634; and MS. 1161 fo. 112v, Asento of the Council of Finance in Goa, 11 September 1630. On the Macao foundry see: M. Teixeira, 'Os Bocarros' in *Actas do Congreso Internacional de História dos descobrimentos* v.2 (Lisbon, 1961), 359–85.

51 Based on the archaeological and historical evidence presented in R. O. W. Goertz, 'Attack and defence techniques at the siege of Chaul, 1570–1' in Albuquerque and Guerreiro, *II seminário*, 265–92. Part of the explanation for the deliverance of Chaul was the failure of the besiegers to cut the town off from the sea, so Portuguese ships were constantly able to land supplies and reinforcements. These warships were also able to use the guns against the besiegers from time to time. The Portuguese were also armed with superior handguns: it was found that their muskets fired a one-ounce shot over 400 metres, while the Indian infantrymen could only send a half-ounce shot for about half that distance.

52 Details from P. E. Pieris, *Some documents relating to the rise of the Dutch power in Ceylon, 1602–1670* (Colombo, 1929), 57 (Batticaloa) and 67–8 (Colombo); and Baldaeus, *Naauwkeurige Beschrijvinghe*, I, 155 (Negapatam) and II, 106 (Colombo). See also the excellent illustrated descriptions in W. A. Nelson, *The Dutch forts of Sri Lanka: the military monuments of Ceylon* (Edinburgh, 1984). Some Portuguese fortresses in India were more impressive, however, such as Diu, or Fort Aguada at the bar of the Mandovi, below Goa.

53 For details see S. Toy, *The strongholds of India* (London, 1957), 53–60 (Golconda) and 123 (Delhi); S. Toy, *The fortified cities of India* (London, 1965), 21, 48–50, and 81–4; Sarkar, *Art of war*, 143–74; and the magnificent plates in V. Fass, *The forts of India* (London, 1986).

54 See, in particular, P. J. Marshall, 'Western arms in maritime Asia in the early phases of expansion', *Modern Asian Studies*, XIV (1980), 13–28. The following part of my argument owes much to discussions with Professor Marshall, whose generous aid I gratefully acknowledge.

55 Figures from P. J. N. Willman, 'The Dutch in Asia, 1595–1610' (St Andrews University M.A. thesis, 1986), 21–2 and 26: based on private calculations made by Grotius from the companies' own papers, and preserved in the Algemeen Rijksarchief, The Hague, *Collectie Hugo de Groot*.

56 Coen to Heeren XVII, 27 December 1614 (from Banten in Java), quoted by H. T. Colenbrander, *Jan Pieterszoon Coen. Levenbeschrijving* (The Hague, 1934), 64. It should be noted, however, the Coen's advice was not always followed. In 1622, he was rebuked by the Directors for fighting too much. Violence, they told him, should be used only in the service of profit: 'One must avoid and eschew war if it is at all compatible with the preservation and safety of our state ... No great attention should be paid to questions of "reputation" ... for we are mere merchants.' (Quoted by Steensgaard, 'The Dutch East India Company as an institutional innovation', 255.) The Directors had good reason for concern: many of their forts and factories in the Orient were returning a loss! See M. A. P. Meilink-Roelofsz, *Asian trade and European influence in the Indonesian archipelago between 1500 and about 1630* (The Hague, 1962), 386.

57 John Fryer, *A new account of East India and Persia, being nine years' travels, 1672–1681*, I (London, 1909; Hakluyt Society, 2nd series XX), 124.

58 Some company officials agreed with the Dutch view, and in the 1680s some of the Directors supported them. Several apposite quotations will be found in I. B. Watson, 'Fortifications and the "idea" of force in early English East India Company relations with India', *Past and Present*, LXXXVIII (1980), 70–87.

59 Quotations from East India Company records in G. J. Bryant, 'The East India Company and its army, 1600–1778' (London University Ph.D. thesis, 1975), 10, 31, 74 and 138. There was a brief period of belligerence in the 1680s, under the leadership of Josiah Child, but it failed (see Bryant, pp. 32–3; interestingly, it coincided with a similar assertiveness by England in her American colonies – S. S. Webb, *The Governor-General. The English army and the definition of the Empire, 1569–1681* [Chapel Hill, 1979], 447–55).

60 The battle of Adyar river (7 November 1746) was well described by the Tamil factor of Dupleix at Pondichéry: J. F. Price, ed., *The private diary of Ananda Ranga Pillai*, III (Madras, 1914), 94–5 and 444–52.

61 See the interesting remarks on this theme by J. A. de Moor, 'Militaire inter-dependentie tussen Europa en de derde wereld. De geschiedenis van "Johnny Gurkha"', *Internationale spectator*, XXXVII (1984), 356–64; de Iongh, *Het krijgswezen*, chap. 4; and Marshall, 'Western arms in maritime Asia', 25f.

62 Exactly how this happened is something of a mystery. A. Martineau, *Dupleix et l'Inde française*, III (Paris, 1927), devoted a few pages to the sepoys (pp. 62–72) but filled them with a sustained diatribe about the shortcomings and vices of all Asian races! E. W. C. Sandes, *The military engineer in India*, I (Chatham, 1933), 64–5, claimed that the French trained some 5,000 Muslims as regular troops in 1741 in order to oppose an invasion of the Carnatic by the Marathas; but Dupleix himself later stated that sepoys were first used by the

French only in 1746. This contradiction is resolved by the records at Pondichéry, which reveal that two companies of 'cypahes' were raised by the French in January 1742 and were drilled, armed and paid in the European manner. But they were disbanded at the end of the year and so Dupleix in 1746 had to start all over again. See H. H. Dodwell, *Sepoy recruitment in the Old Madras Army* (Calcutta, 1922: Studies in Indian Records, I), 3–7; and S. C. Hill, 'The old sepoy officer', *English Historical Review*, XXVIII (1913), 260–91 and 496–514.

63 Dupleix to the Directors of the Compagnie des Indes, 15 February 1751, quoted by H. Furber, *Rival empires of trade in the Orient 1600–1800* (Oxford, 1976), 156.

64 Details from Furber, *ibid*, 147–69 (Saunders quoted at p. 156); and Furber, *John Company at work. A study of European expansion in Indian in the late eighteenth century* (Cambridge, Mass., 1948), 204f. I am most grateful to Professor Blair B. Kling for these references and for invaluable help in formulating the argument of this paragraph.

65 Figures from Bryant, 'The East India Company and its army', 299f; M. P. Singh, *Indian army under the East India Company* (New Delhi, 1976); and P. Mason, *A matter of honour: an account of the Indian army, its officers and men* (2nd edn, London, 1976), 62f. I am grateful to Dr Bryant for sending me further material and additional references on this matter.

66 On the Mughal army's strength, see Raychaudhuri and Habib, eds., *Cambridge economic history of India*, I, 303f, and the sources cited in note 44 above. There is a tendency to discount native Indian power by land in the earlier eighteenth century, perhaps because of the total collapse of native seaborne trade at the same time. But this is wrong: see Das Gupta, *Indian merchants and the decline of Surat*, introduction; 'Indian merchants and the western Indian Ocean: the early seventeenth century', *Modern Asian Studies*, XIX (1985), 481–99; 'Indian merchants'; and in *The Cambridge economic history of India*, I, 425–33.

67 *Reports from Committees of the House of Commons*, IV (1804), 60–1. My thanks go to Professor P. J. Marshall for this reference. The figures are all the more striking when it is remembered that the Company *lost* £2.5 million between 1753 and 1760. The massive new Fort William at Calcutta, built between 1765 and 1771 at a cost of £1 million, is just one example of how the Bengal settlement allowed the Europeans to change the art of defensive warfare in India. See P. J. Marshall, 'Eighteenth-century Calcutta' in Ross and Telkamp, *Colonial cities*, 90.

68 See Ness and Stahl, 'Western imperialist armies in Asia'; J. P. Lawford, *Britain's army in India from its origin to the conquest of Bengal* (London, 1978), 72–81; Bryant, 'The East India Company and its army', chaps. 3–5; and R. Callahan, *The East India Company and army reform, 1783–98* (Cambridge, Mass., 1972), 6. The Dutch East India Company also began to train their Asian troops to fight like Europeans in the 1740s, under Governor-General van Imhoff: see de Iongh, *Het krijgswezen*, 165–8.

69 J. Pemble, 'Resources and techniques in the second Maratha war', *Historical Journal*, XIX (1976), 375–404, at pp. 379f; R. G. S. Cooper, 'Wellington and the Marathas', *International History Review*, XI (1989), 31–8; and P. Barua, 'Military developments in India, 1750–1850', *Journal of Military History*, LVIII (1994), 599–616.

70 On the Marathas' failure, see Pemble, 'Resources and techniques', 386ff. On the sepoys in the Philippines see Mason, *A matter of honour*, 68, 242. On China see L. Dermigny, *La Chine et l'Occident. Le commerce à Canton au XVIIIe siècle*,

1719–1833, II (Paris, 1964), 781. Later in the nineteenth century, sepoys were also sent to conquer East Africa for the Europeans. See also the remarks of Qaisar, *The Indian response to European technology*, 46–57, and 144–6.

71 The suggestion that the Turks introduced Western firearms to China before the Europeans was first made by P. Pelliot, 'Le Hŏǰã et le Sayid Hussain de l'Histoire des Ming', *T'oung Pao*, XXXVIII (1948), 81–292, at pp. 199–207. See also Needham, *The gunpowder epic*, 440–9.

72 Details from R. Huang, 'Military expenditures in sixteenth–century Ming China', *Oriens extremus*, XVII (1970), 39–62; Huang, *1587: a year of no significance*, chap 6; A. Chan, *The glory and fall of the Ming dynasty* (Norman, 1982), 51–63 and A. Waldron, *The Great Wall of China. From history to myth* (Cambridge, Mass., 1990), chap. 5.

73 *Tai-tsu shih-lu* (facsimile edition, Mukden, 1931; reproduced from an edition of 1740 which seems to be based, in turn, on an illustrated chronicle compiled in 1635 – that is, by and for those who might themselves have seen the events they described).

74 See two new accounts of the fall of the Ming by Wakeman, *The great enterprise;* and Struve, *The southern Ming.* See also Spence and Wills, eds., *From Ming to Ch'ing*, chaps. 1 and 2; and Chan, *Glory and fall*, chap. 8.

75 Although the efforts of the Jesuits and other Europeans in Macao and Peking to supply first the Ming and then the Manchu with guns usually monopolize the limelight, this is just another case of Eurocentrism. The bulk of Chinese artillery was produced by Chinese craftsmen: see Needham, *The gunpowder epic*, 392–414; and Chan, *Glory and fall*, 57–63. The same was true in Japan, where production by local workshops far surpassed European imports. The only East Asian country which seems to have been heavily dependent on weapons imported from the West was Vietnam: the Nguyen of the north relied heavily after the 1720s on bronze guns either cast by Westerners living in Hué, or else imported from Macao, in their wars against the Tring of the south, who received (in their turn) supplies from the Dutch in Batavia. But even in Vietnam, local production continued: a French visitor to Hué in 1749 saw 800 bronze and 400 iron guns, by no means all of which were of European manufacture. See P. Y. Manguin, *Les Portugais sur les côtes de Viêtnam et du Campa* (Paris, 1972), 206–8; L. Cadière, 'Le Quartier des Arènes. I. Jean de la Croix et les premiers Jésuites', *Bulletin des amis du Vieux Hué*, XI (1924), 307–32 (La Croix resided in Hué and cast guns for the Nguyen from the 1650s to 1682); and C. R. Boxer, 'Macao as a religious and commercial entrepôt in the sixteenth and seventeenth centuries', *Acta Asiatica*, XXXI (1974), 64–90.

76 Matteo Ricci, in his memoirs (referring to the year 1599), noted that, although the Chinese army drilled 'in proper order', they used gunpowder, 'not so much for their arquebuses, of which they have few, nor for bombards and artillery which are also in short supply, but for firework displays'. Quoted by J. D. Spence, *The memory palace of Matteo Ricci* (London, 1983), 45. It is notable that the very first image in Ricci's 'artificial memory' was *war*. The exact size of the Ch'ing army was an official secret, but the campaign forces in the seventeenth century apparently numbered around 150,000 men, with up to 40,000 men directly involved in battles. See C. Fang, 'A technique for estimating the numerical strength of the early Manchu military forces', *Harvard Journal of Asiatic Studies*, XIII (1950), 192–215.

77 For the precise manner in which Western guns were introduced into Japan, see the definitive account, together with a German translation of Japanese sources,

in C. Schurhammer, *Gesammelte Studien, II. Orientalia* (Rome, 1963: Biblioteca Instituti Historici Societatis Iesu, XXI), 485–579. There is an English translation of one source – the *Teppō-ki* of Nampō Bunshi (1606) – in Tsunoda Ryusaku and others, eds., *Sources of Japanese tradition,* I (New York, 1964), 308–12. It should be noted that the island of Tanegashima, where the first Portuguese guns arrived (which is why early muskets are called in Japanese *Tanegashima*), was an ideal spot for copying them. It was, in 1543, not only an established centre of trade but a major centre of sword production; it proved relatively easy for the sword-smiths to turn out musket-barrels instead, ready for the merchants to distribute.

78 In 1549 Oda Nobunaga was apparently asked to provide '500 musketeers and bowmen', which does not necessarily mean – as many scholars have said – 500 men with muskets (Hora Tomio, *Tanegashima-jū. Denrai to sono eikyō* [Tokyo, 1958], 157). But in 1555, Takeda Shingen definitely deployed 300 musketeers at the battle of Shinano Asahiyamajō (Nagahara Keiji, *Sengoku no dōran, Nihon no rekishi,* XIV [Tokyo, 1975], 947; and Hora, *Tanegashima-jū,* 144–54). Nagashino is depicted in a marvellous series of screen paintings, reproduced in *Sengoku kassen-e Byōbu Shūsei. I.i Kawanakajima kassen-zu Nagashino kassen-zu* (Tokyo, 1980). However, since the screens were all painted several decades after the battle, they may depict later Japanese military practice rather than the actual techniques employed by Nobunaga at Nagashino.

79 The general account of N. Perrin, *Giving up the gun. Japan's reversion to the sword 1543–1879* (New York, 1979), although interesting and provocative, is based almost entirely on Western sources and pushes some of the evidence too far. Greater reliance may be placed on D. M. Brown, 'The impact of firearms on Japanese warfare, 1543–98', *The Far Eastern Quarterly,* VII (1948), 236–53. Hora, *Tanegashima,* 21–3, shows that firearms, almost certainly imported from China, were used in Japan before 1543. They were, however, few in number and limited in effect. The exact nature of early Japanese guns is difficult to establish, because so few survive – perhaps only ten *Tanegashima* from the sixteenth century are known today (personal communication from Dr Yoshioka Shin'ichi of Kyoto). And much the same is true of artillery: very few early modern pieces survive – although here the culprit (according to Japanese sources) was the 'liberation' of most of the beautiful guns collected in the Kudan Museum in Tokyo by American forces after 1945. Only a few firearms are to be found today in the military museum attached to the Yasukuni shrine in Tokyo. There is a concise discussion of the sources and problems in Needham, *The gunpowder epic,* 467–72, which relies (perhaps too heavily) on the utopian vision of Noel Perrin's *Giving up the gun.*

80 Quotation from E. M. Satow, 'Notes on the intercourse between Japan and Siam', *Transactions of the Asiatic Society of Japan,* XIII (1884–5), 145; army sizes in G. B. Sansom, *A history of Japan, 1334–1615* (Stanford, 1961), 322. A recent consideration of the armies commanded by Hideyoshi – which reached a total strength of 280,000 for the invasion of Korea in 1593 – is provided by B. Susser, 'The Toyotomi regime and the daimyō' in J. P. Mass and W. B. Hauser, eds., *The Bakufu in Japanese history* (Stanford, 1985), 129–52, at pp. 135ff.

81 Kodama Kōta, and others, eds., *Nihon jōkaku taikei,* XI (Tokyo, 1980), 261–9 on Kannonji; *ibid.,* 254–60 on Azuchi; plus Naitō Akira, 'Azuchi-jō no kenkyū', *Kokka,* LXXXIII (nos 987–8; 1976), with a brief English summary. A review of Naitō is also helpful: Takayanagi Shun'ichi, 'The glory that was Azuchi', *Monumenta nipponica,* XXXII (1977), 515–24. See also G. Elison and

B. L. Smith, eds., *Warlords, artists and commoners. Japan in the sixteenth century* (Honolulu, 1981), 62–6; and M. Cooper, *They came to Japan: an anthology of European reports on Japan 1543–1640* (London, 1965), 134–5.

82 The verse is quoted by George Elison in Elison and Smith, *Warlords, artists and commoners* 66. On the siege of Odawara, see Sansom, *A history of Japan 1334–1615*, 326–7. Concentrations of troops on this scale caused severe logistical problems and placed an almost intolerable strain on the Japanese economy, weakened by over a century of civil strife. On the link between castle size, army size and tax demands under Hideyoshi, see the richly documented article of G. Moréchand, '"Taikō kenchi": le cadastre de Hideyoshi Toyotomi', *Bulletin de l'École française de l'Extrême Orient*, LIII.1 (1966), 7–69, especially pp. 12–13. For a modern biography of the remarkable *Taikō* – Japan's only commoner ruler before modern times – see M. E. Berry, *Hideyoshi* (Cambridge, Mass., 1982).

83 Kodama, *Nihon jōkaku*, XII (1981), 152–81, and Okamoto Ryōichi, *Nihon jō kaku-shi kenkyū sōsho VIII: Ōsaka-jō* (Tokyo, 1982). Both works are fully illustrated. See also the plates in K. Hirai, *Feudal architecture in Japan* (New York, 1973), chap. 4; the account of W. B. Hauser, 'Osaka castle and Tokugawa authority in western Japan' in Mass and Hauser, *The Bakufu*, 153–72; and the description of the Maeda stronghold at Kanazawa in J. McClain, *Kanazawa: a seventeenth-century Japanese castle town* (New Haven, 1982), 33f.

84 J. W. Hall, 'The castle town and Japan's modern urbanization', *Far Eastern Quarterly*, XV (1955); a classic article reprinted in J. W. Hall and M. B. Jansen, eds., *Studies in the institutional history of early modern Japan* (Princeton, 1968), 169–88 – quotation on p. 177. Possibly the Dutch fortifications at Galle, in southern Ceylon, were in fact larger: see Nelson, *Dutch forts of Sri Lanka*, 48–51.

85 Although we know from several sources that military conversation was one of Nobunaga's chief passions, the Westerners with whom he conversed were mainly regular clergy whose knowledge of military architecture would normally not have extended to the intricacies of defensive architecture. See A. Valignano, *Sumario de las Cosas de Japón* (1583: ed. J. L. Álvarez-Taladriz, Tokyo, 1954), 152. It is true that some Jesuits in the Far East became skilled in metal casting, but this did not necessarily make them into reputable military engineers.

86 Quotations from J. Ouchterlony, *The Chinese War* (London, 1844), 174–5; and H. Knollys, *Incidents in the China War of 1860* (Edinburgh, 1875), 198–9. See also Headrick, *The tools of empire*, 80–1; S. D. Chang, 'The morphology of walled capitals' in G. W. Skinner, ed., *The city in late Imperial China* (Stanford, 1977), 75–100; H. Franke, 'Siege and defence of towns in medieval China' in F. A. Kierman and J. K. Fairbank, eds., *Chinese ways in warfare* (Cambridge, Mass., 1974), 151–201; and J. Needham and R. D. S. Yates, *Science and civilization in China. Volume V: Chemistry and chemical technology, part vi: military technology: missiles and sieges* (Cambridge, 1994).

87 The study of Needham, *Science and civilization in China*, v. vi and vii, replaces all earlier accounts as far as China as concerned. But see also C. R. Boxer, 'Early European military influence in Japan (1543–1853)', *Transactions of the Asiatic Society of Japan*, 2nd series VIII (1931), 67–93; C. R. Boxer, 'Portuguese military expeditions in aid of the Mings and against the Manchus, 1621–1647', *T'ien Hsia Monthly*, VII.1 (August 1938), 24–36; and Cipolla, *Guns and sails*, 114–17.

88 Perrin, *Giving up the gun*, 64–5.

89 Data taken from Itō Tasaburo, 'The book-banning policy of the Tokugawa

shogunate', *Acta Asiatica*, XII (1972), 36–61; B. Susser, 'The Toyotomi regime', 140–5; Fujiki Hisashi and George Elison, 'The political posture of Oda Nobunaga' in J. W. Hall, Nagahara Keiji and Kozo Yamamura, eds., *Japan before Tokugawa: political considerations and economic growth 1500–1650* (Princeton, 1981), 149–93, at pp. 186–93; and J. W. Hall, *Government and local power in Japan, 500 to 1700. A Study based on Bizen province* (Princeton, 1966), 248, 316. There is another parallel here with western Europe's military development: see pages 41–3 above.

90 See the radically new assessment of the development of East Asian history in early modern times offered by R. P. Toby, *State and diplomacy in early modern Japan. Asian in the development of the Tokugawa bakufu* (Princeton, 1984).

5 BEYOND THE REVOLUTION

1 See the useful essays of K. M. Sharpe, 'Crown, Parliament and locality: government and communications in early Stuart England', *English historical review*, CI (1986), 321–50; and J. A. Goldstone, 'State breakdown in the English revolution: a new synthesis', *American journal of sociology*, XCII (1986), 257–322.

2 See J. G. A. Pocock, ed., *The political works of James Harrington* (Cambridge, 1977), 15f and 128f; R. Hutton, *The Restoration. A political and religious history of England and Wales 1658–1667* (Oxford, 1985); L. M. Smith, 'Scotland and Cromwell. A study in early modern government' (Oxford University D.Phil. thesis, 1979); and K. S. Bottigheimer, 'The Restoration land settlement in Ireland: a structural view', *Irish historical studies*, XVIII (1972), 1–21, at p. 6.

3 See the judicious remarks of Corvisier, *Armies and societies*, chap. 6. However, attempts to forge too close a connexion between war and the growth of absolutism can be dangerous. See the much criticized theories advanced by R. Bean, 'War and the birth of the Nation State', *Journal of economic history*, XXXIII (1973), 203–21 (followed by the strictures of D. Ringrose and R. Roehl, *ibid.*, 222–31); and by S. E. Finer, 'State and nation-building in Europe: the role of the military' in C. Tilly, ed., *The formation of nation-states in Western Europe* (Princeton, 1975), 84–163. See also the cautionary remarks of Hale, *War and society*, 246–52. However, the existence of a correlation between militarization and centralization can be clearly demonstrated for certain times and places. See, above all, the essays in Kunisch, ed., *Staatsverfassung und Heeresverfassung*; and also J. Vicens Vives, 'Estructura administrativa estatal en los siglos XVI y XVII' in *XIe congrès internationale des sciences historiques. Rapports*, IV (Stockholm, 1960), 1–24; W. Schulze, *Landesdefension und Staatsbildung: Studien zum Kriegswesen des innerösterreichischen Territorialstaates (1564–1619)* (Vienna, 1973), part 4; V. G. Kiernan, 'Foreign mercenaries and absolutism' in T. S. Aston, ed., *Crisis in Europe 1560–1660* (London, 1965), 117–40; J. A. Maravall, *Estado moderna y mentalidad social*, II (Madrid, 1972), 513–85; the articles of L. Jespersen, J. Lindegren and O. Rian in *Scandinavian Journal of History*, X (1985), 271–363; and C. Jones, 'The military revolution and the professionalization of the French army under the *Ancien Régime*' in Duffy, ed., *The military revolution and the state*, 28–48. In his last historical work, the late Fernand Braudel called attention to the crucial role of early modern armies in breaking down local barriers and unifying the subjects of each state: during the eighteenth century, he claimed, 'Alongside the king's government, the army became the most active instrument in the unification of France' (Braudel, *L'Identité de la France. I. Espace et histoire* [Paris, 1986], 338).

4 See the excellent study by G. A. Craig, 'Delbrück: the military historian' in Paret, ed., *Makers of modern strategy*, 326–53, and the penetrating remarks of T. C. W. Blanning, *The origins of the French revolutionary wars* (London, 1986), 1–68.

5 Details in G. Ritter, *Frederick the Great* (Berkeley, 1968), 129–48; casualty details given in G. Korff, ed., *Preussen: Versuch einer Bilanz*, I (Reinbek bei Hamburg, 1981), 197f. Compare the wastage rates given on pages 53–7 above.

6 See M. Glover, *Wellington's army in the Peninsula, 1808–1814* (Newton Abbot, 1977), 46; and Paret, *Yorck and the era of Prussian reform*, 14f.

7 Details from C. Duffy, *The army of Frederick the Great* (Newton Abbot, 1974), chap. 8.

8 Details from W. L. Dorn, *Competition for empire 1740–1763* (New York, 1940), chaps. 2, 3 and 8; Duffy, *Army*, chap. 8; and Duffy, *Frederick*, chap. 9 ('Frederick and war'). On the other hand, thanks to all these economies, Frederick did end the war with a small profit.

9 Preface to *Histoire de mon temps* quoted by R. R. Palmer, 'Frederick the Great, Guibert, Bülow' in Paret, ed., *Makers of modern strategy*, 91–119, at p. 105. The king was not so keen on preserving the *diplomatic* status quo, however: in 1772, he persuaded Russian and Austria to join him in partitioning Poland.

10 See the detailed discussion in G. A. Craig, *The politics of the Prussian army* (2nd edn, Oxford, 1964), 17–27.

11 Quotation (from Sir Nicholas Wraxall, in Vienna, in 1778) in Kunisch, *Der kleine Krieg*, 29n: an excellent account of the development of the Austrian light infantry. See also G. E. Rothenberg, *The military border in Croatia, 1740–1881. A study of an imperial institution* (Chicago, 1966), chaps. 2 and 3.

12 See the valuable analysis of P. E. Russell, 'Redcoats in the wilderness: British officers and irregular warfare in Europe and America, 1740 to 1760', *William and Mary Quarterly*, 3rd series XXXV (1978), 629–52. Russell notes that the new military techniques were brought to the colonies not only by books and personnel from Europe, but by newspaper reports either printed or distributed in America.

13 Quotation (from a letter of 1756) and details from P. Paret, 'Colonial experience and European military reform at the end of the eighteenth century', *Bulletin of the Institute of Historical Research*, XXVII (1964), 47–59. Both Paret and Russell (see preceding note) argue that techniques of irregular warfare spread from Europe to America in the 1740s and 50s, and not vice versa. But this ignores the fact that irregular warfare had always been a feature of *both* the colonies *and* the Habsburg-Turkish borderlands: see pp. 36–7 and 130–1 above. See also the penetrating remarks of John Shy, *A people numerous and armed. Reflections on the military struggle for American independence* (Oxford, 1976), chap. 6; and idem, *Toward Lexington. The role of the British army in the coming of the American Revolution* (Princeton, 1965), chap. 4.

14 On the tactical deployment of light troops in general see Ritter, *Frederick the Great*, 134ff; and H. Strachan, *European armies and the conduct of war* (London, 1983), 27–32.

15 For the delayed impact of Bourcet, and the *administrative* division, see Quimby, *The background of Napoleonic warfare*, 175–84; and S. T. Ross, 'The development of the combat division in eighteenth-century French armies', *French historical studies*, IV (1965), 84–94. The adoption of the *combat* division, however, was mainly the product of unwieldy armies after the *levée en masse* of 1793: a body of men like the *Armée du Nord*, with 310,000 troops by spring 1794, simply could not operate without divisions. (I am grateful for this point, and for much else in this section, to professor John Lynn.)

16 Details from J. A. Vann, 'Mapping under the Austrian Habsburgs' in D. Buisseret, ed., *Monarchs, ministers and maps* (Chicago, 1992), chap. 6. The Josephine survey was classed 'top secret' until 1864 and only the 'Belgian' sheets, by de Ferraris, were ever published. The Cassini survey was published in 1789 at a cost of 700,000 livres (approximately £33,000). The military survey of Scotland, carried out between 1747 and 1755 in the wake of the Jacobite rebellions, led the way in the field: see Y. O'Donaghue, *William Roy (1726–1790): pioneer of the ordnance survey* (London, 1977). It has been suggested that without contour lines, which only became popular in the 1790s, maps could be of little use to military planners: see F. de Dainville, 'From the depths to the heights', *Surveying and mapping*, XXX (1970), 389–403. But a glance at Roy's exquisite survey maps, which contain a perfectly adequate indication of the exact location of high ground, shows that the British army (at least) possessed serviceable maps from the 1750s onwards. See, in general, the interesting discussion in McNeill, *The pursuit of power*, 158–66. For the influence of roads in slowing down troop-movements see the remarks of J. Milot, 'Un problème operationnel du XVIIe siècle illustré pur un cas régional', *Revue du Nord*, LIII (1971), 269–90.

17 Details taken from Lynn, *Bayonets of the Republic*, 205f; Quimby, *Background of Napoleonic warfare*, 292ff; and Hughes, *Firepower weapons*, 15–36. Again there is an excellent general discussion in McNeill, *The pursuit of power*, 166–72; and in M. Howard, *War in European history* (Oxford, 1976), chap. 5.

18 Figures from J. P. Bertaud, *La Révolution armée. Les soldats-citoyens et la révolution française* (Paris, 1979), 36, 271; and J. Godechot, *Les Institutions de la France sous la Révolution et l'Empire* (2nd edn, Paris, 1968), 362. My thanks go to John Lynn for these two references.

19 Details taken from Bertaud, *Révolution armée*, 239f; Strachan, *European armies*, 33f, 39–41, 50–3; and J. Houdaille, 'Pertes de l'armée de terre sous le premier Empire d'après les registres matricules', *Population*, XXVII (1972), 27–50. For a model study of one of the new-style armies, see Lynn, *Bayonets of the Republic*.

20 See the figures in P. Merino, 'Europäische Kriegsmarinen im 17. und 18. Jahrhundert. Ein Überblick' in J. Schneider, ed., *Wirtschaftskräfte und Wirtschaftswege. Festschrift Hermann Kellenbenz* (Stuttgart, 1981: Beiträge zur Wirtschaftsgeschichte, VIII), 267–82; and Duffy, ed., *The military revolution and the state*, 82f.

21 For the eventual failure of Napoleon's military methods, see the fascinating study of P. Paret, 'Napoleon and the revolution in war' in Paret, ed., *Makers of modern strategy*, 123–42.

22 For the fascinating story of the *Nemesis* see Headrick, *The tools of empire*, chap. 2 (details quoted from pp. 47 and 50); For the 1863 naval campaign see G. A. Ballard, *The influence of the sea on the political history of Japan* (London, 1921), chap. 4. On the subsequent clash of East and West, see L. S. Stavrianos, *The world since 1500: a global history*, (3rd edn, Englewood Cliffs, 1966), chaps. 13–14; and McNeill, *The pursuit of power*, 238ff.

6 AFTERWORD: IN DEFENCE OF *THE MILITARY REVOLUTION*

1 My thanks go to Paul Allen, Thomas Arnold, B. Cox, Paul Dover, Fernando González de León, John F. Guilmartin, John Lynn, Jane Ohlmeyer, Keith Roberts, Jon Sumida and, above all, Clifford J. Rogers for many helpful comments and references. This chapter originally appeared in a slightly different form in C.J. Rogers ed., *The military revolution debate* (Boulder, 1995), 321–49.

2 A good overview of the connection between fortifications, army size and state formation in Japan is offered by Moréchand, '"Taikô Kenchi"'. See also the revised edition of Hora Tomio, *Tanegashima-jū. Denrai to sono eikyō* (Tokyo, 1990).

3 See the useful review articles of J. A. Lynn, 'Clio in arms: the role of the military variable in shaping history', *Journal of Military History*, LV (1991), 83–95; D. A. Parrott, 'The military revolution of early modern Europe', *History Today*, XLII.12 (December 1992), 21–7; A. Espino López, 'La historia militar entre la renovación y la tradición', *Manuscrits*, XI (1993), 215–42; A. Roland, 'Technology and war: the historiographical revolution of the 1980s', *Technology and Culture*, XXXIV (1993), 117–34; and R. A. Stradling, 'A "military revolution": the fall-out from the fall-in', *European History Quarterly*, XXIV (1994), 271–8.

4 Perwez Shafi in *Crescent*, March 1990.

5 B. S. Hall and K. R. DeVries, 'The "military revolution" revisited', *Technology and Culture*, XXXI (1990), 500–7. They take thirty-five lines to show that an early reference to a ship carrying iron guns dates from 1410–12 and not 1338, even though 'Parker's blunder is not, to be sure, fatal to his main line of argument' (p. 503.)

6 'Parker can be rather cavalier with mere facts', Hall and DeVries announce on p. 503, having devoted twenty-six lines to refuting my statement that a musket 'could throw a 2-ounce lead shot with sufficient force to penetrate even plate armour 100 meters away', an error that they claim 'can be traced back (possibly through intermediaries) to Robert Held's *The age of firearms* (2nd edn., Northfield, Ill., 1970)', a work they then dismiss ('Held's readers are unlikely to confuse his work with scholarship'). In fact, I have never read Held's book, in any edition; but I have perused several tracts from the 1590s which made strong claims for the long-range hitting power of the musket. Thus Thomas Digges, a veteran of the Low Countries' Wars, believed that troops should be trained to hit their targets at 'eight to ten score [paces: 120–50 metres]', but conceded that a ball would only carry that far when it fitted the barrel tightly; otherwise effective range was more likely to be 100 paces (75 metres, assuming a 'military pace' of around 75 cm.) See Thomas Digges, *An arithmetical warlike treatise named Stratioticos* (2nd edn, London, 1590), 108 and 122. Similarly, Humfrey Barwick, who had been a soldier for more than forty years, claimed in his *Breefe discourse concerning the force and effect of all manuall weapons of fire* (London, 1591), fo. 10v, that 'The musketes are weapons of great force, and at this day ... will kill the armed of proofe at ten skore paces [150 metres].' Recent test-firing of fourteen early modern firearms from the magnificent collection at the Graz Arsenal in Austria revealed that musket balls can indeed penetrate between 2 and 4 mm of plate armour at 100 metres – precisely the figure given on p. 17 above! See P. Krenn, *Von alten Handfeuerwaffen: Entwicklung – Technick – Leistung* (Graz, 1989: Veröffentlichungen des Landeszeughaus Graz, nr XII), and Krenn, 'Test-firing selected 16th–18th century weapons', *Military Illustrated*, XXXIII (1991), 34–8.

7 On p. 504 Hall and DeVries claim that 'some of Parker's notes in this chapter [chapter 3] play so loosely with book and journal titles that even experienced sleuths in a well-equipped library are going to have trouble tracking them'. However, in subsequent correspondence both authors admitted this charge to be unfounded: Hall conceded that all of the references that he believed to be mistaken were in fact correct (letter of 16 January 1991); DeVries did the same, adding 'I found your notes to be elaborate and intelligent. In fact, I probably

spent more time reading your notes and profiting from them than I did from any other part of the book' (letter of 27 February 1991).

8 Hall and DeVries, 'The "military revolution"', 506. See the critique of H. Dorn, 'The "military revolution": military history or history of Europe', *Technology and Culture*, XXXII (1991), 656–8, criticizing the neo-antiquarianism of Hall and DeVries. The editor of *Technology and Culture* invited the authors to respond to Professor Dorn, but they declined: letter from Robert C. Post, 17 March 1992.

9 See C. J. Rogers, 'The military revolutions of the Hundred Years War', in Rogers, *Military revolution debate*, 55–93, at p. 76.

10 R. Forster and J. P. Greene, eds., *Preconditions of revolution in early modern Europe* (Baltimore, 1970), 1. Surprisingly, the authors of the essays in this collection could find only two sets of early modern events that fully justified the term 'revolution': the Netherlands in the 1570s and England in the 1640s.

11 See J. Black in Rogers, *Military revolution debate*, 98; Volker Smidtchen, *Kriegswesen im späten Mittelalter. Technik, Taktik, Theorie* (Weinheim, 1990), *passim*: and K. R. DeVries, *Medieval military technology* (Peterborough, Ontario, 1992), *passim*.

12 P. Q. Wright, *A study of war* (Chicago, 1942), 227; F. Denton and W. Philips, 'Some patterns in the history of violence', *Journal of conflict resolution*, XII. 2 (1968), 185. Many others have claimed to detect cyclical patterns in military history, from Arnold Toynbee's *Study of history* in 1954 to J. David Singer and Melvyn Small, *The wages of war 1815–1965* (New York, 1972), 215. But how much of this is mere coincidence? Does some sort of Kondratieff cycle explain, for example, the curious fact that a naval arms race has occurred in the last decade of each of the past four centuries – 1590s, 1690s, 1790s and 1890s?

13 See Rogers, *Military revolution debate*, 77.

14 See the recent discussion of the views of Tilly and others in B. D. Porter, *War and the rise of the state. The military foundations of modern politics* (New York, 1994), 1–22.

15 I. A. A. Thompson '"Money, money and yet more money!" Finance, the fiscal-state, and the military revolution: Spain 1500–1650', in Rogers, *Military revolution debate*, 272–98, at p. 290.

16 On this complex issue see also G. Parker, ed., *The Cambridge illustrated history of warfare* (Cambridge, 1995), 14–15; M. Mann, *The sources of social power. I: A history of power from the beginning to AD 1760* (Cambridge, 1986), 433; and F. Tallett, *War and society in early modern Europe, 1495–1715* (London, 1992), 198–205.

17 G. Canestrini, ed., *Opere inedite di Francesco Guicciardini. III: Storia Fiorentina* (Florence, 1859), 105. Interestingly, this passage forms virtually the only analytical break in Guicciardini's detailed narrative of the years between 1494 and 1508, which serves to heighten the impression of shock these events evinced. Twenty-five years later, however, the same Guicciardini recognized that times had changed again: by the 1530s, thanks to the artillery fortress, the balance between offence and defence had shifted back in favour of the latter. See the views cited on p. 10 above, and by Thomas Arnold, 'Fortifications and the military revolution: the Gonzaga experience, 1530–1630', in Rogers, *Military revolution debate*, 201–26, at pp. 212–13 and 223 n. 22.

18 This, the earliest known use of the term 'military revolution', occurs in C. Dalrymple, *A military essay containing reflections on raising, arming, cloathing and discipline of the British infantry and cavalry* (London, 1761), 56. I thank

Jeremy Black for bringing it to my attention. For exponents of the belief that gunpowder weapons distinguished Ancient from Modern warfare, see the quotations on pp. 6 (Williams) and 18 (Barret) above, both from the 1590s; and, rather earlier, Girolamo Garimberto, *Il capitano generale* (Venice, 1557), 125f.

19 An interesting example of the power conferred by Western naval technology even on vessels operating alone occurs in a report made to the English East India Company in 1647, claiming that now 'Any man may trade with India, [and] with £200 worth of powder and shot in the Redd Sea by piracy may waste the Company's estate there and quickly cost them £100,000': E. B. Sainsbury, ed., *A calendar of the Court minutes etc of the East India Company 1644–1649* (Oxford, 1912), 197. The threat to the assets of Asian merchants was similar, although their means of retaliation might prove superior: see p. 108 above.

20 D. Pacheco Pereira, *Esmeraldo de situ orbis*, ed. J. Barradas de Carvalho (Lisbon, 1991), 190f. Pacheco, who had played a prominent role in the exploration of the West African coast in the 1480s and served in Portuguese Asia in 1500–5, wrote his treatise between 1505 and 1508.

21 See details in Rogers, *Military revolution debate*, 68–73; and also H. Dubled, 'L'artillerie royale française à l'époque de Charles VII et au début du règne de Louis XI (1437–69). Les frères Bureau', *Mémorial de l'artillerie française*, L (1976), 555–637.

22 Besides the sources quoted on p. 211 n. 24 above, see K. R. DeVries, 'A 1445 reference to shipboard artillery', *Technology and Culture*, XXXI (1990), 818–29; and N. A. T. Macdougall, '"The greattest schipp that ewer saillit in Ingland or France": James IV's "Great Michael"', in Macdougall, ed., *Scotland and war AD 79–1918* (Edinburgh, 1991), 36–60. On subsequent developments, see the magisterial survey of Jan Glete, *Navies and nations. Warships, navies and state building in Europe and America 1500–1860* (2 vols., Stockholm 1993.)

23 On the latter conflict, see the important article of Weston F. Cook, 'The cannon conquest of Nasrid Spain and the end of the Reconquista', *Journal of Military History*, LVII (1993), 43–70 – infantry outnumbered cavalry by three to one in the Christian army and the standard infantry company included one arquebusier and one crossbowman for every three other soldiers.

24 Thomas Digges, *An arithmeticall militare treatise named Stratioticos, compendiously teaching the science of numbers … requisite for the profession of a soldiour. Together with the moderne militare discipline* (London, 1579), fo. 103. On fo. 105 Digges proposed a 'ring march' to be maintained by detachments of twenty-five men who would fire and retire in sequence 'so as the Head shal be sure always to have charged, before the taile have discharged; and this in a circulare martch, the skirmish all day continued'. Descriptions and diagrams of the 'ring march', again always involving small formations, appear in Thomas Styward, *The pathwaie to martiall discipline* (London, 1581), and William Garrard, *The arte of warre* (London 1591, but completed before 1587). Sir Francis Walsingham, Elizabeth's Secretary of State, in 1588, ordered the musketeers of all county militia units to practice 'in that order which the Frenche men call "à la file," or as we terme yt in ranke', coming forward to fire and then retiring to reload while others did the same. (See A. J. Kempe, ed., *The Loseley Manuscripts. Manuscripts and other rare documents illustrative of some of the more minute particulars of English history, biography and manners* [London, 1835], 296–7.) It is worth recalling that the Japanese had already adopted this technique in the 1560s: see p. 140 above.

25 Martín de Eguiluz, *Milicia, discurso y regla militar* (Madrid, 1592, but written in 1586), fos. 126v–7v, noting that after four rounds an arquebus overheated and could no longer be used accurately.

26 Digges, *Stratioticos* (1590), 122–4. Again on p. 122 Digges notes that he described how 'I would have them trained', not how troops actually did train.

27 It is possible that volley fire was used at the battle of Nieuwpoort in 1600. J. J. Orlers and M. van Haesten, *Den Nassausche Lauren-crans* (Leiden, 1610), fo. 156 and battle plan, show ranks of Dutch musketeers in the Dunes exchanging fire at almost point-blank range with ranks of Spanish musketeers. The accompanying text notes that the troops 'began to fire very fast': 't volck op de Duynen vast aende handt quamen ende met musketten en roers heel dicht begonne te schietene, alsoo inde Caert gehesien werdt'. Other first-hand accounts of the battle – such as the eye-witness accounts of Francis Vere, *Commentaries* (Cambridge, 1657), 81–105, and Lord Grey in *Calendar of the manuscripts of the ... Marquis of Salisbury*, x (London, 1904: Historical Manuscripts Commission), 197–9 – shed no further light on whether this was simply a protracted fire fight, or the first use of the countermarch volley in Europe. However Vere did note (*Commentaries*, pp. 87f) that 'by the situation of the country, that skill and dexterity we presumed to excel our enemies in, which was the apt and agile motions of our battalions, was utterly taken from us'.

28 Data kindly supplied by (respectively) Bernard S. Bachrach and Donald E. Queller.

29 See Contamine, *Guerre, état et société*, 70, 73, 317; John A. Lynn 'Recalculating French army growth', in Rogers, *Military revolution debate*, 117–47, at pp. 121–2; and Cook, 'Cannon conquest', 47, 68.

30 Figures from Lynn, 'Recalculating French army growth', 122–3. Professor Lynn stressed the stability of these figures ('less military growth than might have been expected': p. 123); but some would consider an increase of 100 percent significant.

31 G. Zeller, *Le Siège de Metz par Charles-Quint* (Nancy 1943), 35–6.

32 D. A. Parrott, 'Strategy and tactics in the Thirty Years War: The "military revolution"', in Rogers, *Military revolution debate*, 227–51, at p. 242.

33 Even France, whose military record during the Thirty Years War was indeed abysmal, did not operate without a grand strategy: see Derek Croxton, *Peacemaking in early modern Europe: Cardinal Mazarin and the Congress of Westphalia* (Cranbury, NJ, 1999), with very different conclusions on Richelieu's war from those of Parrott, 'The administration of the French army'.

34 Zeller, *Siège de Metz*, 155, Charles V to Marie, 22 December 1552.

35 See details in H. Lutz, *Christianitas Afflicta: Europa, das Reich und die päpstliche Politik im Niedergang der Hegemonie Kaiser Karls V. (1552–1556)* (Göttingen, 1964), 46–158; Lot, *Recherches sur les effectifs des armées françaises*, 132.

36 For details on this dimension see E. Charrière, *Négociations de la France dans le Levant*, II (Paris, 1850), 178 n. 1: M. de Aramon, French ambassador to the Sultan, 20 January 1552. Charles V's agents intercepted the letter, providing welcome intimation that the Turks would not attack Hungary and thus freeing forces for use elsewhere: see K. Lanz, *Correspondez Kaisers Karl V.*, III (Leipzig, 1846), 137, Instruction to sieur de Rye, 22 March 1552.

37 See p. 45 above, quoting contemporary 'Relaciones' of Charles V's forces.

38 Lynn White Jr, *Medieval religion and technology. Collected essays* (Berkeley, 1986), 149 (from 'Jacopo Aconcio as an engineer', first published in *American historical review*, LXII [1967]).

39 See the important strictures of S. Pepper and N. Adams, *Firearms and fortifi-cations. Military architecture and siege warfare in sixteenth-century Siena* (Chicago, 1986), xxii.

40 See H. Koller, 'Die mittelalterliche Stadtmauer als Grundlage staatliche Selbstbewusstseins', in B. Kirchgässner and G. Scholz, eds., *Stadt und Krieg* (Sigmaringen, 1989: Stadt in der Geschichte, XV), 9–25. France soon took over as the European centre of artillery warfare, but by the 1490s Spain had 180 large and medium pieces and five state-run gun and powder factories: see Cook, 'Cannon conquest', 52.

41 See the important chronology of the increasing force of artillery in Rogers, *Military revolution debate*, 69–71.

42 Bernaldez, *Memorias*, quoted by Cook, 'Cannon conquest', 43; Machiavelli, *Art of War*, quoted p. 10 above. See also the similar views of the late fifteenth-century military engineer di Giorgio discussed in F. P. Fiore, 'L'architettura militare di Francesco di Giorgio: realizzazioni e trattati', in C. Cresti, A. Fara and D. Lamberini, eds., *Architettura militare nell' Europa del XVI secolo* (Siena, 1988), 35–47, at p. 40.

43 Machiavelli's 'Relazione di una visita fatta per fortificare Firenze', in S. Bertelli, ed., *Niccolo Macchiavelli: Arte della guerra e scritti politici minori* (Milan, 1961), 289–302, at p. 295. See also the perceptive discussion of D. Lamberini, 'La politica del guasto. L'impatto del fronte bastionato sulle preesistenze urbane', in Cresti, Fara and Lamberini, *Architettura militare*, 223–4.

44 Zeller, *Siège de Metz*, 219: Guise to Cardinal of Lorraine, 5 December 1552; and J. Rigault, 'Une relation inédite du siège de Metz en 1552', *Annales de l'Est*, 5th series III (1952), 293–306, at p. 298. Metz had been captured in May, and the next few months only allowed time to back the existing walls with earth, bales of wool and other makeshifts (Zeller, *Siège de Metz*, 230). The siege of Haarlem, which lasted for seven months in 1572–3 because the medieval walls were backed by huge earthen ramparts, offers another, later example of Machiavelli's 'third technique': see the contemporary sketches reproduced in G. Schwartz and M. J. Bok, *Pieter Saenredam: de schilder in zijn tijd* (Maarssen, 1989), especially plates 28, 30 and 31 on pp. 38–9.

45 J. A. Lynn, 'The *trace italienne* and the growth of armies: the French case', in Rogers, *Military revolution debate*, 169–99; see p. 175.

46 Fourquevaux, *Instructions sur le faict de la guerre* (Paris, 1548), fo. 85; Laparelli quoted in R. J. Tuttle, 'Against fortifications: the defence of Renaissance Bologna', *Journal of the Society of Architectural Historians*, XLV (1982), 198. For an earlier expression of the superiority of 'bastioni' over 'muro' see G. della Valle, *Vallo libro continente appertinente a capitanii, retenere et fortificare una città con bastioni* (2nd edn, Venice, 1531), book 1 fo. 6. Examples could be multiplied almost endlessly: see the works cited in A. Fara, *Bernardo Buontalenti, L'architettura, la guerra e l'elemente geometrico* (Genoa, 1988), 307–22.

47 See, for example, Archives Nationales, Paris, 261AP45 liasse 1/26, Vauban to Luxembourg, 18 August 1672, minute, and liasse 5/1, Vauban to Turenne, 29 August 1672. My thanks for these references, from Vauban's own archive, go to Paul Sonnino.

48 See the interesting discussion by J. F. Pernot, 'Guerre de siège et places-fortes', in V. Barrie-Curien, ed., *Guerre et pouvoir au XVIIe siècle* (Paris, 1991), 129–50; and by T. Arnold, in Rogers, *Military revolution debate*, 220–2.

49 See A. S. Tosini, 'Cittadelle lombarde di fine '500: il castello di Milano nella prima età spagnola', in Cresti, Fara and Lamberini, *Architettura militare*, 207–17;

and M. E. Mallett and J. R. Hale, *The military organization of a Renaissance state. Venice c. 1400 to 1617* (Cambridge, 1984), 409–28.

50 Data taken from W. Brulez, 'Het gewicht van de oorlog in de nieuwe tijden. Enkele aspecten', *Tijdschrift voor Gechiedenis*, XCI (1978), 386–406, based on (inter alia) a comparison of the town plans made by Jacob van Deventer in the 1560s and by Johan Blaeu in the 1640s. M. van Hemelrijck, *De Vlaamse Krijgsbouwkunde* (Tielt, 1950), 131–307, still provides the best overall survey of fortifications constructed in Belgium and northern France by the Habsburgs.

51 I am most grateful to Ir. B. Cox for sharing with me his fascinating reconstruction of Louis XIV's Grand Strategy, partially deduced from *Le Théâtre militaire du Roi Louis XIV de France* (Paris, 1690).

52 J. Cruso, *Militarie instructions for the cavallrie* (Cambridge, 1632), 105; Boyle quoted on p. 16 above; Behr in C. Duffy, *The fortress in the age of Vauban and Frederick the Great, 1660–1789* (London, 1985), 13f. See also the useful discussion in Tallett, *War and society*, 50–4.

53 Sébastien le Prestre de Vauban, *Mémoire pour servir d'instruction dans la conduite des sièges et dans la défense des places* (c. 1670, but misdated 1704: Leiden, 1740), 3–5, checked against the manuscript copy in the Anne S. K. Brown Military Collection at the Hay Library, Providence, R. I., fos. 1–1v.

54 Vauban, *Traité de l'attaque des places* (manuscript in the Anne S. K. Brown Military Collection at the Hay Library, Providence, R.I.: in the same volume as the *Mémoire*, second pagination, pp. 1–2). This passage does not appear in Sébastien le Prestre de Vauban, *De l'attaque et de la défense des places* (2 vols., The Hague, 1737–42, but written c. 1704), although in other respects the two works are almost identical. The Brown manuscript appears to be an interim draft, written at some point between 1670 and 1704.

55 This ceased to be true only when various governments in the later eighteenth century chose to invest in roads rather than in walls. The cost was much the same, but the speed of movement permitted by the new road network finally rendered a defensive system based on heavily fortified strongpoints both ineffective and uneconomical. See chap. 5 above; reinforced by H. Eichberg, 'Zirkel der Vernichtung oder Kreislauf des Kriegsgewinns? Zur Ökonomie der Festung im 17. Jahrhundert', in Kirchgässner and Scholz, *Stadt und Krieg*, 150–24.

56 Carl von Clausewitz, *On war* (ed. M. Howard and P. Paret, 2nd edn, Princeton, 1984), 487 (book VI chap. 27) and 596 (book VIII chap. 4). The most perceptive modern treatment of this question is A. Beyerchen, 'Clausewitz, non-linearity and the unpredictability of war', *International Security*, XVII.3 (1992–3), 59–90.

57 A. Oschmann, *Der Nürnberger Executionstag 1649–50. Das Ende des dreissigjährigen Krieges in Deutschland* (Münster, 1991), 506–20 and 550–67. In fact Clausewitz did recognize the problem presented by the *trace italienne* in another part of this work: 'In theatres of war where there are plenty of fortresses, almost every movement turns on their possession. the attacker tries to approach them unexpectedly, using various feints, while the defender attempts to forestall this by means of well-planned movements. That was characteristic of almost all campaigns in the Low Countries between the days of Louis XIV and those of Marshal Saxe' (Clausewitz, *On war*, 505 – book VI chap. 30). Actually it remained 'characteristic' from the 1570s, not just the 1670s.

58 *Nueva colección de documentos inéditos para la historia de España*, V (Madrid, 1894), 368: Don Luis de Requeséns to Philip II, 6 October 1574; BL, Additional MS 28,388 fos. 70v–71, Requeséns to Don Gaspar de Quiroga, August 1575.

59 See Simon Adams, 'Tactics or politics? "The military revolution" and the

Habsburg hegemony, 1525–1648', in Rogers, *Military revolution debate*, 253–72.

60 Francis I, considering his bastion-studded northern frontier to be proof against attack, had sent an army to Italy, where a large part of its strength was immediately dissipated in garrisoning sixteen towns and twenty-eight forts. But the king overlooked the fact that his eastern frontier was less secure until the emperor brought this omission dramatically to his attention by leading an army of some 42,000 men through Lorraine and on towards Paris. The scale of Charles V's ambitions appears from his campaign map, which portrays France as his army would have seen it from Lorraine: Fontainebleau, Francis I's favourite residence, is shown at the upper right. (See D. Buisseret, ed., *Monarchs, ministers and maps. The Emergence of cartography as a tool of government in early modern Europe* [Chicago, 1992], colour plate 7.) One set of medieval walls after another fell before the Imperial siege train: Commercy, which Francis I had expected to hold out for three weeks, surrendered after three days; Ligny fell almost as swiftly. Only St Dizier, a mere 125 miles from Paris, resisted – because it was equipped with a *trace italienne* – but the garrison ran out of ammunition and surrendered after six weeks. The Imperial forces went on to capture Vitry, Joinville, Vaucouleurs, Châtillon-sur-Marne, Château-Thierry and (on 10 September) Soissons, while another army in the north besieged and took Boulogne. On 18 September Francis made peace. A better advertisement for the superiority of the *trace italienne* would be hard to find. See C. Paillard and G. Hérelle, *L'Invasion allemande en 1544: fragments d'une histoire militaire et diplomatique de l'expédition de Charles V* (Paris, 1884); R. J. Knecht, *Francis I* (Cambridge 1982), 362–76; and Lot, *Recherches sur les effectifs*, 83, 90–108.

61 On the diffusion, see the sources cited at p. 179 n. 18 above; and the chapters by L. Zangheri, C. van den Heuvel, Z. Wazbinski, and A. M. Porciatti, in Cresti, Fara and Lamberini *L'architettura militare*.

62 Quotations and data from pp. 69 and 203 n. 78 above.

63 Rogers, *Military revolution debate*, 175–8 and 195.

64 See Zeller, *Siège de Metz*, 35, 73–7 and 82.

65 In Rogers, *Military revolution debate*, 177, Lynn admits that his 'sample might invite the criticism that it is not based on first-hand archival research' but argues that 'this is not a fatal flaw' because 'those claiming to see a strong relationship between army size and fortification have not, to my knowledge, presented any such sample, archival or otherwise, in defense of their claims'. True, such a series should be compiled, but the lack of alternatives does not of itself validate a misleading quasi-statistical exercise. Lynn's meticulous archival-based data assembled for his 'French army size' project (Rogers, *Military revolution debate*, chap. 5) is, by contrast, a model of its kind for which all military historians will be grateful, and it shows the way forward.

66 See Rogers, *Military revolution debate*, 177–8 and 198 n. 24.

67 J. Blaeu, *Toonneel de Steden van's Konings Nederlanden met hare Beschrijvingen* (Amsterdam, 1649), sig. iiijB: illustration, history and description of St Omer. The fortifications also stand out clearly in the maps of A. Sanderus, *Flandria illustrata* (Cologne, 1641).

68 Vauban, *De l'attaque et de la défense des places*, I: 203, collated with one of the five surviving original manuscripts in the Anne S. K. Brown Military Collection at the Hay Library, Providence Rhode Island, fos. 2v–3. Far more will become known about Vauban's views when his personal archive in the Collection Rosanbo, at present on deposit in the Archives Nationales, Paris, series AP261, but accessible to few scholars, can be consulted.

69 See, for example, the print of the French siege of Breisach in 1638, which clearly shows an Imperial relief army waiting in its fortified camp, on p. 15 above. For another example, this time from the Low Countries, see the heavily entrenched relief army lurking on the far left beyond the siegeworks around Breda in 1624–5 in the illustrations to S. Zurawski, 'New sources for Jacques Callot's map of the siege of Breda', *The art bulletin*, LXX (1988), 621–39.

70 Rogers, *Military revolution debate*, 181.

71 *Ibid.*, 90–4.

72 Archivio di Stato, Venice, *Misc. Cod. Storia Veneta* 143 no 21, fos. 223ff. I owe this reference to the generosity of Sir John Hale.

73 See M. S. Kingra, 'The *trace italienne* and the military revolution during the Eighty Years' War, 1567–1648', *Journal of military history*, LVII (1993), 431–46, at p. 437.

74 Figures from G. Parker, *The Army of Flanders and the Spanish Road. The logistics of Spanish victory and defeat in the Low Countries' Wars 1567–1659* (Cambridge, 1972), 11–12. Two years earlier a senior officer of the Army of Flanders claimed that garrisons alone required 44,000 soldiers: AGS, *Estado* 2051 fo. 225, Don Miguel de Salamanca to Philip IV, 8 February 1637. On the importance of garrisons in the Dutch army, see H. L. Zwitzer, '*De militie van den Staat.' Het leger van de Republiek der Verenigde Nederlanden* (Amsterdam, 1991), 36–7.

75 See Rogers, *Military revolution debate*, 183. See also the remarkable figures on the size and regional impact of French garrisons in C. Sturgill, 'The French army in Roussillon', in J. M. Ultee, ed., *Adapting to conditions: war and society in the eighteenth century* (Tuscaloosa, AL, 1986), 16–25.

76 In Rogers, *Military revolution debate*, 178, Lynn only partially reproduces Vauban's calculations concerning the size of garrison required to defend an artillery fort: 600 foot and 60 cavalry per bastion, making a total of 3,960 for a stronghold of six bastions. But Vauban went on to note that where outworks exist, the garrison must be increased accordingly – a further 600–700 for each outlying fort capable of resisting artillery bombardment; 600 for each hornwork; 150 for any redoubt. So the total garrison needed for Vauban's new-style defences could be very large indeed. See Vauban. *Mémoire pour servir d'instruction*, 194–5.

77 See Thompson, 'Money, money', in Rogers, *Military revolution debate*, 273–98.

78 See, for example, Contamine, 'Les fortifications urbaines en France'.

79 See H. Soly, 'Cités marchandes et besoins de sécurité: les fortifications d'Anvers au XVIe siècle: coûts économiques et sociaux', in A. Guarducci, ed., *Investimenti e civiltà urbana, secoli XIII–XVIII* (Florence, 1989), 183–97, at pp. 188f. Brulez, 'Het gewicht van de oorlog', 395, calculates the cost of the 43 kilometres of *trace italienne* built in the Netherlands between 1529 and 1572 at 10 million florins, little of it paid from central funds.

80 Mallett and Hale, *Military organization*, 409; see also 468–72.

81 Kingra, 'The *trace italienne*', 440f, argues merely on the basis of the *Staten van Oorlog* of the States-General that 'the Dutch were not building new bastionned fortresses at a rate to match, or bring about, so massive an increase in army size'. This may be true, but his figures do not prove it. For some idea of the complex arrangements used to finance fortifications in the Dutch Republic, see M. C. 't Hart, *The making of a bourgeois state. War, politics and finance during the Dutch Republic* (Manchester, 1993), 81 (and *passim*); van Oerle, *Leiden*, I: 251–349; and W. A. van Ham, *Merck toch hoe sterck. Bijdragen tot de*

geschiedenis van de vestingwerken van Bergen op Zoom (Bergen op Zoom, 1982), 36–72.

82 See K. Roberts, 'Musters and May games: the effect of changing military theory on the English militia', Cromwelliana (1991), 5–9; and J. Stoye, English travellers abroad, 1604–67. Their influence in English society and politics (revised edn, New Haven, 1989), 190. See also, for an earlier period, D. Eltis, The military revolution in sixteenth century Europe (London, 1995), chap. 5; and A. Ayton and J. L. Price, eds., The medieval military revolution: state, society and military change in medieval and early modern Europe (London, 1995), chap. 8.

83 See details in R. Loeber and G. Parker, 'The military revolution in seventeenth century Ireland', in J. H. Ohlmeyer, ed., Ireland from independence to occupation, 1641–60 (Cambridge, 1995), 66–88; and E. M. Furgol, 'Scotland turned Sweden: the Scottish Covenanters and the military revolution', in J. Morrill, ed., The Scottish National Covenant in its British context, 1638–51 (Edinburgh, 1990), 134–54.

84 See R. A. Stradling, The Spanish monarchy and Irish mercenaries. The Wild Geese in Spain 1618–68 (Dublin, 1994), 91: the commanders were Owen Roe O'Neill, who had served Spain between 1605 and 1642, and Robert Monro, who had fought first for Denmark and then for Sweden in Germany from 1627 to 1634.

85 For England, see the review article of H. J. Braddick, 'An English military revolution?', Historical Journal, XXXVI (1993), 965–75 (quotation from p. 975).

86 See L. Zangheri, 'Gli architetti italiani e la difesa dei territori dell'Impero minacciati dai turchi', in Cresti, and Fara and Lamberini Architettura militare, 243–51; and R. Schäfer, 'Festungsbau an der Türkengrenze. Die Pfandschaft Rann im 16. Jahrhundert', Zeitschrift des historiches Vereins für Steiermark, LXXV (1984), 31–59; and above all, Agoston, 'Habsburgs and Ottomans', 129–33.

87 R. Fruin and J. W. Kernkamp, eds., Brieven van Johan de Witt, I (Amsterdam, 1906; Werken uitgegeven door het historisch genootschap, 3rd series XVIII), 326–7: de Witt to Jan van Sijpesteyn, 23 June 1656.

88 On Poland see R. I. Frost, 'The Polish–Lithuanian Commonwealth and the "military revolution"', in J. S. Pula and M. B. Biskupski, eds., Poland and Europe, historical dimensions (New York, 1994), 19–47; and Z. Wazbinski, 'Bernardo Morando e il suo contributo alla difesa dei confini orientali della Polonia', in Cresti, Fara and Lamberini, Architettura militare, 271–8. On Russia, see M. Poe, 'The consequences of the Military Revolution for Muscovy: a comparative perspective', Comparative Studies in Society and History, XXXVIII (1996), 603–18; and W. Reger, 'In the service of the Tsar: European mercenary officers and the reception of military reform in Russia, 1654–1667 (University of Illinois, Ph.D. thesis, 1997). See also further references at p. 189 nn. 78–83 above.

89 See the perceptive review by J. Aubin in Bulletin critique des annales islamologiques, no 6 (1990), 153–5. D. Ralston, Importing the European army: the introduction of European military techniques and institutions into the extra-European world, 1600–1914 (Chicago, 199), sheds little light on this; but see the interesting case studies of C. F. Finkel, 'French mercenaries in the Habsburg – Ottoman war of 1593–1606: the desertion of the Papa garrison to the Ottomans in 1600', Bulletin of the School of Oriental and African Studies, LV (1992), 451–71; R. Murphey, 'The Ottoman attitude towards the adoption of Western technology: the role of the Efrenci technicians in civil and military applications', in J. L. Bacqué-Grammont and P. Dumont, eds., Contributions à l'histoire économique et sociale de l'empire ottoman (Louvain, 1983), 287–98; and S. Christensen, 'European-Ottoman military acculturation in the late Middle Ages', in B. P.

McGuire, ed., *War and peace in the Middle Ages* (Copenhagen, 1985), 227–51.

90 See W. F. Cook, *The Hundred Years War for Morocco. Gunpowder and the military revolution in the early modern Muslim world* (Boulder, 1994), quotation from p. 193. On the spread of Western military techniques to the other Islamic states of North Africa see A. C. Hess, *The forgotten frontier. A history of the sixteenth-century Ibero-African frontier* (Chicago, 1978); on the changing pattern of war in the Muslim states of early modern Indonesia see A. R. Reid, *Southeast Asia in the age of commerce: expansion and crisis 1450–1680* (New Haven, 1993), 87–90 and 224–33.

91 J. F. Richards, *The Mughal Empire* (Cambridge, 1993: The New Cambridge History of India, vol. I.5), 288–9. In Ch'ing China too, despite the keen interest of many government officials in military technology, most innovations involving firearms remained the work of foreigners of limited practical experience: see J. Waley-Cohen, 'China and Western technology in the later eighteenth century', *American Historical Review*, XCVII (1993), 1525–44.

92 W. J. Hamblin, 'Gunpowder weapons and medieval Islamic military theory' (paper graciously sent to me by Dr Hamblin in October 1989). On the remarkable logistical achievements of the Ottoman empire, see C. Finkel, *The administration of warfare: the Ottoman military campaigns in Hungary, 1593–1606* (Vienna, 1988: Beihefte zur Wiener Zeitschrift für die Kunde des Morgenlandes, XIV). On the size of early modern East Asian armies, see pp. 136–45 above.

93 See Reid, *Southeast Asia in the age of commerce*, 271; W. R. Thompson, 'The military superiority thesis and the ascendancy of western Eurasia in the world system', *Journal of World History*, X (1999), 143–78 (quotations from p. 150.)

94 R. Hassig, *Mexico and the Spanish Conquest* (London, 1994), 146. I am grateful to Charles E. Sharpe for reminding me of the 'military might' of the conquistadors: see Sharpe, 'To shake the foundations of heaven: Spanish combat effectiveness and the conquest of Mexico' (Ohio State University Ph.D. thesis, 2000).

95 Information kindly provided by Sanjay Subrahmanyam and Blair B. Kling. For a fuller discussion of the point, see G. Parker, 'The artillery fortress as an engine of European overseas expansion, 1480–1750', in J. D. Tracy, ed., *City Walls* (Cambridge, 2000; forthcoming).

Bibliographical guide

No single work covers precisely the same field as this book. However, three studies plough (as it were) parallel furrows: C. M. Cipolla, *Guns and sails*; W. H. McNeill, *The pursuit of power*; and A. Guillerm, *La pierre et le vent*. Since 1987, when I finalized the typescript of this book, two other works have surveyed global trends in warfare: G. Parker, ed., *The Cambridge Illustrated History of Warefare*, and J. M. Black, *War and the world. Military power and the fate of continents, 1450–2000* (New Haven and London, 1998).

For early modern warfare in Europe, pride of place must go to the work of Sir John Hale, especially his *Renaissance war studies* and *War and society*. Further surveys of great value can also be found (in the chapters on warfare by Hale and others) in volumes I to V of *The new Cambridge modern history*; in M. Howard, *War in European history*; in A. Corvisier, *Armies and societies*; and Pepper and Adams, *Firearms and fortifications*. More recently, J. M. Black, *European warfare, 1660–1815* (London, 1994) provides a magnificent account of western warfare both at home and abroad. Naturally many studies of individual armies have appeared. Two examples must suffice to show how much more we now know: J. A. Lynn, *Giant of the grand siècle. The French Army, 1610–1715* (Cambridge, 1997); and R. MacKay, *The limits of royal authority: resistance and obedience in seventeenth-century Castile* (Cambridge, 1999). John Lynn has also edited two important collections of essays on major military problems: *Tools of war. Instruments, ideas and institutions of warfare 1445–1871* (Urbana, 1989), and *Feeding Mars. Logistics in western warfare from the Middle Ages to the present* (Boulder, 1993). Two other outstanding volumes include material on the making of early modern European strategy: P. Paret, ed., *Makers of modern strategy*; and W. A. Murray, M. Knox and A. Bernstein, eds., *The making of strategy. Rulers, states and war* (Cambridge, 1994). On the evolution of seapower, see the magisterial survey of J. Glete, *Navies and nations. Warships, navies and state-building in Europe and America 1500–1860* (2 vols., Stockholm, 1993), as well as the studies of individual fleets by J. F. Guilmartin, *Gunpowder and galleys*, G. Symcox, *The crisis of French seapower*, and N. A. M. Rodger, *The safeguard of the sea*. For a comparison of military technology in East Asia and Europe, with special reference to developments in China, see the magnificent survey of J. Needham and associates, *Science and Civilization in China*, vol. V, parts VI and VII.

Many recent publications deal with the 'Military Revolution' itself. Most of them are discussed in the 'Afterword' above, but special mention must be made of the articles in C. J. Rogers, *The military revolution debate*; and in the *Journal of Military History*, LXIII, 3 (July 1999), a special issue devoted to 'Warfare and military power'. The *Journal of World History* has also published some essays on the subject: S. Morillo, 'Guns and government: a comparative study of Europe and Japan' (vol. VI, [1995], 75–105); J. Grant, 'Rethinking Ottoman "decline": military technology diffusion in the Ottoman empire, 15th to 18th centuries' (vol. X [1999], 179–201); and W. R. Thompson, 'The military superiority thesis'. Finally, the articles of G. Agoston on the Ottoman empire and the Military Revolution brilliantly fill a yawning gap in our knowledge.

Authors cited

The following list gives the place where a full citation of each work may be found.

Abelinus, J. P. 181 n. 22
Abella, D. 221 n. 85
Åberg, A. 198–9 n. 30
Adams, N. 179 n. 11
Adams, S.: 'Spain' 214 n. 38; 'Tactics or politics?'
  242–3 n. 59; 'The gentry' 195 n. 12
Ade Ajayi, J. F. 222 n. 7
Agoston, G.: 'Habsburgs and Ottomans', 189 n. 77;
  'Ottoman artillery', 226 n. 37; 'Ottoman
  gunpowder', 226 n. 38
Ahmad, A. 220 n. 81
Aho, J. A. 192–3 n. 102
Akveld, L. M. 214–15 n. 40
Albuquerque, B. de 224–5 n. 27
Albuquerque, L. de 216 n. 56
Albuquerque, L. de 210 n. 8
Alcalá-Zamora y Queipo de Llano, J. 214–15 n. 40
Allen, J. de V. 224 n. 23
Allmand, C. T. 182 n. 28
Andaya, L. 225 n. 31
Anderson, M. S. 194 n. 8
Anderson, R. C. 212 n. 27
André, L.: Michel Le Tellier 203 n. 68; Michel Le
  Tellier et Louvois 206–7 n. 94; Testament
  Politique 196 n. 16
Andreopoulos, G. J. 200–1 n. 44
Andrews, K. R.: Drake's voyages 213 n. 31;
  Elizabethan privateering 214 n. 37; Trade 216 n.
  51
Anstey, L. M. 213 n. 34
Aramon, M. de 240 n. 36
Arasaratnam, S. 217 n. 66
Arnold, T. 238 n. 17
Aron, J. P. 201–2 n. 51
Artiñano, G. de 214–15 n. 40
Asaert, G. 210 n. 11
Asgaard, F. 198–9 n. 30
Ashley, M. 202 n. 54
Atkinson, E. G. 204 n. 70
Aubin, J.: 'Albuquerque' 216 n. 57; Bulletin critique
  des annales islamologiques 245 n. 89; 'Ormuz'
  226 n. 33
Avenel, D. L. M. 204–5 n. 78
Axtell, J. L. 222 n. 5
Ayalon, D.: in Encyclopaedia of Islam 226 n. 38;
  Gunpowder and firearms 226 n. 35

Aymard, M.: 'Chiourmes et galères' 211–12 n. 20;
  Dutch capitalism 217 n. 63
Ayton, A. 245 n. 84

Bachrach, B. S.: 'Angevin strategy' 179 n. 4; 'Early
  mediaeval fortifications' 178–9 n. 4; 'Fortifications
  and military tactics' 179 n. 4
Bacqué-Grammont, J. L. 245 n. 89
Baetens, R. 214 n. 39
Baker, W. A. 212 n. 24
Baldaeus, P. 227 n. 46
Barker, T. M. 186 n. 51
Barradas de Carvalho, J. 239 n. 20
Barrie-Curien, V. 241 n. 48
Bartlett, R. J. 179–80 n. 4
Barua, P. 230 n. 69
Barwick, H. 237 n. 6
Bas, F. de 183 n. 35
Basta, G. 205 n. 79
Bastin, J. 220 n. 80
Bathurst, R. D. 220 n. 81
Baumann, R. 201 n. 47
Beerman, V. A. M. 190 n. 88
Bell, H. C. P. 217 n. 65
Bellucci, G. 181 n. 21
Benaglia, G. 207 n. 95
Benecke, G. 203 n. 67
Benzoni, G. 211 n. 19
Bernier, F. 182 n. 29
Berry, M. E. 233 n. 82
Bertaud, J. P. 236 n. 18
Bertelli, S. 241 n. 43
Beyerchen, A. 242 n. 56
Bieganski, W.: Histoire militaire 189 n. 80; Military
  technique 189 n. 80
Birmingham, D. 223 n. 19
Black, J.: European warfare 209 n. 114; 'Military
  revolution' 238 n. 11
Blaeu, J.: Konings Nederlanden 243 n. 67;
  Vereenighde Nederlanden 181 n. 22
Blainey, G. 209 n. 114
Blair, E. H. 220 n. 78
Blanning, T. C. W. 235 n. 4
Bog, I, 203 n. 67
Böhme, K. R. 203 n. 63
Bok, M. J. 241 n. 44

Dalrymple, C. 238–9 n. 18
Das Gupta, A.: 'Indian merchants' 218 n. 70; *Indian merchants* 219 n. 76
Davies, D. W. 190–1 n. 89
Davies, G. 183 n. 37
Davis, R. H. C. 204 n. 75
Day, F. J. 187 n. 58
Dekker, R. 197 n. 20
Delaney, P. 194 n. 9
Denton, F. 238 n. 12
Dermigny, L. 230–1 n. 70
DeVries, K. R.: 'Effectiveness' 210 n. 10; *Medieval military technology* 238 n. 11; 'Military revolution revisited' 237 n. 5; 'Shipboard artillery' 239 n. 22
Dewey, C. 224 n. 24
Díaz del Castillo, B. 223 n. 14
Díaz-Trechuelo Spínola, M. L. 225 n. 30
Dickinson, G. 180 n. 16
Dietz, F. C. 202 n. 56
Digby, S. 226 n. 33
Digges, T. 237 n. 6
Dillingham, W. 190–1 n. 89
Dodwell, H. H. 229–30 n. 62
Donagan, B. 200–1 n. 44
Donnelly, J. A. 186 n. 57
Dorn, H. 238 n. 8
Dorn, W. L. 235 n. 8
Dow, F. 208 n. 101
Dow, J. 196–7 n. 18
Drouot, H. 191 n. 92
Dubled, H. 239 n. 21
Duffy, C.: *Army* 235 n. 7; *The fortress in the age of Vauban* 242 n. 52; *Russia's military way* 189–90 n. 83
Duffy, M. 178 n. 5
Duke, A. C. 200 n. 41
Dukes, P. 189–90 n. 83
Dumont, P.: *Anthropologie du conscrit français* 201–2 n. 51; *Contributions à l'histoire* 245 n. 89
Durand, Y. 195 n. 12
Durange, J. D. 182 n. 24
Dymond, D. 199 n. 34

Edwards, P. R. 205 n. 82
Eguiluz, Martín de 240 n. 25
Ehrman, J. 215 n. 47
Eichberg, H.: 'Geometrie' 185 n. 46; *Militär und Technik* 192 n. 98; 'Zirkel der Vernichtung' 242 n. 55
Ekberg, C. J. 192 n. 99
Elias, J. E. 214–15 n. 40
Elison, G.: *Deus destroyed* 225 n. 29; 'Oda Nobunaga' 233–4 n. 89; *Warlords* 232–3 n. 81
Elliott, J. H.: *Count-Duke of Olivares* 214 n. 38; *Memoriales y cartas* 193 n. 3; *Palace for a king* 177 n. 1
Elphick, R. 224 n. 22
Eltis, D. 245 n. 82
Elvin, M. 178 n. 7
Endres, R. 202 n. 55
Engels, D. W. 208 n. 101
Ennen, E. 186 n. 55

Ernstberger, A.: *Hans de Witte* 203 n. 64; 'Plünderung' 200 n. 42
Espino López, A. 237 n. 3
Evans, J. X. 178 n. 1

Fairbank, J. K. 233 n. 86
Fallon, J. A. 196–7 n. 18
Fang, C. 231 n. 76
Fara, A.: *Architettura militaire* 241 n. 42; *Bernardo Buontalenti* 241 n. 46
Fass, V. 229 n. 53
Fawtier, R. 182 n. 26
Fedorowicz, J. K. 189 n. 80
Feld, M. D. 184 n. 39
Feng, C.: *Dictionary of Ming biography* 210 n. 8; 'Firearms in China' 209 n. 5
Ferguson, C. M. F. 197 n. 19
Ferguson, D. 209–10 n. 7
Ferguson, J. 196 n. 17
Finer, S. E. 234 n. 3
Finkel, C.: *Administration of warfare* 246 n. 92; 'French mercenaries' 245 n. 89
Fiore, F. P. 241 n. 42
Firth, C. H.: *Cromwell's army* 183 n. 35; *Ludlow* 191 n. 93; *Scotland* 187–8 n. 67
Fisher, H. J. 224 n. 24
Fitzsimon, R. D. 197–8 n. 24
Fleming, J. F. von 185 n. 46
Flosom, J. K. 222 n. 12
Forster, R. 238 n. 10
Foster, W.: *Best* 217–18 n. 67; *Downton* 217 n. 60; *English factories 1622–1623* 218–19 n. 73; *English factories 1624–1629* 217–18 n. 67; *English factories 1634–1636* 218–19 n. 73; *Jourdain* 217 n. 60; *Middleton* 222 n. 6
Fowler, K. E. 209 n. 2
Fox, F. 215 n. 47
Franke, H. 233 n. 86
Franz, G. 200 n. 41
Frauenholz, E. von, *Entwicklungsgeschichte* 183 n. 32; *Heerwesen* 185 n. 43
Freeman-Grenville, G. S. P. 223 n. 21
Freitag, A. 209 n. 109
Friedman, E. G. 199 n. 36
Friedrichs, C. R. 202 n. 55
Frost, R. I.: *After the deluge* 189 n. 81; 'Polish–Lithuanian Commonwealth' 245 n. 88
Fruin, R. 245 n. 87
Fryer, J. 229 n. 57
Fujiki, H. 233–4 n. 89
Furber, H. 230 n. 63
Furgol, E. M. 245 n. 83

Gaastra, F. S. 217 n. 64
Gaber, S. 200 n. 41
Gaier, C. 182 n. 27
García de Parades, D. 214–15 n. 40
Gardiner, C. H. 216 n. 51
Garimberto, G. 238–9 n. 18
Garrard, W. 239 n. 24
Gemery, H. A. 224 n. 24
Genard, P. 201 n. 45

Index